Understanding Corporation Law

Practising Law Institute's
Corporate and Securities Law Library

CURRENT TITLES

UNDERSTANDING CORPORATION LAW
by Larry D. Soderquist and A.A. Sommer, Jr.

UNDERSTANDING THE SECURITIES LAWS, 2d ed.
by Larry D. Soderquist

ARBITRATING SECURITIES DISPUTES
by C. Edward Fletcher

CORPORATE LEGAL DEPARTMENTS:
STRATEGIES FOR THE 1990s, 2d ed.
By J. Randolph Ayre, Jr.

21ST ANNUAL INSTITUTE ON SECURITIES REGULATION
by Harvey L. Pitt, Charles M. Nathan, and Stephen R. Volk

Series Editor

Larry D. Soderquist
Professor
Vanderbilt University School of Law

Understanding Corporation Law

LARRY D. SODERQUIST
A.A. SOMMER, JR.

Date of Publication: September 1990

B1-1330
PRACTISING LAW INSTITUTE
NEW YORK CITY

"This publication is designed to provide accurate and authoritative information in regard to the subject matter covered. It is sold with the understanding that the publisher is not engaged in rendering legal, accounting or other professional service. If legal advice or other expert assistance is required, the services of a competent professional person should be sought."

—from Declaration of Principles jointly adopted by Committee of American Bar Association and Committee of Publishers and Associations.

Library of Congress Catalog Card Number: 90-62725

ISBN 0-87224-012-6

About the Authors

LARRY D. SODERQUIST is a Professor of Law at Vanderbilt University and the author of casebooks in both securities regulation and corporation law, the latter of which he coauthors with A.A. Sommer, Jr. Professor Soderquist is active in the American Law Institute and the Federal Regulation of Securities Committee of the American Bar Association. He practiced law with Milbank, Tweed, Hadley & McCloy in New York City before entering teaching, and he continues to play an active role in practice through consulting. Professor Soderquist serves as the editor of PLI's Corporation and Securities Law Library.

A.A. SOMMER, JR. is a partner in the firm of Morgan, Lewis & Bockius in Washington, D.C. He has served as a member of the Securities and Exchange Commission; he is a member of the American Law Institute and the Board of Governors of the American Bar Association; and he chairs the Public Oversight Board of the American Institute of Certified Public Accountants. Mr. Sommer is a frequent contributor to forums on corporation and securities law, and he coauthors, with Larry D. Soderquist, a casebook on corporation law.

Table of Chapters

Table of Contents

Preface

We have tried in this book to provide the information that we wish we had available when we started working in the field of corporation law. Our first goal has been to provide a readable introduction to the major areas of corporation law. In addition, we have attempted to bring the reader along in the field in much the same way a corporate partner might bring along a new associate. This has involved not only discussions of corporation law itself, but of the ways corporate lawyers think and solve problems.

Since corporation law is based on corporation statutes, the question arises as to what statute to use as a starting point for discussion. The clear choice, it seems to us, is the Model Business Corporation Act, because the Model Act is the statute that is most representative of corporation statutes in America today (it being much more representative than the Delaware statute, for example). The Model Act has been amended a number of times, and we have chosen to use the version in existence in 1978 because soon thereafter its drafters adopted changes relating to capital structure that currently are reflected in very few state statutes. Along these same lines, we have chosen not to use the Revised Model Business Corporation Act, which the American Bar Association published in 1984, because it has been adopted in only a handful of states. We have, however, referred to the Delaware statute and the Revised Model Act in a number of places. For the reader's convenience, we have included the 1978 version of the Model Act as appendix A.

In this book we have included a brief introduction to securities law. We have, however, left the more detailed coverage of that subject to UNDERSTANDING THE SECURITIES LAWS, which the Practising Law Institute is publishing in its second edition this September.

We want to thank The Michie Company for allowing us to use material from our casebook, CORPORATIONS: A PROBLEM APPROACH, which is published by them. We also want to express our appreciation to the many people who in diverse ways provided helpful assistance.

Larry D. Soderquist
A.A. Sommer, Jr.

June 1990

CHAPTER ONE

The Corporation in Perspective

Lawyers doing corporate work usually see corporations at close range. Typically, their work is on the details of a client's specific problem or transaction. Only rarely do lawyers have a chance to step back and see corporations in a broader perspective. And yet a broader perspective is important if a lawyer is to do a good job on the bits and pieces of everyday corporate work[1]—and a broader perspective is essential if a corporate lawyer hopes to be more than a technician. This book will provide both close up detail of corporation law and a broader perspective, with the main idea of this chapter being to provide a good initial helping of the latter.

What a Corporation Is

One of the oldest and most interesting questions in corporation law is the question of what a corporation is. We shall approach this question from various directions and then propose an answer.

1. Associates often make mistakes on seemingly simple tasks, like drafting a charter or bylaw provision, because their view of the corporation is not broad enough.

The Corporation as a Creation of the State

It will help, in approaching the question of what a corporation is, to take as a starting point something that is incontestable: A corporation, or at least its legal form,[2] is a creation of the state. Never in the English or American experience have individuals had the power by themselves to create business corporations or, put another way, never have individuals had the power to create enterprises as corporations. In England, before the American Revolution, business corporations were formed by the sovereign or by Parliament.[3] In the United States, business corporations have been formed by the special act of a state legislature[4] or of Congress[5] or, more usually in modern times, by an official[6] acting under the authority of a general corporation statute.[7] Under this system, someone who wishes to form a corporation, or more usually that person's lawyer, drafts the corporate charter[8] and delivers it to the office of the proper state official. If the charter conforms to statutory requirements, the office

2. This parenthetical is necessary because there is a body of scholarship developed by the corporate "realists" during the seventy-five-year period ending in the late 1940s that views the corporation essentially as the corporate enterprise. Adolph Berle, for example, wrote that "the entity commonly known as 'corporate entity' takes its being from the reality of the underlying enterprise." Berle, *The Theory of Enterprise Entity*, 47 COLUM. L. REV. 343 (1947).
3. Case of Sutton's Hospital, 77 Eng. Rep. 937, 968 (K.B. 1613); Williston, *History of the Law of Business Corporations Before 1800*, 2 HARV. L. REV. 105, 114 (1888).
4. Incorporation by a special legislative act was the norm until well into the nineteenth century. See p. 11 *infra*.
5. Probably the most famous private corporation formed by a special Act of Congress was the Second Bank of the United States, which was the subject of McCulloch v. Maryland, 17 U.S. (4 Wheat.) 315 (1819).
6. In 80 percent of the states, the state official involved is the secretary of state. *See* CORP. GUIDE (P-H) ¶ 9002A, B (1988).
7. See p. 11 *infra* for a discussion of the development of universal general incorporation statutes.
8. Throughout this book the general word "charter" is used rather than "certificate of incorporation" or "articles of incorporation"; the charter is called one or the other of these names in most states.

issues the charter in the form presented.[9] The important point here is that even though a lawyer drafts the charter, it is the state that grants it. The system is not very different in this respect from the one prevalent in litigation, where lawyers typically draft the orders that judges sign.

Historical and Judicial Theories of the Corporation

If a corporation, or at least its legal form, is a creation of the state, just what kind of creation is it? In American law, our earliest authoritative answer was by Chief Justice Marshall in the *Dartmouth College* case: "A corporation is an artificial being, invisible, intangible, and existing only in contemplation of law."[10] It seems clear that Marshall took part of this conception from Lord Coke, who in 1613 said that a corporation "is only *in abstracto*; . . . a corporation . . . is invisible, immortal, and rests only in intendment and consideration of the law."[11] The rest of Marshall's conception, that the corporation is an artificial "being," may have originated with Pope Innocent IV,[12] who in the thirteenth century spoke of a particular form of ecclesiastical corporation, one called a collegium or college, as a person, saying, "the college is in corporate matters figured as a

---

9. REVISED MODEL BUSINESS CORP. ACT § 1.26 provides for an appeal, on the order of a mandamus action, for the failure of the secretary of state to grant a charter.

10. Trustees of Dartmouth College v. Woodward, 17 U.S. (4 Wheat.) 518, 636 (1819). Marshall then goes on: "Being the mere creature of law, it possesses only those properties which the charter of its creation confers upon it . . . . " *Id.*

11. Case of Sutton's Hospital, 77 Eng. Rep. 937, 973 (K.B. 1613).

12. Before his ascension to the Papacy, Innocent IV was an Italian jurist, Sinibaldus Fliscus. Koessler, *The Person in Imagination or Persona Ficta of the Corporation*, 9 LA. L. REV. 435, 437 (1949).

person."[13] But perhaps Marshall's direct influence here was Blackstone, who in his *Commentaries* called the corporation an "artificial person."[14]

American judicial comment has tended to follow the Marshall conception,[15] but there are some exceptions, the most notable being from *Farmers' Loan & Trust Co. v. Pierson*:

> [A] corporation is more nearly a method than a thing, and . . . the law in dealing with a corporation has no need of defining it as a person or an entity, or even as an embodiment of functions, rights and duties, but may treat it as a name for a useful and usual collection of jural relations, each one of which must in every instance be ascertained, analyzed and assigned to its appropriate place according to the circumstances of the particular case, having due regard to the purposes to be achieved.[16]

Along this same line is *Scandia Down Corp. v. Euroquilt, Inc.*,[17] in which the Seventh Circuit said that "[t]he corporation is just a convenient name for a complex web of contracts among managers, workers, and suppliers of equity and debt capital."[18] But even cases like *Farmers' Loan* and *Scandia Down* are not so much rejections of Marshall's conception as they are reminders that reference to that conception does not answer specific legal questions about the rights and obligations of a particular corporation and the persons involved with it.

---

13. Translation from Koessler, *id.* at 437. *But see* Williston, *supra* note 3, at 106, who suggests the possibility of an earlier origin of the conception of the corporation as a person.
14. 1 W. BLACKSTONE, COMMENTARIES ON THE LAWS OF ENGLAND 467 (1765).
15. *See, e.g.*, Airvator, Inc. v. Turtle Mountain Mfg. Co., 329 N.W.2d 596 (N.D. 1983), *citing* Asbury Hosp. v. Cass County, 72 N.D. 359, 7 N.W.2d 438 (1943); State v. Luv Pharmacy, Inc., 118 N.H. 398, 388 A.2d 190 (1978), *citing* Boston, C. & M. R.R. v. State, 32 N.H. 215 (1855).
16. Farmers' Loan & Trust Co. v. Pierson, 222 N.Y.S. 533, 544–45 (1927).
17. Scandia Down Corp. v. Euroquilt, Inc., 772 F.2d 1423 (7th Cir. 1985).
18. *Id.* at 1427.

A Structural Theory of the Corporation

Although the historical and judicial conceptions of the corporation are helpful, they are not complete, and their usefulness is limited. We believe that the most useful conception of the corporation begins with a view of the corporation as an entity consisting of a structure within which the corporate enterprise (basically its assets and its personnel taken together as a going concern) is contained, just as one might think of a library of books being contained in a building called a library.[19] At the heart of the structure constituting the corporation is the corporation's charter, but the charter is not the corporation. It merely is legal evidence of the creation of the corporation by the state and of the fact that legal rights and obligations are bestowed on the corporation by the charter and by the corporation statute and other laws. What the state actually creates by the grant of a charter is an entity consisting of a legal structure. This structure is made up of (1) the rules relating to the affairs of the corporation,[20] which rules are contained in the charter,[21] in the corporation statute, and in other laws, and (2) the right to do business within the limits specified in the charter. The instant the state grants a charter, that structure is in place.

---

19. "Just as" is not entirely correct. It should be noted that in the case of a corporation, what is being postulated as the corporation is the structure rather than the enterprise it contains and that in the case of a library, the ordinary conception and the reality is the other way around, for what is in reality the library is the collection of books, not the structure that contains the library. We have here, then, a sort of model of the corporation in mirror image.

20. The affairs of a corporation consist of those actions relating to the corporation's internal workings as an entity as opposed to those actions relating to the conduct of the corporation's business. Examples would be the management structure laid out in the corporation statute, the rules in the statute and the bylaws about the conduct of shareholders' and directors' meetings, and the rules setting voting requirements for various corporate actions.

21. MODEL BUSINESS CORP. ACT § 54 provides, for example, that the charter may contain "[a]ny provision, not inconsistent with law, which the incorporators elect to set forth in the [charter] for the regulation of the internal affairs of the corporation."

We have up until now focused on the structure constituting the corporation that is created by the grant of a charter, and on the corporation's enterprise. Upon reflection it will be seen that there are some items left unaccounted for in our discussion so far. Those are items, such as the rules of corporate governance contained in the bylaws, that relate to the affairs of the corporation rather than to its business. Since these items add to and shore up the corporation's basic structure, we believe that they should be considered part of the corporate entity—not as components of that part of the entity created directly by the state, but as part of the entity as it has been added to in accordance with rules made by the state.[22]

Taking all this into consideration, we can now go this far in saying what a corporation is: A corporation is an entity that consists of an intangible structure for the conduct of the entity's affairs and operations,[23] the essence of which is created by the state, and that possesses the rights and obligations given or allowed it by the state.

The Rights and Obligations of Corporations

It would help in understanding what a corporation is, of course, to know something of the rights and obligations that are given or allowed to corporations by the state. It would especially help if those rights and obligations could be categorized in such a way that a reference to the categorization itself would provide essentially the same information as would an encyclopedic listing of the rights and obligations. There already exists one basis for such a categorization. It is Blackstone's conception of the corporation as an artificial person.[24] The task at this point is to examine the rights and obligations

22. That is, in accordance with rules that appear primarily, although not exclusively, in the corporation statute.

23. The word "operations" is used here rather than "business" so that the definition can be used in the context of other than business corporations, the nonprofit corporation being the commonest example.

24. See p. 4 *supra*.

of corporations in order to see the extent to which they equal or differ from those of natural persons.

The best place to start is with a corporation statute. In the sections of a corporation statute relating to purposes and powers, we find the main recitation of a corporation's rights. Using the Model Business Corporation Act as a paradigm,[25] we see that a corporation may be organized under the Act for any lawful purpose or purposes, except banking and insurance[26] (the idea being that there are special purpose statutes allowing the incorporation of banks and insurance companies[27]). A corporation's purpose or purposes will be specified in its charter, but under the Model Act the purposes can be stated as broadly as "the transaction of any or all lawful business for which corporations may be incorporated under [the] Act."[28]

Turning to the question of a corporation's powers, we find in the Model Act a seventeen-item list of powers possessed by all corporations incorporated under the Act.[29] Sixteen of these items are specific, covering the rights to own and deal in property, make contracts, sue and be sued, and so on. The seventeenth is a catchall

---

25. The Model Business Corporation Act was drafted by the Committee on Corporate Laws of the American Bar Association's Section of Business Law. It has been adopted in whole or in major part by a majority of the states, and substantively it differs little from the Delaware statute. In 1984, the Committee on Corporate Laws issued the Revised Model Business Corporation Act, which is a revised and rewritten version of the Model Act. The Revised Model Act was first adopted in Virginia and Tennessee and has since become law in a handful of other states. Only time will tell whether a large number of states that adopted the Model Act will change to the Revised Model Act. Because the Model Act, as in effect prior to 1979, is more representative of state corporation law than is the Revised Model Act, we shall focus mainly on the Model Act in this book. (The complete text of the Model Act, as of the end of 1978, appears as appendix A.)
26. MODEL BUSINESS CORP. ACT § 3.
27. The single most important of these Acts is the National Bank Act of 1864 (codified in various sections of title 12, United States Code), under which national banks are incorporated.
28. MODEL BUSINESS CORP. ACT § 54(c).
29. *Id.* § 4.

indicating that the corporation has and may exercise "all powers necessary or convenient to effect its purposes."[30] So far as the corporation statute goes, then, it seems that a corporation's powers equal those of a natural person, at least in furtherance of a lawful purpose. And a further look at the statute shows that corporations in fact have the power to act in ways that do not further a lawful purpose, for in the section dealing with such activities the statute provides that "[n]o act of a corporation . . . shall be invalid by reason of the fact that the corporation was without capacity or power to do such Act."[31]

As to both rights and obligations, drafters of statutes of general applicability typically wish to include corporations along with natural persons, and they usually accomplish this by including corporations within the definition of "person." For example, the Securities Act of 1933 provides that "[t]he term 'person' means . . . a corporation."[32] Seeing the wisdom of a general provision to this effect, Congress has provided that "[i]n determining the meaning of any Act of Congress, unless the context indicates otherwise[33] . . . the [word] 'person' . . . [includes] corporations."[34] State codes often provide likewise.[35]

The common law, too, has long considered a corporation to possess the same rights and obligations as a natural person when that seems appropriate. Criminal law offers the most interesting example, with courts having a history, going back at least to the mid-seventeenth century, of treating corporations as they would natural persons in the context of some common-law crimes.[36] By the mid-

30. *Id.* § 4(q).

31. *Id.* § 7.

32. Securities Act of 1933, § 2(2).

33. Typically, it is not difficult to tell whether the context of a particular statutory provision requires that the word "person" be read so as not to include corporations. A statute relating to marriage is a good example.

34. 1 U.S.C. § 1.

35. *See, e.g.*, N.Y. GEN. CONSTR. LAW § 37.

36. *See, e.g.*, Case of Langforth Bridge, 79 Eng. Rep. 919 (K.B. 1635).

nineteenth century the context in which courts would do so had become generalized for crimes other than intentional crimes,[37] and early in the current century this exception largely disappeared.[38]

With respect to federal constitutional rights, the picture changes only a bit. All questions relating to the constitutional rights of corporations as persons have not been answered, but the most important have been. Corporations have the first amendment right of free speech[39] and enjoy the due process and equal protection rights granted to persons by the fifth and fourteenth amendments.[40] Corporations have fourth amendment protection against unreasonable searches and seizures,[41] although the Supreme Court has indicated that this protection is not necessarily as extensive as that enjoyed by natural persons.[42] Finally, the Supreme Court has held, in a case involving the question of whether a corporation must produce its books and papers for a grand jury, that corporations do not enjoy the fifth amendment's protection against self-incrimination.[43] In reaching that decision, the Court developed the theory that (1) the corporation is a creature of the state, (2) the corporation received certain franchises from the state, and (3) the state therefore has a right to inquire whether these franchises "had been abused [and to] demand the production of the corporate books and papers for that

37. *See, e.g.*, State v. Morris & E.R.R., 23 N.J.L. 360 (1852); Commonwealth v. Proprietors of New Bedford Bridge, 68 Mass. (2 Gray) 339 (1854). Crimes for which the only punishment is imprisonment have caused a problem in cases involving corporate defendants, but when courts have wished to do so, they have got around the logical impediments here, too. *See, e.g.*, United States v. Van Schaik, 134 F. 592 (C.C.S.D.N.Y. 1904).
38. *See* New York C. & H.R.R. v. United States, 212 U.S. 481 (1909).
39. First Nat'l Bank v. Bellotti, 435 U.S. 765 (1978).
40. Wheeling Steel Corp. v. Glander, 337 U.S. 562 (1949); Santa Clara Co. v. Southern Pac. R.R., 118 U.S. 394 (1986); Sinking-Fund Cases, 99 U.S. 700 (1878).
41. Hale v. Henkel, 201 U.S. 43 (1906).
42. Oklahoma Press Publishing Co. v. Walling, 327 U.S. 186 (1946).
43. Hale v. Henkel, 201 U.S. 43 (1906).

purpose."[44] A natural person, on the other hand, "owes no duty to the state . . . to divulge his business, or to open his doors to investigation . . . . He owes no such duty to the state, since he receives nothing therefrom, beyond the protection of his life and property."[45]

From this brief survey of the rights and obligations of corporations, it may be said that corporations have largely the same rights and obligations as do natural persons, although the parallel is not exact.

The Corporation Defined

Based on this analysis of the rights and obligations of corporations, we can now complete our statement of what a corporation is: A corporation is an entity that consists of an intangible structure for the conduct of the entity's affairs and operations, the essence of which is created by the state, and that possesses the rights and obligations given or allowed it by the state, which rights and obligations more or less parallel those of natural persons.

The Development of American Business Corporation Law

The law in America relating to business corporations underwent extensive development during the nineteenth century, and that development has continued, along somewhat different lines, to the present time. It will be helpful if we examine those developments one century at a time.

---

44. *Id.* at 74–75.
45. *Id.* at 74.

Nineteenth-Century Developments

There were three separate movements in the development of American business corporation law during the nineteenth century:

1. The movement from incorporation by special legislative acts to incorporation under the provisions of a general corporation statute.
2. The movement from restrictive toward enabling corporation statutes.
3. The movement from unlimited to limited liability of shareholders.

Each movement formed an essential step in creating the modern American business corporation.

From Special Acts to General Corporation Statutes

At the beginning of the nineteenth century, corporations were formed only by the special acts of state legislatures or, occasionally, Congress.[46] That began to change in 1811, when New York passed what might be called the first general corporation statute,[47] although "general" is a bit strained in this context, since the statute provided only for the incorporation of businesses engaged in the manufacture of a few specified products.[48] Other states began following New York's lead, and in 1837 Connecticut adopted a general corporation statute that allowed the incorporation of any lawful business.[49] This process of moving to truly general corporation statutes continued state by state throughout the rest of the nineteenth century, and was complete by the century's end.

---

46. *See* note 5 *supra.*
47. 1811 N.Y. Laws ch. 67.
48. Among these products were glass, mill irons, hoop irons, sheet lead, and goods made from woolen, cotton, or linen.
49. 1837 Conn. Pub. Acts ch. 63.

This is not to say, however, that incorporation by special legislative act ended as soon as a state passed a general corporation statute. In fact, in many states, after the passage of a general corporation statute, incorporations by special act occurred several times as frequently as did incorporations under the general statute. One reason was that those with political influence were able to induce the legislature to issue more favorable charters by special act than the legislature was willing to grant under a general statute. Also, the early general corporation statutes did not meet the needs of some businesses, and the owners or promoters of these businesses had no choice except to seek incorporation under a special act. But by the end of the nineteenth century all states had either drastically limited or prohibited, sometimes by means of a constitutional provision, incorporation except under a general statute.

From Restrictive to Enabling Statutes

At the beginning of the nineteenth century, all the corporate charters granted by special legislative acts were restrictive, and that restrictiveness carried over into the general corporation statutes that states passed with increasing frequency as the century moved on. The statutory restrictions on corporations took many forms, all relating to the widely held fear of the evils that might befall society from the existence of powerful corporations.[50] One restriction was a limit on the amount of capital a corporation could amass. As Brandeis described the reason behind that restriction, "[t]here was a sense of some insidious menace inherent in large aggregations of capital, particularly when held by corporations."[51] The amounts of capital allowed corporations varied widely by state, and often also

50. Jacksonian populism, which was a powerful force during the middle decades of the nineteenth century, played a major role in the continued existence of this fear, but the fear of business corporations in any form, and especially of corporations that were not subject to severe restrictions, long predated Jackson.

51. Louis K. Liggett Co. v. Lee, 288 U.S. 517, 549 (1933) (Brandeis, J., dissenting).

by the type of business a corporation was to conduct. For example, New York's original 1811 general corporation statute, which allowed the incorporation of only a few types of businesses,[52] limited capital to $100,000. And when the New York legislature amended the statute in 1817 to allow the incorporation of additional types of businesses, it set lower capital limits for the newly allowed incorporations, $50,000 for a corporation that was to manufacture salt, for example.[53] A nineteenth-century restriction that went hand in hand with the limitation on capital was a limitation on the amount of indebtedness a corporation could maintain. Another typical provision in the restrictive statutes of the nineteenth century was a limitation on the duration of corporations, with the usual limits ranging from twenty to fifty years. In addition, until late in the century corporation statutes usually limited the types of businesses that could be incorporated under them. Along these same lines, under the restrictive nineteenth-century statutes the powers that a corporation was allowed to exercise in furtherance of its business were, by modern standards, severely limited. Among these limitations was a prohibition on a corporation's owning stock in another corporation, thus preventing a corporation from circumventing statutory restrictions by operating through subsidiaries.

The corporate trust came into prominence in the 1870s as a way to minimize the effect of these restrictions, with the Standard Oil Trust the most famous. The nineteenth-century trust was the forerunner of the modern holding company, and it operated in much the same way. Shareholders in a group of related corporations, each with a restrictive charter, deeded their shares to trustees who managed the corporate group as a single enterprise.

The nineteenth-century corporate trust was short-lived, however, as a device for avoiding restrictive corporation statutes. The reason was simple: Restrictive statutes began to disappear. The movement

---

52. *See* note 48 *supra*.
53. 1817 N.Y. Laws ch. 223.

away from restrictive corporation statutes began in 1875, when New Jersey passed the first relatively nonrestrictive (or enabling) corporation statute.[54] Over the next two decades the New Jersey legislature amended its statute to carry the enabling philosophy further, with the process culminating in a revised and full-blown enabling statute adopted in 1896.[55] As these statutory developments progressed, the New Jersey corporation rather than the trust became the vehicle of choice for large businesses. The Standard Oil Trust was an early convert, incorporating in New Jersey in 1882.[56] During the last quarter of the nineteenth century, other states began following New Jersey's lead. As Brandeis put it, "the great industrial states yielded in order not to lose wholly the prospect of revenue and the control incident to domestic incorporation."[57] Among the states that passed enabling statutes in the nineteenth century was Delaware, but during that century neither Delaware nor any other state was able to push aside New Jersey as the haven for corporations.

From Unlimited to Limited Liability

Perhaps the most important nineteenth-century development in corporation law was the movement from unlimited to limited liability of shareholders. When the century opened, unlimited shareholder liability was the norm for American corporations. That rule eroded as the century progressed, and by 1900 limited liability was virtually universal.[58] In 1911, when Nicholas Murray Butler was

54. N.J. REV. STAT. (1877) 175. For some reason we have not been able to determine, this statute does not appear in the session laws for 1875, but only in the codification of two years later.
55. 1896 N.J. Laws ch. 185.
56. The trust incorporated under the name Standard Oil Company of New Jersey, which is the current Exxon Corporation.
57. Louis K. Liggett Co. v. Lee, 288 U.S. 517, 559–60 (1933) (Brandeis, J., dissenting).
58. California was an exception. Until 1930, shareholders of California corporations were, under the state's constitution, liable pro rata for the corporation's debts. CAL. CONST. art. XII, § 3 (1879).

president of Columbia University, he put the importance of these developments this way:

> I weigh my words when I say that in my judgment the limited liability corporation is the greatest single discovery of modern times. . . . Even steam and electricity are far less important than the limited liability corporation, and they would be reduced to comparative impotence without it.[59]

Because everyone living today takes limited shareholder liability for granted, the cost society pays for limited liability is rarely considered. Nevertheless, a cost is there, and it is substantial. And it grows every time a corporation goes bankrupt leaving creditors unpaid. The point is not, however, that limited liability is bad. The point is that limited liability is not bad only in proportion to the countervailing benefits society receives from it. In the case of the business corporation, what society mainly receives are (1) an increased amount of capital invested for the provision of goods and services and (2) an increase in risk taking with the capital that is invested.

Twentieth-Century Developments

During the twentieth century, developments in American business corporation law have been along three lines. First, there has been the emergence of Delaware as the leading corporate state, accompanied by the trend toward congruence with Delaware in the laws and the approach to corporations of the other states. Second, there has been a perfection of the enabling concept in corporation statutes. Third, there has been the movement from corporate regulation by the states to increasing coregulation by the federal government.

---

59. Quoted in 1 W. FLETCHER, CYCLOPEDIA OF THE LAW OF PRIVATE CORPORATIONS § 21 (1917).

Emergence of Delaware and the Trend Toward Congruence in Other States

When the twentieth century began, New Jersey was the premier corporate state. That soon changed. Woodrow Wilson became governor in 1911, and he immediately mounted an effort to return to a restrictive approach to corporations.[60] The legislature agreed and in 1913 gutted the enabling provisions from New Jersey's corporation statute. Consequences followed quickly. Corporations flocked to Delaware, which had a statute very much like the old New Jersey statute. And under the commerce clause of the federal Constitution, these corporations had the right to operate in New Jersey and in any other state so long as they were engaged in interstate commerce. From New Jersey's viewpoint the net results were these: salutary effect from corporate reforms, zero; loss of revenues from corporations, substantial. New Jersey stood that for only four years. In 1917, with Woodrow Wilson in the White House, the New Jersey legislature again amended its corporation statute, this time to undo the Wilson-era reforms.

By 1917, however, large corporations had come to like their home in Delaware, and they had no interest in moving back to New Jersey. Delaware ever since has continued to be hospitable to corporations. Its legislature has moved quickly in response to corporate desires for changes in its corporation statute.[61] Its approach to corporate taxation has always been a gentle milking, with care being taken not to squeeze enough to hurt. Its secretary of state's office has been run like a good service business. And its courts, which like those of all states have the power to hear cases involving domestic corporations no matter where a controversy arises, have had judges

60. This effort was one of the themes in Wilson's inaugural address as governor. Minutes of Assembly of N.J., Jan. 17, 1911, at 65, 69; *reprinted in* 2 PUBLIC PAPERS OF WOODROW WILSON 273–75 (Baker & Dodd, eds.).

61. The usual impetus for change in Delaware's corporation statute comes from the Delaware corporate bar.

who are knowledgeable in corporation law. As a result, most of America's largest corporations have been incorporated in Delaware.

During the twentieth century, however, there has developed a great congruence in corporation statutes and to a lesser degree in the ways in which the states approach corporations. All states have and have had for decades an enabling corporation statute. This has resulted from two forces. First, each state knows that having a restrictive corporation statute will cost it revenues and will have no real effect, as New Jersey learned to its great cost. Second, the Model Business Corporation Act and, since 1984, the Revised Model Business Corporation Act have been available for easy adoption, as a majority of the states have done.[62] The Committee on Corporate Laws of the American Bar Association's Section of Business Law, which drafted these Model Acts, is made up of some of the country's best corporate lawyers. The committee has worked hard to perfect these Acts to the point that they are not only generally congruent with the Delaware statute, but are in certain respects superior to the Delaware statute, at least from the point of view of corporations and their lawyers. This is a subject to which we shall return in chapter 4, when we discuss choosing the state of incorporation.

Perhaps because of competition from Delaware, other states also have tended at least to approach Delaware's general treatment of corporations. States have realized that it does no good to set corporate taxes that are out of line with Delaware's, and this has led to congruence. Most secretaries of state run their offices along the lines of Delaware's, or at least more like Delaware's than like a classic bureaucracy. It is in the area of judicial decision-making that other states are furthest from Delaware, because no other state has Delaware's high percentage of judges who are experts with respect to corporation law and because much more litigation about corporation law occurs in Delaware than in any other state.

62. *See* note 25 *supra*.

Perfection of the Enabling Concept

The enabling concept has been fine-tuned throughout this century, and it has also taken on a slightly different cast than it had when the century began, for most of the examples of fine-tuning during this century have related to internal matters of corporate decision-making rather than to the corporation's interactions in society. Here are some examples that are found both in the Delaware statute and in both Model Acts. First, short-form mergers: If one corporation owns 90 percent of the stock of another corporation, the corporations can merge without the approval of either corporation's shareholders, which would usually be required in a merger.[63] Second, preferred stock issuable in series: A corporation's charter may provide that the board of directors can set the terms of individual series of preferred stock without the approval of shareholders.[64] Third, consents in lieu of meetings: The shareholders and the board of directors may act without a meeting, so long as each shareholder (or, under Delaware law, enough shareholders to pass on the action in question, which is usually a majority) or director agrees in writing to the action.[65] As a final twist to this respect, when Tennessee adopted its version of the Revised Model Act, effective in 1988, it provided that the written agreement by the shareholders or directors on a particular matter may be by the percentage vote that would be required at a meeting, so long as all the shareholders or directors agree in writing to vote on the matter without a meeting.[66]

63. Del. Gen. Corp. Law §§ 251, 253; MODEL BUSINESS CORP. ACT §§ 73, 75; REVISED MODEL BUSINESS CORP. ACT §§ 11.03, 11.04.
64. Del. Gen. Corp. Law § 151; MODEL BUSINESS CORP. ACT § 16; REVISED MODEL BUSINESS CORP. ACT § 6.02.
65. Del. Gen. Corp. Law §§ 141, 228; MODEL BUSINESS CORP. ACT §§ 44, 145; REVISED MODEL BUSINESS CORP. ACT §§ 6.04, 7.04.
66. TENN. CODE ANN. §§ 48-17-104, 48-17-206, 48-18-202, 48-18-205.

State Regulation to Coregulation with the Federal Government

At the turn of the twentieth century, the regulation of corporations was virtually the sole concern of the states, and that was especially true with respect to regulation of the internal affairs of corporations. The New Deal securities legislation, especially the Securities Exchange Act of 1934 (the Exchange Act), changed this substantially. Most of this legislation relates directly to the issuance or trading of securities and is properly considered securities regulation rather than corporate regulation. Some of this legislation, however, serves almost purely to fill gaps that Congress saw in the state scheme for the regulation of the affairs of corporations.

The best example is the regulation of the proxy solicitation process that the Exchange Act mandates for publicly held corporations.[67] State corporation statutes provide no regulation of the solicitation of proxies,[68] and because of the pressure on state legislatures not to place restrictive provisions in their corporation statutes,[69] the states are never likely to provide such regulation.[70] Congress filled that gap with a highly formalized and detailed scheme of regulation that begins with the Exchange Act and carries

67. *See* pp. 30–31 *infra* for the meaning of "publicly held" in this book.

68. The only proxy regulation in the Model Business Corporation Act, for example, comes from the provisions in section 33 that a proxy must be in writing and that a proxy is valid for eleven months from the date of execution unless the proxy provides otherwise.

69. *See* pp. 16–17 *supra.*

70. Because of the practical inability of states to institute restrictive corporate regulation, many writers have called for the federal incorporation of publicly held corporations or, as an alternative, the passage of federal legislation that would regulate those corporations in a more systemic way than they are now regulated by the federal securities laws. *See, e.g.*, R. NADER, M. GREEN & J. SELIGMAN, TAMING THE GIANT CORPORATION (1976); Cary, *Federalism and Corporate Law: Reflections upon Delaware*, 83 YALE L.J. 663 (1974).

over into voluminous rules of the Securities and Exchange Commission. This regulation, along with other federal securities law having regulatory attributes in common with the proxy rules, is in fact so involved in corporate regulation that it has come to be called federal corporation law. We shall return to federal corporation law later in the book.

CHAPTER TWO

Approaching Corporation Law

This chapter continues the broad perspective of the preceding chapter, but here the focus is brought closer to the everyday concerns of corporate lawyers. We shall look first at the types of American corporations that exist today, and then turn to an examination of the distinguishing features of corporate practice.

Types of American Corporations

There are four types of corporations in America: business, nonprofit, government, and public. We shall take these up in reverse order, starting with the type furthest removed from the center of this book's concerns.

Public Corporations

Public corporations are corporations that function as governments. The most common examples are municipalities such as cities, towns, and villages.[1] Also common are governmental authorities of various sorts that serve some special purpose, airport authorities being a common example. Public corporations are sometimes formed by a special legislative act. This would be most common in

1. The legislatures in the various states determine the distinguishing characteristics of these municipalities, with population being the most common distinguishing feature.

the cases of authorities and of large cities, in each case because of the need to tailor the charter to fit a unique situation. In most situations, however, incorporation is by the secretary of state or another state official acting under the authority of a general incorporation statute. Typically, under these statutes the residents of an unincorporated area that meets statutory requirements[2] vote to incorporate under a chosen name, the vote is certified by a specified official,[3] and the secretary of state then issues a charter. As in the case of all corporations, the rights and obligations of public corporations are spelled out by statute, and typically these rights and obligations are in general similar to the rights and obligations of business corporations.[4]

Although public corporations have the basics of their existence in common with business corporations, the two types of corporations share few other characteristics, and for this reason we shall not discuss public corporations further in this book.

Government Corporations

Government corporations are corporations that are wholly or partly owned by a government and that were formed by that government to perform some special purpose. Examples are Amtrak and the Tennessee Valley Authority, the first of which is partly owned and the second of which is wholly owned by the federal government. These corporations and twenty-two others were formed by special Acts of Congress and are subject to a common set of laws

---

2. The most common statutory requirement is population. For example, a particular statute might require there to be at least 200 people in an area before it can be incorporated as a village. If the area to be incorporated is within a specified distance from an incorporated area, some statutes require the concurrence of the incorporated area before the unincorporated area may be incorporated.
3. The county clerk often is the official who certifies such votes.
4. *See* pp. 6–10 *supra*.

relating, in the main, to their finances.[5] The reason Congress formed these government corporations was to take their organization, their operations, and their finances out of the governmental sphere and place them in a more businesslike structure.[6]

The best-known government corporation is the United States Postal Service. In the statute establishing the Postal Service, Congress avoided calling the Service a corporation, describing it instead as "an independent establishment of the executive branch of the Government of the United States."[7] When one examines what kind of "independent establishment" the Postal Service is, however, it becomes obvious that the Postal Service is a corporation. This is seen most clearly in the sections of its establishing statute that deal with the Service's powers and organization, for these are the standard powers and organization of a corporation.[8] The reason Congress did not call the Postal Service a corporation may well have been to distinguish it from the other government corporations, discussed in the previous paragraph, that it wished to subject to a common set of laws.

Government corporations are highly specialized entities. The legal rules relating to them are hybrids of the rules relating to business corporations and government agencies, and the affairs of government corporations are handled by only a few lawyers. For these reasons we shall not return to those corporations.

Nonprofit Corporations

There is a great deal of confusion in the public's mind about what it means to be a nonprofit corporation.[9] A usual idea is that such

---

5. 31 U.S.C. §§ 9101–9109.
6. An indication of this is the requirement that wholly owned corporations subject to the laws cited in note 5 *supra* must prepare and submit to the president "a business-type budget." 31 U.S.C.A. § 9103.
7. 39 U.S.C. § 201.
8. *See* 39 U.S.C. §§ 202–404.
9. These corporations are sometimes called not-for-profit corporations.

corporations may not make profits, or that they must arrange their affairs in such a way that profits are unlikely. These ideas are far from the mark. At the heart of what distinguishes nonprofit from business corporations is the fact that nonprofit corporations do not have shareholders, or owners of any kind. They may or may not have members.[10] If they do, the members may function very much like shareholders.[11] In a nonprofit corporation, however, profits may not be paid to the members as dividends.[12] This does not mean, however, that the corporation may not or should not make profits. Many hospitals, for example, are operated by nonprofit corporations, and their managers try hard to earn profits. The difference in this respect between nonprofit and business corporations simply is in what may be done with the profits.

Nonprofit corporations are of two types: eleemosynary (or charitable) and mutual-benefit. The distinguishing characteristic is whether the purpose of the corporation is to benefit its members or to benefit some other group or groups. Hospitals, private universities, and charities of all descriptions are typically organized in the form of eleemosynary nonprofit corporations, while social clubs offer a common example of mutual-benefit nonprofit corporations.

The tax treatment of nonprofit corporations varies depending upon whether the corporation is eleemosynary or mutual-benefit. Basically, an eleemosynary corporation does not pay taxes on its

---

10. In the typical statute relating to nonprofit corporations, such a corporation is not required to have members. If a corporation does not have members, the directors usually take over the typical functions of members.
11. The members, for example, may elect the directors and vote on extraordinary matters such as charter amendments, sales of assets, and mergers. Under the typical nonprofit corporation statute, however, a corporation may have members, but give them no power to vote on any matter. In that case, the concept of "member" is empty of any content other than the personal satisfaction or prestige that flows from membership.
12. It is true, however, that under the typical nonprofit corporation statute, the assets of at least some nonprofit corporations may be distributed to the members upon dissolution. *But see* note 16 *infra*.

profits,[13] and contributions to the corporation are deductible by the donors.[14] As in the case of an eleemosynary corporation, a mutual-benefit nonprofit corporation escapes taxes on its profits,[15] but contributions to the mutual-benefit corporation are not deductible by the contributors. In each case, these tax treatments will be available only when a corporation qualifies for them under the Internal Revenue Code and when the corporation files the proper application with the Internal Revenue Service.[16] Also, profits of nonprofit corporations that arise from essentially commercial activities are taxable in a manner comparable to profits of business corporations.

All states now have general corporation statutes for nonprofit corporations, and incorporation under these statutes usually follows the same procedure as for business corporations.[17] But there are exceptions. Under some statutes, for example, the approval of one or more state agencies is necessary before an eleemosynary corporation may be incorporated.[18] There is no general corporation statute for nonprofit corporations at the federal level, but Congress occasionally creates a nonprofit corporation by special Act.[19]

Nonprofit corporation statutes are often less detailed than are business corporation statutes, and the case law relating directly to nonprofit corporations is sparse. As a result, a lawyer dealing with a

---

13. *See* I.R.C. § 501(c)(3).
14. *See* I.R.C. §§ 170(c)(2), 2055(a), 2522(a).
15. *See, e.g.*, I.R.C. § 501(c)(4).
16. Regardless of what a state's corporation statute provides with respect to how assets may be distributed upon dissolution, *see* note 12 *supra*, an eleemosynary corporation cannot receive the tax treatment described above unless its charter provides that upon dissolution the assets may not be distributed to the members, but rather must be given to another corporation having the same type of tax-exempt status or to another suitable donee.
17. *See* pp. 2–3 *supra*.
18. *See, e.g.*, N.Y. NOT-FOR-PROFIT CORP. LAW § 404.
19. Recent examples are Vietnam Veterans of America, Inc. and Army and Navy Union of the United States of America. *See* 36 U.S.C. §§ 3801, 3901. Approximately eighty other nonprofit corporations have federal charters. Most are patriotic organizations.

nonprofit corporation is sometimes left to wonder just what the law is on a particular point. The correct conclusion usually can be reached by making the right analysis. A good way to begin is with the idea of trying to determine what a court would decide the law to be if it got the question. Assuming there is no statutory provision or nonprofit corporation case law on the particular point in the state of incorporation, there are only two places a court could reasonably look for an answer to the question. One is the case law outside the state relating to nonprofit corporations and the other is the law of the same or other states relating to business corporations. If there is relevant case law in another state relating to nonprofit corporations, and if the nonprofit corporation statute in the other state is analogous to the one in the state in question, a court likely will accept that case law, at least if it is not contrary to the state's law relating to business corporations. In the more usual situation, however, there is available no case law on point in any jurisdiction relating to nonprofit corporations. In that situation, a court would look to the law relating to business corporations in the state of incorporation, or in other states if necessary, to answer the question by analogy.

This can be seen best by example. Assume the question is whether the members of a nonprofit corporation, who in this particular corporation have the power to elect directors at annual meetings, also have the power to fill vacancies occurring on the board of directors between annual meetings. Assume further that the state's nonprofit corporation statute is silent on the question of the members' power to fill vacancies on the board, but that, as is not unusual, the statute specifically gives the remaining directors this power. Finally, assume that there is no nonprofit corporation case law on the question in any state. The answer to the question then would be found by looking at the law relating to business corporations. The likely result of research on the point would be that neither the state's business corporation statute nor its case law speaks to the question. A look at the case law outside the state quickly will provide the answer, however: Shareholders have the inherent power to fill vacancies on the board, and silence in the business corporation statute, coupled with a provision in the statute allowing directors to fill such vacancies, should not be taken to indicate otherwise.[20] It is a small and sure step from that point to the conclusion that the same rule would apply in the case of members in a nonprofit corporation.

We shall come back specifically to nonprofit corporations only a few times in this book. As may be surmised from the preceding paragraphs, however, much of the law relating to business corporations carries over to nonprofit corporations. To a large degree, therefore, the rest of this book can be viewed as being about business and nonprofit corporations.

Business Corporations

Business corporations are of two types: publicly held and close.[21] A number of courts have attempted at least a partial definition or characterization of the close corporation. Some judges have described close corporations as little more than chartered partnerships[22] or incorporated partnerships.[23] Though descriptive, these characterizations are not by themselves analytically helpful. Most courts speaking on the subject, however, have focused on specific attributes of close corporations. Various judges taking this approach

---

20. *See, e.g.*, Campbell v. Loew's, Inc., 36 Del. Ch. 563, 571, 134 A.2d 852, 857 (1957).
21. One sometimes sees "closed" substituted for "close," perhaps because the latter strikes the unaccustomed ear as strange. "Close" is the word of choice, however, among corporate lawyers. The use of the word in this context likely was derived from its early use as a description of a piece of land that is enclosed by a fence or hedge. "Closely held" is also used sometimes. For a fuller discussion of the matters dealt with in this section of the chapter, *see* Soderquist, *Reconciling Shareholders' Rights and Corporate Responsibility: Close and Small Public Corporations*, 33 VAND. L. REV. 1387 (1980).
22. Ripin v. United States Woven Label Co., 205 N.Y. 442, 447, 98 N.E. 855, 856 (1912).
23. Cuppy v. Ward, 187 A.D. 625, 639, 176 N.Y.S. 233, 243 (1919) (Shearn, J., dissenting).

have viewed the close corporation as one in which (1) the corporation's stock is held in a few hands or in a few families; and (2) the corporation's stock is never or only rarely dealt in by buying or selling;[24] or (3) as one in which the management and ownership of the corporation are substantially identical.[25] In the leading case of *Donahue v. Rodd Electrotype Co.*,[26] the court, while avoiding a definition, accepted some aspects of these earlier formulations and stated that the close corporation is "typified by (1) a small number of stockholders, (2) no ready market for the corporate stock, and (3) substantial majority stockholder participation in the management, direction, and operations of the corporation."[27] Most scholars who have examined the nature of close corporations have focused on one or more of the characteristics enumerated in *Donahue*, and the largest number of these scholars seems to have regarded the last of these characteristics as the most important.[28]

We think it is incorrect, however, in attempting to distinguish close from publicly held corporations, to focus on the substantial involvement of majority shareholders in the management, direction, and operations of the corporation. Certainly this involvement is typically found in close corporations, but it is not always found. For example, second-generation owners of a family corporation may have no interest in the business and may turn its management over to

24. Brooks v. Willcuts, 78 F.2d 270, 273 (8th Cir. 1935); Galler v. Galler, 32 Ill. 2d 16, 27, 203 N.E.2d 577, 583 (1965); Lavene v. Lavene, 162 N.J. Super. 187, 192, 392 A.2d 621, 623 (1978).

25. Kruger v. Gerth, 16 N.Y.2d 802, 806, 210 N.E.2d 355, 357 (1956) (Fuld, J., dissenting). See Helms v. Duckworth, 249 F.2d 482, 486–87 (D.C. Cir. 1957); Thisted v. Tower Management Corp., 147 Mont. 1, 14, 409 P.2d 813, 820 (1966).

26. Donahue v. Rodd Electrotype Co., 367 Mass. 578, 328 N.E.2d 505 (1975).

27. *Id.* at 586, 328 N.E.2d at 511.

28. *See, e.g.*, Chayes, *Madam Wagner and the Close Corporation*, 73 HARV. L. REV. 1532, 1533 (1960); Israels, *The Close Corporation and the Law*, 33 CORNELL L.Q. 487, 488 (1948); Scott, *The Close Corporation in Contemporary Business*, 13 BUS. LAW. 741, 741 (1958).

professionals. Moreover, at some point even first-generation shareholders in a family corporation may hire professional managers because of age, health, retirement, or the desire to devote effort to other ventures. This formulation of a close corporation definition is, thus, too narrow. In another sense, however, it is too broad, because many corporations that have stock trading on a stock exchange and that are without question publicly held are managed by their majority owners.[29]

Defining the close corporation as a corporation having few shareholders also presents problems. In most close corporations, there are only a few shareholders. In some, however, the concept of "few" becomes strained. In most close corporations, the number of shareholders will tend to increase over the years. This will especially be true if restrictions are not placed on the transfer of shares, but it will be true in any case as shares find their way into the hands of second and later generations. Moreover, while questions of how few is "few" can obviously be resolved on an ad hoc basis, one surmises that in answering the question of whether a corporation is close, courts or others would look to factors other than simply the number of shareholders. For example, in deciding whether a corporation with 200 shareholders meets the test of having only a few shareholders, a court might wish to know whether the corporation's stock is publicly traded or whether its shareholders are active in the management of the corporation. This definition, then, presents problems that in some cases would not be resolved by a literal interpretation of the term "few."

---

29. In the usual situation of a close corporation selling shares to the public for the first time, the current owners wish to retain control of the corporation after the public sale. Accordingly, the owners of the corporation usually retain over 50 percent of the stock when the corporation initially becomes a publicly held corporation. Also, the owners of a close corporation going public sometimes retain control by creating two classes of common stock and selling to the public shares of the class with lesser or no general voting rights.

We believe the best way to define the close corporation is by reference to the other factor discussed in *Donahue*: whether there is a ready market for the corporation's stock. For one thing, using this test as a definition avoids the problems, just discussed, that one faces when using other suggested definitions. More important, we believe that whether or not there is a ready market for a corporation's stock is the major determinant in how a shareholder views his or her relationship to the corporation. In a corporation whose stock cannot easily be traded, a shareholder is likely to take a personal, long-term interest in the corporation. This shareholder is likely to view himself or herself as an owner of the corporation in a direct sense, and one can view this kind of shareholder relationship as a secondary characteristic of a close corporation. In a corporation having stock with a ready market, however, a shareholder is much more likely to view himself or herself primarily as the owner of a corporation's shares rather than as an owner of the corporation itself in any real sense. The owner of a small percentage of the stock of a local foundry may say, "I own a piece of that foundry." If he or she owns a small percentage of the shares of General Motors Corporation, the statement is more likely to be, "I own some GM stock."

Finally, of course, the opposite of "close" is "publicly held," and when one looks at the publicly held corporation, one almost necessarily focuses on the ease with which shares of the corporation trade in the public markets, which is another way of saying that there is a ready market for the corporation's stock. To be pure in our definition, we should focus on whether the shares of a particular corporation are publicly traded with some regularity. We should, that is, consider a corporation to be a close corporation even if its stock is sometimes publicly traded in the over-the-counter market, so long as its stock cannot be traded there with any certainty. However, since there exists a well-known and easy-to-apply test that nearly fits the pure requirements for distinguishing between close and publicly held corporations, we would use that test as a rule of thumb. The test is whether the corporation is required to file the reports called for by section 13 of the Securities Exchange Act of 1934 (the Exchange Act). This filing requirement arises in one of three ways: (1) the corporation has securities registered under section 12(b) of the Exchange Act because these securities trade on a securities exchange, (2) the corporation has securities registered under section 12(g) of the Exchange Act because it has assets exceeding $5 million[30] and a class of equity security held of record by 500 or more persons, or (3) the corporation is required, under the provisions of Exchange Act section 15(d), to file section 13 reports because it has in the past registered securities for public sale under the Securities Act of 1933. If a corporation meets any one of these requirements, it becomes what corporation lawyers call a "reporting company." The reporting company/nonreporting company dichotomy almost exactly duplicates the publicly held/close corporation dichotomy insofar as corporations go, because this duplication is exactly what the Exchange Act is designed to accomplish with its reporting requirements. If a corporation's stock is traded in the public markets, Congress wanted to ensure that the corporation would make public the information that is contained in the reports required to be filed by Exchange Act section 13.

There are consequences of the determination as to whether a corporation is close or publicly held. First, close corporations are allowed greater latitude than publicly held corporations in their internal management. For example, while informal decision-making outside of board meetings may be unacceptable in a publicly held corporation, it may be tolerated in a close corporation.[31] Moreover, some types of agreements among shareholders as to the conduct of

30. To get to the $5 million test one needs to read Exchange Act rule 12g-1 along with section 12(g). The statute contains the figure $1 million, but this is increased to $5 million by the rule.

31. *See, e.g.*, Trager v. Schwartz, 345 Mass. 653, 189 N.E.2d 509 (1963).

corporate affairs may be allowed in a close corporation but forbidden in a publicly held corporation.[32] The second consequence of being classified as a close corporation can be more important. In a series of decisions going back over three decades, courts have developed the doctrine that shareholders in close corporations stand in a fiduciary relationship to each other.[33] This can have serious consequences, as will be discussed in chapter 10. Finally, and what may be most important, corporations having securities registered under Exchange Act section 12 are subject to a whole range of special requirements and constraints under other sections of the Exchange Act. For example, these corporations must comply with the proxy rules of the Securities and Exchange Commission when soliciting proxies from their shareholders, and their officers, directors, and substantial shareholders must follow the so-called short-swing trading provisions of Exchange Act section 16. These and other Exchange Act requirements will be introduced later in the book.

These differing treatments of close and publicly held corporations are important, but what is more interesting is the fact that in the bulk of corporation law, close and publicly held corporations are treated exactly the same. For example, the typical corporation statute contains one set of provisions that applies to all corporations. What makes the statute work for the smallest, one-shareholder corporation as well as the largest publicly held multinational is the flexibility built into the statutory provisions. The Model Business Corporation Act, for example, allows a corporation's board of directors to "consist of one or more members."[34] With this flexibility, the statute serves the needs of the large publicly held corporation that wishes to have a fifteen-person board and the desires of the sole shareholder who wants to be the corporation's only director.

32. *See, e.g.*, Glazer v. Glazer, 374 F.2d 390 (5th Cir. 1967); Galler v. Galler, 32 Ill. 2d 16, 203 N.E.2d 577 (1965); Kantzler v. Benzinger, 214 Ill. 589, 73 N.E. 874 (1905); Clark v. Dodge, 269 N.Y. 410, 199 N.E. 641 (1936).

33. *See* chapter 10 *infra*, text accompanying notes 22 & 23.

34. Model Business Corp. Act § 36.

Along these same lines, the Model Act provides that a corporation may split management functions among the shareholders, directors, and officers as it chooses, so long as the corporation specifies in its charter the person or persons who are to perform the usual tasks of directors.[35] This would allow a corporation's sole shareholder to avoid the formalities of board action by providing in the corporation's charter that the shareholder or shareholders of the corporation will perform the usual functions of directors.[36] Notwithstanding the flexibility of statutes like the Model Act, however, some states have passed statutes relating only to close corporations, and the Revised Model Act has a close corporation supplement.

Distinguishing Features of Corporate Practice

A number of features distinguish the practice of corporation law from other practices. Some other practices share certain of these features with corporate practice, of course, but no other practice comes close to being quite the same. The features discussed below distinguish corporate practice by a typical good corporate lawyer.

Prospective Viewpoint

Corporate lawyers work as planners, viewing transactions prospectively. They take the law as a given and structure transactions around it. Litigators, on the other hand, view transactions retrospectively. They take the facts as a given and attempt to portray the law, by analysis and argument, as fitting the facts in a manner favorable to the client. This prospective/retrospective dichotomy leads corporate lawyers and litigators to approach law quite differently. For

35. *Id.* § 35.

36. Interestingly, this is almost never done because lawyers and shareholders find that there are benefits in doing things the ordinary way. *See* pp. 148–149 *infra*, for a discussion of this subject and the related subject of whether the Model Act requires a corporation to have a board of directors.

example, whether a particular statement by a court is dictum may be important to the litigator but virtually irrelevant to the corporate lawyer. The litigator does not mind working in the vanguard, and sometimes that is the only place from which a case can be won. The corporate lawyer, on the other hand, wishes to take no avoidable chance of running afoul of the law, and so if a court has interpreted a statutory provision to say a particular act may not be done, that usually is enough to dissuade the corporate lawyer, whether the court's interpretation was in dicta or holding.[37]

Skill as a Drafter

In much the same way as a dexterous use of the hands distinguishes the surgeon, skill as a drafter distinguishes the corporate lawyer. The prototypical corporate lawyer is a consummate drafter. Care and precision, along with elegant use of the language, are points of the corporate lawyer's pride. That being true, corporate lawyers heavily judge other corporate lawyers on their drafting skill. New associates rarely are careful or precise enough in drafting to satisfy the seasoned corporate lawyer, but that is usually forgiven if the associate seems intent on measuring up. A lack of interest in care and precision, however, will keep an associate from ever being accepted as a corporate lawyer.[38]

---

37. This assumes that the corporate lawyer can find a way to accomplish a client's basic desires without going against the court's dictum. If the lawyer believes the court is wrong, and there is no other way to accomplish what the client wants accomplished, the good corporate lawyer does not shy away from subjecting a client to risk if that is what the client wants.
38. Consistency in definitional forms offers an example. A corporate lawyer cannot stand to see "(herein called the 'Company')" coupled with "(hereinafter called the 'Partnership')." "Hereinafter" is okay and "herein" is fine, as long as the drafter is consistent. (Actually, the following definitional form is probably most favored, because of its simplicity: (the "Company").)

One often hears about the predilection of surgeons to solve patients' problems by an operation. And perhaps litigators see lawsuits as the solution to clients' problems more frequently than do other lawyers. Along these same lines, corporate lawyers think first about drafting to solve a client's problem. If in structuring a transaction a corporate lawyer comes across a legal ambiguity, his or her inclination is not to do research to resolve the ambiguity, it is rather to avoid the ambiguity by drafting around it.[39] Here is an example. Suppose a corporation lawyer practicing in Illinois is presented with a provision in a contract that says, "This Agreement shall be governed by and construed in accordance with the laws of the State of Illinois." The lawyer probably would like the idea of using Illinois law, but might reasonably wonder what the Illinois choice-of-law rules would provide as to the contract. Would they, for example, provide that the substantive law of another place rather than Illinois would govern the contract? Rather than research the question, the corporate lawyer likely will rewrite this provision along these lines: "This Agreement shall be governed by and construed in accordance with the local laws of the State of Illinois and not its choice-of-law rules."

Predilection Against Telling a Client No

The mindset of the corporate lawyer is to find a way to accomplish what the client basically wants. Good corporate lawyers not only listen to the specific questions clients ask them, but they try to discern what at base the client wants to accomplish. Corporate lawyers might have to say no to the specific question, but if at all possible they will present an alternative designed to accomplish the real, often unspoken, goal. A president of a client might say, for example, that the corporation wants to pay a dividend of one dollar

39. New associates need especially to be aware of this mindset of corporate lawyers, because the law school training of new associates typically emphasized finding legal answers to legal questions.

on its common stock. Realizing that the corporation has no earned surplus available for dividends under the governing statute, the lawyer may have to say that that cannot be done. The good lawyer would not leave the matter there, however. Understanding that what the client really wants is to take one dollar per share out of the corporation and give it to its shareholders, the good lawyer would look for a way to do so. If there is enough capital surplus available, a distribution of one dollar per share will probably be allowed under the governing statute. If there is no capital surplus, it can be created, if necessary by a charter amendment changing the par value of the corporation's stock.[40]

Involvement in Clients' Affairs

Corporate lawyers do not merely give clients advice. Usually, corporate lawyers are intimately involved in the accomplishment of corporate transactions about which they give advice, and very often these transactions are accomplished almost solely by the effect of documents drafted by the lawyer. The corporate distribution used as an example in the preceding paragraph serves also as an example here, because the lawyer is likely to draft every document involved in the distribution, including the letter to shareholders explaining the distribution and transmitting the corporation's check. One consequence of this involvement in clients' affairs is that if anyone raises a problem about the legality or propriety of a corporate transaction, it is not unlikely that the corporation's lawyer will be in the middle of the controversy.

Main Client Contact

The corporate lawyer is typically a law firm's main contact with a corporate client, even if most of the firm's work for the client is

40. Each of the corporate concepts mentioned in this paragraph will be discussed in a later chapter.

done by other specialists. Here the corporate lawyer's role is reminiscent of that of the internist in medical practice, who tends to be the intake physician in a group practice. Another way of describing this role of the corporate lawyer is that it is the role of a traffic cop. One thing this means is that the corporate lawyer has to know enough about other specialties to decide (1) whether the client has a legal problem and (2) if the client does have a legal problem, what other lawyer to get involved.

Conservatism

Corporate lawyers are conservative in their risk-taking. In everything they do for clients they ask themselves where problems might lie and what they can do to avoid them. Corporate lawyers often are willing to go to or have others go to whatever trouble it takes to avoid even the extremely remote possibility of a problem. For example, when a corporation opens a bank account, the bank will require that the board of directors pass a resolution defining the banking relationship. Typically, the board gives certain officers the unlimited power to borrow from the bank. If, however, when the corporation goes to the bank for a loan the bank involves its lawyer, that lawyer invariably will require that the corporation's board of directors pass a new resolution specifically authorizing the loan.[41] But how much extra safety does the bank's lawyer add by insisting on the new resolution? Virtually none.

One can question the application of the conservative approach to a specific situation,[42] but that approach in general is exactly the

41. A resolution of the board's executive committee will suffice if the committee has been properly constituted and has been given enough power. Executive committees will be discussed in chapter 8.

42. Being corporate lawyers, the authors do not question the decision by bank lawyers to insist on specific borrowing resolutions, as discussed in the preceding paragraph. Here it can be pointed out that the last sentence of that paragraph reads "Virtually none," which to the corporate lawyer is very different from "None."

correct one. The corporate lawyer works prospectively, but he or she continually tries to look at a transaction being planned through the eyes of a court viewing the transaction retrospectively. The good lawyer knows that objective truth, if it exists at all, is not nearly so important as what a plaintiff's lawyer can make the truth seem to be. The good lawyer also knows that even more important than the facts in a lawsuit is how a judge or jury views the equities. And finally, the good lawyer knows that it is impossible to tell when planning a transaction how a judge or jury might someday view the equities. The lawyer's only course is to button up both the facts (by documentation) and the legalities (usually by precisely drawn contractual provisions) of a transaction so tightly that the equities do not matter—that is, so tightly that no matter how much a court may wish to find against the corporation, it will have no basis for doing so.[43]

Collegial Approach

Corporate lawyers working on a transaction typically find corporate lawyers working on the other side. The relationship between these lawyers almost invariably is collegial rather than adversarial. Negotiations on documents, for example, are characterized by good-natured civility. So much is this the case that to an outside observer it often might appear that the lawyers are working for the same client. This illusion may come partially from the fact that each client does want basically the same thing: the transaction done smoothly and quickly. It comes also from the fact that the two lawyers share approaches and values, and so they understand each other. The borrower's lawyer, for example, does not argue when the

---

43. Perhaps the conservatism of corporate lawyers goes back to the railroad lawyers of the nineteenth century, who knew that in many courts the railroad would lose a case brought against it if there were any basis for the plaintiff's claim.

bank's lawyer requests a specific borrowing resolution from the borrower's board of directors.

Involvement of Securities Law

Corporate practice is intertwined with the practice of securities law to such an extent that they are virtually two parts of the same whole. Much of this intertwining arises from the fact that some federal securities law serves to fill gaps in state corporation law and is, in reality, federal corporation law.[44] But some of the intertwining also comes from the fact that a corporation cannot avoid some involvement in pure securities law. All corporations need to sell stock, for example, and anytime the corporation—or one of its shareholders—sells stock, the sale involves securities law questions. This does not mean, of course, that all corporate lawyers need to be full-blown securities lawyers. What it does mean is that every corporate lawyer needs to be expert in some areas of securities law.[45]

Special Ethical Problem

Corporate lawyers face a special ethical problem that arises from the fact that their corporate client does not exist in a form that can be dealt with directly. Since the corporation is a legal creation only, everything the corporation does must be done through agents. The special ethical problem arises when the interest of an agent with whom the lawyer deals differs from the corporation's interest. The first problem of the lawyer is to see the conflict. That is not always as easy as it might seem, partly because the lawyer often does not know enough facts to discern, for example, that a proposed action is good for the corporation's president but bad for the corporation. The

44. *See* pp. 19–20 *supra*.

45. Securities law will be introduced briefly in later chapters. For a fuller introduction, see the companion to this book entitled UNDERSTANDING THE SECURITIES LAWS (2d. ed. 1990), which also is published by the Practising Law Institute.

second problem is to handle the conflict without damaging the lawyer's relationship with people in the corporation. That typically can be done if the lawyer exercises enough skill.

Perhaps the clearest example of this conflict arises when the president of the corporation asks the corporation's lawyer to draft the president's employment contract. There is more than one acceptable way the lawyer might handle this situation. A good and practical way would be to have the president secure the agreement of the board of directors that the lawyer will draft the contract as he or she believes the contract likely would come out if negotiated by two good corporate lawyers, and further that the corporation will pay for the legal work. (Essentially this would mean that the contract would include a full array of protective provisions for each party and no overreaching provisions favoring either.)

CHAPTER THREE

Choosing the Corporate Form and Preincorporation Transactions

In this chapter we shall discuss matters relating to the time before a corporation is formed. During that period, those forming a new business and their lawyers concern themselves with two kinds of issues. One issue is whether to incorporate the new business. The other issue is whether, to what extent, and under what circumstances contracts should be entered into for the benefit of a corporation that is not yet in existence.

Choosing the Corporate Form: The Corporation and Its Alternatives

The decision to choose the corporate form for a new business can be made intelligently only after considering the alternatives. Usually the corporate form is best, but that is not always true. There are still in existence a few examples of exotic business entities such as joint stock companies,[1] but those entities would not be rational choices

1. Joint stock companies were most popular in England before the advent of general corporation statutes, when it was sometimes difficult—or expensive—to talk the King or Parliament into granting a corporate charter. The term "stock" here relates to stock in trade, with the idea being that the owners of the company "join," or pool, their goods for sale. The joint stock company shares with the corporation a centralized management structure, and to the outsider it looks much like a corporation. It operates, however,

for a newly formed business. In almost all cases,[2] the practical choices for a new business would be limited to these: sole proprietorship, general partnership, limited partnership, and corporation.

Sole Proprietorship

The sole proprietorship is the most popular form in America for operating a business, with most small start-up ventures operating in that form. Sometimes the form is chosen because the sole proprietorship is the best form for a particular business. Often, however, the owner of a business chooses this form without legal advice, sometimes to his or her regret.

The greatest draw of the sole proprietorship is its simplicity. A sole proprietorship is just a business owned directly by one person, with the property used in the business being the direct property of the owner.[3] Since there is no business entity involved in the sole proprietorship, there is no entity to form. What is at least as important, there are no formalities to follow or statutory requirements to meet in operating the business: no shareholders' or directors' meetings, no separate financial records and bank accounts, no annual reports, and no corporate tax returns.[4] With no entity to form and no formalities to follow, there obviously are no costs for those items

---

without the benefit of a charter, and what is most important, it does not offer its owners limited liability.

2. In a few situations, mostly relating to tax planning, it makes sense to operate a business in the trust form.
3. The natural word to use at the end of this sentence might seem to be "proprietor," but this would connote that the owner of the sole proprietorship manages the business as well as owns it. This usually is the case, but there are many exceptions. Probably the most common exception occurs when the owner retires and turns the management of the business over to others while retaining ownership.
4. In some states, however, if a sole proprietorship is to be operated in a name other than that of the owner, a filing to that effect must be made under a fictitious-name statute.

in a sole proprietorship, so in this particular, simplicity translates to a direct cost saving.

The sole proprietorship suffers from serious disadvantages, however. For one thing, it offers no structure for the management of other than a small business. Take, for example, a large manufacturing company that has a few hundred employees. The company likely will have several different operating divisions, and it necessarily will have a number of different departments to take care of the company's internal affairs. The owner can make up a management structure, with the heads of each division or department given whatever responsibilities and titles the owner wishes, but that structure will not exist until the owner devises it, and unless the owner uses traditional corporate titles, the titles the owner chooses likely will not carry a widely understood meaning.

But the problem of management structure is a small matter that is overwhelmed by the main problem in a sole proprietorship. That is the unlimited liability of the owner. The attribute of unlimited liability and problem of management structure are related, however. In a business in which the owner is the sole decision-maker and worker, unlimited liability is not much of a detriment if the owner's main fear is tort liability, because a tortfeasor can always be sued in his or her individual capacity. But as the operation of the business gets increasingly complex, with a widening spread of managers and workers, the sole proprietor becomes subject to more and more risk of vicarious liability arising from the acts of others. And on any rational ground, considering the availability of the corporate form, the sole proprietorship is an unacceptable form for operating a business when it subjects the owner to significant risks of vicarious liability.

General Partnership

Under the Uniform Partnership Act, which has been adopted in all states except Louisiana, a general partnership[5] is "an association of two or more persons to carry on as co-owners a business for profit."[6] If the partners wish, they can operate a partnership with the same simplicity and lack of formality as can an owner of a sole proprietorship. No agreement, written or otherwise, between the partners is necessary either to form or to operate a partnership. If the definition set out above is met, a partnership exists, and that is true regardless of whether the partners want a partnership to exist and regardless of whether they know it exists. Likewise, the partners can operate a partnership without any agreement relating to the partnership's management, in which case the management rules spelled out in the Uniform Partnership Act will serve in place of an agreement among the partners.

Under those rules each partner has the power to bind the partnership in connection with the usual business of the partnership,[7] and in the event of disagreement among the partners, the majority rules.[8] Also, in a partnership operating without a partnership agreement, the partners share equally in the partnership's profits and losses.[9] The rule as to profits and losses usually matches partners' desires when the partners make equal investments and contribute equal efforts, but in the case of disproportionate efforts or investments the partners usually will want profits and losses to be shared disproportionately.

That desire is easily accommodated by the Uniform Partnership Act, since it provides that the statutory split of profits and losses may be varied at will, so long as the partners reach an agreement on the

5. General partnerships usually are referred to simply as "partnerships," and we shall follow this convention from here on.
6. UNIFORM PARTNERSHIP ACT § 6(1).
7. *Id.* § 9 (1).
8. *Id.* § 18(e), (h).
9. *Id.* § 18(a).

split.[10] The rules as to management of the partnership also may be varied by agreement among the partners, so as to take away a partner's authority to bind the partnership, to opt out of majority rule, or to make virtually any other management change the partners wish.[11] Notice, however, that once an agreement among the partners is necessary, the benefit of simplicity—and its attendant cost saving—is decreased in proportion to the complexity of the agreement.

Still, the partnership is a good form for some businesses. In this respect, however, it is important to emphasize the word "some," for there are in America many more partnerships than there would be if their partners had sought the advice of good lawyers. No partnership should ever be formed without carefully considering the detriments of a partnership. We believe that there are three that are the most important. First, the death or bankruptcy of any partner dissolves a partnership.[12] Under the Uniform Partnership Act, the other partners will then have to wind up the business and affairs of the partnership and distribute its assets unless the remaining partners (and the estate of any deceased partner) can come to an arrangement for the formation of a new partnership.[13]

The second major detriment of the partnership form flows from the fact that the partnership is not an entity separate from its partners. This, of course, is not always a detriment. In most respects, a partnership's nonentity status is immaterial, and with respect to taxation this status is a clear benefit, for at the federal level and usually also under state law the partnership is not subject to income taxation. The partnership merely files an information return, and

10. *Id.* § 18.

11. *Id.* §§ 9(1), 18. What cannot be avoided, however, are the effects of apparent authority. If a partner without authority to bind the partnership nevertheless acts to do so in connection with the partnership's usual business, and if the person on the other side of the transaction does not know of the partner's lack of authority, the partnership is bound by the partner's act. *See id.* § 9(1).

12. *Id.* § 31(4), (5).

13. *Id.* §§ 29–43.

then each partner pays tax on his or her proportionate share of the partnership's profits or takes a deduction for the proper share of its losses. The detriment from the partnership's nonentity status arises upon the death of a partner. Since each piece of partnership property is considered to be part owned by the deceased partner, all of the partnership's property is subject to probate. This can be at least a nuisance in any partnership. In the case of a partnership owning property in several states, multiple probate can be an expensive nightmare.

As in the case of the sole proprietorship, the biggest detriment of the partnership is the fact that its owners do not enjoy limited liability. Rather, each partner is liable for all debts of the partnership.[14] In a large percentage of co-owned businesses in America, the owners could live with the other detriments of doing business in the partnership form, but not with the attribute of unlimited liability. Investment banking firms offer a good example. Prior to the 1970s, almost all such firms were partnerships, and they operated with no significant problems flowing from their status as partnerships. When a changing judicial and regulatory climate fostered the widespread fear of liability, however, investment banking firms began incorporating, and during the 1970s their movement from the partnership to the corporate form became virtually complete.

Limited Partnership

The limited partnership form was devised to remove the attribute of unlimited liability from some of the partners in a general partnership. The limited partnership is much like a general partnership, but it has a group of limited partners—who have limited liability—grafted on. Most of the legal rules in a general partnership are carried over to the limited partnership insofar as they relate to the general partners (of whom there must be at least one), with a special

---

14. *Id.* § 15.

set of rules applying to the limited partners. One large and important difference between general and limited partnerships is that a limited partnership cannot be created informally. In all states, to form a limited partnership, a certificate of limited partnership must be filed in one or more state offices.[15]

There are two separate Uniform Limited Partnership Acts, one adopted in 1916 and the other in 1976. The 1916 Act ultimately was adopted in all states except Louisiana, but that Act has now been superseded by the 1976 Act in about two-thirds of the states. The new Act creates no revolution. In large measure, it can be viewed as a cleaning up and streamlining of limited partnership law. The new Act is, nevertheless, a helpful improvement for those involved in limited partnerships, especially those serving as limited partners.

Under both the old and the new Acts, the main feature that distinguishes limited from general partners, along with the difference in their liability, is the placement of management power solely in the hands of the general partners.[16] It is perhaps in their treatment of the details of the liability and management rules of the limited partnership that the differences between the 1916 and 1976 Acts are most important. The 1916 Act's provision on the question of limited partners' liability and involvement in management is very simple: A limited partner has no liability to creditors unless he or she "takes part in the control of the business."[17] If a limited partner does take part in the control of the business, he or she loses limited liability. One problem with the 1916 Act is that there can be a good deal of argument about what constitutes taking part in the control of a business.

The drafters of the new Act started with the same concept for determining a limited partner's liability as did the drafters of the old

15. UNIFORM LIMITED PARTNERSHIP ACT (1916) § 2; UNIFORM LIMITED PARTNERSHIP ACT (1976) § 201.

16. UNIFORM LIMITED PARTNERSHIP ACT (1916) §§ 9, 10; UNIFORM LIMITED PARTNERSHIP ACT (1976) §§ 303, 404.

17. UNIFORM LIMITED PARTNERSHIP ACT (1916) § 7.

Act, and they used essentially equivalent operative words (substituting "participates in" for "takes part in" the control of the business), but then they added substantial elaboration in an attempt to reduce the area of uncertainty. This elaboration takes the form of an eight-item "safe harbor" list of actions that do not constitute participation in the control of the business. Examples are (1) consulting with a general partner with respect to the business of the partnership, (2) requesting or attending a meeting of partners, and (3) voting on any matter relating to the business of the partnership that under the partnership agreement is subject to the approval or disapproval of the limited partners.[18]

The new Act also made a more fundamental change with respect to limited partners' liability. Under the new Act, a limited partner who does participate in the control of the business is liable "only to persons who transact business with the limited partnership reasonably believing, based upon the limited partner's conduct, that the limited partner is a general partner."[19] In a large percentage of cases involving conduct by a limited partner that arguably constitutes participation in the control of the business, this provision may prove to be the Act's most effective liability shield.

There is one more change from the 1916 Act to the 1976 Act that deserves mention. The old Act makes no mention of the possibility of limited partnerships' operating across state lines. This presents a substantial problem for a business operating in more than one state, because it is not clear how a particular state may treat a foreign limited partnership, with the risk being that a state will treat it as a general partnership. This uncertainty often has led careful lawyers to form separate limited partnerships in each state in which a business will operate. The 1976 Act, on the other hand, devotes an entire article to the question of foreign limited partnerships and provides

---

18. UNIFORM LIMITED PARTNERSHIP ACT (1976) § 303.
19. *Id.*

that limited partnerships formed in other states may register under the Act as foreign limited partnerships.[20]

Limited partnerships tend to be used in three types of business situations. First, a business operating as a general partnership sometimes finds it convenient to recast itself as a limited partnership for the purpose of attracting new capital from investors who will share in the profits of the business but who have no desire to participate in its management. Second, a general partnership sometimes recasts itself as a limited partnership upon the retirement of a partner who wishes to leave capital invested in the partnership, and thus share in its profits, but who does not wish to be subjected to the unlimited liability of a general partner in a business that he or she no longer manages. These first two uses of the limited partnership are obviously closely related. The third use is quite different. It is the use of the limited partnership as a vehicle for tax-shelter investments. A good example is a limited partnership that is formed to build and operate a real estate venture, say an apartment complex or a shopping center. In those types of ventures, promoters have looked for investors anxious to make an investment that (1) will generate losses while the project is under construction, so that the investors can write these losses off against their other income and (2) will later make profits that can be passed through to the investors without taxation at the partnership level (in each case with these tax consequences flowing from the fact that partnerships are exempt from federal and most state income taxation).[21] Under the Internal Revenue Code of 1986, the tax benefits available from the use of such tax shelters are substantially less than under the prior Code, and so many fewer limited partnerships are now being formed.

---

20. *Id.* art. 9

21. See pp. 45–46 *supra.*

Corporations

Since the rest of this book will deal with corporations, we would get ahead of ourselves if we attempted to discuss the corporation completely at this point. In order to appreciate the reasons the corporate form is usually chosen for a business, however, it will be helpful to examine briefly the advantages and disadvantages of operating a business as a corporation.

Advantages of the Corporate Form

The advantages of operating a business as a corporation flow from these six attributes of the corporation:

1. Limited liability of shareholders
2. Management structure
3. Capital structure
4. Separate entity status
5. Tax status
6. Usual form for most businesses

1. Limited Liability of Shareholders

For most businesses operating in the corporate form, limited liability of shareholders is the most important advantage. This can be seen by imagining that the liability rules of corporation and partnership law have been switched while keeping all other aspects of these laws unchanged, so that partners enjoy limited liability, but shareholders do not. Even though, as will be seen in the discussions below, the corporate form presents many advantages lacking in the partnership form, there is little doubt that most corporate businesses would switch to the partnership form if this were necessary to preserve limited liability.

This may be a good point at which to return to the statement of Nicholas Murray Butler, set out in chapter 1,[22] about the significance of the limited liability corporation:

> I weigh my words when I say that in my judgment the limited liability corporation is the greatest single discovery of modern times. . . . Even steam and electricity are far less important than the limited liability corporation, and they would be reduced to comparative impotence without it.[23]

Butler was right, and the reason is that the nineteenth-century industrial revolution could not have advanced significantly without the availability of massive amounts of capital, which investors would not have provided without the guarantee of limited liability.

2. Management Structure

As we have seen, the attribute of limited liability makes the corporation an extraordinarily effective device for amassing capital. The management structure of the corporation makes it an equally effective device for managing capital. The strengths of the corporate form in this regard flow from two factors. First, the traditional management structure created in corporation statutes works perfectly for most businesses. This should not be surprising, since the traditional structure has evolved over a long period, during which the evolution has been driven by the desire of businesses to find the most usable management structure. Second, modern corporation statutes give corporations broad authority to vary their structure as their owners wish, so that any unusual needs are easily served.

The traditional management structure is three-tiered, consisting of shareholders, directors, and officers. In this structure, (1) shareholders elect directors and approve certain extraordinary corporate actions, (2) directors elect officers and have authority to manage or

---

22. See p. 15 *supra*.
23. Quoted in 1 W. FLETCHER, CYCLOPEDIA OF THE LAW OF PRIVATE CORPORATIONS § 21 (1917).

direct the management of the corporation that is unfettered except for the limited power of shareholders, and (3) officers use power delegated by the directors to manage the corporation in whatever ways the directors allow. As is apparent, there is substantial flexibility inherent in this traditional structure, in that the directors can decide how much authority to retain and how much to delegate to officers.

Section 35 of the Model Business Corporation Act offers a good example of a provision allowing variations from this traditional structure:

> All corporate powers shall be exercised by or under authority of, and the business and affairs of a corporation shall be managed under the direction of, a board of directors except as may be otherwise in this Act or the articles of incorporation.

If those forming a corporation wish to do away with the board of directors, this sentence in Model Act section 35 merely requires that provision for this be made in the charter. In such an instance, the next sentence of section 35 needs to be considered:

> If any such provision is made in the articles of incorporation, the powers and duties conferred or imposed upon the board of directors by this Act shall be exercised or performed to such extent and by such person or persons as shall be provided in the articles of incorporation.

Under this sentence, the powers of the board could be given to the shareholders or to one or more officers, or the board's powers could be distributed among the shareholders and the officers, as the drafter of the charter wishes. Or, under Model Act section 35, the board may be left in place but with some of its powers given to the shareholders or to the officers.[24]

24. In practice, only close corporations ever deviate from the traditional management structure, and they do so infrequently.

3. Capital Structure

As in the case of management structure, the advantage of the corporate form in capital structure flows from the existence of a simple, traditional form of structure that perfectly serves the needs of most corporations, coupled with the flexibility to vary the traditional structure almost at will. In the simplest capital structure, a corporation has one class of stock, typically called common stock, which represents the sole ownership interest in the corporation. That is all the capital structure the average corporation needs when it begins its existence.

The first move away from this simplest structure typically is the issuance of a promissory note to evidence a loan taken by the corporation, thus leaving the corporation with one type of equity interest, the common stock, and one type of debt interest, the note. From here the permutations in capital structure are almost endless. A corporation might have two classes of common stock, with the rights of ownership in the corporation split between the classes in any way those controlling the corporation wish. For example, the classes might be equal in every way except that one class carries the right to vote and the other does not. A corporation might have one or more classes of preferred stock in addition to common stock.[25]

Debt interests can vary as much as can equity interests. A corporation might issue several different promissory notes having varying provisions with respect to interest payable and the terms of payment. The corporation might also issue a number of different bonds and debentures.[26] One type of interest in the corporation may also be made convertible into another type of interest. For example, a bond might be convertible into common or preferred stock at the

25. Preferred stock is simply stock that is preferred in some respect or other, or in several respects, to the common stock. For example, the holders of the preferred stock might have the right to receive a certain dollar amount of dividends before any dividends are paid to the holders of the common stock.

26. The differences between notes, bonds, and debentures are discussed in chapter 5. *See* p. 103 *infra*.

option of the bond holder, or preferred stock might be convertible into common stock. Or, for that matter, preferred stock or a class of common stock might be convertible into bonds or debentures.

In short, those controlling a corporation have virtual carte blanche to create any capital structure they wish. That being true, those wanting to exercise financial creativity have the full chance to do so. What is more important in the usual situation is that a full range of permutations in capital structure is already in existence and well known to corporate lawyers, so that the need for the creation of a unique structure is rare. What almost any client wants in a capital structure is available "off the shelf."

4. Separate Entity Status

The status of the corporation as a separate entity creates advantages in at least two ways. First, since the corporation is an entity separate from its owners, the death or bankruptcy of an owner, which would dissolve a partnership,[27] has no institutional effect on the corporation. In the case of bankruptcy, a shareholder simply continues as a shareholder, and when a shareholder dies, his or her shares are distributed to the heirs as personal property.

The fact that upon the death of a shareholder his or her shares are distributed to heirs as personal property points up the second benefit that flows from a corporation's status as a separate entity. Remember that since a partnership is not an entity separate from its partners, a deceased partner's estate must be probated in each state where the partnership owns property.[28] The expense and trouble of multiple probate is avoided in a corporation, since, as personal property, corporate shares are subject to probate only in the deceased shareholder's state of domicile.

27. *See* p. 45 *supra.*
28. *See* pp. 45–46 *supra.*

5. Tax Treatment

Whereas a partnership is not subject to federal income taxation because it is not an entity separate from its partners,[29] a corporation is subject to federal income taxation precisely because it is a separate entity. When a corporation distributes its after-tax profits to its shareholders as dividends, those dividends are subject to taxation as the ordinary income of the shareholders. Thus corporate income that is distributed to shareholders is twice subjected to taxation. This double taxation most definitely is not an advantage of the corporate form. Double taxation can be avoided, however, and once it is avoided, the corporate form does provide tax advantages.

Congress has provided certain close corporations with the most straightforward way of avoiding double taxation. Under the Internal Revenue Code, a corporation meeting specified requirements can choose to be treated for federal tax purposes as if it were a partnership.[30] In that case, the corporation will file merely an information return, and any corporate profits or losses will flow through to its shareholders for inclusion in their individual income tax returns. Such corporations are called type S corporations, with that designation coming from the fact that the provisions in the Code dealing with such corporations were originally contained in subchapter S of the Internal Revenue Code of 1954. Here are the requirements for type S treatment:

1. No more than thirty-five shareholders.
2. Incorporation in the United States.
3. Only one class of stock.
4. Shareholders must be individuals, estates, or specified types of trusts.
5. No shareholder may be a nonresident alien.

---

29. *Id.*
30. I.R.C. §§ 1361–1379.

6. May not be a life insurance company or certain other excluded types of businesses.
7. All shareholders must agree to the type S election.[31]

In some corporations that have not elected type S treatment, double taxation can be avoided to an extent, or at least deferred, by not paying dividends. The shareholders do not necessarily see this as a hardship, because they usually want their corporation to keep available cash invested in the corporation, rather than pay it out in dividends, so that the corporation will grow and the shareholders' shares will become more valuable. This is especially true in a close corporation that is owned and managed by the same group of people, since the group can take money out of the corporation as salaries and directors' fees, which are deductible expenses for the corporation and thus not subject to double taxation.

Not only do corporations avoid double taxation by reinvesting available cash and paying salaries to their owner-managers, they may minimize or at least defer even single taxation by the same means. Good managers often are able shrewdly to spend cash that otherwise would end up as a profit on an expansion of the business. If the managers are successful at this technique, the corporation can become larger and more successful each year, while paying substantially minimized income taxes.

Perfection in this technique is not easily achieved, and the corporation looks for other ways to minimize taxes. There are some expenditures for officer and employee benefits that are deductible to the corporation and not taxable to the recipients. Generally, these expenditures are those relating to medical payment and disability plans, group term life insurance up to $50,000, death benefits up to $5,000, and certain deferred compensation plans.[32] The availability

31. *Id.* §§ 1361, 1362.
32. *Id.* §§ 79, 101, 105, 401–425.

of this tax-free treatment can be especially valuable to owner-managers, because as officers or employees they themselves can receive these tax-free benefits.

6. Usual Form

The corporation is the usual form for the operation of a business of any size, and the advantages of operating in the usual form should not be underestimated. In the business world, things work more smoothly if one operates in the usual way. Take, for example, something as simple as opening a bank account. When a corporation wishes to open an account, any customer service clerk in the bank can provide the standard forms. This would also be true for a partnership, but it would not be true for a business trust or any other exotic form of business. The same sort of experience will be encountered when a business wants to sign a lease or buy expensive equipment. Those on the other side of the transaction are used to dealing with corporations and are familiar with how documents are signed on behalf of corporations. With other forms of business, save perhaps the partnership, that usually is not the case.

Disadvantages of the Corporate Form

There are three clear disadvantages of operating a business in the corporate form:

1. Expense and trouble of formation and maintenance
2. Required initial and continuing formalities
3. Tax treatment

1. Expense and Trouble of Formation and Maintenance

To form a corporation, a charter needs to be drafted in accordance with the statutory requirements and then filed in one or more offices in the state of incorporation. After incorporation, bylaws need to be drafted for adoption. All this work should be done by a knowledgeable lawyer, with attendant fees of at least a few hundred dollars. The state's fees will not be substantial for a close corporation, but they will add perhaps $100 to the total costs. If the corporation is to operate in any state other than the one in which it is incorporated, it will have to qualify to do business in that state. Qualification will entail drafting and filing other forms and paying additional fees.

In addition to these one-time costs of incorporation and qualification to do business, the filing of an annual report and the paying of an annual fee will be required in the state of incorporation and in most states in which the corporation is qualified to do business. In addition to the legal fees corporations pay initially and each year in connection with the filing of annual reports, a corporation will almost certainly incur legal fees on a continuing basis for advice on corporation law, for drafting charter and bylaw amendments, for drafting minutes of meetings, and for other work relating to the corporation's internal affairs.

All such corporate expenses could be avoided in a sole proprietorship, and they could be avoided in a partnership if the partners choose to operate without a partnership agreement. Operating without a partnership agreement is usually unwise, however, and drafting a proper partnership agreement often gives rise to higher legal fees than does the drafting of a corporation's charter and bylaws, because a partnership agreement often involves more custom drafting than do a corporation's charter and bylaws. Still, the total legal expenses and fees to states typically will be more in a corporation than in a partnership.

2. Required Initial and Continuing Formality

A sole proprietorship and a partnership, and to a degree a limited partnership, can be operated without formalities and without records of decisions that are made. The rules are quite different in a corporation. Both the shareholders and the directors must have meetings, or take action by formal written consent in lieu of meetings, and proper records must be kept of shareholders' and directors' actions. Further, the funds of the corporation must be kept separate from those of its owner or owners, and proper financial records must be maintained.

None of these requirements typically seems onerous to lawyers, but clients often view them as needless bothers. Unless their lawyers convince them otherwise, managers of close corporations tend to ignore some or all of these formalities. As will be seen in chapter 7, the cost of ignoring formalities might be that a court will disregard the corporate form and allow creditors to collect from a corporation's shareholders.

3. Tax Treatment

The tax disadvantage of operating in the corporate form is, of course, double taxation, which has been discussed above.[33] Even though double taxation often can be avoided, the fact that it exists as a possibility and that corporate managers must devote efforts to avoiding it makes double taxation a clear disadvantage of operating in the corporate form.

Preincorporation Transactions

Before a corporation can be formed for the operation of a business, those behind the business often desire to enter into one or more contracts on behalf of the corporation that is to be formed. There are many ways these contracts can be handled, some of which may have results that are not desired by those who make these contracts. The rules relating to these contracts are part of the common-law doctrine of promoters' contracts, and questions relating to these contracts can most helpfully be divided into two categories.

---

33. *See* p. 55 *supra.*

The first category is the rights and liabilities of corporations on promoters' contracts, and the second is the rights and liabilities of promoters on promoters' contracts.

Rights and Liabilities of Corporations on Promoters' Contracts

No matter what a contract by its terms provides about the liabilities of a corporation that is not yet formed, the corporation is not bound by the contract unless after it is formed it takes some action to make the contract its own or takes some action that will cause a court to estop the corporation from denying that it is bound by the contract.

Ratification

The doctrine of ratification is so generally useful in the corporate context that when faced with the problem of how to make a promoters' contract a corporation's own, lawyers often think first of having the corporation ratify the acts of a promoter in making the contract. The way ratification would be accomplished formally is for the board of directors to adopt a resolution saying that the acts of the promoter in executing and delivering the contract are ratified. The problem with ratification, however, is that it relates back to the point in time when the action that is being ratified occurred. That is, the effect of ratification is retroactively to authorize whatever act is being ratified, as of the time of the act. Since, in the case of a promoter's contract, no corporation was in existence at the time the promoter executed and delivered the contract, ratification is a logical impossibility.

Adoption

In the case of promoters' contracts, the way for a corporation to bind itself to the contract is by adoption, which works in much the same way as ratification, except that adoption does not have retroactive effect. A corporation may adopt a contract in one of two ways, formally or informally. For a formal adoption, the board of directors passes a resolution stating that it adopts the contract. This is the safest course if a corporation has any question about the desire of the party on the other side of the contract to go through with the contract. Usually, however, adoption is informal, with the typical adoption scenario seeing the newly formed corporation performing obligations under the contract with knowledge of the contract's terms.[34]

Rights and Obligations of Promoters on Promoters' Contracts

Promoters generally are personally liable under promoters' contracts, largely because, to be enforceable, a contract has to have at least one party on each side, and as we have just seen, a corporation cannot be bound to a contract when it is not yet in existence. In the garden-variety promoters' contract, where the promoter simply signs on behalf of the to-be-formed corporation, if the promoter were not bound by the contract, there would not be a contract. In terms of agency principles, this result is explained by the rule that if an agent purports to act for a nonexistent principal, the agent is personally bound. The general rule of promoters' liability does not always hold true, however, and whether or not a promoter is bound by a promoters' contract often turns on (1) what the parties seem to have intended and (2) how the contract is drafted.

Intent of the Parties

Care is needed in dealing with the question of intent of the parties in the context of promoters' contracts, because the question of what

34. For a leading case discussing both ratification and adoption of promoters' contracts, see McArthur v. Times Printing Co., 48 Minn. 319, 51 N.W. 216 (1892)

the parties intended needs to be approached in a special way. Suppose, as is often the case, a promoter negotiates a contract on behalf of a nonexistent corporation without telling the other party that the corporation has not yet been formed and then the promoter signs in the name of the corporation. In such a situation, the parties clearly intended that the corporation and not the promoter be bound. This situation, however, is an example of the classic, garden-variety promoters' contract that is covered by the general rule that the promoter is liable and the corporation is not. So looking for "what the parties intended" cannot be taken literally.

If the facts of the situation are changed slightly, however, to include the knowledge by the other party that no corporation was in existence when the contract was signed, courts sometimes will alter the general rule and find that the promoter is not liable. This is especially likely if the equities seem to be on the side of the promoter. *Sherwood & Roberts-Oregon, Inc. v. Alexander*[35] offers a good example. In that case, the plaintiff was a mortgage lender and the defendants were real estate developers. One of the defendants executed a promissory note, bearing 12 percent interest, in the name of a corporation to be formed. That interest rate would have been usurious if the borrower were an individual, and the plaintiff therefore told the defendants that the loan would have to be made to a corporation. The defendant who signed the note gave the plaintiff the name of the corporation to be formed, and the defendants accepted the note, knowing that the corporation was not yet in existence. In those circumstances, the Oregon Supreme Court found that "the plaintiff looked solely to the to-be-formed corporation for payment of the note."[36]

---

35. Sherwood & Roberts-Or., Inc. v. Alexander, 269 Or. 389, 525 P.2d 135 (1974).

36. *Id.* at 396, 525 P.2d at 139. Quaker Hill, Inc. v. Parr, 148 Colo. 45, 364 P.2d 1056 (1961), involved a situation similar to the one in *Sherwood*, except that

How a Contract Is Drafted

How a contract is drafted also significantly affects a promoter's possible liability. Any language that a court can interpret as indicating an intent that the promoter is not to be personally liable may be used by the court to relieve the promoter of liability. But unless the language is clear beyond argument, a court can be expected to be guided in its contract interpretation, subconsciously at least, by how it perceives the equities of the situation. That being the case, the only safe course for a promoter who wishes to escape personal liability on a standard promoters' contract is to include clear language in the contract saying explicitly that the other contracting party will look only to the to-be-formed corporation for performance. A pitfall to be avoided here, of course, is lack of consideration, so the promoter should ensure that the other party receives something in the bargain that will provide the necessary consideration.

Another possibility for a promoter is to secure a written option from the other contracting party by which the other party grants to the promoter, for the benefit of the to-be-formed corporation, an option to enter into a specified contract. This is often the most artful way to ensure that the promoter escapes personal liability while also assuring the right of the to-be-formed corporation to enter into a desired contract. As in the case of the standard promoters' contract, of course, the promoter needs to be sure that the option is supported by sufficient consideration.

Promoter's Liability After a Corporation's Adoption

Assume that a promoter enters into a standard promoters' contract under which he or she is bound, and assume further that the

---

in *Quaker Hill* the other contracting party actually suggested that the promoter sign a contract in the name of a corporation to be formed. The result was the same as in *Alexander*: The promoter was held not to be liable.

corporation that is to have the benefit of the contract is formed and adopts the contract. Is the promoter thereby released from personal liability? The promoter probably will assume so, but that is not the case. Absent a novation whereby the other contracting party releases the promoter from liability upon accepting a substituted party, the promoter will remain liable along with the now formed corporation.[37] To guard against promoters' liability, then, either (1) language contemplating an automatic novation upon adoption of the contract by the to-be-formed corporation must be included in the contract or (2) a novation (either formal or one that can be inferred from words or actions of the other contracting party) must be effected after the to-be-formed corporation has adopted the contract.

Ethical and Practice Issues

The area of promoters' contracts is one that is ripe for ethical and practice issues for the corporate lawyer. One reason for this is that the lawyer may originally have been representing the promoter and then, upon the formation of a corporation, the lawyer begins representing the corporation instead of the promoter. Suppose, for example, that the promoter signs an ordinary promoters' contract without seeking the lawyer's help and then, after the corporation is formed and has a number of shareholders in addition to the promoter (who, let us assume, serves as the corporation's chief executive officer and the lawyer's main contact with the corporation), questions arise in the lawyer's mind about whether it is in the best interests of the corporation to adopt the contract. There exists here, of course, a classic conflict of interest problem of the type discussed in chapter 2.[38]

The lawyer's duty to the corporate client is clear, but the way the lawyer can handle the conflict ethically and without alienating the

37. *See, e.g.*, Jacobson v. Stern, 605 P.2d 198 (Nev. 1980).

38. *See* pp. 39–40 *supra*.

lawyer's main contact with the client is not nearly so clear. A smaller and more easily managed problem will arise if the corporation wants to adopt the contract and the promoter wants to seek a novation. Perhaps going to the other contracting party for a novation will upset an already delicate relationship for the corporation. In that case the lawyer is again facing a conflict of interest. Typically, however, the only ethical or practice problem in seeking the novation would relate to whether the corporation or the promoter is to pay for the legal work involved. Sometimes the amount of the fee involved in a situation like this does not justify the friction that may be created by resolving such issues. It sometimes may be best, for example, just to handle the novation as a courtesy and write off the legal time involved.

CHAPTER FOUR

Incorporation

Once the decision is made to form a corporation for the operation of a business, the next decision to make is where to incorporate. When that decision is made, the question arises as to how best to accomplish incorporation in the chosen state to the maximum benefit of the clients. In practical drafting terms, the question of where to incorporate affects what must go in the corporation's charter, since requirements vary from state to state, and the question of how best to accomplish incorporation affects what goes in the charter beyond the bare requirements of the chosen state of incorporation.

Where to Incorporate

The discussion in chapter 1 of the major twentieth-century developments in corporation law showed the widespread congruence of corporation law among the various states.[1] This congruence usually makes easy the choice of the state of incorporation. For the typical corporation, the clear choice is the state where the corporation is principally to operate. Virtually without exception, the corporation law of that state will be based on a modern enabling statute that offers any options necessary for the efficient operation of a start-up corporation. Some desirable options, such as the ability of the board of directors to conduct business by written consents in lieu of

1. *See* pp. 16–17 *supra*.

meetings or by telephone, admittedly may not be available in the home state's corporation statute, but usually it is preferable to forgo such options rather than to incorporate in another state. The reasons for this preference relate to expense and trouble. If a business is incorporated in a state other than its home state, it will have to qualify to do business in its home state and will have to file reports and pay fees each year not only in its state of incorporation but in its home state as well.

This is not to say, of course, that home state incorporation is always desirable. Suppose, for example, that the proposed directors of a particular corporation live in different states, so that getting together for board meetings is impractical. In such a corporation, it is necessary to incorporate in a state that allows either telephone board meetings or written consents in lieu of board meetings. Also, for some corporations there will be tax savings to be had by incorporating elsewhere than in the home state. For the typical start-up corporation, the tax rates of the various states are irrelevant, since in almost all cases the corporation will pay the state's minimum tax, typically $100 or so. The rates become relevant for some corporations, however. Typically those are corporations that expect to have their shares publicly held by a large number of shareholders, since taxes often are based on the number of shares that the corporation is authorized to issue.

Advantages of Delaware Incorporation

Delaware's corporation statute allows both written consents in lieu of board meetings[2] and telephone board meetings,[3] along with a full range of other options a particular corporation may find necessary. And when it comes to tax savings for corporations that are to have a large number of public shareholders, Delaware often wins out as the state of incorporation, since its corporate tax structure has

2. Del. Gen. Corp. Law § 141.
3. *Id.*

been carefully designed to beat the competition.[4] For the large publicly held corporation that does business in many states, Delaware also is often the state of choice for incorporation because of its judiciary, which is highly competent in corporation law, and its large and well developed body of existing corporate case law, which sometimes adds a legal certainty that may be lacking in other states.[5] For such corporations, which already have to stand the expense and trouble of qualifying to do business in many states, the possible extra expense of qualifying in the corporation's home state is too small to worry about. Also, the fast and efficient service available from the Delaware Secretary of State's office adds a benefit to Delaware incorporation. Finally, the appeal to lawyers or clients of Delaware's law on one or more particular matters, such as directors' liability,[6] may be enough to make them settle on Delaware incorporation.

Disadvantages of Delaware Incorporation

Even for the large publicly held corporation, there are disadvantages to incorporating in Delaware that are important in some situations. The first disadvantage is that by incorporating in Delaware, a corporation and its lawyers forgo the benefits of operating under the Revised Model Business Corporation Act, which is a better statute than the one now in existence in Delaware. Delaware's corporation

4. See p. 16 *supra*.
5. See pp. 16–17 *supra*.
6. As will be seen in chapter 9, Delaware has been a leader in creating both statutory and case law on directors' liability. That area offers a good example, however, of corporation law congruence among the various states. Within a few months after Delaware in 1986 passed a new statute on directors' liability, about half the other states passed statutes of their own, most of which were copies or near copies of Delaware's. It should also be noted that the Delaware statute was triggered in large measure by a legislative desire to counter a Delaware Supreme Court decision on directors' liability that corporations and their lawyers generally disfavored.

statute has not been overhauled since 1953, but it has been subjected to continual amendment. In many ways, it is a jumble that is difficult to use. The Revised Model Act, on the other hand, was new in 1984, and it is the product of painstaking drafting designed to maximize its benefit to businesses, including the benefit of being easy to use. The Revised Model Act is a rewrite of the Model Business Corporation Act, and to understand why the Revised Model Act is so good, one has to understand something of both model Acts. Each is the product of the Committee on Corporate Laws of the American Bar Association's Section of Business Law. Over several decades the members of this committee drafted and refined the Model Act, always with an eye to what Delaware was doing with its corporation statute. The Model Act and the Delaware statute ended up being very much alike in substance, but perhaps because of better drafting, it was the Model Act rather than the Delaware statute that states around the country chose to copy. Ultimately, the Model Act served as the basis for the corporation laws of over half the states. In the early 1980s the Committee on Corporate Laws decided it was time to rewrite the Model Act, and in 1984 the committee came out with the Revised Model Act as a completely rewritten and streamlined statute. The Revised Model Act has now been adopted in a handful of states, in each case with some modifications. Of the various versions of the Revised Model Act, the Tennessee Business Corporation Act is one of the most refined, and we therefore shall use it as our Revised Model Act example.

Substantively, the Tennessee statute differs from the Delaware statute in several ways. Here are some of them:

1. The Revised Model Act does away with the archaic concepts of par value, stated capital, and treasury stock, and with the consequences that follow from them, whereas the Delaware statute retains those concepts. The Revised Model Act's approach leads to simplified accounting and

corporate decision-making and also avoids the liabilities that can flow from violating the rules that accompany those outmoded concepts.

2. Delaware's statute allows a corporate charter to provide that shareholders are liable for a corporation's debts, but under the Tennessee version of the Revised Model Act that is not possible. Since under each statute a corporation may amend its charter freely upon the majority vote of its shareholders, the Tennessee approach avoids the mischief that could flow to minority shareholders if a majority of the shareholders decided to amend the corporation's charter to provide for shareholder liability.
3. Compared to the Revised Model Act, the Delaware statute contains some niggling provisions that serve mainly as traps for the unwary. Under the Delaware statute, for example, oral notice of shareholders' meetings is never sufficient, but rather notice must be in writing no matter what the circumstances. Along those same lines, under the Delaware statute elections of directors are to be by written ballot unless a corporation's charter specifically provides otherwise, regardless of whether written ballots serve any purpose in a particular situation. At first glance, provisions like those may seem unimportant. And they are, so long as those managing a corporation never run afoul of them. But there the problem lies, for compliance with provisions like those does not come naturally to corporate managers for the simple reason that the formalities mandated by such provisions often do not make any sense. The drafters of the Revised Model Act made a real effort to save the managers of corporations from worrying about needless formalities.
4. In order to protect a Tennessee corporation from claims to the contrary, the Tennessee version of the Revised Model Act provides, in its section allowing charter amendments,

> that shareholders do not have vested property rights resulting from any provision in the charter or bylaws, including provisions relating to management, control, capital structure, dividend entitlement, or purpose or duration of the corporation. The Delaware statute offers no such protection.

A second disadvantage of incorporation in Delaware is felt by corporations that desire their state of incorporation to pass aggressive antitakeover legislation. Delaware has not passed such legislation, and it is not likely to do so. One reason for that reticence is that the Delaware legislature is pulled both ways on the issue. There are powerful Delaware corporations that want the unfettered opportunity to take over other Delaware corporations, and there are Delaware corporations that want protection from being taken over. In that situation, the safest course for Delaware probably is to steer a middle course, which is what the legislature has done in the takeover area.[7]

How to Incorporate

In determining how to incorporate, the first place to look for guidance is the corporation statute in the state of incorporation. Since the Model Business Corporation Act, as in effect prior to 1979, is the statute that is most representative of the statutes found in states around the country, we shall use it as our main example throughout the book. (For the convenience of readers, the complete text of the Model Act, as of the end of 1978, is included as appendix A.) Incorporation is covered in Model Act sections 53 through 56. Section 53 provides that: "One or more persons . . . may act as

7. The Delaware legislature has adopted legislation that requires a three-year delay before a large shareholder can effect a merger, unless certain conditions are satisfied. Del. Gen. Corp. Law § 203.

incorporator or incorporators of a corporation by signing and delivering in duplicate to the Secretary of State articles of incorporation for such corporation." Section 54 tells what the articles of incorporation must contain, and section 55 details what the secretary of state's office is to do with articles of incorporation delivered by incorporators. Basically, if the articles comply with the statute, one of the duplicates is to be filed in the secretary of state's office and the other is to be returned to the incorporators along with a certificate of incorporation attesting to the validity the articles.[8] Finally, section 56 gives the effect of the issuance of a certificate of incorporation:

> Upon the issuance of the certificate of incorporation, the corporate existence shall begin, and such certificate of incorporation shall be conclusive evidence that all conditions precedent required to be performed by the incorporators have been complied with and that the corporation has been incorporated under this Act, except as against the State in a proceeding to cancel or revoke the certificate of incorporation or for involuntary dissolution of the corporation.[9]

Under the corporation statutes that were in existence several decades ago, incorporation was a multistep procedure, perhaps requiring the publication of notice of intent to incorporate, then the filing of articles of incorporation in a state office, then the filing of the articles in one or more county offices, then publication of notice

8. The terminology relating to articles of incorporation and certificates of incorporation varies from state to state. Most follow the Model Act. Some, however, call the document that is filed by the incorporator a certificate of incorporation. In those states, the secretary of state's office, or the office of some other official, attaches to the certificate of incorporation a certificate attesting the validity of the certificate of incorporation. "Charter" is the generic term for a certificate of incorporation and for articles of incorporation (or, more properly, articles of incorporation with the accompanying certificate of incorporation attached by the secretary of state's office).

9. Under some statutes, including the Revised Model Act, the corporate existence begins upon the filing of the articles by the secretary of state's office. (Notice that that is not the delivery of the articles to that office by the incorporator.)

of incorporation, then the payment to the corporation by shareholders of a specified amount of capital. Under those old statutes, it sometimes was difficult to tell at just what point the corporation came into existence, causing promoters and their lawyers to wonder when a contract could safely be signed on behalf of the corporation, without worrying about promoters' liability. Model Act section 56 is an example of the care the drafters of the Model Act took to create a statute free of such problems, since under that section there can be no confusion about the exact moment when the corporation comes into existence—even if there are underlying problems, such as a defect in the articles of incorporation not caught by the secretary of state's office.[10]

Articles of Incorporation

After looking at the corporation statute's incorporation requirements, the next step in incorporation is to obtain a copy or example of the state's charter form. In some states, one fills in the blanks in a form provided by the secretary of state. In others, one types out the entire charter. In yet other states, one has a choice between those two procedures. In any case, it is necessary to obtain a form or an example of a charter that has been accepted by the secretary of state, so that one can see exactly what the secretary of state requires, since

---

10. Defects in articles occur with some frequency because those drafting articles of incorporation too often do not check the statutory requirements. Unless a defect is quite clear on the face of the articles, the secretary of state's office is not likely to catch it, since the clerks in the office typically give filed documents only cursory review.

that may not be entirely apparent from a reading of the statute. Here is the Model Act's form of articles of incorporation:

ARTICLES OF INCORPORATION

OF

____

The undersigned, acting as incorporator(s) of a corporation under the [State] Business Corporation Act, adopt(s) the following Articles of Incorporation for such corporation:

FIRST: The name of the corporation is ____________.

SECOND: The period of its duration is ____________.

THIRD: The purpose or purposes for which the corporation is formed are: ________________________________.

FOURTH: The aggregate number of shares which the corporation shall have authority to issue is ____.

FIFTH: Provisions granting preemptive rights are: ____.

SIXTH: Provisions for the regulation of the internal affairs of the corporation are: ____.

SEVENTH: The address of the initial registered office of the corporation is ________________, and the name of its initial registered agent at such address is ________________.

EIGHTH: The number of directors constituting the initial board of directors of the corporation is ______, and the names and addresses of the persons who are to serve as directors until the first annual meeting of shareholders or until their successors are elected and qualify are:

Name	Address
____________________________	____________________________
____________________________	____________________________
____________________________	____________________________

NINTH: The name and address of each incorporator is:

Name	Address
______________________	______________________
______________________	______________________
______________________	______________________

Dated _________, 19__

____

____

____
Incorporator(s)

This form will serve as a good organizational device for a discussion of many of the issues encountered during the course of incorporation. In using the form in that way, we shall simply start at the top and work through to the end, discussing the various issues as they present themselves.

Corporate Name

In the heading of the articles and in Article First, the name of the corporation needs to be filled in. There are more tricks here than there might seem. First, all corporation statutes contain requirements and limitations on corporate names. For example, section 8 of the Model Act requires that the name contain the word "corporation," "company," "incorporated," or "limited," or an abbreviation of one of those words.[11] That section also provides that a corporate name cannot imply that the corporation is organized for a purpose

11. That requirement actually serves as a good example of how enabling the Model Act is. Notice that the word "company" is typically used in the name of a sole proprietorship or a partnership and that the term "limited" is usually

that is not covered in its charter and further that a name may not be the same as or deceptively similar to the name of another corporation that is incorporated or qualified to do business in the state. One can check with the secretary of state's office to see if a desired name is available, and if it is, Model Act section 9 provides a procedure for reserving the name until articles of incorporation can be drafted and filed. If a name is unusual enough that it is not likely to be taken by someone else within a few days, corporate lawyers typically do not bother with the reservation procedure.

Simply clearing the desired corporate name in the state of incorporation often is not enough. Good lawyers ask which states the corporation plans to do business in within the foreseeable future. Even small startup businesses often at least hope to do business in contiguous states. With a list of states in hand, a lawyer can contact the office of the secretary of state in each state on the list and check on the availability of the desired name, looking forward to the time when qualification to do business will be required there. Sections 10 and 11 of the Model Act provide procedures for a foreign corporation to register its name and to renew that registration so as to prevent others from beating the corporation to the name.

It is easy to see that a large amount of time and effort can be expended in clearing, reserving, and registering a corporate name. What may not be so apparent is that a fair amount of experience may be necessary to accomplish that process. Sometimes a member of the secretary of state's staff will say that a particular name is not available because another corporation has a name that is too similar. That presents a number of questions, which the staff member likely will have leeway in answering. If the staff member believes the name is not so close that the public will be misled, he or she may allow the name to be used if written permission is obtained from the corporation with the similar name. Or the staff member may allow the name

used in America to designate a limited partnership. Those terms do not put members of the public on notice that they are dealing with a corporation.

to be used with the addition of a modifying word or two to the name. For example, "River City Corporation" may be unacceptable, but "River City Gas Corporation" may be fine. In situations like that, there is no substitute for experience, especially experience in dealing with a particular secretary of state's office.

For that reason and for reasons of general efficiency a lawyer often is wise to turn over to a corporation service company all matters relating to a corporate name. Those companies, of which the Corporation Trust Company is one of the better known, provide a number of services to lawyers in addition to clearing and reserving corporate names, among them filing charters and other corporate papers. They are experts in handling matters with the offices of secretaries of state and often know what a particular office will accept as a solution when a desired corporate name is too close to that of another corporation.

Duration

Article Second calls for the period of the corporation's duration. As indicated in chapter 1,[12] in an earlier era the duration of corporations typically was limited to twenty to fifty years. Under all modern corporation statutes, a corporation's duration may be perpetual, and under some statutes, a corporation's duration is perpetual unless its charter specifies otherwise. Unless a lawyer sees an overwhelming reason for doing otherwise, a corporation's duration should be made perpetual. Suppose, for example, that those starting a mining exploration corporation wish to ensure that the venture will go on for only five years unless each shareholder agrees otherwise. The corporation's duration could be limited to five years, but since the charter typically could be amended by majority votes of the directors and the shareholders,[13] steps also would have to be taken to limit the ability of the shareholders to approve a charter amendment

12. See p. 13 *supra*.
13. *See, e.g.*, MODEL BUSINESS CORP. ACT §§ 58, 59.

by less than a unanimous vote.[14] At the end of the corporation's stated life, it would have to distribute its assets in accordance with the corporation statute, which would give the board of directors substantial discretion in deciding whether to distribute assets in kind or to sell them and distribute cash,[15] unless steps were also taken to limit the board's discretion in that respect.[16]

In some cases, taking all those steps may be the proper course for accomplishing the clients' desires, but before doing so the careful lawyer would want to explore the possibility of creating the desired protections by a contract among the prospective shareholders. Exactly the protections desired could be fine-tuned in the contract, and that would avoid the undesirable consequences that might flow from a charter limitation on the corporation's duration. What are those consequences? There are at least four. First, if the corporation's duration is to be extended, the corporation will have to go to the expense and trouble of a charter amendment. Second, since a charter is often put in a corporation's files and forgotten, it is not unlikely that the corporation's duration will run out without the shareholders' giving much thought to it, especially if the venture is doing well during the last couple of years of its existence. Third, each shareholder will have the power to extort perhaps unreasonable concessions in exchange for a vote in favor of a charter amendment even if it is clear on rational grounds that the corporation's duration should be extended. Finally, the corporation will find it impossible to enter into bank loans or contracts that run beyond the end of its duration, and that can affect it severely in the final years of its life.

---

14. See p. 85 *infra* for a discussion of how that could be accomplished.
15. *See, e.g.*, MODEL BUSINESS CORP. ACT § 87, read along with § 35.
16. See pp. 84–85 *infra* for a discussion of how that could be accomplished.

Corporate Purposes

Article Third calls for a specification of the corporation's purpose or purposes. The first thing a lawyer needs to do with respect to corporate purposes is check the corporation statute for requirements, because they vary from state to state. The Model Act provisions are typical of an approach followed in many states. Section 3 provides that corporations may be incorporated for any lawful purpose or purposes, except banking and insurance,[17]and section 54 tells us that in the charter a corporation's purpose or purposes may be stated to be "the transaction of any or all lawful business . . .." In a number of states, however, a corporation's exact purposes must be stated explicitly in the charter. In those states the drafter has no choice but to draft a specific purposes clause. In states that follow the approach of the Model Act, the question arises as to whether it is better to state specific purposes or to state the purposes as "the transaction of any or all lawful business."[18]

In making that decision, it is necessary first to understand the consequences when a corporation engages in activities that are not covered by the purposes clause in its charter. Such activities are termed ultra vires, or beyond the corporation's power, and there is a large body of corporation law covering the consequences of ultra vires acts. In assessing those consequences, the first place to look is the corporation statute. Section 7 of the Model Act provides a representative example. Under that section, no act of a corporation is invalid because the corporation "was without capacity or power to do such Act," but the lack of authority may be asserted in three ways: (1) in a proceeding by a shareholder to enjoin the act; (2) in a proceeding by the corporation directly, by a trustee in bankruptcy or

17. Banking and insurance are carved out of the Model Act because its drafters assumed that banks and insurance companies would be incorporated under special-purpose statutes.

18. Even corporations incorporated in states that do not require a specific recitation of purposes may nevertheless have to state specific purposes in the papers they file to qualify to do business in another state.

other representative, or by a shareholder suing derivatively, against the current or former officers or directors for damages; or (3) in a proceeding by the attorney general to enjoin the act or to dissolve the corporation.

The first thing that might be said about section 7 is that it presents a logical impossibility, for if a corporation truly is without capacity or power to do an act, the act could not be done by the corporation. In the case of section 7, the drafters quite properly have opted for practicality over logic, for to provide that unauthorized corporate acts are invalid would cause parties on the other side of corporate transactions continually to worry over the question of corporate authority. The second thing that might be said about section 7 is that while suits for injunctions against ultra vires acts as contemplated in that section are far from happy consequences to corporate managers, the far less attractive consequence to them is the possibility of being sued for damages if the corporation engages in ultra vires activities that lose money.

In evaluating the likelihood of ultra vires activities, it will be helpful to understand how they typically occur. Under modern statutes, which allow incorporation for any lawful purpose and also allow charters to be amended freely,[19] ultra vires acts usually occur for one of two reasons. First, due to a lawyer's poor understanding of a corporation's needs or the lawyer's bad drafting, a purpose clause reciting specified purposes may not be broad enough to encompass the corporation's planned activities. Second, the direction of a corporation's business activities may shift without anyone thinking to amend the purposes clause of its charter.

Partly to avoid those problems, it is usually better to draft a purpose clause as broad as the corporation statute will allow. Another and not insignificant reason to do that is that it can take some hours of legal work, with substantial attendant expense, to

---

19. Under Model Act section 58, for example, a corporation may amend its charter freely at any time.

learn from the clients exactly what they intend for a corporation and then to draft a purposes clause that covers all of the clients' plans. Sometimes prospective owners of a corporation will request that a corporation's purposes be limited in order to protect them from having the managers of the corporation change the corporation's agreed direction. Usually, the better way to handle those concerns is by a contract among the prospective shareholders, in which they agree on the corporation's direction. As will be discussed in chapter 6, a contract among the prospective shareholders will probably be desired for other reasons, so the added expense of covering that concern would not be great.

One final thought needs to be kept in mind about ultra vires acts: Acts that at first glance may seem clearly to be ultra vires may not be. A hundred years ago, when corporations were forced to operate under restrictive corporation statutes, courts sometimes struggled to find ways to approve corporate actions that clearly were not covered directly in a corporation's purposes clause. Those courts developed the doctrine of incidental powers, under which acts that are beyond a corporation's explicitly stated purposes are nevertheless authorized if they are sufficiently related to a stated purpose.

One of the most famous such cases is *Jacksonville M.P. Railway & Navigation Co. v. Hooper*,[20] decided by the Supreme Court late in the last century. There a railroad company, without explicit authority to do so, leased and operated a hotel but failed to insure the hotel as required by its lease. The hotel was on a Florida beach at the end of the rail line, with no other accommodations nearby. When the hotel burned down, the lessors of the hotel obtained a money judgment for breach of the covenant to insure the hotel. On appeal, the defendant corporation argued that it should not be bound by the lease because the lease was ultra vires. The Supreme Court disagreed based on the doctrine of incidental powers, saying that a corporation may "engage in transactions which are incidental

20. Jacksonville M.P. Ry. & Navigation Co. v. Hooper, 160 U.S. 514 (1895).

or auxiliary to its main business, which may become necessary, expedient, or profitable in the care and management of the property which it is authorized to hold under [its charter]."[21]

Capitalization

Article Fourth calls for information on the shares of stock the corporation is authorized to issue. A number of decisions need to be made before that article may be drafted, among them the classes of stock the clients want authorized and the rights to be provided for each class, the number of shares of each class the clients want the corporation to be able to issue, whether the corporation's stock is to have par value, and if it is to have par value, how much. The entire next chapter is spent discussing those and other issues relating to corporate capitalization, and so we shall not attempt to deal further with those issues here.

Preemptive Rights

Article Fifth calls for any provisions granting preemptive rights. A preemptive right is the right of a shareholder to purchase a pro rata portion of the shares that the corporation may in the future offer for sale,[22] and the purpose of that right is to allow a shareholder to maintain his or her proportionate ownership in the corporation. Corporation statutes tend to treat preemptive rights in one of two ways: Either the shareholders have no preemptive rights unless those rights are provided in the charter, or the shareholders do have those rights unless the charter provides otherwise.

---

21. *Id.* at 515.
22. Typically, there are exceptions to preemptive rights. Those rights usually relate only to a sale of shares of the same class as those held by a shareholder, and certain sales are usually excluded from those rights, for example, sales otherwise than for cash (e.g., the exchange of shares for assets or shares of another corporation) and sales under an employee stock ownership plan. Those exceptions may be found in the corporation statute, *see, e.g.*, MODEL BUSINESS CORP. ACT § 26A, or in a corporation's charter.

The right of a shareholder to maintain a proportionate interest in a corporation can be of critical importance to a shareholder. Take, for example, a corporation without a preemptive rights provision that is owned equally by three shareholders. If one shareholder has a falling out with the others, the two-thirds owners may be able to sell themselves a large number of shares and thus decrease the ownership interest of the other shareholder without that shareholder's consent.

This is not to say, however, that a preemptive rights provision is the only way to protect shareholders from that eventuality. That might be handled by a contract among the shareholders, whereby each agrees not to buy any shares in the corporation without the approval of each of the other shareholders. It should also be realized that the mere existence of preemptive rights, without more, often will provide little protection to a shareholder. For example, preemptive rights provide only first refusal rights, and without such a contract as the one mentioned above, a shareholder without funds equal to those of the other shareholders may find that a preemptive right provides little real protection from purchases by other shareholders.

Regulation of the Corporation's Internal Affairs

Article Sixth calls for the addition of provisions regulating the internal affairs of the corporation. A typical such provision would be one increasing the usual percentage vote required by directors or shareholders for the approval of some action—for example, amendment of the charter. The area of preemptive rights offers another good example. Going back to the previous example of a three-shareholder corporation with each shareholder owning one-third of the shares, it can be seen that merely having a preemptive rights provision in the corporation's charter provides each shareholder little protection if the charter can be amended by a two-thirds vote to remove the provision. To provide the needed protection, a provision might be added in Article Sixth to the effect that a unanimous vote of the shareholders is required for an amendment of the charter's preemptive rights provision.[23]

Registered Office and Registered Agent

Article Seventh calls for the name and address of the corporation's initial registered agent in the state and for the address of the corporation's initial registered office in the state. Those requirements are meant to allow the state and others a means of contacting the corporation and serving it with process. If a corporation does not intend to maintain an office in its state of incorporation, one of the corporation service companies will provide a registered office and a registered agent for a modest yearly charge.

Directors

The number of the corporation's initial directors and their names and addresses are required to be stated in Article Eighth. Traditionally, corporation statutes required at least three directors, and often those statutes required that the directors be shareholders. Under modern statutes like the Model Act, those requirements have been abolished, and so a corporation, if it chooses, may have only one director, who need not be a shareholder.[24]

Considering how enabling modern statutes have become in that respect, one might wonder why the Model Act requires that a corporation's first directors be named in the charter, especially since

23. Note that authority for any provision regulating the internal affairs of the corporation must be found in the corporation statute. If, for example, the statute provides that a charter amendment may be approved by a majority vote of the shareholders, and if it does not provide any authority to modify that rule by a charter provision, any provision in the charter that does not comply with the statute will be ineffective.

24. *See, e.g.*, MODEL BUSINESS CORP. ACT § 36.

the Delaware statute does not require that.[25] To understand why naming the directors in that statute is a good idea, one must first look at the alternative, which is to have the incorporator or incorporators choose the first directors. What if there is a defect in the action taken by an incorporator in electing the directors, or as is more usual, the persons forming the corporation decide who the directors are to be and those persons begin acting as directors, but the incorporator never takes action to elect them? In those cases, there will be a question as to whether the corporation has directors and thus whether actions taken by the persons who purport to be directors have any validity. By naming the directors in the charter, those problems are avoided.

Sometimes a person who is to serve as a director does not wish to have his or her name appear in the public records. That presents no problem, since naming a particular person as a director may be avoided by starting with a smaller board than is planned and simply adding the new director soon after the corporation is formed. If all the persons who are to serve as directors wish to have their names kept out of the charter, a so-called dummy director may be named. In that case the person named, perhaps an employee or friend of one of the people behind the corporation, will serve as the corporation's initial director. But soon after incorporation, the dummy will elect the "real" directors as his or her successors and then resign.

Incorporators

Finally, Article Ninth requires that the name and address of the incorporator or incorporators be provided. Under the Model Act, the only job of incorporators is to sign the charter and deliver it to the secretary of state's office.[26] When, however, under some other statutes the directors are not named in the charter, the incorporators also adopt the corporation's bylaws and elect its first board of

25. Del. Gen. Corp. Law § 102.
26. Model Business Corp. Act § 53.

directors, and perhaps also its first officers. Under either form of statute, the jobs of an incorporator tend to be ministerial, since any adoptions or elections by an incorporator typically are agreed to by the persons for whom the corporation is being formed, assuming those persons are not themselves the incorporators.

Considering the ministerial nature of the incorporator's job, the question often arises as to whether the lawyer who drafts the charter should simply sign it as incorporator. That usually is the most efficient way to proceed, but two considerations should be kept in mind. First, clients who are not yet jaded with respect to corporate formalities sometimes derive personal satisfaction from signing the charter, and such clients should be given the opportunity to do so. Typically, however, the clients do not care who serves as the incorporator. In those instances, the lawyer should keep the second consideration in mind, which is that the lawyer's name will be on the corporation's charter in perpetuity, and there is no way for the lawyer to tell who may own the corporation in the future or what business the corporation might get into. If, for example, the corporation someday becomes a slumlord or opens a pornographic bookstore, and if an investigative reporter wants to find out who is "behind" the corporation, the first thing the reporter will do is check the corporation's file at the office of the secretary of state. Prominent in that file will be the name of the incorporator, which likely will appear in the next day's newspaper as the name of one of the people connected with the corporation.

The lawyer who drafts the charter can, after it is signed by the incorporator, calculate the fees and taxes that will be payable, have a check drawn, and see to the filing of the charter personally or through someone in the lawyer's office. Sometimes that makes good sense. Often, however, and especially if the lawyer does not deal often with the secretary of state's office, it makes better sense to turn the charter over to a corporation service company for filing. Those companies can accomplish an incorporation efficiently, and they know about changes in the secretary of state's fee schedules before most lawyers.

Qualifying to Do Business

While working on the charter, a lawyer should also be working on the papers required to qualify to do business in other states. The requirements for qualification vary from state to state, and a good source of information about those requirements usually is a corporation service company.[27] Those companies are also the most convenient source of the forms required by the various states. Ideally, by the time the charter is drafted, the lawyer will have ready all the forms necessary for qualifying to do business, so that those forms can be signed and filed as soon as the incorporation process is completed.

27. The Corporation Trust Company publishes a paperback book, WHAT CONSTITUTES DOING BUSINESS, which discusses requirements for qualification to do business in the various states, and it provides that book to lawyers on request.

CHAPTER FIVE

Capitalization

Those approaching corporation law without any business background often have initial problems with capitalization. There seem to be two reasons for that. First, many of the terms in use are new. Although the concepts to which those terms relate are quite simple, the concepts obviously cannot be understood by someone who has not been given the necessary vocabulary. Second, those new to corporation law sometimes expect more complexity in the area of capitalization than in fact exists. That is, they may understand a concept, but feel a sense of unease because they do not realize how well they understand it. Some of the concepts discussed in this chapter are introduced in Reading Financial Statements, which appears as appendix B. Those without a business background will find it helpful to read that appendix along with this chapter.

Basically, a corporation's capitalization (which we can take roughly to mean the cash or other assets put into the corporation on a long-term basis) consists of equity and, if desired, debt. Focusing on the initial capitalization of a new corporation, the equity capitalization will be the cash or other assets contributed by shareholders in exchange for stock. "Equity," then, is an ownership interest in the corporation. "Debt," of course, is cash or other assets that are borrowed. Nothing prevents a person from contributing some capital as equity and some as debt, making the person both a shareholder and a creditor. In fact, for reasons that will be discussed below, that is often done.

Equity

Equity is represented by some form of security, typically stock of one or another type. Modern corporation statutes allow great flexibility in devising forms of stock, but in most cases corporations will start out simply with common stock. In that situation, the holders of the common stock will be the only owners of the corporation, and they will share among themselves, in proportion to the number of shares they own, all the rights shareholders have in a corporation. Chief among those are a right to vote on certain matters, a right to the corporation's profits, and a right to the corporation's assets if the corporation is liquidated. Sometimes corporations establish more than one class of common stock, so as to distribute the traditional rights of common shareholders in some way other than equally to all common shareholders. For example, a corporation might have two classes of common stock, one of which carries the right to vote for directors and the other of which does not.[1]

Some corporations have preferred stock in addition to common stock. Preferred stock will virtually always be preferred over the common stock as to the shareholders' right to receive assets if the corporation is dissolved. Almost as often it will carry with it the preferred shareholders' right to receive a portion of the corporation's profits, in the form of a dividend, before the common shareholders receive a dividend. Almost always, however, the preferred shareholders' call on the corporation's profits will be limited to stated amounts. That is, preferred shareholders do not typically share in the corporation's successes beyond an agreed level. A particular preferred stock, for example, may have a per share preference as to dividends of ten dollars per year. No matter how successful the

1. Exchange Act rule 19c-4 limited the use of multiple classes of common stock in certain publicly held companies, but this rule was vacated in Business Roundtable v. SEC, [1990] Fed. Sec. L. Rep. (CCH) ¶ 95,291.

corporation becomes, an annual payment of ten dollars per share is all the dividend a holder of that stock will ever receive.

Preferred stock dividends usually are made cumulative, which means that no dividends may be paid to the common shareholders until all dividends that should have been paid to the preferred shareholders have been paid. Typically, preferred shareholders do not have a right to vote on most matters that are submitted for a shareholders' vote. If, however, preferred stock dividends are not paid for a stated period, often twelve months, many corporations give their preferred shareholders the right to elect some or all of the corporation's directors until all dividends in arrears are paid. Unlike the typical common stock, preferred stock usually is callable. That is, the board of directors usually is able to force the preferred shareholders out of the corporation upon the payment to them of an amount of cash that is stated in the charter. In the usual case that amount is equal to the original purchase price of the stock plus one year's dividends. As may be apparent from this discussion, although preferred stock is technically an equity security, in practical terms it usually seems closer to debt than it does to common stock.

Par Value

Under the typical modern corporation statute, any form of stock may have a "par value" stated in the corporation's charter, or the charter may state that the stock is without par value. The concept of par value is often baffling to the uninitiated. A common problem is the belief that there must be more substance to the concept than there is. In fact, there is very little to the concept of par value. The best way to view par value is as a dollar figure specified in the charter, from which certain well-defined consequences flow. Once one understands those consequences, one understands par value. We shall be getting ahead of ourselves if we go too deeply into that, but here is a short introduction to the three main consequences: First, stock typically cannot be issued by the corporation for less than par value. Second, when par value shares are issued by the corporation, a dollar figure equal to the par value is shown on the corporation's books as stated capital (as discussed in Reading Financial Statements and below in this chapter), and there are limitations, spelled out in the corporation statute, about what can be done with stated capital. No dividends, for example, may be paid out of it. Third, fees and taxes payable to the state of incorporation often are based on par value. A typical arrangement sets fees or taxes as a percentage of a number that is derived by multiplying par value by the number of shares authorized in the corporation's charter. Here an interesting twist is that stock without par value typically is taxed as if it had relatively high par value, such as $100 per share, thus making stock without par value an unpopular choice in states, such as Delaware, that follow that practice.

Mechanics of Equity Capitalization

The best way to learn more about capitalization is to go through the mechanics involved in a corporation's equity capitalization. The starting point is a corporation statute, and again we shall use the Model Business Corporation Act as an example. Section 15 of the Model Act provides that a corporation has authority to issue the number of shares that are stated in its charter, and that those shares may be divided by classes if the corporation so desires. That section also provides that the corporation must state in its charter the par value of its shares, or state that the shares are without par value.

As would be expected, section 18 of the Model Act provides two separate rules for the consideration that a corporation must charge for its shares upon their original sale (called an "issuance") by the corporation, one rule for par value shares and the other for shares without par value. In each case, the consideration is to be that set by the board of directors, but for par value shares the board may not set the consideration at less than par value.

Section 19 needs to be read along with section 18, because it specifies what kind of consideration is allowable in payment for the issuance of shares. Basically, under section 19 the consideration must be paid in money, in property other than a promissory note, or in labor or services actually performed for the corporation in the past. No matter what form of consideration is accepted by the board, section 18 says that the board of directors must express the consideration in dollars. That allows the consideration to be entered properly in the corporation's books, which are kept in terms of dollars.

At this point it will be helpful to look at how a corporation accounts on its books for the consideration it receives upon the issuance of shares, using both par value and no par value shares as examples, and then to look at the legal consequences of that accounting. The accounting involved in our discussion will be very simple and will require no more than an understanding of how to read the most basic balance sheet. For readers without any business background, Reading Financial Statements (appendix B) will provide all the help that is needed.

Section 21 of the Model Act provides that the par value of shares issued constitutes stated capital and that the excess of the consideration over par value constitutes capital surplus. For no par value stock, section 21 provides that all consideration received for the issuance of shares constitutes stated capital unless the board of directors determines within sixty days that only a part of the consideration is to be stated capital. In that case, any amount the board wishes, short of all the consideration, can be made capital surplus.

All that will be seen more easily by looking at examples. Suppose that a corporation issues 1,000 shares of one-dollar par value stock for ten dollars per share. After the issuance the corporation's balance sheet will look like this:

ASSETS		LIABILITIES	$ 0
Cash	$10,000	SHAREHOLDERS' EQUITY	
		Stated Capital	$ 1,000
		Capital Surplus	9,000
			$10,000

In the case of no par value stock the balance sheet would show $10,000 in stated capital unless the board of directors decided to place some portion of the consideration in capital surplus.

Suppose that the corporation then invested its $10,000 in some venture that returned $15,000 on the investment. Taking into account the results of that investment, the corporation's balance sheet will look like this in the case of one-dollar par value stock:

ASSETS		LIABILITIES	$ 0
Cash	$15,000	SHAREHOLDERS' EQUITY	
		Stated Capital	$ 1,000
		Capital Surplus	9,000
		Earned Surplus	5,000
			$15,000

That is about all there is to the basic mechanics of equity capitalization, except that at this point we have not said anything about what difference it makes whether a particular amount appears in stated capital, capital surplus, or earned surplus. To understand that, it is necessary briefly to discuss dividends and distributions. Section 45 of the Model Act, relating to dividends, is a good place to start. Under that section, the board of directors may declare dividends out of earned surplus. That makes sense, since, as we have seen in our example, earned surplus comes from earnings and since dividends are typically considered to be a payout to the shareholders of a corporation's earnings.

Under section 46, the board of directors can make a distribution to shareholders out of capital surplus, provided that the charter gives that power to the board or provided that the shareholders vote to approve the board's action. From the standpoint of the typical shareholder, a dividend and a distribution look very much alike. In each case, the shareholder receives a check in the amount of the per share dividend or distribution, multiplied by the number of shares owned by the shareholder. But while a dividend typically is a payout to the shareholders of a corporation's earnings, a distribution usually is a payback to shareholders of amounts previously invested by them in the corporation. (There is not in the Model Act or in any other corporation statute a provision for a payback to shareholders of a corporation's stated capital.)

That is not the end of the Model Act's story about those capital accounts, however, because that statute, like most others, allows certain transfers between those accounts. Under section 21, the board of directors can transfer capital surplus to stated capital. That is understandable, since the drafters of the statute had no reason to prevent a board from placing a restriction on the corporation's ability to make distributions if the board wants to do that. However, under sections 69 and 70, upon the vote of the board and of the shareholders, amounts may be transferred from stated capital to capital surplus as long as an amount is left in stated capital that is more than equal to the total par value of the corporation's issued stock (except if the corporation has issued certain preferred shares, in which case a special rule applies). What that comes down to is that if the board transfers an amount of capital surplus to stated capital, in the usual case the board and the shareholders later can transfer out of stated capital most of what the board transferred in. Under section 70, the board can transfer earned surplus to capital surplus, thus restricting its own ability to pay dividends. Finally, under that section, if the corporation has a deficit in earned surplus, the board can transfer from capital surplus to earned surplus any amount necessary to eliminate the deficit.

Here the question may arise as to how a corporation may have a deficit in earned surplus. Suppose, in our example above, that from the corporation's investment of $10,000 it received only $5,000 in return, thus losing $5,000. After that loss, the corporation's balance sheet would look like that, with parentheses indicating a negative number:

ASSETS		LIABILITIES	$ 0
Cash	$5,000	SHAREHOLDERS' EQUITY	
		Stated Capital	$1,000
		Capital Surplus	9,000
		Earned Surplus	(5,000)
			$5,000

As indicated above, if the board wishes to eliminate that earned surplus deficit, it may do so by a transfer from capital surplus. It may not, however, transfer from capital surplus any greater amount than that necessary to eliminate the deficit.

Duly Authorized, Validly Issued, Fully Paid, and Nonassessable

Corporation lawyers are often asked to give an opinion that certain shares of a corporation's stock are duly authorized, validly issued, fully paid, and nonassessable. That typically occurs when a corporation sells shares to the public or to private investors or when a shareholder in a close corporation sells to a new investor. "Duly authorized" simply means that when the shares were issued the corporation had sufficient shares authorized in its charter to cover the issuance. For example, if the opinion relates to 100 shares issued on May 1, the lawyer would check to be sure that, when the 100 shares were issued, the corporation had authorized in its charter at least 100 shares in excess of the shares that were already outstanding on that date.

"Validly issued" indicates that the issuance of shares was in accordance with corporation law, including that the board and the officers of the corporation took the proper steps to issue the shares. All corporation statutes give the board the power to approve the issuance of stock.[2] The first question for a lawyer to answer, then, is whether the board approved the issuance of stock. Another question a lawyer needs to answer is whether the consideration set by the board was in an amount and of a type allowed by the statute. For example, was the consideration at least equal to par value if the shares had par value.[3] Yet another question is whether the officers took the proper steps to issue the stock against payment of the consideration set by the board.

"Fully paid" overlaps with "validly issued" and also with "nonassessable." It will be best if we discuss "nonassessable" first, since in almost all cases if stock is fully paid, it is nonassessable or, put another way, if stock is fully paid, the owner cannot be assessed for further payments. There are two ways that stock could be assessable. Once in a great while a corporation's charter authorizes "assessable stock," which simply means that in certain specified circumstances the corporation has the right to demand future payments from the holders of that stock. Stock can also be assessable if the consideration that was to have been paid upon its issuance was not paid.

If, on the other hand, the consideration that was to have been paid upon issuance has been paid, the stock is "fully paid." Under a statute like the Model Act, it is usually easy to determine if the statutory requirements as to type and amount of consideration have

2. That power typically is covered in the section of the statute giving the board of directors general management power. In the Model Act, that power is granted by section 35, which says: "All corporate powers shall be exercised by or under authority of, and the business and affairs of the corporation shall be managed under the direction of, a board of directors . . . ."
3. That would be required by MODEL BUSINESS CORP. ACT § 18.

been meet, since those requirements are clearly spelled out.[4] Usually, the only additional requirement the lawyer has to worry about is whether the consideration set by the board has actually been paid. The lawyer would first determine that the consideration set by the board met the statutory requirements, for example, that the transfer of a piece of real estate appraised at $10,000 is proper consideration for 1,000 shares of one-dollar par value stock. The lawyer would then check to see if title to the real estate actually passed to the corporation in exchange for the stock.

So as not to leave any doubt about what it takes to have stock that is fully paid and nonassessable, the drafters of the Model Act wrote in two related and somewhat redundant provisions. The first appears in section 19:

> When payment of the consideration for which shares are to be issued shall have been received by the corporation, such shares shall be deemed to be fully paid and nonassessable.[5]

The other provision appears in section 25:

> A holder of . . . shares of a corporation shall be under no obligation to the corporation or its creditors with respect to such shares other than the obligation to pay to the corporation the full consideration for which such shares were issued or to be issued.

Stock that is not fully paid is called "watered stock." While determining whether stock is watered is straightforward under the Model Act, which embodies what is called the statutory obligation theory of watered stock liability, that is not true under all corporation statutes. That being the case, a brief look is necessary at the common-law doctrines of watered stock liability. Under the most traditional view of watered stock liability, a shareholder was liable

4. *See* pp. 92–93 *supra.*

5. Note that stock is not fully paid and nonassessable just because the shareholder paid the amount set by the board. The consideration must meet the statutory requirements or it will not meet the test of being "the consideration for which shares are to be issued."

for the difference between the amount paid for a share and the share's par value. That view made good sense in the nineteenth and early twentieth centuries, when most watered stock cases were decided, because the practice then was to sell stock at its par value, which traditionally was $100 per share. If that practice is assumed, (1) not paying par value for shares and (2) not paying the consideration set by the board in accordance with statutory requirements (which is what constitutes watered stock under the Model Act) would come down to the same thing. Put another way, in the old days the target amount for avoiding watered stock liability would be par value under both the traditional and the Model Act's formulations.

In the traditional view, the amount of a stock's par value had great importance to a corporation's creditors. There have been two theories about that, the trust fund theory and the misrepresentation theory. Under the trust fund theory, a corporation's stated capital[6] was viewed as analogous to a trust for the benefit of a corporation's creditors. That theory is defective on two counts. First, stated capital does not consist of anything remotely like a trust. Second, stated capital is not a fund. To see that clearly, consider this balance sheet:

ASSETS		LIABILITIES	$ 0
Inventory	$15,000	SHAREHOLDERS' EQUITY	
		Stated Capital	$10,000
		Earned Surplus	5,000
			$15,000

It will be apparent from analyzing this balance sheet that stated capital is simply a concept from which flow certain legal consequences, such as the corporation's inability to pay dividends or distributions "out of" stated capital. Stated capital does not exist in any physical sense, and nothing may in any real sense be paid out of

6. Stated capital in the case of par value shares, remember, is basically the aggregate par value of all the outstanding shares.

it. If one wants to determine what assets the corporation has that creditors might be able to attach, it is necessary to look at the assets side of the balance sheet, which is the only part of the balance sheet that shows items that exist in a physical sense. Looking at the balance sheet above, the question arises as to how valuable the inventory is to creditors. The inventory may consist of items that can readily be sold at their balance-sheet value, but just as easily it may consist of specialized and hard-to-sell items that have virtually no value to creditors.

This is not to say, however, that stated capital offers creditors no protection. It is just to say that the trust fund theory of watered stock liability is based on invalid premises. That was recognized in the last century by courts that began adopting the misrepresentation theory of watered stock liability. Under the classic application of that theory, liability flows to shareholders who pay less than par value for their stock because, it is said, creditors rely on the existence of stated capital in the amount shown in a corporation's balance sheet, and if shareholders have not paid at least par value for their stock, the stated capital account must necessarily be inflated by the difference between the amount paid and the par value.[7] That is the reasoning behind the misrepresentation theory of watered stock liability, which is likely to be followed, at least in some form, in a state that does not have a statutory formulation along the lines of the Model Act's.[8]

---

7. That ignores the possibility of transfers to stated capital, which were not part of corporate culture when the theories of watered stock liability were being developed.
8. Section 19 of the Model Act provides that "[i]n the absence of fraud in the transaction, the judgment of the board of directors . . . as to the value of the consideration received for shares shall be conclusive." In a state having such a provision in its statute, it is harder to make the case that consideration has been overvalued, thus creating watered stock liability. However, "fraud" does not mean common-law fraud, and courts have discretion in deciding when "fraud" has existed in a valuation. Also, a court may hold that that provision does not apply except in an arm's-length transaction involving a prospective

Since stated capital does not provide a fund for the protection of creditors, it can be said that a focus on a misrepresentation in stated capital is misplaced. Look at this balance sheet, which we shall assume shows the initial capitalization of a corporation by means of an exchange by a shareholder of property constituting inventory for stock having an aggregate par value of $10,000:

ASSETS		LIABILITIES	$ 0
Inventory	$10,000	SHAREHOLDERS' EQUITY	
		Stated Capital	$10,000
			$10,000

If this corporation's stated capital is inflated, it is inflated because the inventory has been overvalued. That is, for a court to find stated capital to be inflated by $4,000, the court would have to find that the proper value of the inventory was $6,000 rather than $10,000. Or put another way, if the proper valuation of the inventory were $10,000, then stated capital would be shown properly at $10,000 because in that event $10,000 of property would have been exchanged for $10,000 in par value of stock. All that being true, the real focus under the misrepresentation theory might better be on the assets shown on a balance sheet and not on stated capital, since creditors need to look at the assets side of a balance sheet to determine what assets might be available for attachment.

Stated capital arguably does provide creditors protection in that it may be said to set a limit on what amounts can be taken out of the corporation by dividends or distributions. For example, a creditor looking at the above balance sheet could rightly conclude that at that point the corporation could take no money out of the corporation as dividends or distributions. Notice, however, that "at that point" is an important qualifier. As discussed above, if at any time

---

shareholder without a material preexisting relationship to the corporation. *See, e.g.*, Pipelife Corp. v. Bedford, 37 Del. Ch. 467, 145 A.2d 206 (1958).

stated capital is in excess of the aggregate par value of a corporation's outstanding stock, the board and shareholders can vote to transfer most of the excess stated capital to capital surplus,[9] and all of a corporation's capital surplus may be taken out of the corporation by a distribution to shareholders.[10] Also, a corporation at any time can amend its charter to change the par value of its stock[11] so as to create an excess in stated capital that may be transferred to capital surplus. All in all, then, the protection that stated capital gives creditors is more illusory than real.

Treasury Stock

Treasury stock is treated differently from nontreasury stock in the rules relating to capitalization. Model Act section 2(h) provides a standard definition:

> "Treasury shares" means shares of a corporation which have been issued, have been subsequently acquired by and belong to a corporation, and have not . . . been canceled or restored to the status of authorized but unissued shares. Treasury shares shall be deemed to be "issued" shares, but not "outstanding" shares.

The reader may have noticed that in our earlier discussions of the rules relating to consideration for shares, we phrased those rules as being applicable upon the "issuance" of shares, not merely on the "sale" of shares.[12] The reason for that is that those rules do not apply upon the sale by a corporation of treasury stock. For example, treasury shares having a par value may be sold for whatever consideration the board sets, regardless of their par value.[13] That is the case because when shares held as treasury shares initially were issued, an amount equal to their par value was placed in stated capital, and that

9. *See* p. 95 *supra*.
10. *See* pp. 94–95 *supra*.
11. *See, e.g.*, Model Business Corp. Act § 58(e).
12. *See* p. 92 *supra*.
13. *See, e.g.*, Model Business Corp. Act § 18.

amount remains in stated capital so long as the shares retain their status as "issued" shares.[14] In other words, the sale of treasury shares has no relevance insofar as the rules we have discussed are concerned.

Debt

Debt capitalization takes a number of forms. The most common is simply long-term (at least one-year) loans from banks, private investors, or shareholders. Such loans typically are represented by notes. In larger corporations, bonds and debentures are sometimes encountered. The term "bond" is usually used to describe a long-term debt instrument secured by a mortgage or deed of trust on corporate property, while a long-term debt instrument that is unsecured usually is called a "debenture." A note, of course, may be secured or unsecured. In either case, a note differs from a bond or a debenture in that bond and debenture holders are protected by contractual provisions contained in an indenture covering a multitude of corporate financial matters. An indenture is a contract between the corporation and an indenture trustee, usually a bank, that acts for the benefit of the bond or debenture holders. A note holder also may be protected by contractual provisions, but in the case of a note the contract, which often is a loan agreement, is between the corporation and the lender. No indenture or indenture trustee is involved.

There can be many advantages to a corporation and to its shareholders in having the corporation include debt in its capital structure. From the point of view of the corporation, an important

14. A corporation's board of directors may cancel the issuance of treasury shares and thus restore them to the status of authorized but unissued shares at any time it wishes. Once that is done, all the capitalization rules apply just as they would if the shares had never been issued.

advantage to debt is that interest payments on debt are tax deductible, while dividends on stock are not. If, therefore, the corporation is considering issuing either long-term notes or preferred stock, issuing notes likely will be much less expensive, largely because of the tax advantage inherent in the notes. Often shareholders wish to put into a corporation some of their total contribution as equity and some as debt, and often a prospective investor wishes to be a creditor rather than a shareholder—usually a creditor having the right to convert his or her debt into common stock if all goes well for the corporation. Of major interest to debt holders is that (1) debt may be repaid without any tax consequences, but if stock is redeemed when the corporation has had profits, the redemption may be taxed as a dividend; (2) if the corporation goes bankrupt, debt holders have the right to be repaid before any payments are made to preferred or common shareholders; and (3) if debt holders are not repaid, they can qualify for a current income tax deduction in the amount of their loss more readily than can a holder of equity who has suffered an investment loss. Largely for those reasons, owners of a corporation often wish to split their own contribution to the corporation between equity and debt, hoping to avoid some taxes if all goes well, and hoping also to salvage at least some of their investment if the corporation goes bankrupt.

Thin Incorporation

There are dangers for shareholders if they go too far with their use of shareholder debt or if they are not careful enough in establishing and maintaining their debtor-creditor relationship with the corporation. In each case, the problem is that there may be found to exist what is called thin incorporation. The consequences of thin incorporation fall into two categories. First, the Internal Revenue Service may consider the debt to be equity for tax purposes, causing the interest payments on the debt to be treated as nondeductible dividends. Second, a court may subordinate the shareholders' debt to that of other creditors in the event of bankruptcy or other financial calamity.

Many considerations go into determining if a corporation is thinly incorporated. A primary consideration is the ratio of the shareholders' equity to the debt owed to shareholders. There is no universally accepted dividing line between an acceptable and an unacceptable ratio, but a one-to-one debt/equity ratio is considered very conservative. As the ratio goes up, the danger increases, and it increases more rapidly if the debt in question has any unusual features that make it seem more like equity than like debt. Besides exercising care in establishing the debt/equity ratio, it is important to structure shareholder debt in an ordinary, commercially sensible way and then to ensure that the relationship between the shareholder as debtor and the corporation is as much like one at arm's length as possible. For example, a note should be signed at the time of the loan, the loan should have a commercially reasonable interest rate and other terms, and the interest and principal on the loan should be repaid on time. Perhaps especially to be avoided is tying the interest rate to the earnings of the corporation.[15]

Leverage

By having their corporation borrow some of its capital from others, shareholders get the benefit of leverage. The benefits of leverage exist for the shareholders any time the corporation can make a return on borrowed money that is greater than the cost of the borrowed money. The easiest example of leverage for most people is the leverage enjoyed by homeowners during periods of rising real estate prices. Assume, for example, that a young lawyer buys a house for $100,000, paying $10,000 down and borrowing $90,000. If the lawyer later sells the house for $110,000 after

15. For interesting cases relating to the subordination aspects of thin incorporation, *see* Costello v. Fazio, 256 F.2d 903 (9th. Cir. 1958); Obre v. Alban Tractor Co., 228 Md. 291, 179 A.2d 861 (1962).

expenses, the gain has been $10,000. If the lawyer had paid cash for the house, his or her gain on the invested funds would have been 10 percent. Since the lawyer's investment was highly leveraged, however, the gain on invested funds was 100 percent. (Notice, of course, that if the house had sold for $90,000 after expenses, the lawyer's loss would have been 100 percent, so leverage can be a disadvantage as well as an advantage.)

Shareholders can use leverage in the same way as can a homeowner, by causing their corporation to borrow money at a lower rate of interest than it can earn by using the money it borrowed. If, for example, a corporation borrows from a bank $50,000 at 10 percent interest and its shareholders contribute $50,000 in exchange for all the corporation's common stock, and then the corporation makes a 15 percent return on its $100,000 capital, the shareholders' return on their investment is $10,000, or 20 percent on the funds they had invested. That is calculated as follows: $15,000 profit, minus $5,000 interest paid on the debt, equals $10,000, which is 20 percent of the $50,000 that the shareholders had invested.

Since, as indicated above,[16] preferred stock is in financial terms more like debt than it is like common stock, the common shareholders can leverage their investment by causing their corporation to issue preferred stock just as easily as they can by having the corporation issue debt. In that case, for leveraging to be beneficial, the hoped-for return on the money obtained from the preferred shareholders must be greater than the dividends payable on the preferred stock.

The corporation can, of course, issue both preferred stock and debt, thus maximizing the common shareholders' leverage. Public utility corporations, for example, typically do just that, with a usual capitalization of one of those corporations being 30 percent common stock, 15 percent preferred stock, and 55 percent debt. One might ask why the entire leveraging amount of such a corporation is

16. *See* pp. 90–91 *supra*.

not made up of debt, since dividends on preferred stock are not tax deductible. A major reason is that public utility commissions have to approve the capital structures of public utilities, and those commissions will not allow public utilities to obligate themselves to make interest payments on more than about 55 percent debt. But those commissions usually will allow public utilities further to leverage their common shareholders by the issuance of perhaps 30 percent preferred stock.[17]

17. Since preferred shareholders are not promised dividend payments, dividends are not a corporate obligation in the way that interest payments are.

CHAPTER SIX

Organizing the Corporation

The terms "incorporation" and "organization" of a corporation are often confused. Not infrequently, lawyers use them interchangeably. Actually, incorporation and organization are two separate events in the life of a corporation. Incorporation occurs when the state issues the corporate charter.[1] At that point only the barest corporate skeleton exists, one consisting basically of the few items covered in the charter, such as the corporation's name and the type of business in which it may engage.[2] It is during the process of organization that the corporation is given bylaws, shareholders, officers, and often its first directors. It is only at the completion of that process that enough meat has been added to the corporate bones to establish the corporation as an entity ready to do business.

Organization Meeting

Corporation statutes provide for the holding of an organization meeting after the issuance of a corporation's charter, to accomplish the organization of a corporation. Model Business Corporation Act section 57 is typical: "[A]n organization meeting . . . shall be held . . . for the purpose of adopting bylaws, electing officers and transacting such other business as may come before the meeting."

1. See p. 73 *supra*.
2. See pp. 74–88 *supra* for a discussion of what a charter contains.

Whether the meeting is to be held by the incorporator or by directors depends on whether directors are named in the charter.[3] If directors are named in the charter, then they hold the organization meeting. If directors are not named in the charter, then one of the most important items on the agenda of the organization meeting is the election of the corporation's first directors.

Consent in Lieu of Meeting

Modern corporation statutes typically provide a convenient alternative to holding an organization meeting: written consent in lieu of meeting. Under statutes that allow that procedure, the incorporator or incorporators or the directors may forgo the organization meeting and act by written consent in lieu of meeting. Usually, the consent must be unanimous, but that rule is not without exception. For example, under one state's version of the Revised Model Business Corporation Act, the incorporators, or directors if there are any, may act in writing by majority vote on any matter relating to the organization of the corporation, so long as all those who have a right to vote agree in writing to act without a meeting.[4]

There is much to be said for organizing a corporation by written consent. For one thing, in cases where directors are not named in the charter and thus available to hold an organization meeting, there typically is only one incorporator. While it is possible for a sole incorporator to hold an organization meeting, doing so is either cumbrous or strange. The cleanest way for a sole incorporator to conduct an organization meeting is to ask another person to preside as chairman and then to interact with the chairman. The organization meeting can also be held with only the incorporator present, with the only requirement being that the incorporator actually

3. Many statutes require directors to be named in the charter. *See, e.g.*, MODEL BUSINESS CORP. ACT § 54.

4. TENN. CODE ANN. § 48-12-105(b).

accomplish the necessary tasks, such as the adoption of bylaws and the election of directors and officers. The incorporator could go through the agenda out loud ("I hereby elect Mary Smith as the sole director of the corporation"), but presumably the incorporator's actions would be equally valid if done in the incorporator's head. But either way, holding a meeting with oneself is outside the norms of ordinary conduct.

Even if there is more than one person who has power to act at an organization meeting, it is usually better to organize the corporation by written consent in lieu of meeting. As will be seen in the course of this chapter, there are a number of technical items to handle in connection with a corporation's organization, but at that point in a corporation's life there usually is not much that needs to be discussed at a meeting. Even critical decisions, such as who the officers are to be, typically will have been decided informally before the organization of the corporation. As a result, an organization meeting tends to be merely tedious rather than productive in terms of decision-making.

Finally, the kind of technical matters involved in organizing a corporation can be handled most reliably and at the least cost in a written consent drafted by the corporation's lawyer. In resolving the issue of whether to operate by written consent, an important question to consider is whether those who would conduct the meeting can be relied upon to take all the proper actions that need to be taken, and even if they can, whether they will draft proper minutes showing those actions. Considering the importance of starting the corporation's life without defects in its organization, and the expense of having a lawyer supervise the organization meeting and the preparation of accurate minutes in an attempt to ensure correctness, it turns out to be rare that holding an organization meeting makes more sense than operating by written consent.

Bylaws

Position in the Hierarchy of Regulation

The adoption of bylaws is the first step in the organization of a corporation. Model Act section 27 provides a good starting point for discussing bylaws. The last sentence of that section provides: "The bylaws may contain any provision for the regulation and management of the affairs of the corporation not inconsistent with law or the articles of incorporation." Compare that provision with the first sentence of section 35, which is the usual statement of the power of the board of directors: "All corporate powers shall be exercised by or under authority of, and the business and affairs of a corporation shall be managed under the direction of, a board of directors except as may be otherwise provided in this Act or the articles of incorporation."

Each of those provisions relates to the hierarchy of authority in a corporation, and the first important thing to understand about bylaws is their place in that hierarchy. Notice first that section 27 relates only to the power of the bylaws over the affairs of a corporation, whereas section 35 speaks about the power of the board over both business and affairs. Remember that the affairs of a corporation consist of those actions relating to the corporation's internal workings as an entity, as opposed to those actions relating to the conduct of the corporation's business.[5] It is clear from section 27 that the bylaws have a place in the hierarchy of corporate regulation only in relation to the corporation's affairs, not its business.

This being said, one might perceive a conflict between sections 27 and 35, in that section 27 says the bylaws may contain any provision relating to the regulation of a corporation's affairs "not inconsistent with law or the articles of incorporation" and section 35 may seem

5. *See* p. 5 *supra*, note 20.

to give the board plenary power to manage the affairs of the corporation "except as may be otherwise provided in this Act or the articles of incorporation." In other words, under section 27, the hierarchy of corporate regulation with respect to a corporation's affairs has the bylaws directly after the charter, whereas under section 35 the board of directors may seem to occupy that position.

Actually there is no conflict between sections 27 and 35. In section 27 the drafters did intend to set out a hierarchy of corporate regulation. In section 35, on the other hand, what the drafters intended was merely to say where one would look (in the Act or the charter) to find exceptions to the general rules that all corporate powers are to be exercised by the directors and that all of a corporation's business and affairs are at least to be supervised by a board of directors. The Model Act contains a number of such exceptions to the plenary power of directors, for example, the requirement that shareholders must vote to approve a charter amendment.[6] And section 54 of the Model Act provides that the charter may contain any provision for the regulation of the internal affairs of a corporation, so long as the provision is not inconsistent with law. Section 35 thus does not speak to the general position of the bylaws in the hierarchy of regulation. That being said, here is the correct corporate hierarchy, through the level of the board of directors:

1. Law
2. Charter
3. Bylaws (affairs only)
4. Board of Directors

What Bylaws Cover

As indicated above, bylaws may contain any provision relating to the affairs of the corporation, so long as the provision does not conflict with law or the charter. In point of fact, however, bylaws

6. MODEL BUSINESS COMP. ACT § 59.

prepared by experienced corporate lawyers are highly stylized, with the subjects covered and the way those subjects are covered being marked by little variation. Official Model Act form bylaws are included as appendix C, and that form represents the prototypical bylaws drafted by skilled corporate lawyers. A brief examination will show that those bylaws are divided into articles and sections. The major articles relate to the shareholders, the directors, and the officers, and those articles are followed by others relating to such subjects as certificates for shares and the corporate seal. Within the articles, detailed sections cover a multitude of rules relating to the subjects at hand. With respect to the shareholders, for example, each of the following are covered: annual meeting, special meetings, place of meetings, notice of meetings, closing of transfer books, voting record, quorum, proxies, voting of shares, informal action by shareholders, and (as an optional provision) cumulative voting.

Bylaw Conflicts

More often than the uninitiated might suppose, corporate bylaws are defective because they conflict either with the corporation statute or, less often, with the corporation's charter. Examples of the first type of conflict are found in the well-known New York Court of Appeals case, *Benintendi v. Kenton Hotel, Inc.*[7] There a corporation had bylaws that required the unanimous vote of shareholders for the election of directors, whereas the New York corporation statute provided for the election of directors by a plurality of shareholder votes. Not surprisingly, the New York Court of Appeals found the bylaw provision to be of no effect. Another of that corporation's bylaws required the unanimous vote of directors for the taking of any action. On that subject there was no unequivocal conflict with the corporation statute. In fact, the statute's provision most on point

7. Benintendi v. Kenton Hotel, Inc., 294 N.Y. 112, 60 N.E.2d 829 (1945). For an example of bylaws in conflict with a corporation's charter, *see* Paulek v. Isgar, 551 P.2d 213 (Colo. Ct. App. 1976).

provided that "[A]ction may be taken by the directors . . . acting by a majority of a quorum, except when otherwise expressly required by law or the bylaws."[8] At first glance, that provision would seem to allow a bylaw requiring a unanimous vote of directors. Looking, however, at the common-law rule that directors may act by majority vote, and at the legislative history of the New York corporation statute, the court determined that there was no legislative intent to change the common-law rule, and it therefore declared the second bylaw also to be of no effect. (The official comment to Model Act section 40 indicates that, under the Model Act, bylaws may require the unanimous vote of directors.)

There are many ways bylaw conflicts may arise. Sometimes they arise because the lawyer doing the drafting uses a form of bylaws as a model without carefully checking the form against the statute and charter. Often, also, a lawyer drafts a new bylaw provision without checking the statute and charter. And even if all bylaw provisions are correct when drafted, they may come into conflict when the statute or the charter is changed without the change's being reflected in a bylaw amendment.

The way to avoid bylaw conflicts is simple in theory (except for the kind of exotic conflict found in one of the bylaws in *Benintendi*, which admittedly would require a high degree of sophistication to avoid): Do not draft bylaws or any bylaw provision without a careful checking against the statute and corporate charter. Actually avoiding conflicts is not so simple in practice, because most corporate law firms have office forms of bylaws that lawyers are encouraged to use without much checking. Still, use of office forms without checking, even in the best firms, results in more risks than one would imagine. Meticulously check the office form bylaws in twenty good law firms, and you probably will find at least one or two problems. Not infrequently, one at least will find upon checking that the lawyer who was supposed to look after updating corporate forms has not

8. N.Y. Stock Corporation Law of 1923, § 28.

done so frequently enough. If office form bylaws have not been updated at least as recently as the latest changes to the state's corporation statute, a lawyer should view them with more than ordinary suspicion.

Bylaws as a Contract

If a particular bylaw provision is ineffective as a bylaw, a court may in some circumstances decide to interpret the bylaw as a contract between the persons who agreed to it. That only would occur in a close corporation, and it is much more likely to occur when the bylaw provision in question is not invalid as a bylaw because of a conflict with the statute or the corporation's charter. A provision that is ineffective as a bylaw because of a procedural defect in its passage, for example, would be the best candidate for treatment as a contract between the persons who agreed to it.[9]

Election of Directors

If directors are not named in the charter, the incorporator typically adopts bylaws, which usually contain a provision on the number of directors, and then elects the corporation's first directors. Depending on the corporation statute involved and sometimes on the preference of the lawyer handling the organization of the corporation, the incorporator may continue with the organization or the new directors may take up the job at that point. The latter is preferable, if for no other reason than that one item that needs to be handled immediately—even if not technically a part of the organization of the corporation—is the sale of stock to the first shareholders; virtually all corporation statutes require that item to be handled by

9. For a good case discussing the treatment of invalid bylaw provisions as a contract, *see* Jones v. Wallace, 291 Or. 11, 628 P.2d 388 (1981).

the directors. Other important items, such as fixing the compensation of officers, also need to be done by the directors rather than the incorporators under most statutes, and so it usually is best simply to have the directors finish the whole task of organization. If the organization is being accomplished by consent in lieu of meeting, that simply means having two separate consents, one of the incorporator or incorporators and one of the directors.

Election of Officers

After the adoption of bylaws and if necessary the election of directors, the next step in organizing a corporation is the election of officers. All corporation statutes have a provision on the question of required officers, although Delaware's provides simply that the corporation shall have the officers stated in the bylaws or in a resolution of the directors.[10] Most states require certain named officers, however, and then allow the board to appoint any other officers it desires. A typical provision requires that a corporation have a president and a secretary, and some statutes go further and also require a treasurer.

The Model Act may or may not go even further, depending on how one interprets its section 50: "The officers of a corporation shall consist of a president, one or more vice presidents as may be prescribed by the bylaws, a secretary, and a treasurer . . . ." From that language, it is impossible to tell whether or not at least one vice president is required.[11] Since it has not been traditional for corporation statutes to require a vice president, one can argue that unambiguous language to the opposite effect would be required before section 50 could be interpreted to change that tradition. However, since having a vice president usually either makes sense or at least

10. Del. Gen. Corp. Law § 142.

11. It may seem that that language is unambiguous. From informal surveys, however, it is clear that people read it differently.

causes no harm, the wisest course in a Model Act state is simply to elect at least one vice president.

Especially in small close corporations, the question arises as to whether one person may hold more than one office. The answer is that a person may hold any number of offices, with the almost universal exception that a person may not hold the offices of president and secretary.[12] The reason for that prohibition, as will better be seen in chapter 8 (which deals with the subject of corporate authority), is that the secretary is the principal officer who certifies the correctness of corporate actions, such as the signing of documents in the corporate name, and the president is the most likely officer to take those actions. That being so, it is not surprising that the drafters of corporate statutes usually have decided that the president and the secretary should be different persons.

Bylaws have been mentioned in a number of places in the foregoing discussion of corporate officers. Bylaws typically list the officers a corporation is to have, along with a brief recitation of their basic powers and duties, and then give the board of directors (and perhaps certain officers, depending on what the corporation statute provides) the power to elect or appoint additional officers. Obviously, in planning the organization of a corporation, decisions on corporate officers need to be made before the lawyer finishes drafting the bylaws.

Other Organizational Matters

Once a corporation has bylaws, directors, and officers, the basics of its organization have been completed. There are, however, other matters that should be handled at the time of organization. If they are not handled then, some of those matters will need to be handled

---

12. *See, e.g.*, MODEL BUSINESS CORP. ACT § 50. Since, however, the Delaware statute does not require any particular officers, it also does not refuse to allow one person to be both president and secretary.

almost immediately, probably to the annoyance of clients who thought the details of getting their corporation started were out of the way.

Sale of Stock

Without question, the most important of those additional organizational matters is the sale of stock to the first shareholders. Corporation statutes provide that the directors must authorize the sale of stock against consideration approved by them. If the consideration is other than cash, then the directors must put a dollar value on the consideration.[13] Those details need either to be memorialized in the minutes of an organization meeting or handled in a written consent in lieu of meeting. In addition to covering such details, the directors typically authorize certain corporate officers to issue the agreed number of shares against the specified consideration.

Modern corporation statutes typically allow shares to be issued without certificates.[14] Especially in corporations with only one or two owners, that option can be useful in achieving simplicity and minimizing costs. If the corporation is to issue stock certificates, the lawyer handling the organization of the corporation needs to obtain from a corporate stationer certificates that meet the requirements of the corporation statute.[15] The board then should approve the form of those certificates at the time it authorizes the first stock issuance.

---

13. *See, e.g.*, MODEL BUSINESS CORP. ACT § 18, read along with section 35. Corporation statutes also specify allowable consideration. *See, e.g., id.* § 19, which provides: "Neither promissory notes nor future services shall constitute payment or part payment for the issuance of shares of a corporation." *See* chapter 4 *supra* for a discussion of corporate capitalization.
14. *See, e.g., id.* § 23.
15. Id. § 23, which is representative, provides:

> Each certificate representing shares shall state upon the face thereof:
> (a) That the corporation is organized under the laws of this State.
> (b) The name of the person to whom issued.
> (c) The number and class of shares, and the designation of the series, if any, which such certificate represents

If the corporation issues stock certificates, each certificate should have a legend along the following lines placed on its face anytime the shares being issued have not been registered under federal and state securities laws:

> THE SECURITIES REPRESENTED BY THIS CERTIFICATE HAVE NOT BEEN REGISTERED UNDER THE SECURITIES ACT OF 1933 OR ANY STATE SECURITIES LAW AND MAY NOT BE TRANSFERRED UNLESS SO REGISTERED OR UNLESS AN EXEMPTION FROM APPLICABLE REGISTRATION REQUIREMENTS IS AVAILABLE.

If the corporation issues shares without certificates, the corporation statute likely requires that each owner be provided a statement in writing setting forth the same information that a stock certificate would provide. Whether or not that is required, the corporation often provides each shareholder with a letter confirming the issuance of shares. That letter or the required statement of information (which may take the form of a letter) should contain a statement like the one set out in the above legend.

The securities law aspects of the issuance of stock are beyond the scope of this book.[16] For the purposes of explaining the above legend, it may be enough to note that for any offering or sale of securities there must be registration with the Securities and Exchange Commission, and usually with one or more state agencies, unless exemption from the registration requirement is available. For the issuance of stock to a founder of the corporation who will be an actual owner-manager[17] or for the issuance of stock in situations that meet other specified criteria, exemptions should be available.

(d) The par value of each share represented by such certificate, or a statement that the shares are without par value.

16. For a basic discussion of that and other securities law topics, *see* L. SODERQUIST, UNDERSTANDING THE SECURITIES LAWS (2d ed. 1990), which also is published by the Practising Law Institute.
17. Although that may sound simple, it requires a fair understanding of securities law to determine who may be issued securities without registration in such a situation.

Those exemptions can be lost, however, unless the corporation that issues the stock prevents the sale or other transfer of that stock into new hands. That is the main reason behind the above legend.

Considering the substantial civil and criminal liabilities that may flow to a corporation that illegally issues securities and to others involved in such transactions (including the corporation's lawyers), a lawyer should not assist in the issuance of unregistered securities to anyone unless he or she is satisfied that exemptions from the registration requirements of federal and state securities laws are available.

Promoters' Contracts and Expenses

Often, clients enter into promoters' contracts on behalf of a corporation before it is formed. Whether or not clients have entered into promoters' contracts, typically they have taken some actions on the corporation's behalf (such as having preliminary discussions with prospective suppliers and customers) and in so doing have incurred expenses. Usually, clients wish to have the board of directors adopt such actions that were taken before incorporation and ratify those taken between the corporation's incorporation and its organization.[18] Also, clients often wish to be reimbursed by the corporation for costs they have incurred on behalf of the corporation. The clients' desires in those regards can all be taken care of at the time of organization by a simple resolution of the directors.[19]

---

18. The legal rule is that a corporation may only ratify an action that it could itself have taken originally, and actions occurring before incorporation clearly fall outside that possibility. The major difference between adoption and ratification, in terms of legal effect, is that ratification relates back in time, putting the corporation's stamp of approval on the ratified action as of the time of the action, whereas adoption has no retroactive effect. See pp. 60–61 *supra*, for a fuller discussion of adoption and ratification.
19. Note that, absent a novation, mere adoption or ratification of a contract by the corporation will not release a promoter from any liability the promoter may have on the contract. See pp. 63–64 *supra*.

Compensation of Directors and Officers

At the time of organization, the directors should pass a resolution approving the compensation of directors, or at minimum approving the reimbursement of their costs, and also approving the compensation of at least the chief executive officer. It may be legally possible for the chief executive officer to approve his or her own salary, but no one believes that to be good practice. And in the typical close corporation, the board approves all or most officers' salaries.

Adoption of Corporate Seal

Corporation statutes do not require corporate seals, but they do authorize them.[20] While from the standpoint of contract law seals have come to be viewed as quaint anachronisms, that is not the case for corporations. Most corporations have a seal, and the use of it often is called for in connection with the execution of corporate documents. When that is the case, it can be easier to have and use a seal than to explain that the corporation does not have one. Besides that practical benefit, the use of a corporate seal often has evidentiary effect, usually serving either as prima facie evidence of due authorization or due execution of the sealed document. If a corporation is to have a seal, the form of the seal should be approved in connection with the corporation's organization.

Qualification to Do Business

If the corporation is to do business in other than its state of incorporation, the corporation will have to qualify to do business in

---

20. Model Business Corp. Act § 4(c) provides, for example:

> Each corporation shall have power:
>
> . . . .
>
> (c) To have a corporate seal which may be altered at pleasure, and to use the same by causing it, or a facsimile thereof, to be impressed or affixed or in any other manner reproduced.

each state in which it intends to operate. At a minimum, the board should pass a general resolution authorizing and directing the officers to take all necessary steps to effect those qualifications. A better practice is promptly to obtain the documents that will be required for qualification and then determine if a specific board resolution is necessary in connection with any qualification.[21]

Banking Relationship

The lawyer handling the organization of a corporation should ask the client where the corporation intends to open a bank account and then should obtain from that bank, or ask the client to obtain from the bank, the form of board of directors' resolutions the bank will require before opening an account. Those resolutions should then be passed in connection with the organization of the corporation. If that is not done, immediately after the organization is complete and the corporation has received checks from its shareholders in payment for their stock, a corporate officer will be confronted with the need for those resolutions as soon as he or she attempts to open a bank account.

Those resolutions authorize specified persons to open a corporate checking account, sell commercial paper, take out loans, and so on. In handling those resolutions, a lawyer can save the corporation future trouble by listing corporate offices, rather than the names of individuals, as those the board of directors authorizes to act for the corporation. That way, the banking resolutions will not have to be passed again and again as new persons are elected to corporate offices.

21. The documents can be obtained directly from each state involved, usually from the office of the secretary of state, but they also can be obtained quickly and more easily from one of the corporation service companies.

Agreements Among Shareholders

Chapter 12 deals with distributing control within the corporation, and so we would be getting ahead of ourselves if we went too deeply at this point into the kinds of agreements shareholders may wish to enter into with respect to their corporation. It is important to note two things about such agreements, however, in connection with the discussion of the organization of corporations. First, in close corporations owned by more than one person, there usually is a need for one or more agreements among shareholders on such matters as voting for each other as directors and officers and on such questions as to whom a shareholder may sell his or her stock. Second, the best time for entering into such agreements is at the very beginning of a corporation's life.

CHAPTER SEVEN

Personal Liability for Corporate Obligations

The usual rule is that shareholders have no liability for their corporation's debts, absent the shareholders' signing a personal guaranty or otherwise agreeing to assume a corporate liability.[1] There are, however, two sets of circumstances under which the shareholders, and sometimes officers and directors, may be held liable for obligations they expect to be only the obligations of their corporation. The first of those circumstances involves corporations that have a defect in their incorporation. The second involves situations where a court determines to disregard the existence of what inarguably is a properly formed corporation.

Defective Incorporation

In their early development, corporation laws set up technical multistep procedures for establishing a corporation. For example, an incorporator might have to publish notice of intent to incorporate, file properly executed papers with the secretary of state and with one or more county officers, publish notice of those filings, and then capitalize the corporation at a certain level, all before a court would recognize the existence of what is called a de jure corporation, or a corporation "of right." To stumble over one of those

1. Banks usually require that one or more shareholders guarantee the repayment of corporate loans, unless the corporation is well established.

procedures, and to operate a business that only appeared to be a corporation, was to risk being held personally liable for the business's debts. To alleviate the perceived inequities of personal liability in some of those circumstances, courts established two doctrines, the de facto corporation doctrine and the corporation by estoppel doctrine.

De Facto Corporation Doctrine and Corporations by Estoppel

In order to establish the existence of a de facto corporation, there are three things that one must prove:

1. There is a law under which the purported corporation could have been incorporated;
2. There was a good faith attempt to incorporate under that law; and
3. There was a use of corporate power in the honest belief that a corporation existed.[2]

For all of this century, the first requirement has been met in each American jurisdiction, and in situations involving real-world questions about the existence of a de facto corporation, the third requirement also tends to be met without much question. The real issue usually is whether there has been a good faith attempt to incorporate.

One of the more interesting modern de facto corporation doctrine cases is *Cantor v. Sunshine Greenery, Inc.*,[3] and that case nicely illustrates how the question of whether a good faith attempt has been made to incorporate can arise. In *Cantor*, the incorporators signed a corporate charter on December 3 and on that same day mailed the charter to the office of the secretary of state. Evidently

2. *See, e.g.*, Cranson v. IBM, 234 Md. 477, 200 A.2d 33 (1964). *See also* Harrill v. Davis, 168 F. 187 (8th Cir. 1909).
3. Cantor v. Sunshine Greenery, Inc., 165 N.J. Super. 411, 398 A.2d 571 (1979).

believing that the charter had been received by that office and filed, one of the incorporators signed a lease in the corporation's name on December 16. In fact, the charter was not filed by the secretary of state until two days later. Those facts were enough to allow a New Jersey court to find a bona fide attempt to incorporate and, with the other elements of the de facto corporation doctrine met, also to find the existence of a de facto corporation. "To deny such existence because of a mere technicality caused by administrative delay in filing runs counter to the purpose of the *de facto* concept," the court said, "and would accomplish an unjust and inequitable result in favor of plaintiffs contrary to their own contractual expectations."[4] The most important learning from *Cantor* is probably found in that quoted explanation by the court of its decision, i.e., that to reach another result would be inequitable. The theme of equity in the judicial resolution of liability questions is one that runs through this chapter.

Perhaps it is the courts' appraisals of who ultimately will suffer liability that cause them to show little sympathy when it is a lawyer rather than the secretary of state who delays filing a corporate charter. For example, in *Asplund v. Marjohn Corp.*,[5] incorporation papers evidently had been signed and left with a lawyer for filing, but the lawyer had neglected to file them before a contract was entered into in the corporate name. In those circumstances, the court, which happened to be the same court that decided *Cantor*, found no bona fide attempt to incorporate and laid on personal liability. Could it be that the court was at least somewhat of the opinion that it was the lawyer, or more likely his insurance company, who ultimately should stand the liability?[6]

---

4. *Id.* at 415–16, 398 A.2d at 573.
5. Asplund v. Marjohn Corp., 66 N.J. Super. 255, 168 A.2d 844 (1961).
6. That is not to say that lawyers always could be liable in such circumstances. For one thing, the liability of a lawyer should depend on what the lawyer tells the client. Partially with that in mind, lawyers should tell clients not to begin

The corporation by estoppel doctrine is a misnomer. The effect of the application of that doctrine is not to create a corporation. The effect, rather, is simply that a court in applying the doctrine will estop a plaintiff from arguing the nonexistence of a corporation that patently does not exist as a de jure corporation. As might be expected, the occasion for a court to invoke the doctrine relates to its appraisal of the equities of the situation before it in litigation, with the basic question for the court being, "Is it equitable to allow the plaintiff to collect from persons who thought they were officers, directors, or shareholders of a corporation?" Perhaps the best statement of the corporation by estoppel doctrine is found in one of Ballantine's classic works on corporation law:

> The so-called estoppel that arises to deny corporate capacity does not depend on the presence of the technical elements of equitable estoppel, viz., misrepresentations and change of position in reliance thereon, but on the nature of the relations contemplated, that one who has recognized the organization as a corporation in business dealings should not be allowed to quibble or raise immaterial issues on matters which do not concern him in the slightest degree or affect his substantial rights.[7]

Although some courts get confused on the subject,[8] the corporation by estoppel doctrine and the de facto corporation doctrine are two distinct doctrines, and the elements of a de facto corporation do not have to be found before a court can find a corporation by estoppel. Some of the confusion is understandable, however, because each doctrine ultimately is underpinned by concepts of equity, and the facts that support one doctrine often also support the other. For example, a typical fact situation finds a defendant facing personal liability for a contract that both the defendant and the plaintiff believed was a corporate debt, thus leading to questions

---

operating in the corporate form before the lawyer has told them that a charter has been issued.

7. H. BALLANTINE, MANUAL OF CORPORATION LAW AND PRACTICE 92 (1930).
8. *See, e.g.*, the discussion in Cranson v. IBM, 234 Md. 477, 200 A.2d 33 (1964).

about the equity of allowing the plaintiff to collect from an individual defendant because of a technical problem in the incorporation of the defendant's corporation. A further look at the facts may indicate that they fit the required elements of the de facto corporation doctrine, and so the overlap between the two doctrines may be fairly extensive. Perhaps it can most helpfully be said that the usual effect of the corporation by estoppel doctrine is to backstop the de facto corporation doctrine by allowing courts to excuse defendants from liability, where doing so would work equity, in situations where one or more elements of the de facto corporation doctrine are not met.

Statutory Developments

Over the last few decades, questions of defective incorporation have been answered to an increased degree by reference to corporation statutes. Those statutes, typified by the Model Business Corporation Act, now universally make establishing a corporation a simple one-step process, thus arguably lessening the need for the de facto corporation doctrine and, perhaps to a lesser extent, for the corporation by estoppel doctrine as well. Some of those statutes also include language speaking directly to the question of liability for those who assume to act as a corporation without authority to do so. Here are the two relevant Model Act sections, each of which has been widely adopted:

Section 56. Effect of Issuance of Certificate of Incorporation.

Upon the issuance of the certificate of incorporation, the corporate existence shall begin, and such certificate shall be conclusive evidence that all conditions precedent required to be performed by the incorporators have been complied with and that the corporation has been incorporated under this Act, except as against this State in a proceeding to cancel or revoke the certificate of incorporation or for the involuntary dissolution of the corporation.

Section 146. Unauthorized Assumption of Corporate Powers.

All persons who assume to act as a corporation without authority so to do shall be jointly and severally liable for all debts and liabilities incurred or arising as a result thereof.

We know that the intent of the Model Act's drafters was to abrogate the de facto corporation doctrine, because they said as much in the official comment to section 56: "Since it is unlikely that any steps short of securing a certificate of incorporation would be held to constitute apparent compliance [with the de facto corporation requirement that there be a good faith attempt at incorporation], the possibility that a de facto corporation could exist under such a provision is remote."

The drafters said nothing about the corporation by estoppel doctrine, and the best conclusion from their silence is that they did not mean also to do away with that doctrine. Leaving the corporation by estoppel doctrine untouched by statutory law seems inarguably the best course, since the doctrine merely allows a court to use its general equity powers to mitigate the unfairness that otherwise might flow from the application of legal rules. That, of course, is what equity is all about.

Nevertheless, the case law on that subject is in conflict. The two main cases are *Robertson v. Levy*[9] and *Timberline Equipment Co. v. Davenport*,[10] each of which was decided under a statute that contained Model Act sections 56 and 146. In *Robertson*, the District of Columbia Court of Appeals held that "the impact of those sections, when considered together, is to eliminate the concepts of estoppel and de facto corporateness."[11] When the Oregon Supreme Court later considered the question of the post-Model Act existence of the corporation by estoppel doctrine, it refused to follow *Robertson*. Because in *Timberline* the lower court had found that the facts of

9. Robertson v. Levy, 197 A.2d 443 (D.C. Ct. App. 1964).
10. Timberline Equip. Co. v. Davenport, 267 Or. 64, 514 P.2d 1109 (1973).
11. Robertson v. Levy, 197 A.2d at 477.

the case would not support the application of the doctrine, the supreme court did not officially reach the question of whether the doctrine exists in Oregon under the Model Act, but its discussion of the issue indicates its clear predisposition to find that it does.

Interestingly, the District of Columbia Court of Appeals does not seem inclined to follow its *Robertson* holding when the equities of a particular situation pull it in another direction. The facts in *Robertson* involved a defendant who had signed a lease in a corporate name before the certification of incorporation was issued, there being no indication in the court's decision that the defendant mistakenly thought the corporation had been formed. In those circumstances, there would seem to be no justification for the imposition of the corporation by estoppel doctrine. Two years later, the same court had before it *Namerly v. Generalcar.*[12] In that case, the same panel that decided *Robertson* reversed field and found that a party was estopped to deny the existence of a corporation. The facts of *Namerly* easily explain the court's desire to apply an equitable doctrine. There the court was faced with a defendant who attempted to escape a contractual debt, which equitably seemed clearly to be his, on the grounds that the plaintiff—which the defendant had dealt with as a corporation—had failed to prove its corporate existence. Strangely, the *Namerly* court did not mention its decision in *Robertson*. Perhaps the court thought it best simply to ignore its earlier too-quick casting aside of its power to do equity.

Even if the corporation by estoppel doctrine is not available in a given situation, the liability result of Model Act section 146 may not be what it first seems. That section, which places liability on "[a]ll persons who assume to act as a corporation without authority" may appear clearly to place personal liability at least on all owners of the noncorporate enterprise. In *Timberline*, however, the Oregon Supreme Court concluded that that section "does not include those

12. Namerly v. Generalcar, 217 A.2d 109 (D.C. Ct. App. 1966).

whose only connection with the organization is as an investor,"[13] but rather "those persons who have an investment in the organization and who actively participate in the policy and operational decisions of the organization."[14] That conclusion, which flows from an interpretation of the statutory language "assume to act," means that section 146 can have a less far-reaching result than would exist in its absence. Without a statutory provision on the question, all the owners of the enterprise would be treated as partners, since the enterprise would meet the partnership definition of "an association of two or more persons to carry on as co-owners a business for profit."[15] And, of course, all partners share joint and several personal liability for a partnership's obligations.[16]

When the drafters of the Model Act revisited, in connection with the creation of the Revised Model Act, the question of personal liability for the debts of a defectively incorporated enterprise, they found an interesting phenomenon: "A review of recent case law indicates . . . that even in states with [statutes like the Model Act] courts have continued to rely on common-law concepts of de facto corporations, de jure corporations, and corporations by estoppel . . . ."[17] *Cantor v. Sunshine Greenery, Inc.*, discussed above, is one of the examples cited, and a look at those examples and other cases like them shows an even more interesting phenomenon: Courts too often do not discuss the corporation statute when deciding cases involving possible personal liability, but rather rely on case law that predates the statute. That is bad judicial decision making, which almost certainly can be blamed in part on lawyers who did not properly brief the courts on the corporation statutes. Nevertheless, that decision making can be taken in part to indicate a desire on

13. Timberline Equip. Co. v. Davenport, 267 Or. at 74, 514 P.2d at 1113.
14. *Id.* at 75, 514 P.2d at 1114.
15. UNIFORM PARTNERSHIP ACT § 6 (1).
16. *Id.* § 15.
17. Official Comment to REVISED MODEL BUSINESS CORP. ACT § 2.04 (1985).

the part of judges to retain more flexibility than the Model Act gave them in the area of defective incorporation.

As a result of those decisions, the ABA Committee on Corporate Laws gave up on Model Act sections 56 and 146. Here is what they came up with as a substitute in the Revised Model Act:

Section 2.04. Liability for Preincorporation Transactions.

All persons purporting to act as or on behalf of a corporation, knowing there was no incorporation under this Act, are jointly and severally liable for all liabilities created while so acting.

On the question of estoppel, the official comment to that section indicates that "the section does not foreclose the possibility that persons who urge defendants to execute contracts in the corporate name knowing that no steps to incorporate have been taken may be estopped to impose personal liability on individual defendants." Not wanting to see estoppel intrude too far into the scheme of the Revised Model Act, however, its drafters added that "persons who knowingly participate in [an unincorporated] business under a corporate name . . . may not argue that plaintiffs are 'estopped' from holding them liable because all transactions were conducted on a corporate basis."[18] As with all matters concerning the Revised Model Act, major questions are how many states will adopt the Act and how soon? Here there is an additional serious question: Even in states that adopt the Revised Act, will courts pay any attention to it, or will they apply old case law?

18. *Id.* It should be noted here that in the circumstances stated, it would be rarely if ever possible that a defendant could escape liability under the corporation by estoppel doctrine.

Disregard of the Corporate Entity

Incorporation does not guarantee that in all circumstances the shareholders will be safe from personal liability for their corporation's debts. Even though the limited liability of shareholders is provided by corporation statutes, courts nevertheless will hold shareholders personally liable for a corporation's debts, or in popular terminology will "pierce the corporate veil," in accordance with well-established—if loose—precedent.

One way to approach this area is theoretically. The cases discuss two theories for piercing, the alter-ego theory and the instrumentality theory. The focus of the first theory is on the indistinctness of the boundaries between a corporation and its owners, while the focus of the second is on the use of a corporation by its owners in ways that benefit them rather than the corporation. Under those theories, a court will analyze whether a corporation is the "alter ego" or "instrumentality" of its owners. If a court finds that it is, it will hold the shareholders liable for the corporation's debts.

In actual practice, those theories are almost useless in decision making. First of all, judges' discussions of those theories tend to be a jumble, with the terms "alter ego" and "instrumentality" often being used in the place of each other. Second, judges tend merely to use those terms in a conclusory way without any real analysis, so that "talisman" might be a better word to use than "theory" when discussing the terms.

If the alter-ego and instrumentality theories do not provide an analytical underpinning for disregarding the corporate entity, what is the underpinning? As Professor Latty said a half century ago in the context of a discussion of the instrumentality theory as it relates to multiple corporate enterprises: "What the formula comes down to, once shorn of verbiage about control, instrumentality, agency, and corporate entity, is that liability is imposed to reach an equitable result."[19] This is not to say, of course, that courts often make ad hoc decisions about the equities of a given situation without reference to factual precedent. They do not. To understand this area, it is necessary to examine the various factual constructs upon which courts have based decisions to pierce.

Inadequate Capital

A lack of adequate capital is one of the most often cited bases for disregarding the corporate entity. The best known articulation of that basis is by Ballantine:

> If a corporation is organized and carries on business without substantial capital in such a way that the corporation is likely to have no sufficient assets available to meet its debts, it is inequitable that shareholders should set up such a flimsy organization to escape personal liability. . . . If the capital is illusory or trifling compared with the business to be done and the risks of loss, this is a ground for denying the separate entity privilege.[20]

The last sentence of that quotation appears repeatedly in the case law, and from that one might conclude that courts require substantial capitalization if a corporation's owners are to escape personal liability. In fact, however, the courts' statements on inadequate capital are a matter of all smoke, no fire. For one thing, some courts have focused on the "a" in Ballantine's statement that inadequate capital "is a ground for denying the separate entity privilege," with the idea being that inadequate capital is not enough by itself to deny the privilege.[21] That clearly was not Ballantine's intent, as evidenced by his statement to the contrary appearing in the same paragraph as the language last quoted: "The attempt to do corporate business without providing any sufficient basis of financial responsibility to

---

19. E. Latty, Subsidiaries and Affiliated Corporations 191 (1936).
20. H. Ballantine, Corporations 302–03 (rev. ed. 1946).
21. *See, e.g.*, Harris v. Curtis, 8 Cal. App. 3d 837, 87 Cal. Rptr. 614 (1970), which uses the Ballantine quotation as earlier adopted by a California court.

creditors is an abuse of the separate entity and will be ineffectual to exempt the shareholders from corporate debts."[22]

The main way courts have avoided piercing the corporate veil based on inadequate capitalization is simply to quote strong language such as Ballantine's and then ignore it. Rarely does one find any real attempt to discern what amount of capital would be "illusory or trifling compared to the business to be done and the risks of loss." Admittedly, that may be difficult to do. But let us take an amount, say $1,000, that clearly would meet the illusory or trifling test in the case of most businesses. Search the cases on disregard of the corporate entity, and you will be hard pressed to find even one where a corporate veil was pierced when at least $1,000 had been paid in as capital and where no other basis for piercing existed.

One wonders, in fact, if there is not some magic in the number $1,000. That was the traditional amount that corporation statutes, including an earlier version of the Model Act, required to be paid in before the corporation was supposed to begin its operations. Although those statutory requirements have almost all disappeared, the collective memory in the legal profession of the figure $1,000 seems vivid. Does that mean that a shareholder is safe from personal liability if a corporation is capitalized at that level? Certainly not, if for no other reason than that virtually any court that wants to can quote the Ballantine language as the law and then take that language seriously when applying it to the facts. It does mean, however, that corporations should not be capitalized at less than $1,000, for to do so may cause them to fall short of what a court may view as a minimum number.

Failure to Follow Formalities

Aside from such problems as the use of the corporation to commit fraud, virtually all bases for disregarding the corporate entity,

22. H. BALLANTINE, *supra* note 20, at 302.

other than inadequate capital, may be thought of largely as a failure to follow formalities.[23] Take, for example, the commingling of personal and corporate funds, which is one of the more likely problems that will lead to piercing. Commingling can be viewed, of course, as a substantive rather than a formal problem. When one breaks down a commingling situation into its constituent parts, however, one finds either that the various components are themselves formal problems or that the problems inherent in the components could be cured by establishing the proper formalities. For example, a sole-shareholder corporation that is financed out of its owner's checking account rather than an account of its own, and that neither pays dividends nor salaries but has the owner use the corporation's funds as if they were his own, has a substantive commingling problem. But the failure to maintain a separate bank account is largely a formal problem, and one that can easily be cured by the formality of establishing and maintaining a separate account. Likewise, using a corporation's funds as if they were personal property can be viewed as a formal problem, and again the problem largely can be cured by formal means. For starters, the owner can cause the corporation to establish a reasonable salary, combined as desirable with bonuses, dividends, an expense account, and fringe benefits such as a health plan. Beyond those means of getting money out of the corporation, the corporation could authorize and properly document loans to the owner on a revolving basis, so that the owner could take money out of the corporation and pay it back as needed. The loans would need to bear reasonable interest, but in a one-owner corporation, and especially a corporation that has elected type S corporation tax treatment, that, too, ends up being largely a formality.

In order better to understand the role of formalities in piercing cases, it may be helpful to look at the facts of one of the best-known of those cases, *DeWitt Truck Brokers, Inc. v. W. Ray Flemming*

23. Here the term "formalities" is used to include actions the substantive consequences of which make little or no difference to the people involved.

Fruit Co.,[24] which the Fourth Circuit decided in 1976. In that case, the plaintiff sought to impose personal contract liability on the president and major shareholder of W. Ray Flemming Fruit Co. Here is how the court described in part the situation relating to corporate formalities:

> [The corporation] began in 1962 with a capitalization of 5,000 shares . . . . In some manner which Flemming never made entirely clear, approximately 2,000 shares were retired. At the times involved here Flemming owned approximately 90% of the corporation's outstanding stock, according to his own testimony, though that was not verified by any stock records. Flemming was obscure on who the other stockholders were . . . . His testimony on who were the officers and directors was hardly more direct. He testified that the corporation did have one other director, Ed Bernstein . . . . It is significant, however, that . . . there were no corporate records of a real directors' meeting in all the years of the corporation's existence . . . . Flemming countered that by testifying that Bernstein traveled a great deal and that his contacts with Bernstein were generally by telephone. The evidence indicates rather clearly that Bernstein was . . . "nothing more than [a] figurehead[s]," [sic] who had "attended no directors meeting . . . ."[25]

Those problems by themselves were enough to sustain a verdict for the plaintiff. Sadly, problems like those are not uncommon. At least as sad is the fact that problems like the ones described easily can be avoided. For example, holding necessary board meetings—including by telephone so long as the corporation statute allows that—or having the directors act by written consent in lieu of meetings, taking and recording the proper corporate action to "retire" shares, keeping clear stock records, and electing officers and directors annually are tasks easily accomplished.

---

24. DeWitt Truck Brokers, Inc. v. W. Ray Flemming Fruit Co., 540 F.2d 681 (4th Cir. 1976).
25. *Id.* at 687.

Importance of Equities

Although the formalities problems just discussed were enough to support piercing in the *Flemming* case, there was something additional relating to formalities that may have been more important:

> The District Court found, also, that the corporation never had a stockholders' meeting. This accorded with Flemming's own testimony when originally deposed. Later, it is true, he sought to disown this admission and produce minutes of five stockholders' meetings, which incidentally were identical in form. He would explain his earlier admission by saying he had misunderstood a simple question such as whether the corporation had ever had a stockholders' meeting. The trial judge, who observed the witnesses and their demeanor on the stand, found the defendant's disavowal of his earlier testimony in this regard unconvincing and concluded that his earlier admission was correct.

Whatever the truth in *Flemming*, that brings up the practice of simply drafting minutes of a meeting that did not occur or of inserting into minutes of a meeting that did occur resolutions concerning matters that were not discussed at the meeting.

Regrettably, some lawyers involve themselves in those practices, presumably on the grounds either that the practices are innocuous or that they are at least unlikely to be discovered. Lawyers who believe that are wrong on both counts. The ethical problems involved are obvious and we shall not labor them, but rather focus on the damage those practices can do to defendants in a piercing case. First, it is important to realize that in such cases the judge's or jury's perceptions of the relative equities are nearly everything. To win a piercing case, the job of the plaintiff's lawyer is first to convince the court that the equities are on the plaintiff's side and then to provide the court with some basis for a decision in the plaintiff's favor. If a corporation has not had proper meetings, a court can brush that aside as a minor technicality if it wishes. But if in addition to not having proper meetings, persons involved in the corporation falsify its minutes, the defendant's case likely will be lost at the instant the court hears the facts.

How likely are falsified minutes to be discovered? Almost certainly, if the plaintiff is well represented. The falsification of minutes is not a secret in the legal community, so lawyers often know what to look for in a piercing case. Proving the falsification usually is easy. A matching of supposed meeting dates with subpoenaed travel or telephone records often will show that persons who were recorded as being at a meeting were either out of town or involved in long-distance telephone calls at the time of the supposed meeting. Deposing the clerical secretary who typed the minutes may get at the truth, since he or she often will know the truth and likely will not want to risk false testimony. But such aggressive discovery usually is not required. Few directors or shareholders want to risk perjury charges in a deposition when they cannot be sure what others who know the facts will say. And if it is the corporation's lawyers who drafted the fake minutes, directors or shareholders being deposed easily can be made to sing "The lawyers did it, the lawyers did it" faster than the court recorder's fingers can move.[26]

Multiple Corporations

Enterprises consisting of multiple corporations present special problems in the context of piercing the corporate veil. In those situations, two different kinds of piercing are possible. First, as in the

---

26. In this discussion we have assumed the lack of involvement by a lawyer except in connection with the drafting of false minutes. A corporation's lawyer who knows minutes are false can find himself or herself in serious trouble as time goes by, even if he or she was not involved in the falsification. Consider, for example, the position of the lawyer when the corporation's minutes are subpoenaed in connection with litigation, when they are asked for by the Internal Revenue Service in connection with an audit, or when they are requested by the lawyers for a private party in connection with a securities sale or a bank loan. If the lawyer is a party to turning over false minutes, he or she may face such charges as fraud on a court, committing or aiding and abetting tax fraud, or fraud on the other party to a planned transaction.

single-corporation situation, any one or more of the corporations can have their separate entity status disregarded to the end that the owners are held personally liable for a corporation's debts. Second, the separate entity status of the corporations involved in the enterprise may be disregarded to the end that the assets of all the corporations are pooled and made available to the creditors of any of the corporations.

As in the case of single corporations, corporate entity status in the multiple-corporation enterprise is disregarded most often as a result of the failure to follow formalities. Usual problems that may lead to piercing are (1) failing properly to approve and document intercorporate transactions, (2) treating multiple corporations as if they were one business, and (3) setting up contractual arrangements that favor one corporation at the expense of another. It does not help if each corporation has the same officers and directors and operates out of the same office, but often business realities limit the possibilities in those regards. Factors such as those are not fatal, however, so long as steps are taken to avoid the bigger problems.

To avoid the kinds of problems outlined above, two different kinds of steps should be taken. First, care must be taken to follow scrupulously all formalities in each corporation. If there are to be intercorporate loans, for example, the loans need to be properly approved and documented. Second, all intercorporate transactions should be as much like ones at arm's length as one can make them, to the extent that real arm's-length bargaining is not possible. For example, each corporation that enters into a contract with a related corporation should have a reasonable chance of making a profit on the contract.

Often, it makes no business sense for each corporation in a multicorporation complex to handle all of its own affairs. For example, a corporate complex may consist of a number of restaurants, each of which is operated by a separate corporation. Each corporation will need legal and accounting services, insurance services, janitorial services, personnel services, and so on. It would be economically foolhardy for each corporation to contract for or handle each of those services itself, yet dangerous for the jobs of providing those services to be shared among the corporations willy-nilly. The way to handle the provision of such services is to establish a service corporation whose business it is to provide those services to each of the operating corporations under contract. Risks of piercing thus should be avoided, so long as the contracts are fair to each corporation.

CHAPTER EIGHT

Corporate Authority

Corporate authority is an especially important subject for lawyers because questions about corporate authority arise frequently. Most of those questions involve one or both of the following aspects:

1. What person or corporate body has power to take action?
2. What formalities are required for the action to be taken?

In terms of who can take action, there usually are three choices: the shareholders, the directors, or one or more of the officers.[1] We shall discuss the choices of who may take action in the order just stated, and we shall blend into that discussion a consideration of the required formalities of decision-making.

Functions and Authority of Shareholders

Shareholders of close corporations tend to assume that they have broad powers to make corporate decisions. Such was the case with the shareholders of the Rawhide Ranch Gold and Silver Mining Company when, in 1865, they met and voted to sell the corporation's mine and its other assets, thus setting the stage for one of the classic cases on shareholders' power, *Gashwiler v. Willis*.[2] In that

1. As will be seen in the discussions that follow, often there is more than one person or corporate body having power to act on a particular matter.
2. Gashwiler v. Willis, 33 Cal. 11 (1867).

case, the California Supreme Court held that the shareholders had no power by themselves to authorize a sale of the corporation's assets, even though the shareholders were all assembled at a meeting and even though they voted unanimously. The reason was simple: The corporation statute did not give the shareholders that power (and they did not have it at common law).

Although it surprises many clients, the universal rule in corporation law is that shareholders have no general power in the management of a corporation. Rather, shareholders have only those powers specifically given them, mostly by the corporation statute, but in some instances by common law. The overwhelmingly important power of shareholders, of course, is to elect directors, and it is that power to choose directors of their liking that gives shareholders their greatest power, especially when combined with the ability to remove directors at any time with or without cause, which is the modern statutory norm,[3] and when combined with the further ability to elect new directors to fill vacancies thus created.[4]

Some corporation statutes give the shareholders the power to amend the corporation's bylaws, unless the charter provides that the directors have that power. The Model Act goes in just the opposite direction with respect to bylaw amendments by providing that the authority to amend bylaws resides with the directors, unless the charter gives that power to the shareholders.[5] All or almost all other instances of shareholders' power relate to specific consents required

3. *See, e.g.*, MODEL BUSINESS CORP. ACT § 39.
4. Corporation statutes typically are silent on the power of shareholders to fill vacancies on the board of directors. The usual provision, of which Model Act section 38 is an example, simply provides that the remaining directors can fill such vacancies. The shareholders' power to fill vacancies comes from common law. *See, e.g.*, Campbell v. Loew's, Inc., 36 Del. Ch. 563, 134 A.2d 852 (1957).
5. MODEL BUSINESS CORP. ACT § 27. That section does provide, however, that directors' actions with respect to bylaws are "subject to repeal or change by action of the shareholders." Just how broad is the shareholders' mandate arising from the statutory word "change" is uncertain.

for particular corporate actions. In each of those instances there is the statutory requirement that the board of directors first vote on the action and then send it on to the shareholders for their consent. Examples are distributions from capital surplus,[6] charter amendments,[7] mergers and consolidations,[8] sales of all or substantially all corporate assets,[9] and voluntary dissolution.[10]

In order for a lawyer to be prepared for questions about the authority of shareholders, it will be helpful to understand the contexts in which those questions tend to arise. One is when a shareholders' meeting is imminent or in progress and a lawyer is asked whether the shareholders can vote on a particular matter or whether the matter has to wait for directors' action. Another is when it is possible to assemble a quorum of the shareholders but not of the directors or, along those same lines, where shareholders are available to sign consents in lieu of a meeting but the directors are not. When the need exists for the corporation to take action quickly, it is sometimes hard to convince shareholders that they lack the necessary power. That especially is the case where (1) the shareholders and the directors are exactly the same persons, which is not an unusual situation, and (2) a quorum for a directors' meeting cannot be obtained, but a quorum for a shareholders' meeting can be (the difference being that shareholders can be represented at a meeting by proxy holders while directors cannot[11]).

---

6. *See, e.g., id.* § 46.
7. *See, e.g., id.* § 59.
8. *See, e.g., id.* § 73.
9. *See, e.g., id.* § 79.
10. *See, e.g., id.* § 83.
11. *See, e.g., id.* § 33 regarding shareholders acting through proxy holders.

Functions and Authority of Directors

A popular misconception about the authority of directors, which goes along with misconceptions about shareholders' power, is that the directors get their authority from the shareholders. The issue of where directors get their power is nicely exposed in *Manson v. Curtis*,[12] a case decided by the New York Court of Appeals during World War I. In *Manson*, shareholders of the Bermuda-Atlantic Steamship Company entered into an agreement providing that one person was to manage the corporation, and that agreement, in the words of the court, "necessitated . . . passive directors." Holding that the agreement was void because the shareholders did not have the power to limit the power of the corporation's directors, the court laid out the basis for directors' authority this way: "In corporate bodies, the powers of the board of directors are, in a very important sense, original and undelegated. The stockholders do not confer, nor can they revoke, those powers. They are derivative only in the sense of being received from the state in the act of incorporation."[13]

Although it is a century and a quarter old, *Gashwiler v. Willis*,[14] the shareholders' authority issues of which are discussed at the beginning of the preceding section, also is one of the classic cases on the power of directors. As indicated in the prior discussion of that case, the California Supreme Court held in *Gashwiler* that the shareholders of the Rawhide Ranch Gold and Silver Mining Company had no power by themselves to authorize the sale of the corporation's mine and other assets. For the assets to be sold, the court found, the directors, acting at a meeting by the vote of a majority of the quorum, would have to authorize the sale.[15]

---

12. Manson v. Curtis, 223 N.Y. 313, 119 N.E. 559 (1918).
13. *Id.* at 322, 119 N.E. at 562.
14. Gashwiler v. Willis, 33 Cal. 11 (1867).
15. On the question of whether the directors could on their own sell the assets without shareholder approval, the court indicated that, although it was not

The court based that conclusion on two provisions in the California statute authorizing the incorporation of mining companies. The first provided that "the corporate powers of the corporation shall be exercised by a Board of not less than three Trustees, who shall be stockholders,"[16] and the second provided that "[a] majority of the whole number of Trustees shall form a Board for the transaction of business, and every decision of a majority of the persons assembled as a Board shall be valid as a corporate act." Those provisions still state the essentials of directors' power.

Model Business Corporation Act section 35 is the prototypical modern statutory grant to directors of their general power over the management of a corporation. Its most essential provision is: "All corporate powers shall be exercised by or under authority of, and the business and affairs of a corporation shall be managed under the direction of, a board of directors except as may be otherwise provided in this Act or the articles of incorporation." Until into the 1970s, the first clause of section 35 left out the language "or under authority of," so that, in the words of the statute, all corporate powers were to be exercised "by" the board. Even though it had long been clear that directors are not required to manage a corporation directly on a day-to-day basis, but may do so through delegation and oversight,[17] the drafters added the "under authority of" language to make the statute more transparent.

---

formally deciding the question since the question was not involved in the case, "[i]t may be conceded for the purposes of that case that the [directors] could not authorize a conveyance of the property in question without the consent of the stockholders." Consent of the shareholders for the sale of all or substantially all of a corporation's assets is the rule under modern statutes, so long as the sale is outside the regular course of a corporation's business. *See, e.g.*, MODEL BUSINESS CORP. ACT § 79.

16. "Trustees" is a synonym for "directors." That term now is seldom used in the case of business corporations, but it retains popularity in nonprofit corporations.

17. *See, e.g.*, Barnes v. Andrews, 298 F. 614 (S.D.N.Y. 1924).

The "except as may be otherwise provided in this Act or the articles of incorporation" provision in section 35 serves two purposes. First, it warns the reader of the statute that limitations on the board's power are found in other statutory sections. Second, it introduces the concept, fairly new to corporation law, that management schemes other than one featuring a supremely powerful board may be established in the charter. That brief provision, read along with language in Model Act section 54 allowing a charter to contain any provision not inconsistent with law "for the regulation of the internal affairs of the corporation," gives corporate planners nearly carte blanche to vary the corporate management scheme. The charter could, for example, limit the board's power in specific areas or take away all of the board's power and give it to the shareholders. (The official comment to Model Act section 35 indicates that, although the board's power can be taken away, a corporation nevertheless must retain a board. Since this makes no sense, and can only lead to confusion on the part of those who deal with the corporation, it is questionable whether the drafters of the Model Act actually intended this result (regardless of the official comment, which may have been written somewhat later) and also questionable whether courts would require the retention of a powerless board.)

Management flexibility was written into the Model Act and other statutes as a result of suggestions that traditional corporation statutes did not fit the needs of close corporations. It has been thought by some, for example, that it is preferable in the typical small close corporation to simplify corporate decision-making by having only shareholders and officers, and that is allowed under some statutes. Actually, however, the main effect of the flexible management options of modern statutes has been to show the usefulness inherent in the traditional management structure. Exceptionally few corporations operate without a board, for example, and those that do pay a high price for apparent simplicity.

Their trouble begins as soon as they attempt the early corporate act of opening a bank account, since banking procedures are set up to handle accounts that have been authorized by a corporation's board of directors. At minimum, the officer attempting to open an account encounters resistance from clerks. At maximum, the bank's officers insist on consulting their lawyers before opening an account for a directorless corporation. That sort of problem follows such a corporation throughout its life, coming up every time the corporation wants to enter into a transaction that traditionally is accompanied by an authorizing board resolution.

Referring again to the statute discussed in *Gashwiler*, one may remember that it required a board of at least three directors, each of whom must be a shareholder. Those have been traditional statutory requirements, and they are still found in some corporation statutes. The most modern statutes have done away with such requirements, however. The Model Act, for example, requires only one director, and it does not require that directors be shareholders.[18] Experience taught that those traditional requirements serve no purpose. In the one- or two-shareholder corporation, requiring three directors typically ends up a meaningless formality, since any nonshareholder director can be replaced at will by the shareholder or shareholders. Likewise the requirement that each director be a shareholder: In a corporation with one real owner, such a requirement merely leads to the issuance of what are referred to as directors' qualifying shares. Typically, a certificate representing one share is issued to each "extra" director, who immediately indorses the certificate for transfer and gives it back to the corporation with the understanding that the transfer will be effective as soon as the director's term is over.

The requirement in the statute in *Gashwiler* that the board act by majority decision at a meeting at which a majority of the whole number of directors is present also has been the traditional norm. There is a trick here for the uninitiated. Suppose that a corporation's charter or bylaws provide for a board of nine members, but that because of resignations or failures to fill all the spots the corporation

18. Model Business Corp. Act §§ 35, 36.

has only five directors. How many directors are necessary for a quorum? The answer is "five," because the phrase "whole number of directors" (usually stated as "whole board," "full board," or "entire board" in modern statutes) is a term of art meaning the number of directors the corporation would have if there were no vacancies. Because corporation statutes have been drafted and refined by practical lawyers who have tried hard to make the statutes easily usable by corporate managers, statutory provisions usually track the expectations of those managers. The rules on quorums are one place where that is not the case. Unless they are taught otherwise, clients almost invariably assume that quorum requirements are based on the number of directors the corporation actually has, not on the number it is authorized to have.

While the *Gashwiler* statutory quorum and voting requirements do state the traditional norm, modern statutes often contain some important differences. Under the Model Act, for example, both the percentage of directors that constitutes a quorum and the percentage of the quorum whose agreement is required to take action may be increased beyond a mere majority in a corporation's charter or bylaws.[19] A far more important addition in modern statutes is the opportunity given directors to act by unanimous written consent in lieu of meeting,[20] which is a possibility that is discussed in the preceding chapter.[21]

Note that under neither the traditional nor the more liberal modern statutory approaches to directors' decision-making do directors have any power as individuals. Their power is collective only. The theory behind the traditional rule that directors may act only as a group, and only while assembled at a meeting, is that the give and take of a group discussion will help ensure the best corporate decisions. Since directors' written consents in lieu of meetings almost

19. *Id.* § 40.
20. *See, e.g., id.* § 44.
21. *See* pp. 110–111 *supra.*

always must be unanimous, they fit within that theory by virtue of the idea that if all the directors are already of one mind on an issue, there would be no give and take at a meeting.

There is one final exception to the rule that directors must act together and at a meeting: Under modern statutes directors may act through a committee they have established. The typical statutory provision on board committees provides that, by the vote of a majority of the whole board,[22] the board may designate from among its members any committees it wishes, and may delegate to a committee any of the board's powers, except for certain powers that the statute prohibits to committees. The Model Act's prohibitions are representative:

> [N]o . . . committee shall have authority to (i) declare dividends or distributions, (ii) approve or recommend to shareholders actions or proposals required by this Act to be approved by shareholders, (iii) designate candidates for the office of director . . . or fill vacancies on the board of directors or any committee thereof, (iv) amend the bylaws, (v) approve a plan of merger not requiring shareholder approval, (vi) reduce earned or capital surplus, (vii) authorize or approve the reacquisition of shares unless pursuant to a general formula or method specified by the board of directors, or (viii) authorize or approve the issuance or sale of, or any contract to issue or sell, shares or designate the terms of a series of a class of shares [except in limited, specified circumstances].[23]

The first committee that a board usually appoints is an executive committee, which traditionally is a committee having all the powers

22. Note the special vote required for the establishment of committees. Unless clients are reminded of that requirement, they are inclined to consider valid board action to be taken if there is an affirmative vote of a majority of a quorum, which is the usual rule in directors' decision-making. What saves the situation in many cases is that votes by directors tend to be unanimous—after whatever discussion is necessary to reach consensus. Thus, if a quorum is present and if a vote is unanimous, the special voting requirement of a majority of the full board (which also is the quorum requirement) is met automatically.

23. MODEL BUSINESS CORP. ACT § 42.

of the board when the board is not in session, except those powers prohibited to a committee by statute. To call a committee an executive committee and then give it substantially different powers than that is to invite trouble, since everyone dealing with the corporation will assume that its executive committee has standard authority. Often a corporation has a board made up of both inside and outside directors.[24] Because of their everyday involvement in the corporation's affairs, inside directors are usually more available for meetings on short notice than are outside directors. Partly for that reason, it is common for an executive committee's members to be all or almost all inside directors.

So far, our discussion of directors has focused on what directors have the power to do—which is just about anything relating to the business and affairs of a corporation, save for those few things for which directors need the shareholders' consent.[25] That is important, but it also is important to understand what directors actually do in corporations and what they tend to leave to others.

Here it is necessary to distinguish between corporations whose directors are substantial shareholders and those whose directors are not, because in the former corporations directors can be expected to take an unusually active role in decision making. Partially because the director who is a substantial shareholder is much more likely to be found in the close than in the publicly held corporation, close corporations more often have active directors than do publicly held ones. Beyond that, it is hard to generalize about what directors actually do in close corporations, because the distribution of real power in those corporations varies so greatly. In many close corporations, one majority shareholder dominates all corporate decisions, rendering board action a mere formality. In other close corporations, a board of equally powerful director-shareholders meets

24. Inside directors are directors who, as officers, work full-time for the corporation. For outside directors, their directorship is their only position in the corporation.

25. See pp. 146–147 *supra*.

often to argue out all important decisions. On the continuum between those two extremes there exists a seemingly infinite variety of director involvement in corporate decision-making.

There is more consistency in the level and type of director decision-making in the publicly held corporation, once you set aside those publicly held corporations whose directors also are substantial shareholders.[26] Miles Mace of the Harvard Business School conducted extensive research on what outside directors do and don't do in the typical large or medium-sized publicly held corporation. He reported his findings in a now famous book, *Directors: Myth and Reality*,[27] and in a not so well known but more widely available article, "The President and the Board of Directors."[28]

Mace found that in the kinds of corporations he studied, outside directors typically do three things: "[S]erve as a source of advice and counsel, offer some sort of discipline value, and act in crisis situations."[29] They do not, he found, establish objectives, strategies, or major policies, but rather leave those jobs to the corporation's officers.

From reading Mace's findings, it is easy to underestimate the value to the corporation of the things Mace says directors do. That is a mistake. In their advisory role, directors discuss troublesome corporate matters with the chief executive officer, almost exclusively on the telephone or in informal settings outside board meetings. Considering that outside directors are familiar with the corporation in a way that management consultants typically cannot be, and considering that outside directors tend to be chief executive officers of other

---

26. Admittedly, that means setting aside a substantial percentage of publicly held corporations, because in the small publicly held corporation, the original investors typically still own a large percentage of the corporation after it has gone public, and a majority of the directors often are original investors.
27. Harvard University Press, 1971.
28. Mace, *The President and the Board of Directors*, HARV. BUS. REV. 37 (Mar.-Apr. 1972).
29. *Id.* at 38.

corporations or to have other significant management or professional experience, outside directors provide a chief executive officer with a source of help in decision-making that is unavailable from anyone else.

Mace describes the discipline value of directors this way:

> Presidents and other members of top management in describing the discipline value of boards, indicated that the requirement of appearing formally before a board of directors consisting of respected, able people of stature, no matter how friendly, motivates the company managers to do a better job of thinking through their problems and of being prepared with solutions, explanations, or rationales.[30]

One also can easily see how that discipline value carries over into corporate actions generally, not just actions that are formally presented to the board. Because directors typically are given fairly broad information about their corporations, officers know that any significant decision they make may come to the directors' attention.

The role of directors in crisis situations can be a critical one. One classic crisis that Mace describes is the sudden death of the chief executive officer when succession has not been decided upon in advance. Another is when the chief executive officer's performance is so poor that a replacement must be found promptly. In situations such as those, it is only the directors who have either the statutory power or the real-world ability to act.

In the years since Mace did his research, two developments have influenced the behavior of directors. First, lawsuits against directors, alleging mismanagement, have become much more numerous. Second, there has been a widespread agreement among both scholars and corporate managers that the main function of directors should be to monitor the performance of the chief executive and other principal officers. As a result of those two developments, the first of

30. *Id.* at 39.

which pushed directors toward being more active and the second of which told directors the way they should be more active, monitoring must be added to Mace's list of what directors do.

Functions and Authority of Officers

Corporation statutes have very similar provisions with respect to corporate officers. The structure and most of the substance of Model Business Corporation Act section 50 is typical. The section first provides what officers a corporation must have and who shall choose them: "The officers of a corporation shall consist of a president, one or more vice presidents as may be prescribed by the bylaws, a secretary, and a treasurer, each of whom shall be elected by the board of directors at such time and in such manner as may be prescribed by the bylaws." That provision is found in many state statutes, but even in Model Act states, and more so in other states, there exists much variance in the list of required officers. In a high percentage of states, at least a president and a secretary are required.[31]

In addition to requiring a corporation to have certain officers, all statutes allow corporations to have whatever other officers they wish. Again, Model Act section 50 is typical: "Such other officers and assistant officers and agents as may be deemed necessary may be elected or appointed by the board of directors or chosen in such other manner as may be prescribed by the bylaws." The phrase "as may be deemed necessary" should not be taken literally. If the board elects an assistant secretary after deciding that it would be convenient for the corporation to have one, it is unlikely that a court later would hold the election to be invalid because the board did not go so far as to deem the assistant secretary to be necessary. Perhaps

31. As discussed in chapter 6, Model Act section 50 is ambiguous on the question of whether a corporation is required to have at least one vice president. *See* p. 117 *supra*.

"necessary" here should be interpreted to mean something like "necessary to the most efficient operation of the corporation," because necessity in an absolute sense almost never exists in the context of corporate officers. The corporation could exist and operate at some level with no officers at all.

It should also be noted that in connection with the statutory provision just discussed, the significant difference between required and nonrequired officers is that only required officers must be elected by the board of directors. Others may be chosen in any way the corporation wishes, so long as the procedure is spelled out in the bylaws. If a corporation opts for the choosing of nonrequired officers otherwise than by the board, the almost universally chosen alternative is to allow those officers to be appointed by another officer or officers. Both required and nonrequired offices may be held by the same person, except that statutes almost invariably prohibit one person from being both president and secretary. That too is covered in Model Act section 50.

So far we have discussed what officers a corporation must or may have and how they are to be chosen. The equally important question is: What are their powers? Model Act section 50 contains a standard provision on officers' powers: "All officers and agents of the corporation, as between themselves and the corporation, shall have such authority and perform such duties in the management of the corporation as may be provided in the bylaws, or as may be determined by resolution of the board of directors not inconsistent with the bylaws." That provision is somewhat misleading, as it seems to indicate that for an officer to have authority, the authority must either be spelled out in the bylaws or in a formal resolution of the board.

It is uncertain why the drafters of the Model Act chose to use the term "resolution" in that provision, rather than simply say that officers would have such authority "as may be determined by the board." In fact, the board often "determines" the exact powers of officers by acquiescence rather than by formal resolution. Not uncommonly, the only formal action the board of directors takes with respect to the powers of a particular officer is to adopt a bylaw provision containing a general statement of the officer's powers. After that, it may "give" an officer power simply by allowing the officer to continue doing what he or she has been doing, which often is something the officer has been told to do by another officer. There is no real doubt about the effectiveness of the board's grant of power by acquiescence in such a case—there being no significant chance, for example, that a court would allow the corporation to disavow a contract signed by an officer in the exercise of such authority—and there is little chance that the drafters of the Model Act wished that to be otherwise. The reference to board action by resolution probably is simply a case of less than perfect drafting.

The Model Act provision we have been discussing actually is misleading in a more basic way. As indicated above, the Model Act seems to say that for an officer to have authority, the authority must either be spelled out in the bylaws or in a formal resolution of the board. Explaining the problem with the part of that provision relating to a resolution still lets the provision create the impression that the board must focus specifically on the question of whether an officer has a particular power. That leaves unsaid anything about a number of types of authority, arising under the principles of agency law, that the board grants to officers simply by electing them to specified offices.

Those are inherent authority, incidental authority, and apparent authority. Simply by being elected to a particular office, the officer is automatically granted the powers that are inherent in that office, save when the board specifically indicates that the officer will not have a particular power. An example of an inherent power is the power of the vice president to act for the president when the president is incapacitated.

Incidental authority of an officer is the authority to perform acts that are incidental to acts for which the officer has actual authority (actual authority includes inherent authority and also any authority that is specifically granted, for example in the bylaws or by the board). Suppose that the board gives the treasurer the authority to invest the corporation's funds in common stocks. In that situation, the treasurer probably would have the incidental power to contract with an investment banking firm for investment advice, so long as the terms of the contract were reasonable in the circumstances.

Apparent authority of officers can be the most troublesome form of authority for a corporation, because that form of authority cannot easily be controlled. The apparent authority of an officer is coextensive with the authority that usually resides in the office held. That sounds complicated, but apparent authority is quite simple. If the board of directors elects a person to the office of vice president, but indicates that the person will not have the power to act for the president if the president becomes incapacitated, the vice president obviously will not have the actual authority to act in that situation. Nevertheless, since the power to act when the president is incapacitated usually resides in the office of vice president, the vice president will have the apparent authority to act. The result is that if, when the president is incapacitated, the vice president signs a contract that the president could have signed, the corporation ordinarily will be bound. Apparent authority is only defeated if a person dealing with an officer having apparent authority knows of the officer's lack of actual authority.

With that background in mind, it may be helpful to examine the authority inherent in the more common corporate offices: president, chairman of the board, vice president, secretary, and treasurer.

President

One of the most famous cases dealing with the authority of the president is *Joseph Greenspon's Sons Iron & Steel Co. v. Pecos Valley Gas Co.*[32] Although it is only a Delaware superior court case,

32. Joseph Greenspon's Sons Iron & Steel Co. v. Pecos Valley Gas Co., 34 Del. 567, 156 A. 350 (Super. Ct. 1931).

its instructional value is so high that law students have studied it for decades. *Greenspon's Sons* consists of a charge to the jury in a case involving a contract signed by the president of a gas company for the purchase of forty-five miles of gas pipe. The gas company attempted to repudiate the contract, and the question for the jury was whether or not signing the contract was within the president's power. On the question of inherent power, the court told the jury that: "[B]y virtue of his office [the president] may enter into a contract and bind his corporation in matters arising from and concerning the usual course of the corporation's business."[33] The question for the jury was whether buying forty-five miles of pipe was within the usual course of the gas company's business. In answering that question, a number of facts would be relevant, among them whether the gas company ever bought its own pipe or whether its practice was to hire a contractor to buy and lay pipe. (Regrettably, the reported case gives us only the charge to the jury, not the jury's verdict.)

Greenspon's Sons nicely states the general rule for a president's inherent authority: The president has the power to bind the corporation in the usual course of its business. For matters outside the usual course of business, the board of directors generally must give its approval for corporate action to be valid.[34] But even though that is the general rule, courts sometimes stretch to find that a corporation is bound by the actions of the president, and less often those of another officer, that technically needed the board's approval. The New Mexico Supreme Court put it that way:

> [I]t is recognized that, with the swift pace of modern business life, it is impossible to expect action by the directors in every transaction, even though it may be termed "unusual." Many courts have refused to permit a corporation to disclaim unauthorized agreements by officers

33. *Id.* at 571, 156 A. at 352.
34. Here it is important to remember the doctrine of ratification, under which the board could give its after the fact approval to an action of the president or another officer.

> as working an injustice as to parties dealing with the corporation . . . .[35]

Sometimes the president is the corporation's chief executive officer and sometimes not. Does that affect the general rule about the authority inherent in the presidency? The answer is no, but that brings us to a discussion of the authority of another officer at the top of the corporate hierarchy, the chairman of the board.

Chairman of the Board

Most corporations do not have a chairman of the board. The use of that title becomes increasingly common, however, as the size of a corporation increases, and most of the largest corporations do have a chairman. The chairman of the board is usually an officer, but not always. Sometimes, especially in smaller corporations, the title is simply given to the director who is chosen to preside at meetings, without also making the director an officer.

Assuming that the chairman of the board is an officer, what are his or her inherent powers? It is not possible to say with certainty. The widespread use of that title is relatively recent, and litigation about officers' authority is not common. Nevertheless, the opinions of courts are not too difficult to predict. Usually, if a corporation has a chairman, the chairman is the corporation's chief executive officer. In that case, the president almost always is the chief operating officer. Whatever role the president plays, as discussed above, the president will have the power to bind the corporation in connection with its usual course of business. That being the case, it is virtually certain that a court faced with determining the inherent authority of a chairman who is chief executive officer will determine that the chairman has the same inherent powers as the president to bind the corporation. That seems especially likely when one considers how

---

35. Yucca Mining & Petroleum Co. v. Howard C. Phillips Oil Co., 69 N.M. 281, 365 P.2d 925 (1961).

such a case is likely to arise: Typically, it would involve a corporation that attempts to avoid a contract within the corporation's usual course of business that was signed by its chairman. It is hard to postulate such a case in which the equities would be on the side of such a corporation, and it is highly unlikely that in such a situation a court would go against the equities.

It is not unusual, however, for the office of chairman of the board to be largely ceremonial. Often, the office is occupied by a former chief executive officer who is serving out his or her time until retirement or until a suitable position outside the corporation becomes available. In such cases, there probably are no powers that are inherent in the office of chairman, save arguably the power to preside at directors' meetings (and even that power is not the power of an officer, but rather of a director). Even so, corporations should not be surprised if courts do not allow them to avoid a contract entered into by a chairman of the board, whatever the chairman's actual authority. One suspects that courts often will be inclined to make the chairman's corporation, rather than the other party to a contract, suffer from the ambiguity of the title "chairman of the board."

Vice President

The vice president has but one inherent power: to serve in the place of the president, most usually in the event of the president's death, incapacity, or absence.[36] In that connection, there are two problems. First, if there is more than one vice president, do they share those powers or is there an order of succession? Second, what constitutes "incapacity" or "absence."

The first of those problems is the easiest to answer. In the absence of a bylaw or board action on the question, there seems to be no basis for distinguishing between vice presidents, and so each would seem to have the same power to substitute for the president. Well-

36. *See* Anderson v. Campbell, 176 Minn. 411, 223 N.W. 624 (1929).

drafted bylaws always speak to that question, however. The Model Act official form bylaws, for example, provide that "in the event there be more than one vice-president, the vice-presidents in the order designated at the time of their election, or in the absence of any designation, then in the order of their election,"[37] shall serve in the place of the president. The usual way to set one vice president apart from others is to use a different title, such as "executive vice president" or "senior vice president." That should be enough to establish the order of succession.

Determining just when a vice president may step in for a president is more difficult. Take incapacity as an example. Is it enough that the president be home with a cold, or must the president be in a coma before he or she will be considered incapacitated? Questions such as those are particularly troubling to those on the other side of a corporate transaction, because they do not wish to run the risk that a vice president's authority later will be denied by his or her corporation. In order to make it easier for their vice presidents to serve when needed, many corporations place in their bylaws language like the following: "The performance of any duty by a vice president shall, in respect of any other person dealing with the corporation, be conclusive evidence of the vice president's power to act."

Besides the inherent power to serve in the place of the president, certain vice presidents may be given additional inherent authority by virtue of their specialized titles. For example, it seems unlikely that a corporation that has elected someone to the office of vice president–purchasing could later avoid a contract for the purchase of office supplies that was signed by that vice president. Here the more interesting question relates to how far that additional authority might go. If that vice president purported to commit the corporation to purchase multimillion-dollar manufacturing equipment, for

---

37. Model Business Corp. Act Official Long Form Bylaws, art. IV, § 6.

example, would the corporation be bound? Answers to those questions cannot be reached in the abstract, but will depend on how a court views the facts and, probably more important, the equities.

Secretary

Unlike the inherent authority of the president and the vice president, the power inherent in the office of secretary relates only to the internal affairs of the corporation and not to its business. Those are powers to keep minutes of meetings and other nonfinancial corporate records, to have custody of the corporate seal, to attest the seal, to certify corporate records, and so on.

Insofar as dealings with those outside the corporation go, the certification of corporate records and particularly of minutes of meetings is by far the most important function of the secretary. Often, in connection with a corporate transaction, the person on the other side of the transaction will demand a certified copy of the board of directors' resolution approving the transaction. The person may also demand a certified list of the corporation's officers along with an attestation of the officers' signatures. The secretary has the inherent power to deliver those certifications and attestations, and once the secretary has done so, the corporation will not be allowed to deny their accuracy.[38]

Treasurer

In terms of inherent authority, the treasurer has much in common with the secretary, for the treasurer's power, too, relates to the affairs of the corporation. The treasurer has the power to care for the funds of the corporation. That includes depositing the funds in

38. *See, e.g., In re* Drive-In Dev. Corp., 371 F.2d 215 (7th Cir. 1966). That assumes that the person to whom a certification or attestation is delivered knows of no problem. If, for example, someone takes a certified copy of minutes that he or she knows or should know is false, that person cannot rely upon the certification.

proper depositories and disbursing them in accordance with orders from the board of directors or a proper officer, maintaining records of the funds, and rendering reports on the corporation's funds to the board of directors. In opposition to what most people believe, and as some have learned to their sorrow, the treasurer has no inherent power to sign a promissory note for the corporation.[39]

One final word about the authority of officers: Most vice presidents and treasurers, and many secretaries, have substantial corporate powers in addition to those inherent in their offices. The important thing to remember is that when considering any alleged power beyond that which is inherent, the power must ultimately have been given by the board, either directly or through another officer. The board may have granted the power formally in a bylaw or a resolution or it may have acted by acquiescence, but the board must have granted the power in some way—or the power does not exist.

39. *See, e.g.*, Jacobus v. Jamestown Mantel Co., 211 N.Y. 154, 105 N.E. 210 (1914).

CHAPTER NINE

Directors' Duty of Care

Directors are fiduciaries. "But," as Justice Frankfurter pointed out, "to say that a man is a fiduciary only begins analysis; it gives direction to further inquiry. . . . What obligations does he owe as a fiduciary?"[1] The obligations of directors can be grouped under two concepts, the duty of care and the duty of loyalty. The first of those duties will be discussed in this chapter and the second in the chapter immediately following.

We use the term "duty of care" because it is the longstanding term that describes the subjects we are about to discuss. The term is somewhat unhelpful, however, in that it seems to focus on the standard by which a director's performance is measured rather than on the more primary question of just what it is that directors are required to do. First, of course, a decision has to be made about the nature of directors' duties. Only then can one reasonably turn to the question of their liability for a failure to discharge those duties. It is with that in mind that the first section of the chapter is headed "Directors' Duty to Direct and Their Liability for Negligence."[2]

---

1. SEC v. Chenery Corp., 318 U.S. 80, 85–86 (1943).
2. For an expanded discussion of most of the material in this section, see Soderquist, *The Proper Standard for Directors' Negligence Liability*, 66 NOTRE DAME L. REV. (1990)

Directors' Duty to Direct and Their Liability for Negligence

Corporation statutes have typically provided that a corporation is to be managed "by a board of directors" or more recently "under the direction of a board of directors."[3] At first glance, the first quoted formulation may seem to require direct, day-to-day management by directors. But, as discussed in the preceding chapter,[4] that has never been required, and the addition of language in some statutes clearly providing for indirect management was a semantic clarification rather than a substantive revision. Taking that as a starting point, it will be helpful first to examine some of the major cases dealing with what it is that directors are supposed to do and the circumstances in which they may be held liable for negligence in management.

Case Law on Directors' Negligence Liability

Barnes v. Andrews,[5] which was decided by Learned Hand in 1924, is one of the best-known early modern cases on directors' negligence liability. Charles Andrews became a director of the Liberty Starters Corporation during its start-up period, and he served for about eight months. Judge Hand described the company's situation: "[T]he period before production was possible . . . was unduly prolonged by the incompetence of the factory manager, and disagreements between him and the engineer . . . .The officers were unable to induce these men to compose their differences, and the work languished from incompetence and extravagance."[6] "[Andrews's] only attention to the affairs of the company consisted

3. *See, e.g.*, MODEL BUSINESS CORP. ACT § 35.
4. *See* p. 147 *supra*.
5. Barnes v. Andrews, 298 F. 614 (S.D.N.Y. 1924).
6. *Id.* at 615.

of talks with the president as they met from time to time."[7] After the corporation went into receivership, the receiver sued Andrews for mismanagement.

The court first examined the question of whether Andrews could be charged with neglect in not attending board meetings. Judge Hand determined that Andrews could not be so charged, because of the two meetings held during his tenure as a director, Andrews attended one and had an adequate excuse for missing the other. The importance for our purposes of the court's handling of that issue is Judge Hand's clear intimation that failure to attend board meetings would be a basis for a finding of mismanagement. So much we would expect.

Judge Hand then turns to the more difficult question of just what Andrews should have done in addition to attending board meetings. Andrews did have a number of informal discussions with the president, but that was not enough:

> [H]e did not press [the president] for details, as he should. It is not enough to content oneself with general answers that the business looks promising and that all seems prosperous. Andrews was bound . . . to inform himself of what was going on with some particularity, and, if he had done so, he would have learned that there were delays in production which were putting the enterprise in most serious peril.[8]

As a result of those failures, the court found that Andrews was chargeable with mismanagement.

But that was not the end of story for Andrews, because Judge Hand also determined that Andrews could not be held liable for the corporation's losses unless the receiver could show causation: "The plaintiff must accept the burden of showing that the performance of the defendant's duties would have avoided loss, and what loss it

7. *Id.*
8. *Id.* at 616.

would have avoided."[9] In his discussion of causation, Judge Hand differentiated losses stemming from specific, identifiable causes and those arising from more general problems, and he made it clear that directors run significantly more risk in the former situation:

> When the corporate funds have been illegally lent, it is a fair inference that a protest would have stopped the loan, and that the director's neglect caused the loss. But when a business fails from general mismanagement, business incapacity, or bad judgment, how is it possible to say that a single director could have made the company successful, or how much in dollars he could have saved?

Stated that way, proof of causation not only was a required link in the receiver's case against Andrews, it was a link that was impossible to forge, and Andrews thus escaped liability.

During the same era as *Barnes*, the United States Supreme Court gave us *Bates v. Dresser*,[10] with an opinion by Oliver Wendell Holmes. *Bates* involved a small bank in Cambridge that was driven into bankruptcy by the embezzlements of its bookkeeper, Coleman, who covered his thefts by false balances in the deposit ledger. The bank's receiver sued the directors, alleging mismanagement. The Supreme Court's opinion is helpful to us for two purposes: its institution of the one-bite rule in the context of directors' actions and its differing treatment of inside and outside directors.

It seems that the way in which Coleman covered his tracks "was a novelty in the way of swindling a bank so far as the knowledge of any experience had reached Cambridge . . . ."[11] Noting that "[s]ome animals must be given at least one exhibition of dangerous propensities before the owner can be held,"[12] the Supreme Court agreed with

9. *Id.*
10. Bates v. Dresser, 251 U.S. 524 (1920).
11. *Id.* at 529.
12. *Id.*

the court of appeals' reversal of a judgment against the outside directors, saying that

> [t]heir confidence [that all was right] seemed warranted by the semi-annual examinations by the government examiner and they were encouraged in their belief that all was well by the president, whose responsibility, as executive officer; interest, as large stockholder and depositor; and knowledge, from long daily experience in the bank, were greater than theirs.[13]

The story was different when the Court turned to the question of Dresser, the president: "Practically he was the master of the situation. He was daily at the bank for hours, he had the deposit ledger in his hands at times and might have had it at any time. He had hints and warnings [about Coleman]."[14] One warning came from a man named Filmore, who "advise[d] the president to look after Coleman, that he believed he was living at a pretty fast pace, and that he had pretty good authority for thinking that he was supporting a woman."[15] Along those same lines, Dresser knew that Coleman had acquired an automobile, even though Coleman's weekly salary never was more than twelve dollars. Based on those and like facts about Dresser's "mastery of the situation," the Court upheld the lower courts' finding of mismanagement by Dresser. Thus was an inside director held liable while his outsider director colleagues were not.

The next significant directors' liability case we want to discuss, *Litwin v. Allen*,[16] shows a real contrast to the relative leniency of *Barnes* and *Bates*, insofar as outside directors are concerned. *Litwin* is the first modern case in which a court held outside directors liable simply for negligent management. That, by itself, gave the case major importance. That it involved famous and prestigious banking

13. *Id.* at 530.
14. *Id.*
15. *Id.*
16. Litwin v. Allen, 25 N.Y.S.2d 667 (1940).

houses and unusual facts helped ensure *Litwin's* position as the traditional leading case on directors' negligence liability.

The story behind *Litwin* began in early 1929, just before the start of the Great Depression, when clients of J.P. Morgan & Co. organized Alleghany Corporation to engage in the railroad business. By October 1930, the Depression was one year old, and Alleghany needed $10 million to pay for railroad terminals in Kansas City and St. Joseph, Missouri. Because of a borrowing limitation in its charter, a loan was not possible, but Morgan came to the rescue by agreeing to transactions designed to substitute for a loan. Morgan purchased from Alleghany $10 million face amount of debentures issued by Alleghany's subsidiary, Missouri Pacific Railroad. Because the debentures were convertible into Missouri Pacific common stock and because Alleghany did not want that stock to fall into the hands of outsiders, Alleghany retained the option to repurchase the debentures, at the price paid by Morgan, within six months. Since Morgan would receive the interest accrued on the debentures during the time it owned them, the sale and repurchase would have essentially the financial attributes of a loan, but without violating Alleghany's charter.

The direct road to *Litwin v. Allen* began when Morgan sold a $3 million participation in the transactions to its affiliate, Guaranty Trust Company of New York, upon the approval of the Trust Company's directors. What happened next, of course, is that the Depression deepened, the market value of the Missouri Pacific debentures fell precipitously, and Alleghany never exercised its option to repurchase the debentures. Trust Company shareholders then sued the directors for negligence in approving the Trust Company's participation in the Alleghany transactions. The court's discussion of what it called "the rules to be applied in determining the liability of directors"[17] was brief. "Directors," the court said, "are liable for negligence in the performance of their duties," adding, "In the last

17. *Id.* at 677.

analysis, whether or not a director . . . has been negligent . . . depends upon the facts and circumstances of a particular case . . . . A director is called upon 'to bestow the care and skill' which the situation demands."[18]

Turning to the Alleghany situation, the court found that the "directors plainly failed . . . to bestow the care which the situation demanded."[19] "I find liability in that transaction," the judge said, "because the entire arrangement was so improvident, so risky, so unusual and unnecessary as to be contrary to fundamental conceptions of prudent banking practice."[20] And then the court asked an intriguing question: "What sound reason is there for a bank . . . to buy securities under an arrangement whereby any appreciation will inure to the benefit of the seller and any loss will be borne by the bank?"[21] Plainly, there was no sound reason for the directors to approve the arrangement, the defects of which are so clear in hindsight. But since the directors did approve it, the interesting question is, Why?

One writer has suggested that "the answer lay in the complex interdependencies of high finance in those troubled times."[22] The problem with that theory is that the finance involved was very basic. Any first-year business-school student can appreciate that, with Alleghany having a call,[23] the Trust Company needed a put.[24] It is so obvious that if the Trust Company had requested a put, Alleghany could not have refused.

---

18. *Id.* at 678, citing New York Cent. R.R. v. Lockwood, 17 Wall. 357, 382–83 (1873).
19. *Id.* at 699.
20. *Id.*
21. *Id.*
22. Dyson, *The Director's Liability for Negligence*, 40 IND. L.J. 341, 370 (1964).
23. A "call" is a right to buy securities on terms agreed to in advance.
24. A "put" is a right to sell securities on terms agreed to in advance.

The question is, then, why did the directors not demand a put? Two obvious possibilities come to mind: incompetence and double-dealing. But it is almost inconceivable that directors of a major bank were in over their heads at so basic a level of finance, and the court took pains to dispel any suggestions of dishonesty. The likely possibility is that the directors did not "see" the defect in the Alleghany arrangements when the arrangements were presented to them for approval. That is, the directors heard a description of the arrangements and an explanation of what the arrangements were designed to accomplish, determined that in the context in which they were presented the arrangements made sense, and approved the arrangements without its having crossed their minds that inherent in the arrangements was a monumental defect.[25] If that is true, one can question the fairness and efficacy of holding the Trust Company directors liable for "mismanagement."

Although *Litwin* clearly established a precedent for holding directors liable for negligence, as time went by without many cases decided against them,[26] directors for a time fell into a comfortable complacency. As the British life peer Lord Boothby put it:

> If you have five directorships it is total heaven, like having a permanent hot bath . . . . No effort of any kind is called for. You go to a meeting once a month in a car supplied by the company, you look grave and sage, on two occasions say, "I agree," say "I don't think so" once, and if all goes well you get 500 pounds a year.[27]

---

25. For possible explanations of why the directors did not "see" the defect, based on well-known psychological phenomena, *see* Soderquist, *supra* note 2.
26. Joseph Bishop commented in 1968: "The search for cases in which directors of industrial corporations have been held liable in derivative suits for negligence uncomplicated by self-dealing is a search for a very small number of needles in a very large haystack." Bishop, *Sitting Ducks and Decoy Ducks: New Trends in the Indemnification of Corporate Directors and Officers*, 77 YALE L.J. 1078, 1095 (1968).
27. Chamberlain, *Why It's Harder and Harder to Get a Good Board*, FORTUNE 109 (Nov. 1962).

That continued until the late 1960s. The turning point was the decision in *Escott v. BarChris Construction Corp.*,[28] a case under section 11 of the Securities Act of 1933 in which directors were held liable for defects in their corporation's registration statement. After *BarChris*, Boothby's "hot bath" took on new meaning for directors as they became more and more concerned about what courts expected of them and what they could do to protect themselves from a negligence claim.

Regrettably, although *BarChris* served to raise the consciousness of directors, it could not provide them any guidance about what is or is not negligence, since the case involved the application of a narrow statutory criterion of behavior[29] rather than a general negligence standard. Two major directors' negligence cases of the 1970s and early 1980s, *Stern v. Lucy Webb Hayes National Training School for Deaconesses and Missionaries*[30] and *Francis v. United Jersey Bank*,[31] did provide helpful general guidance by emphasizing the directors' monitoring or supervisory role within the corporation.[32] But they could not provide a meaningful analysis of directors' conduct against the negligence standard because the directors

28. Escott v. BarChris Constr. Corp., 283 F. Supp. 643 (S.D.N.Y. 1968).

29. The criterion being one of "reasonable investigation" before a director can take advantage of the general "due diligence" defense provided by Securities Act section 11(b). "Reasonable investigation" is defined as "that required of a prudent man in the management of his own property." Securities Act of 1933, § 11(c).

30. Stern v. Lucy Webb Hayes Nat'l Training School for Deaconesses & Missionaries, 381 F. Supp. 1003 (D.D.C. 1974).

31. Francis v. United Jersey Bank, 87 N.J. 15, 432 A.2d 814 (1981).

32. *See, e.g.*, Stern v. Lucy Webb Hayes Nat'l Training School for Deaconesses & Missionaries, 381 F. Supp. at 1014 ("A director whose failure to supervise permits negligent mismanagement by others to go unchecked has committed an independent wrong against the corporation"); Francis v. United Jersey Bank, 87 N.J. at 32, 432 A.2d at 822 ("Directorial management does not require a detailed inspection of day-to-day activities, but rather a general monitoring of corporate affairs and policies").

involved in those cases did either nothing, in *Francis*,[33] or next to nothing relevant to the facts at hand, in *Lucy Webb Hayes*.[34]

Smith v. Van Gorkom,[35] decided by the Delaware Supreme Court in 1985, is the most important directors' liability case since *Litwin*. Like *Litwin*, it involved alleged mismanagement by directors in connection with their approval of a proposed corporate transaction, the transaction in that case being a merger in which the shareholders of Trans Union Corporation would receive fifty-five dollars per share. The merger had been negotiated by the chief executive officer of Trans Union without the knowledge of the board and was approved at a board meeting after two hours' consideration. Without any substantial discussion of the standard against which the directors' conduct was to be judged, the Delaware Supreme Court determined that the directors had failed adequately to inform themselves about various matters including the intrinsic value of the corporation, and that the directors were, at a minimum, grossly negligent in approving the merger.[36] As a result, the court held the directors liable for the difference between what the shareholders received in the merger and the fair value of the corporation, which value was to be determined at an evidentiary hearing. At that point,

33. "[The defendant-director] did not pay any attention to her duties as a director or to the affairs of the corporation." Francis v. United Jersey Bank, 87 N.J. at 27, 432 A.2d at 819.
34. "In short, those [directors] have . . . failed to exercise even the most cursory supervision over the handling of Hospital funds and failed to establish and carry out a defined policy." Stern v. Lucy Webb Hayes Nat'l Training School for Deaconesses & Missionaries, 381 F. Supp. at 1008.
35. Smith v. Van Gorkom, 488 A.2d 858 (Del. 1985).
36. Under Delaware law, the standard used to determine whether a director has breached his or her duty of care is gross negligence. Aronson v. Lewis, 473 A.2d 805 (Del. Sup. Ct. 1984).

the plaintiffs' lawyers were projecting damages of up to $200 million, with the directors having only several million in liability insurance.[37] Ultimately, the case was settled for $23.5 million,[38] without an evidentiary hearing having been held. But $23.5 million was sufficient to keep the fears of directors from abating.

The president of the National Association of Corporate Directors has said that *Van Gorkom* "created perilous times for corporate directors,"[39] and he has called the decision "the straw that broke the camel's back" as far as directors are concerned.[40] Clearly, the case had the direct effect of frightening directors. In an article discussing the fallout of the decision, for example, a business school dean who is a director of eight corporations was quoted as saying: "I would probably resign from every board on which I serve if I am liable beyond my directors' and officers' insurance."[41] Regrettably for that and other directors, *Van Gorkom* also had the indirect effect of making directors' liability insurance harder to get and substantially more expensive.[42] By mid-1986, a directorship had become what one business writer called "a job that nobody wants."[43]

---

37. Glaberson & Powell, *A Landmark Ruling That Puts Board Members in Peril*, BUS. WEEK 56, 57 (Mar. 18, 1986). The authors understand that $10 million was covered by insurance, $10 million was put up by the corporate purchaser or an affiliate, and the directors made up the rest.
38. Baum, *The Job Nobody Wants*, BUS. WEEK 46 (Sept. 8, 1986).
39. *Id.* at 56.
40. Mauro, *Liability in the Boardroom*, NATION'S BUS. 45, 46 (May 1986).
41. Presumably meaning he would resign if he were in danger of any liability beyond the policy limits. Glaberson & Powell, *supra* note 37, at 57. *See also, e.g.*, Mauro, *supra* note 40, at 46.
42. Shortly after *Van Gorkom*, a director of the leading directors' liability insurer at Lloyd's of London said, "Any buyer who thinks the cost of his insurance will only double is a dreamer." Newport, *Protecting Directors Suddenly Gets Costly*, FORTUNE 61 (Mar. 18, 1985). Two years after *Van Gorkom*, Korn/Ferry International estimated that the premiums for directors' liability insurance "went up more than 900 percent in just two years." Powell, *Is It Safe to Go Back in the Boardroom*, NEWSWEEK 45, 46 (May 4, 1987).
43. Baum, *supra* note 38, at 56.

Charter Limitations on Money Damages

In June 1986, the Delaware legislature stepped in. Its response to what some were now calling a crisis was this amendment to the Delaware General Corporation Law:

> [T]he certificate of incorporation may . . . contain . . . [a] provision eliminating or limiting the personal liability of a director to the corporation for monetary damages for breach of fiduciary duty as a director[, except] for any breach of the director's duty of loyalty to the corporation or its stockholders [and except] for acts or omissions not in good faith . . . .[44]

Delaware corporations rushed to amend their certificates of incorporation, and a sizable number of out-of-state corporations reincorporated in Delaware to take advantage of the new provision.[45] Other states quickly began adopting copies or near copies of the Delaware amendment, and a majority of the states have now done so.

The extent of the protection afforded directors by that provision is uncertain. By excluding "any breach of the director's duty of loyalty," the Delaware legislature left a large, gaping, uncertain hole in the protections it apparently intended to afford directors. Already Delaware court decisions have shown the dimensions of that hole. In *Mills Acquisition Co. v. Macmillan, Inc.*,[46] a case involving the sale of a corporation to competing bidders (often called an auction), the Delaware Supreme Court said that it "entertain[ed] no doubt that [the] board's virtual abandonment of its oversight functions in the face of [others'] patent self-interest was a breach of its fundamental duties of loyalty and care in the conduct of [the] auction."[47] At another point it reinforced that statement bluntly:

44. *See* Del. Gen. Corp. Law § 102(b)(7). The "except" clause also included acts and omissions constituting the unlawful declaration of dividends, intentional misconduct, or a knowing violation of law. These are derelictions that involve something other than negligence.

45. *See, e.g.*, Powell, *supra* note 42, at 45.

46. Mills Acquisition Co. v. Macmillan, Inc., 559 A.2d 1261 (Del. 1989).

47. *Id.* at 1284 n.32.

> Following *Revlon, [Inc. v. MacAndrews & Forbes Holdings, Inc.*, 506 A.2d 173], there appeared to be a degree of "scholarly" debate about the particular fiduciary duty that had been breached in that case, i.e. the duty of care or the duty of loyalty. In *Ivanhoe [Partners v. Newmont Mining Corp.]*, 535 A.2d at 1345, we made it abundantly clear that both duties were involved in *Revlon*, and both had been breached.

Similarily, it will, of course, be up to the courts to determine what "good faith" means in that context. That term is used in a wide variety of legal contexts, and it means different things in different of those contexts, with large cross-contextual variations.[48] Certainly the term always includes something like "pure-heartedness." And just as certainly it means more than simply that in the context of the directors' negligence standard. In trying to discern the meaning of "good faith" in that context, it will be helpful to remember that corporation statutes give a number of responsibilities to directors, and that a director cannot ignore those responsibilities without being intentionally derelict. Whatever else "good faith" may encompass, it does not include intentional dereliction.

As a starting point, therefore, one can say that to be in good faith, a director necessarily must engage in conduct aimed toward discharging his or her responsibilities.[49] In judging such conduct, a court would have to look not at the efficacy of the conduct, but at the director's state of mind about the conduct. The most appropriate inquiry here would seem to be into whether the director reasonably believed his or her conduct was for the good of the corporation, but only time will tell how courts will interpret the good faith standard and how much protection it will give directors.

---

48. For a broad treatment of the term "good faith" as used in various contexts, see 18A WORDS AND PHRASES 83–131; WORDS AND PHRASES CUM. ANN. SUPP. 56–73. Examples of the use of the term are collected under eighty-four separate headings.

49. The conduct could, of course, be the act of deciding to do nothing in a given situation.

Statutory Standards of Care and Protections

In addition to the statutory provisions allowing a corporation's charter to limit the liability of directors for money damages discussed in the preceding section, corporation statutes have long contained provisions setting the standard by which a director's conduct is to be judged. Model Business Corporation Act section 35 contains a representative example:

> A director shall perform his duties as a director, including his duties as a member of any committee of the board upon which he may serve, in good faith, in a manner he reasonably believes to be in the best interests of the corporation, and with such care as an ordinarily prudent person in a like position would use under similar circumstances.

The Model Act and many state statutes go on to provide some further guidance to directors in discharging their obligations and also to afford them some significant protections. Here is the provision from section 35:

> In performing his duties, a director shall be entitled to rely on information, opinions, reports or statements, including financial statements and other financial data, in each case prepared or presented by:
>
> (a) one or more officers or employees of the corporation whom the director reasonably believes to be reliable and competent in the matters presented,
>
> (b) counsel, public accountants or other persons as to matters which the director reasonably believes to be within such person's professional or expert competence, or
>
> (c) a committee of the board upon which he does not serve, duly designated in accordance with a provision in the articles of incorporation or the bylaws, as to matters within its designated authority, which committee the director reasonably believes merits confidence,
>
> but he shall not be considered to be acting in good faith if he has knowledge concerning the matter in question that would cause such reliance to be unwarranted. A person who so performs his duties

shall have no liability by reason of being or having been a director of the corporation.

Especially when combined with a charter provision limiting directors' liability for negligence when they act in good faith, these statutory provisions provide directors with substantial protections.

Business Judgment Rule

Overlaying the entire area of the director's duty of care, or at least that part relating to mismanagement as opposed to failure to manage, is the business judgment rule. There are various formulations of the rule, one of the more helpful being that:

> Directors of corporations discharge their fiduciary duties when in good faith they exercise business judgment in making decisions regarding the corporation. When they act in good faith, they enjoy a presumption of sound business judgment, reposing in them as directors, which courts will not disturb if any rational business purpose can be attributed to their decisions. In the absence of fraud, bad faith, gross overreaching or abuse of discretion, courts will not interfere with the exercise of business judgment by corporate directors.[50]

Analytically, the main underpinnings of the rule seem to be two. First, it would be unfair, and ultimately counterproductive, to allow shareholders to elect directors of their choosing and then to collect damages from those directors when their judgment — as opposed to their honesty and diligence — proves faulty. Otherwise, in the words of an early case, "no man of ordinary prudence would accept a trust surrounded by such perils."[51] Second, the courts are ill-suited for the job of corporate decision making and would not have the time for it if they were.

The business judgment rule and its application can be fairly easily criticized. For one thing, it is well understood that shareholders of

50. Panter v. Marshall Field & Co., 486 F. Supp. 1168, 1194 (N.D. Ill. 1980).
51. Godbold v. Branch Bank, 11 Ala. 191, 199 (1847)

publicly held corporations do not, other than as a formal matter, choose directors. Either the chief executive officer chooses them, or the directors pick their own replacements, and then the shareholders go through the formality of an election. In light of that, it can be argued that any base for establishing shareholder responsibility is entirely illusory. Further, while almost no one believes the business judgment rule should be abolished, many people believe that courts apply it too freely and without more than a perfunctory examination of directors' decision-making. Finally, the rule is not supposed to apply when a director has a conflict of interest. There is strong sentiment among many that in that connection the courts have misapplied the rule.

Some of the more interesting examples of the rule's application have arisen in two specialized contexts. The first is where the board of directors establishes a special litigation committee to decide whether the corporation should bring a suit against certain of its directors or officers, or to decide whether a shareholder's derivative action already filed against officers or directors should be dismissed. Many people question whether the directors who serve on such a committee reasonably can be expected to exercise disinterested judgment about the actions of colleagues in management. The second situation occurs when one corporation makes a tender offer for the shares of another corporation. Often, management of the target corporation decides to fight the tender offer by filing lawsuits on various grounds, through a media campaign directed at the shareholders, and by other means. Whether the target corporation's directors should be considered "interested" when making decisions about the tender offer, basically because they stand to lose their positions if the tender offer is successful, has been hotly debated.

Most of the significant cases involving the business judgment rule have been decided by the Delaware Supreme Court. Since the late 1970s, that court has delineated the details of the rule in general usage and in the contexts both of special litigation committees and defenses to tender offers. The leading case outside those two specialized areas is *Aronson v. Lewis*,[52] in which the Delaware Supreme Court outlined the business judgment rule as "a presumption that in making a business decision the directors of a corporation acted on an informed basis, in good faith and in the honest belief that the action taken was in the best interests of the company,"[53] adding that the protections of the rule "can only be claimed by disinterested directors."[54] In *Aronson*, the court also looked at the level of care directors must exercise to avail themselves of the rule and decided that ordinary negligence will not cast directors outside the rule's protections, but gross negligence will.

The *Aronson* formulation of the business judgment rule got a major test in *Smith v. Van Gorkom*,[55] which is discussed in a preceding section of this chapter.[56] In *Van Gorkom*, the Delaware Supreme Court found that directors of Trans Union Corporation were chargeable with gross negligence when, after two hours' consideration, they approved a merger that had been negotiated by Trans Union's chief executive officer without their knowledge. The directors had sought the protection of the business judgment rule, but the court held that the rule did not protect their conduct because the rule offers "no protection to directors who have made 'an unintelligent or unadvised judgment,'"[57] and because in Delaware a finding of gross negligence answers in the negative the question of whether a decision is an informed one.

The Delaware Supreme Court's main exposition of the business judgment rule in the context of special litigation committees is

52. Aronson v. Lewis, 473 A.2d 805 (Del. 1984).
53. *Id.* at 812.
54. *Id.*
55. Smith v. Van Gorkom, 488 A.2d at 858.
56. See pp. 174–175 *supra*.
57. Smith v. Van Gorkom, 488 A.2d at 872, quoting Mitchell v. Highland-W. Glass, 167 A. 831, 833 (1933).

Zapata Corp. v. Maldonado.[58] That case dealt with the situation where, based on a decision of a special litigation committee, a corporation moves to dismiss a shareholder's derivative action. The Delaware Supreme Court said in *Maldonado* that, in such a situation, the chancery court should apply a two-step test to determine if it should grant the motion. "First, the Court should inquire into the independence and good faith of the committee and the bases supporting its conclusions."[59] Second, "[t]he Court should determine, applying its own independent business judgment, whether the motion should be granted."[60] The first part of that test should come as no surprise, since the mandated inquiries are at the heart of the business judgment rule. The second is an astonishing rule of judicial decision-making, especially since one traditional underpinning of the business judgment rule is that exercising business judgment is the proper realm of directors rather than judges. One partial explanation is that perhaps the Delaware Supreme Court views Delaware chancellors as being unusually well suited, compared to the average trial court judge, to make business judgments because of the amount and sophistication of corporate litigation found in Delaware courts.[61]

The leading Delaware business judgment rule case involving defenses to tender offers is *Unocal Corp. v. Mesa Petroleum Co.*[62] Under *Unocal*, if a defensive maneuver by directors is challenged, the directors must meet some threshold tests. First, the "directors must show that they had reasonable grounds for believing that a danger to corporate policy and effectiveness existed."[63] That burden

58. Zapata Corp. v. Maldonado, 430 A.2d 779 (Del. 1981).
59. *Id.* at 788.
60. *Id.* at 789.
61. Interestingly, the Second Circuit adopted the *Zapata* tests in Joy v. North, 692 F.2d 880 (2d Cir. 1982), a case that involved Connecticut law.
62. Unocal Corp. v. Mesa Petroleum Co., 493 A.2d 946 (Del. 1985).
63. *Id.* at 955.

may be satisfied "by showing good faith and reasonable investigation."[64] Second, the directors must establish that the defensive maneuver was "reasonable in relation to the threat posed."[65] If the directors' actions meet those tests, they are not necessarily home free. Rather, with the tests met the burden shifts to the plaintiffs, who then still can attempt to prove that the directors were not entitled to the benefits of the business judgment rule.

Indemnification and Insurance

Corporation statutes typically provide for the indemnification of directors (and of officers, employees, and agents as well) in connection with litigation against them that arises out of their corporate duties. Indemnification provisions vary somewhat from statute to statute, but the Model Business Corporation Act is representative. Its section 5 provides for broad indemnification for both civil and criminal liability, and the costs of defending or settling either type of action, if the director "acted in good faith and in a manner he reasonably believed to be in or not opposed to the best interests of the corporation, and, with respect to any criminal action or proceeding, had no reasonable cause to believe his conduct was unlawful."

If a director successfully defends against a claim, the statute requires that the director be indemnified. If the director loses, or settles a claim before judgment, indemnification is discretionary with the corporation, with one important exception. In the case of a shareholder's derivative action or other suit by or in the name of the corporation, in which the director is found to be liable for negligence or misconduct, a corporation may indemnify the director only upon the approval of the court in which the action was brought. As can be imagined, that exception to liberal, corporation-granted

64. *Id.*
65. *Id.*

indemnification is responsible for the settlement of many shareholder's derivative actions before trial. In a lot of cases, it simply is too risky to go to trial and chance losing easy access to indemnification.

Many corporation statutes permit indemnification by contract, bylaw, or other means beyond that provided for in the statute, although some forms of indemnification might be invalidated as contrary to public policy (e.g., indemnification of a director for expenses in the unsuccessful defense of a criminal charge). As a consequence of a perceived danger that in the event of a change in the control of the corporation, those newly in control might seek to change the bylaw in which the indemnification provisions are contained, or refuse to exercise the right to indemnify under the statute, many corporations have entered into contracts with their directors and officers providing for their indemnification as a matter of contract right.

Modern corporation statutes, many of which are patterned after Model Act section 5(g), also universally give corporations the right to purchase liability insurance to protect their directors, officers, employees, and agents from liability for actions that arise out of corporate duties. Typically, those provisions allow the corporation to pay the full premium for the insurance, and usually they further allow the insurance to cover acts, such as those not done in good faith, for which the corporation would be prohibited from paying indemnity.

CHAPTER TEN

Directors' and Shareholders' Duties of Fairness

Directors and shareholders have duties to their corporations and to the corporations' shareholders that can best be described as duties of fairness. For directors, that duty traditionally has been known as the duty of loyalty. The duty of shareholders has not had a specific label, but it relates to the duty of shareholders, and particularly of those who control the corporation, to treat their fellow shareholders fairly.

Directors' Duty of Loyalty

Questions involving directors' duty of loyalty typically arise in one of two contexts. First, they come up in connection with corporate transactions in which a director has a personal interest. Second, they appear in situations where a director appropriates some opportunity that arguably belonged to the corporation.

Transactions Involving Interested Directors

Courts have applied different common-law formulations in deciding cases involving interested directors, but fairness to the corporation has been the courts' primary concern. Many corporation statutes, including the Model Business Corporation Act in its section 41, now contain a provision covering those transactions. A typical provision gives protection to such a transaction (1) if the interest of the director is known or disclosed to the board of directors, which then approves or ratifies the transaction by a majority vote of the disinterested directors; (2) if the interest of the director is known or disclosed to the shareholders entitled to vote, who then approve or ratify the transaction; or (3) if the transaction is fair and reasonable to the corporation. While those statutory provisions give interested directors very substantial protection if there has been full disclosure of the director's involvement in the transaction, in other situations it is up to the courts to decide what is "fair and reasonable." Partly in an attempt to understand how courts might decide that issue, and partly to help understand courts' handling of duty of loyalty cases not governed by statutes, it will be helpful to look at two of the major cases involving interested director transactions.

Perhaps the most famous interested director case is *Globe Woolen Co. v. Utica Gas & Electric Co.*,[1] which was decided by the New York Court of Appeals in 1918, with an opinion by Benjamin Cardozo. John Maynard was the major shareholder, the president, and a director of Globe Woolen Co. and also a director of Utica Gas & Electric Co. Over the years, the electric company suggested a number of times to Maynard that the woolen company switch from steam to electric power, but Maynard always declined because the electric company could not guarantee a saving from the change. Finally, the woolen company opened its books to an electric company executive named Greenidge, who himself calculated the relative costs of steam and electric power for the woolen company. As a result, the electric company proposed contracts—which were approved by the board of the electric company, with Maynard not voting—that called for electricity to be supplied at the maximum rate of $.0104 per kilowatt hour and guaranteed a total of $600 per month in savings over the same month in the preceding year. After a several-month trial period, the contracts were to run for five years,

1. Globe Woolen Co. v. Utica Gas & Elec. Co., 224 N.Y. 483, 121 N.E. 378 (1918).

with an additional five-year renewal term. The woolen company accepted the contracts and switched its operations to electricity. Justice Cardozo tells the story of what came next:

> It quickly appeared that the defendant made a losing contract; but only gradually did the extent of the loss, its permanence, and its causes unfold themselves. Greenidge had miscalculated the amount of steam that would be required to heat the dye houses. The expenditure for coal mounted by leaps and bounds. The plaintiff dyed more yarn and less slubbing than before. But the dyeing of yarn takes twice as much heat as that of slubbing . . . . Finally . . . the defendant gave notice of rescission. At that time it had supplied the plaintiff with electricity worth $69,500.75 . . . . Yet not only had it received nothing, but it owed the plaintiff under its guaranty $11,721.41. The finding is that a like loss prolonged to the end of the term would amount to $300,000.[2]

The question for the court was whether the electric company could void those contracts because of Maynard's involvement on both sides of the transaction. One problem the court saw was Maynard's dealing with Greenidge: "There was an influence here, dominating perhaps, and surely potent and persuasive, which was exerted by Mr. Maynard . . . . In all stages of preliminary treaty, he dealt with a subordinate, who looked up to him as a superior, and was alert to serve his pleasure."[3] But what really seemed to bother the court was Maynard's failing to warn his fellow electric company directors of the dangers latent in the contracts: "The trustee is free to stand aloof, while others act, if all is equitable and fair. He cannot rid himself of the duty to warn and to denounce, if there is improvidence or oppression, either apparent on the surface, or lurking beneath the surface, but visible to his practiced eye."[4] Finding Maynard's conduct wanting, the court allowed the electric company to void the contracts.

---

2. *Id.*, 121 N.E. at 379.
3. *Id.* at 380.
4. *Id.*

It is interesting to note here that there was absolutely no evidence that Maynard saw the defects that were latent in the contracts. The court seemed simply to assume that he did, and it did that while at the same time excusing the other electric company directors for their failure to see the defects: "[Maynard's] fellow members, hearing [the terms of the contracts] for the first time, and trustful of his loyalty, would have no thought of latent peril."[5] Actually, it is not unlikely that Maynard, too, failed to see the latent peril, perhaps making *Globe Woolen* the second case discussed in this book, the other being *Litwin v. Allen,*[6] in which a director or directors suffered because of a failure to "see" a defect in a transaction that is completely clear in hindsight.

The Pennsylvania Supreme Court was easier on the interested director in another major duty of loyalty case, *Dravosburg Land Co. v. Scott.*[7] There the interested director, Howard Scott, owned a one-acre piece of land, which had his house on it, and his corporation owned an adjacent sixty-five acres, which it had been trying to sell for years. Carnegie-Illinois Steel Corporation offered to buy the two properties together for $75,000, indicating that it could not use one without the other. The trial court had found that the corporation's property was worth at least four times as much as Scott's, but Scott had held out for $40,000 for his plot. Finally, the corporation agreed to take $35,000 for its sixty-five acres and then, after the sale, sued Scott to recover the excess it said he received over his fair share of the $75,000 total price.

The lower court found that the corporation was not entitled to any relief, and the Supreme Court agreed: "While defendant may have taken harsh and selfish advantage of the circumstances which placed him in a strategic position—although obviously the company

5. *Id.*
6. See pp. 169–172 *supra.*
7. Dravosburg Land Co. v. Scott, 340 Pa. 280, 16 A.2d 415 (1940).

enjoyed an equally strategic position against him—he was not precluded, merely because of his being a stockholder and director of the company, from demanding whatever price he might see fit for the sale of his own property."[8] While the court in *Globe Woolen* may have been too hard on Maynard, the court in *Dravosburg* can be criticized for being too easy. Perhaps they reached the right decision, especially since Scott's one-acre plot contained the house he had lived in for many years with his since-deceased wife. Maybe courts should not intrude into questions such as the price a director should take for a piece of land like that one. But allowing Scott to take advantage of what the court called his "strategic position" put the corporation at a disadvantage that the court seemed not to appreciate. The court said that the corporation "enjoyed an equally strategic position against [Scott]," but that was not true. Technically each could drive as hard a bargain as desired, but Scott held a special advantage: From his position as a director, he knew how badly the corporation wanted to sell its land and how long it had tried to do so. What the court allowed Scott to do was play poker after seeing the other player's hand.

Reading *Globe Woolen* and *Dravosburg* together, perhaps the best lesson that can be learned is one we have encountered before: How a corporation law case comes out often depends on how the court views the equities. In *Globe Woolen,* the court obviously very badly wanted to allow the electric company to void its contracts on grounds of unfairness, whereas in *Dravosburg,* the court seemed satisfied that the director's hard bargaining was a fair tactic. Those involved in interested-director transactions should expect a judicial perception of the equities to play as large a role in a court's view of their transaction as it did in *Globe Woolen* and *Dravosburg* once they fall outside the protective boundaries established by such statutory provisions as Model Act section 41. (Here it might be noted that under section 41, the contracts in *Globe Woolen* would not have

8. *Id.*, 16 A.2d at 416.

been voidable, since Maynard's conflict of interest was known to the woolen company; and that the *Dravosburg* situation would not be covered by section 41, since the situation did not involve a transaction between a director and his or her corporation.)

Corporate Opportunity Doctrine

The corporate opportunity doctrine says that if a director (or an officer, to whom the doctrine is equally applicable) usurps an opportunity that rightfully belonged to the corporation, then the director must make the corporation whole. The traditional leading case is *Guth v. Loft, Inc.*,[9] decided by the Delaware Supreme Court in 1939. Charles Guth was a director and the president of Loft, Inc., a company that made and sold candy, syrups, and beverages. In 1931, the opportunity presented itself for Guth to become one of the two major shareholders of a new Pepsi-Cola company that was to acquire the Pepsi-Cola trademark and formula from a trustee in bankruptcy. Guth took that opportunity and then used Loft assets to aid the Pepsi-Cola business.

Later, Loft sued Guth, asking the court to require Guth to turn over to Loft all of the Pepsi-Cola stock he owned. Guth lost in the trial court, and the Delaware Supreme Court affirmed. Here is the court's explanation of the doctrine:

> [I]f there is presented to a corporate officer or director a business opportunity which the corporation is financially able to undertake, is, from its nature, in the line of the corporation's business and is of practical advantage to it, is one in which the corporation has an interest or a reasonable expectancy, and by embracing the opportunity, the self-interest of the officer or director will be brought into conflict with that of his corporation, the law will not permit him to seize the opportunity for himself.[10]

---

9. Guth v. Loft, Inc., 23 Del. Ch. 255, 5 A.2d 503 (1939).
10. *Id.*, 5 A.2d at 511.

If an officer or director does appropriate a corporate opportunity, the court said, "the corporation may elect to claim all of the benefits of the transaction for itself, and the law will impress a trust in favor of the corporation upon the property, interests and profits so acquired."[11]

Inherent in *Guth v. Loft, Inc.* is a two-part test for determining if an officer or director has violated the duty of loyalty. The first part of the test is an inquiry into whether the opportunity was reasonably related to the business of the corporation. The second is an inquiry into whether the corporation was financially able to undertake the opportunity. Although some courts place little weight on the question of financial ability,[12] most follow that two-part analysis in resolving duty of loyalty issues.[13]

Shareholders' Duty of Fairness

Corporation statutes contain no provisions outlining the duty of shareholders to their corporation or to fellow shareholders. Courts have developed, however, some rules of their own. Certain of those rules relate to what is called "sale of control," or the sale of a majority or other controlling interest in a corporation. Others relate to the relations among shareholders in the operation of the corporation.

Sale of Control

Shares constituting a controlling interest in voting power usually can be sold at a premium because of the added benefits to the buyer that flow from the ability to control the corporation. A controlling shareholder in general may sell his or her interest for whatever price

11. *Id.*
12. *See, e.g.*, Irving Trust Co. v. Deutsch, 73 F.2d 121 (2d Cir. 1934).
13. *See, e.g.*, Miller v. Miller, 301 Minn. 207, 222 N.W.2d 71 (1974).

may be obtained, including a price that includes the value of control. Courts have found, however, that in making such a sale the controlling shareholder has a fiduciary obligation to protect the corporation and the other shareholders. A shareholder may not sell a controlling block of stock to a person or group who intends to loot the corporation[14] or otherwise to misappropriate some corporate opportunity or benefit. The Sixth Circuit's discussion of that duty in *Seagrave Corp. v. Mount*[15] is particularly helpful:

> [Appellants contend] that majority stockholders are at liberty to dispose of their shares at any time and for any price to which they may agree without being liable to other stockholders.
>
> As a general proposition appellants are correct in that contention. However, there are recognized exceptions to the general rule, such as where fraud is involved in the actions of the dominant . . . stockholders, where controlling stockholders turn over their shares to purchasers who mismanage the corporation or loot the corporate assets, where non-controlling stockholders are induced to sell their shares by concealment of the fact that a premium is to be paid to the controlling stockholders, [or] where controlling stockholders . . . make a secret profit from a transaction . . . .[16]

A famous case involving misappropriation is *Perlman v. Feldman.*[17] There the dominant shareholder sold a controlling block of stock in Newport Steel Corp. for a substantial premium over the market price during the Korean War, when there was a serious steel shortage. After taking control, the purchasers bought Newport's entire steel production for their own use, to the detriment of the corporation's longterm business, including a detriment resulting from bad relations with its regular customers. Minority shareholders sued the seller of the controlling block, alleging breach of fiduciary

---

14. *See, e.g.*, Insuranshares Corp. v. Northern Fiscal Corp., 35 F. Supp. 22 (E.D. Pa. 1940).
15. Seagrave Corp. v. Mount, 212 F.2d 389 (6th Cir. 1954).
16. *Id.* at 395.
17. Perlman v. Feldman, 219 F.2d 173 (2d Cir. 1955).

obligations. Although the district court held for the defendant, the Second Circuit reversed, found that there had been a breach of fiduciary duty, and set damages at the amount of the control premium (which, on remand, the district court determined to be $5.33 per share out of a $17 selling price[18]). Such a result can occur whenever a controlling shareholder receives a control premium and the purchasers thereafter manage the corporation to the benefit of themselves rather than the shareholders generally.[19]

Operation of the Corporation

Violations of the fiduciary duties of shareholders in connection with the sale of a controlling interest can occur either in the close or the publicly held corporation, and in either type of corporation the duties of controlling shareholders are the same. When one focuses on the ongoing relations of shareholders in corporations, however, there are significant differences in the duties of shareholders in close and publicly held corporations.

There are general fiduciary duties of controlling shareholders in both close and publicly held corporations. Those are well stated in two United Supreme Court cases, *Southern Pacific Co. v. Bogert*[20] and *Pepper v. Litton*.[21] In *Bogert* the Court laid out the basic rule: "The rule of corporation law and of equity is well settled and has been often applied. The majority has the right to control; but when it does so, it occupies a fiduciary relation toward the minority, as much so as the corporation itself or its officers and directors."[22] That basic theme was reiterated and expanded upon by the Court in *Pepper v. Litton:*

---

18. Perlman v. Feldman, 154 F. Supp. 436 (D. Conn. 1957).
19. By itself, receiving a control premium will not likely result in liability for the controlling shareholder. *See, e.g.*, Essex Universal Corp. v. Yates, 305 F.2d 572 (2d Cir. 1962).
20. Southern Pac. Co. v. Bogert, 250 U.S. 483 (1919).
21. Pepper v. Litton, 308 U.S. 295 (1939).
22. Southern Pac. Co. v. Bogert, 250 U.S. at 487–88

> A director is a fiduciary. . . . So is a dominant or controlling stockholder or group of stockholders. . . . Their powers are powers in trust. . . . Their dealings with the corporation are subjected to rigorous scrutiny and the burden is on the . . . stockholder not only to prove the good faith of the transaction but also to show its inherent fairness from the viewpoint of the corporation and those interested therein.[23]

The relationship of shareholders in close corporations typically is much different from that among shareholders in publicly held corporations. For that reason, courts have found there to be a special fiduciary duty owed each other by shareholders in a close corporation. That line of cases goes back at least as far as *Helms v. Duckworth*,[24] which the Second Circuit decided in 1957. The leading case is *Donahue v. Rodd Electrotype Co.*,[25] which was handed down by the Massachusetts Supreme Judicial Court in 1975.

In *Donahue,* most of the stock of Rodd Electrotype Co. was owned by the Rodd family, but a small percentage was held by the Donahue family. As Harry Rodd, the dominant shareholder, neared retirement, the corporation repurchased some of his shares at a favorable price. The Donahues wanted the corporation to purchase their shares at the same price, but the corporation was not interested. One of the Donahues then brought suit against the corporation, its directors, and Harry Rodd, alleging a breach of the defendants' fiduciary duties toward her.

In deciding the case, the Massachusetts Supreme Judicial Court first examined the relationship among shareholders in a close corporation. It found two things of significance. First, the court found that the relationship of shareholders in a close corporation is like that of partners in a partnership: "[T]he close corporation bears a striking resemblance to a partnership. Commentators and courts have noted that the close corporation is often little more than an 'incorporated'

23. Pepper v. Litton, 308 U.S. at 306.
24. Helms v. Duckworth, 249 F.2d 482 (D.C. Cir. 1957).
25. Donahue v. Rodd Electrotype Co., 367 Mass. 578, 328 N.E.2d 505 (1975).

or 'chartered' partnership."[26] Second, the court found that minority shareholders in a close corporation are extremely vulnerable to overreaching by the majority: "[T]he minority stockholder may be trapped in a disadvantageous situation. No outsider would knowingly assume the position of the disadvantaged minority. The outsider would have the same difficulties."[27]

As a result, the court found for Mrs. Donahue in a far-reaching holding: "[W]e hold that stockholders in a close corporation owe one another substantially the same fiduciary duty in the operation of the enterprise that partners owe to one another."[28] For shareholders in close corporations that was a critically significant holding, for the duty of one partner to another is the highest fiduciary duty there is, one that the Massachusetts court described as "utmost good faith and loyalty."[29] *Donahue* quickly became a famous case, and shareholders should expect that it will be a rare court that does not follow it. Before *Donahue*, corporate lawyers systematically warned clients about the dangers of becoming minority shareholders in a close corporation. That continues after *Donahue*, but with less vehemence and with much more hope that a minority shareholder will have a remedy in the case of majority oppression.

26. *Id.*, 328 N.E.2d at 512.
27. *Id.* at 515.
28. *Id.*
29. *Id.*

CHAPTER ELEVEN

Dividends and Distributions

While some corporation statutes jumble dividends and distributions together, analytically dividends and distributions are entirely different. In a pure sense, dividends represent a payment to the shareholders of a corporation's profits, whereas distributions are a return to the shareholders of a portion of their capital contributions. As will be seen in the discussions that follow, however, even such statutes as the Model Business Corporation Act, which treat dividends and distributions differently, allow so many transfers among a corporation's financial accounts that the pure distinctions between dividends and distributions become blurred.[1]

Mechanics of Dividends and Distributions

Not only do distributions differ from dividends, but different types of dividends differ from each other. It will be helpful if we first discuss dividends in cash or other property, then handle stock dividends (and stock splits, which are closely related), and finally turn to distributions.

1. See pp. 207–208 *infra*. See also p. 95 *supra*.

Dividends in Cash or Other Property

Model Business Corporation Act section 45 is representative of modern statutory provisions governing the payment of dividends in cash or other property. The first requirement noted in that section is that it is the board of directors that declares dividends, the statutory language being that the directors may declare dividends "from time to time." The second requirement is that the directors may not declare a dividend, nor may the corporation pay a dividend, if the corporation is insolvent[2] or if the payment of the dividend would make the corporation insolvent. The third requirement of section 45 is that a dividend may not contravene a restriction on dividends contained in the corporation's charter.

The fourth Model Act requirement is the one that goes to the heart of what dividends are all about. Except for corporations that are in the business of exploiting natural resources, which have a special rule, section 45 provides that "[d]ividends may be declared and paid in cash or property only out of the unreserved and unrestricted earned surplus of the corporation." Earned surplus is defined in Model Act section 2(l), and some of the more obscure details of that definition will be discussed below in the section of this chapter entitled "Limitations on Dividends." For now, we shall confine our discussion to the more straightforward elements of earned surplus, as shown on a corporation's balance sheet.

So far as we are concerned here, then, earned surplus comes from a corporation's earnings. The other kind of surplus is capital surplus, and it usually comes from the capital that is paid in by shareholders in exchange for their stock. In the case of one-dollar par value stock that is issued for ten dollars, for example, the amount of the par

---

2. In financial usage, there are two different definitions of "insolvent." The first is insolvent in the balance sheet sense. That is, liabilities are greater than assets. The second definition, which is the one used in the Model Business Corporation Act, is "the inability of a corporation to pay its debts as they become due in the usual course of its business." MODEL BUSINESS CORP. ACT § 2(n).

value will constitute stated capital and the excess in the purchase price over par value, or nine dollars, will be capital surplus. What is surplus? As defined in Model Act section 2(k), it is "the excess of the net assets of the corporation over its stated capital," with net assets being the amount one gets upon subtracting all of the corporation's liabilities from all of its assets.

Here it might help to remember that surplus is one of the accounts, stated capital being the other, that make up the shareholders' equity section of a corporate balance sheet. All that is covered in some detail in chapter 5, relating to capitalization, and also in appendix B, which is entitled "Reading Financial Statements." For convenience and brief review, however, it may be helpful to set out a simple balance sheet here, so that the relationships of the accounts just mentioned can be seen easily. Here is a balance sheet as it would appear just after a corporation has issued 1,000 shares of one-dollar par value stock for ten dollars per share:

ACADEMAIR, INC.
December 31, 1992

ASSETS		LIABILITIES	$ 0
Cash	$10,000	SHAREHOLDERS' EQUITY	
		Stated Capital	$ 1,000
		Capital Surplus	9,000
		Earned Surplus	0
			$10,000

Academair, Inc. could pay no dividends, because it has no earned surplus. As soon as that corporation has profits, they will show up in earned surplus, and then the board could declare and the corporation could pay dividends in the amount of the earned surplus. Assume, for example, that Academair immediately invests its $10,000 cash in an option to purchase an airplane and then one month later sells that option for $15,000 after expenses. Here is how the new balance sheet would look:

ACADEMAIR, INC.
January 31, 1993

ASSETS		LIABILITIES	$ 0
Cash	$15,000	SHAREHOLDERS' EQUITY	
		Stated Capital	$ 1,000
		Capital Surplus	9,000
		Earned Surplus	5,000
			$15,000

Many states' corporation statutes follow the Model Act's basic rule, just discussed, that says dividends may be declared and paid only out of earned surplus. A number of states follow a more liberal rule, however, one that is called a "nimble dividends" provision. That provision, which is contained in Model Act alternative section 45(a), allows dividends to be declared and paid either out of earned surplus or "out of the unreserved and unrestricted net earnings of the current fiscal year and the next preceding fiscal year taken as a single period."

The nimble dividends provision can be useful to a corporation that has had losses in previous years, which losses have prevented it from having any earned surplus even though the corporation currently is generating profits. To see how that works, it will be helpful to look at another balance sheet of Academair, Inc., this one showing the result of a $50,000 loss, with a $35,000 loan taken out to raise cash to cover the loss, in the month following the last balance sheet shown above.

ACADEMAIR, INC.
February 28, 1993

ASSETS		LIABILITIES		
Cash	$ 0		Note Payable	$35,000
		SHAREHOLDERS' EQUITY		
			Stated Capital	$ 1,000
			Capital Surplus	9,000
			Earned Surplus	(45,000)
				$0

Notice that the $50,000 loss has wiped out the corporation's $5,000 earned surplus and has created a $45,000 deficit in earned surplus. (Deficits are shown on financial statements in parentheses.) The corporation could continue having losses, and therefore amassing deficits in earned surplus, for some time. It could then begin generating profits, but it could take some years of profits before the earned surplus deficits are eliminated. Unless the statute under which this corporation is incorporated has a nimble dividends provision, it will not be able to pay dividends until those deficits are eliminated completely and until it thereafter generates earned surplus.

Notice that Model Act section 45 refers not simply to "earned surplus," but to "unreserved and unrestricted earned surplus." The board of directors may reserve a portion of earned surplus, or a specified amount of earned surplus may be restricted by a provision in the charter or some other document. Typically, reservations and restrictions are placed on earned surplus as a result of a covenant in a loan agreement, or an agreement among the shareholders, not to pay dividends unless an established amount of earned surplus will remain after the dividend.

Although corporation statutes typically do not explicitly state how dividends are to be spread among shareholders, dividends must be paid to the various classes of shareholders (e.g., preferred and common) as specified in the charter and, within classes of shareholders, pro rata on a share-for-share basis. An attempt by the directors to favor one shareholder over another in the payment of dividends, in a way not sanctioned by the charter, would be considered an illegal dividend or an unauthorized distribution of corporate assets. Under Model Act section 48, which is a representative statutory provision, directors who vote for or assent to an unauthorized distribution of corporate assets, or to a dividend that is not allowed under the statute, are liable to the corporation jointly and severally for the amount of the distribution or dividend.

Shareholders are never given the legal right to dividends that are not yet declared and announced. Especially in the case of preferred stock, there may be every expectation that dividends will be paid annually in agreed amounts, but there will be no contract to that effect. If a corporation has preferred stock, however, its charter typically contains provisions designed to force the declaration and payment of dividends by making the alternative unpalatable. For example, at a minimum, preferred dividends in a set amount usually are made cumulative, and the charter typically provides that no dividends may be declared on the common stock until all accumulated dividends on the preferred stock have been paid. It is not uncommon for the charter to go further and to provide that if dividends are not paid on the preferred stock for four consecutive quarters, the preferred shareholders rather than the common shareholders will have the right to elect some or all of the directors. Once dividends are declared and announced to the shareholders, they become liabilities of the corporation. At that point, shareholders can sue to collect dividends if the corporation does not pay them voluntarily.

Stock Dividends and Stock Splits

Stock dividends are dividends payable to a corporation's shareholders in the corporation's own stock rather than in cash or other property. Stock splits have much in common with stock dividends, in that both stock splits and stock dividends have the same effect of getting a greater number of a corporation's shares into the hands of its shareholders without their paying for the shares, but the mechanisms involved are entirely different, as are certain of the consequences. An important consideration that should be noted at the outset is that neither a stock dividend nor a stock split changes the equity participation of a shareholder in the corporation. Each simply changes the number of shares representing that participation.

Model Business Corporation Act section 45 contains typical provisions on stock dividends and stock splits. The main provision on stock dividends is that, with respect to par value stock:

> (d) Dividends may be declared and paid in [a corporation's] own authorized but unissued shares out of any unreserved and unrestricted surplus of the corporation upon the following conditions:
>
> . . . If a dividend is payable in its own shares having par value, such shares shall be issued at not less than the par value thereof and there shall be transferred to stated capital at the time such dividend is paid an amount of surplus equal to the aggregate par value of the shares to be issued as a dividend.[3]

Note here that section 45 merely requires that stock dividends be paid out of "surplus," not "earned surplus" as in the case of cash dividends. As a result, a corporation that has capital surplus but no earned surplus may pay a stock dividend.

The requirement that an amount equal to par value be transferred from surplus to stated capital is necessary if the amount of stated

---

3. For stock without par value, the board must fix a stated value and then transfer to stated capital an amount equal to the stated value. MODEL BUSINESS CORP. ACT § 45(d).

capital is at all times to be equal to the aggregate par value of a corporation's outstanding stock, which is what is at the heart of stated capital.[4] That requirement is lifted when the dividend is paid in treasury stock, which is stock that at one time was issued and outstanding, but which has been repurchased by the corporation and is now retained in its "treasury."[5] Since an amount equal to the par value of treasury shares was transferred to stated capital at the time the shares were issued, there is no need to make such a transfer when treasury shares are given to shareholders as a stock dividend. For that reason, the Model Act provision on stock dividends payable in treasury shares is very simple: "Dividends may be declared and paid in [a corporation's] own treasury shares."[6]

The only provision in the Model Act on stock splits is the last paragraph of section 45, which merely says that: "A split-up or division of the issued shares of any class into a greater number of shares of the same class without increasing the stated capital of the corporation shall not be construed to be a share dividend within the meaning of this section." No particular statutory authority is needed for a stock split. Since a stock split is accomplished by an ordinary charter amendment, the regular authorization for a charter amendment is all the authority needed.[7]

The amendment to effect a stock split would first, if need be, increase the number of authorized shares. Then, using one-dollar

---

4. MODEL BUSINESS CORP. ACT § 2(j), which is the definition of stated capital, indicates that the concept of "stated capital" begins with "the par value of all shares of the corporation having a par value that have been issued."
5. *See, e.g.*, MODEL BUSINESS CORP. ACT § 2(h). Treasury shares, then, are issued but not outstanding. If the board of directors cancels the issuance of shares, which it can do simply by passing a resolution saying the issuance is canceled, then the shares revert to the status of being authorized but unissued.
6. MODEL BUSINESS CORP. ACT § 45(c).
7. *See, e.g.*, MODEL BUSINESS CORP. ACT § 59, which provides for charter amendments upon the vote of the directors and the consent of the shareholders. Under that provision, the charter amendment may contain any provision that would be, at the time of the amendment, allowed in an original charter.

par value stock being split two for one as an example, the amendment would accomplish the split with language like the following: "Upon the effectiveness of this amendment, each issued share of common stock, par value $1, is split up into two shares of common stock, par value $.50." Stated capital will remain the same, because the aggregate par value of all the shares outstanding is exactly the same before and after the split.

In the case of stock dividends, additional stock certificates showing the newly issued shares are sent to each shareholder. The mechanics of issuing stock certificates are not so simple after a stock split involving par value stock, because all of the existing certificates will show an incorrect par value and because corporation statutes typically require that stock certificates include the correct par value.[8] As a result, the corporation will have to issue new certificates for all outstanding shares, which it will do by exchanging the new certificates for the old ones. All that is an expensive proposition in a publicly held corporation, and one that never can be accomplished with respect to all old certificates if the number of shareholders involved is very great, since some shareholders will not respond to requests to exchange their old certificates.[9] Largely for those reasons, publicly held corporations do stock dividends much more often then stock splits. As a result, however, of financial convention and pressure from the accounting profession,[10] corporations paying stock dividends often refer to the dividend as a stock split, especially if the number of shares outstanding after the dividend is at least 20 percent greater than before the dividend.

That handles how stock dividends and stock splits can be accomplished. The equally important consideration is why corporations do stock splits or stock dividends. Here it is important to realize that

8. *See, e.g.*, MODEL BUSINESS CORP. ACT § 23.

9. If the shares are without par value, such an exchange is not necessary.

10. Accounting convention regards any distribution in excess of 20 or 25 percent of the stock outstanding as a split rather than a dividend, regardless of how the action is taken.

since stock dividends and stock splits do not increase each shareholder's interest in the corporation, all that either a stock split or a stock dividend accomplishes is a cutting up of the corporate pie into smaller pieces. Take, for example, a corporation that has three shareholders, each owning 100 shares. If the corporation does a two-for-one stock split, each shareholder will now own 200 shares, each share representing exactly half the ownership percentage that a share in the corporation used to represent. As a result, each new share will be worth exactly half of what an old share was worth. With that in mind, one might question whether there is any good reason for a corporation to pay a stock dividend or to do a stock split.

There are three primary reasons corporations issue stock dividends or do stock splits. Perhaps the most common reason is to force down the price of stock in a publicly held corporation that has risen to "too high" a level in the trading markets. Stock is traded in 100-share lots, and there is an extra commission payable for trading in odd lots. For that reason and for others relating more to tradition than logic, the markets favor shares that trade at particular levels, say from fifteen dollars to forty dollars a share for seasoned companies. If the price of a stock approaches $100, a corporation probably will do a 200 percent stock dividend or split it three for one in order to drive the stock's price down to about thirty dollars per share, with the hope that its rise from there will be easier than if the price were left at $100.

Sometimes corporate managers issue small stock dividends, not exceeding a few percent, to communicate to shareholders that the company is prospering and would be in a position to distribute cash dividends but for the management decision to reinvest profits in the business.

Finally, a stock split or a stock dividend may occur as a necessary financial expedient when a corporation is planning to sell its shares to the public for the first time. In the usual close corporation, there are no more than a few thousand shares outstanding. A typical initial public offering might involve the sale of 500,000 new shares representing a 25 percent interest in the corporation. In that case, the corporation will need to do a stock split or stock dividend to cause the shares currently outstanding to be increased to 1,500,000, so that after the public offering that number of shares will represent a 75 percent interest in the corporation.

Notice that if the corporation in that example has par value stock, a stock split of the magnitude required probably would cause the stock after the split to have a par value at some fraction of a cent. That would look unusual, and the corporation would wish to avoid it. Doing so would be easy. Since the corporation will file a charter amendment to effect the stock split, it can in the same amendment change to no par value stock or change the par value of the stock to some acceptable amount, such as ten cents or one cent. The only requirement in the latter cases would be to transfer from surplus to stated capital whatever amount is necessary to have stated capital equal to at least par value times the number of shares outstanding.

Distributions

Distributions are simpler than dividends. Model Business Corporation Act section 46 gives the board of directors the power to make distributions out of a corporation's capital surplus, subject to a few conditions, the most important of which are these: (1) There may be no distribution if the corporation is insolvent or if the distribution would make the corporation insolvent; (2) the distribution must be approved by the shareholders unless the charter gives to the board the sole power over distributions; and (3) each distribution must be identified to the shareholders as a distribution from capital surplus at the time it is made.

Sometimes a lawyer is faced with a corporate client that wants to distribute cash or other property to its shareholders, but has neither earned nor capital surplus. Considering the freedom to amend corporate charters given in modern statutes such as the Model Act, creating capital surplus out of which to make a distribution presents no problem. What first is necessary is a charter amendment either decreasing the par value of the corporation's shares or changing from par value to no par value stock. Then the corporation, upon the vote of the board of directors and the approval of the shareholders as provided in Model Act section 69, may reduce the corporation's stated capital. Under Model Act section 70, the amount of the reduction will become capital surplus, out of which the desired distribution may be made.[11]

Limitations on Dividends

The major limitation on a corporation's ability to declare and pay dividends is that, as discussed above, under a statute like the Model Business Corporation Act, dividends must come out of earned surplus. Over the years, the main question relating to that limitation on dividends is whether a corporation can consider unrealized appreciation in its assets in calculating earned surplus for dividend purposes. May, for example, a corporation that owns a $10 million piece of land, which it purchased for $1 million, treat for dividend purposes the $9 million increase in value the same way it would treat a $9 million profit on the sale of a piece of land?

Ask an accountant that question and he or she will think you are crazy for asking it, for to accountants it is almost a sacred idea that assets are to be valued at no higher than their cost. But one might notice that judges have not necessarily listened to accountants in deciding corporation law questions (perhaps because cases are pleaded by lawyers rather than accountants) and corporation statutes do not incorporate accounting theory wholesale. Corporation statutes do not, for example, require that corporations follow generally accepted accounting principles.

11. All steps in the process can be approved at the same directors' and shareholders' meetings, so that only one meeting of each group is required.

One place we might begin the search for an answer to our question is with the major case on using unrealized appreciation in assets to support dividends, *Randall v. Bailey*.[12] In *Randall*, a trustee sued former directors of a bankrupt corporation alleging that they had declared illegal dividends. The trustee's two allegations most relevant to our purposes are these: first, that in calculating amounts available for dividends, it was improper for the directors to take into account unrealized appreciation on a piece of land; second, that it was improper for the directors not to take into account unrealized depreciation in the corporation's investments in and advances to certain subsidiaries.

The relevant New York statute prohibited a corporation from declaring or paying dividends that would "impair its capital or capital stock, [or] while its capital or capital stock is impaired." In modern statutory language, that provision prohibited declaring or paying dividends when to do so would require a corporation to invade its stated capital, or when its stated capital already was less than the required amount, or, in other words, when the corporation had or would have no surplus. The statutory language did not give guidance on how surplus was to be calculated. The court looked at the history of changes in the corporation statute and divined a legislative intent to allow unrealized appreciation to be used in the calculation of surplus, along with an intent also to require unrealized depreciation to be taken into account in making that calculation.

The statute in *Randall v. Bailey* is now quite old-fashioned. The question therefore arises as to whether the *Randall* result would obtain under a modern statute. Model Business Corporation Act section 45 provides a good example. Under that section, as discussed above, a corporation can declare and pay dividends out of earned surplus. The place to start our inquiry about the *Randall* result is

12. Randall v. Bailey, 23 N.Y.S.2d 173 (Sup. Ct. 1940).

with section 2(*l*), the definition of earned surplus. In relevant part, section 2(*l*) provides:

> "Earned surplus" means the portion of the surplus of a corporation equal to the balance of its net profits, income, gains and losses from the date of incorporation, or from the latest date when a deficit was eliminated by an application of its capital surplus or stated capital or otherwise, after deducting subsequent distributions to shareholders and transfers . . . made out of earned surplus.

The reference in section 2(*l*) to the elimination of a deficit in earned surplus is necessary because under Model Act section 70 the board of directors may transfer from capital surplus any amount necessary to eliminate a deficit in earned surplus.[13] The reference to deductions from earned surplus as a result of distributions to shareholders is meant to cover the fact that dividends are paid out of earned surplus and therefore reduce earned surplus. And the reference to deductions from earned surplus as a result of transfers to stated capital and capital surplus is necessary because under Model Act sections 21 and 70 amounts in earned surplus may be transferred to stated capital or capital surplus.

With those adjustments to earned surplus coming from dividends, transfers, and so on out of the way, let us focus on the main part of the earned surplus definition: "'Earned surplus' means the portion of the surplus of a corporation equal to the balance of its net profits, income, gains and losses . . . ." Does that definition include unrealized appreciation in earned surplus? The key elements in the definition are net profits, income, and gains. It is a basic tenet of statutory interpretation to assume that each word in a statute adds something of substance. It is somewhat difficult to discern separate meanings for "profits" and "income," although one can try. Perhaps, for

13. Why that section speaks of an application of stated capital to eliminate an earned surplus deficit is obscure, since that would not be lawful under the Model Act. Perhaps that language is designed to provide that such an application of stated capital might sometimes be effective, even though unlawful.

example, the drafters thought of "profits" as coming from active business activities and "income" as arising from investments. In any case, it it much easier to separate out "gains." If one starts with the idea that for purposes of the statute "gains" must be something different from "profits" or "income," it becomes clear that "gain" may well refer to unrealized appreciation. That, as a matter of fact, comports with ordinary usage. If a landowner is asked whether he or she has had a profit on a piece of land the landowner still owns, now worth twice what was paid for it, the answer will be no. Likewise with income. But if one asks the landowner if he or she has experienced a "gain" from the increase in the land's value, the answer likely will be yes.

There is further support for the idea that the Model Business Corporation Act supports taking into account unrealized appreciation in calculating earned surplus. As a one-time member of the American Bar Association committee that oversees the Model Act pointed out in a 1952 article,[14] the original Model Act section on dividends was based on a section in the Illinois corporation statute. That section contained the following provision, which the Model Act's drafters chose to omit: "No dividend, except a dividend payable in its own shares, shall be declared or paid out of surplus arising from unrealized appreciation in value, or revaluation, of assets."

The Model Act gives less guidance on the question of whether unrealized depreciation in assets must be taken into account in calculating earned surplus for dividend purposes. Section 2(*l*) contains only the one word "losses," so the language of the statute really does not answer the question in the way it does for unrealized appreciation. But here it can be pointed out that words other than the word "losses" that are analogous to "profits," "income," and "gains" do not exist in the English language. The words of the

14. Seward, *Earned Surplus—Its Meaning and Use in the Model Business Corporation Act*, 38 VA. L. REV. 435 (1952).

statute at least, then, should not be read as saying that unrealized depreciation does not have to be taken into account.

With that out of the way, the answer to the question about unrealized depreciation is quite easily come to. If the statute allows unrealized appreciation to be taken into account, it is almost unthinkable that the drafters would not also require unrealized depreciation to be considered. Clearly, what is behind allowing directors to consider unrealized appreciation in declaring dividends is the idea that the directors should focus on what the corporation currently is worth in the real world, rather than on historical accounting data. That being the case, the directors necessarily must consider assets that have depreciated as well as those that have appreciated.

None of this is to say that directors should take unrealized appreciation into account when deciding if a dividend is lawful. A court would not necessarily agree with the above analysis, and the penalty for being wrong can be personal liability for the directors.[15] But the idea that unrealized appreciation may be taken into account in calculating earned surplus can be very useful in litigation. If directors have been sued for declaring dividends that appear to be unlawful, it may be that taking unrealized appreciation into account will save them from personal liability.

The net effect of the above analysis probably is more likely to hurt directors than help them, however. Few directors will consider taking unrealized appreciation into account when planning a dividend, since that goes against ordinary accounting conventions. But even fewer would be likely to consider the need to take unrealized depreciation into account, and here is where directors may get into trouble.

---

15. That is the result under Model Act section 48 for unlawful dividends.

Judicial Review of Dividend Policy

Corporation statutes provide that a corporation's board of directors may declare dividends when certain conditions are met. Those statutes never require directors to declare dividends. In some situations, however, courts have been willing to require corporations to pay dividends. The leading case is *Dodge v. Ford Motor Co.*[16] The dispute in that case arose in 1917 after the Ford Motor Company, which then was a close corporation, changed its previous policy of paying substantial dividends to shareholders. The Michigan Supreme Court saw the situation this way:

> The record, and especially the testimony of Mr. Ford, convinces that he has to some extent the attitude toward shareholders of one who has dispensed and distributed to them large gains and that they should be content to take what he chooses to give. His testimony creates the impression, also, that he thinks the Ford Motor Company has made too much money, has had too large profits, and that although large profits might be still earned, a sharing of them with the public, by reducing the price of the output of the company, ought to be undertaken.

That was too much corporate social responsibility for judges to stomach in 1919, and the Michigan Supreme Court therefore upheld a lower court verdict mandating an immediate $20 million dividend.

More modern cases involving suits by shareholders over nondeclaration of dividends give plaintiffs a heavy burden. That is well exemplified by *Gay v. Gay's Supermarkets, Inc.*,[17] decided by the Maine Supreme Court in 1975. There the court indicated that to justify judicial intervention, the plaintiff must show "that the deci-

16. Dodge v. Ford Motor Co., 204 Mich. 459, 170 N.W. 668 (1919).
17. Gay v. Gay's Supermarkets, Inc., 343 A.2d 577 (Me. 1975).

sion not to declare a dividend amounted to fraud, bad faith or an abuse of discretion on the part of the [directors]."[18] Further, the court indicated, "If there are plausible business reasons supportive of the decision of the board of directors, and such reasons can be given credence, a Court will not interfere with a corporate board's right to make that decision."[19]

18. *Id.* at 580.
19. *Id.*

CHAPTER TWELVE

Control Distribution Devices

The corporation lawyer has available a large number of diverse tools for fine-tuning the control relationships within a corporation. Theoretically, that fine-tuning may occur at any time during a corporation's life, but most of the tools require shareholder agreement for their use. That means that often those tools cannot be used in the midst of struggles for control or other corporate strife. For that reason, good corporate lawyers attempt to foresee possible control problems and to use those tools prophylactically. Typically, the best time for their use is at the beginning of a corporation's life.

Cumulative Voting and Classification of Directors

Corporation statutes vary in their requirements for the election of directors by the shareholders. Most require so-called straight voting unless the charter provides otherwise, but some mandate cumulative voting unless the charter calls for straight voting. In straight voting, the shareholders have one vote per share, which they may cast to fill each vacant directorship. If there are five directors to be elected, a shareholder having 100 shares could vote those shares five times, once for each favored candidate. Notice that in that example, someone owning as few as 101 shares could outvote that shareholder and fill each vacancy. In other words, under straight voting, a shareholder or shareholder group owning a majority of a corporation's voting stock can elect all of the directors.

The Model Business Corporation Act describes cumulative voting this way: "[A]t each election of directors every shareholder entitled to vote at such election shall have the right . . . to cumulate his votes by giving one candidate as many votes as the number of [directors to be elected] multiplied by the number of his shares shall equal, or by distributing such votes on the same principle among any number of such candidates."[1] Under cumulative voting, the shareholder in the above example who holds 100 shares at a time when five directors are to be elected would have 500 votes, and those votes could be given to one candidate or could be spread among the candidates in any way the shareholder wishes.

The question immediately arises, of course, as to how a shareholder can use his or her votes most effectively. There is a formula a shareholder can use to determine how many directors can be elected with a particular number of shares. Here is the formula:

$$X = \frac{(N - 1)(D + 1)}{S}$$

X = Number of directors who can be elected with N shares
N = Number of shares controlled by a shareholder or shareholder group
D = Number of directors to be elected at the meeting
S = Number of shares to be voted by all shareholders

Here is how the formula would work, using the above example of 500 shares owned by one shareholder (N = 500) and five directors to

1. Model Business Corp. Act § 33. In that section of the Model Act, the drafters did not choose either straight or cumulative voting as the norm. Rather, they provided alternative language so that state legislatures could make the choice.

be elected (D = 5), assuming that all the shareholders will vote a total of 1,500 shares in the election of directors (S = 1,500):

$$X = \frac{(500 - 1 = 499)(5 + 1 = 6)}{1{,}500} = 2994$$

$$\text{or } X = 1.996$$

Here the shareholder would be able to elect one director. Since 500 shares will get that shareholder so close to being able to elect two directors, perhaps an alliance can be formed to put together a few additional votes. With that in mind, the shareholder may wonder how many shares it would take to elect two directors. Here again, there is a formula the shareholder can use, this time one that will show the number of shares needed to elect a particular number of directors:[2]

$$X = \frac{S \times N}{D + 1} + 1$$

X = Number of shares needed to elect N directors
S = Number of shares to be voted by all shareholders
N = Number of directors a shareholder or shareholder group wishes to elect
D = Number of directors to be elected at the meeting

Using the numbers in the above example, here is the answer to the question of how many shares would be needed to elect two directors:

$$X = \frac{1500 \times 2 = 3000}{5 + 1 = 6} + 1$$

$$\text{or } X = 501$$

After determining the number of directors who can be elected by a given number of votes, shareholders wishing to maximize their

2. A. Hoffman, Israels on Corporate Practice 148 (4th ed. 1983).

cumulative voting power simply need to distribute their votes as evenly as possible among their candidates. In the above example, that would mean casting 251 votes for one candidate and 250 for the other.

As is obvious from this discussion, the fewer directors there are to be elected at a particular meeting, the less chance there is that a minority shareholder or shareholder group can elect even one director. In order to minimize the effective voting power of minority shareholders, corporations sometimes divide their directors into classes, with only one of the classes coming up for election each year. That scheme, which is called "classification of directors" or "staggering the board," is allowed by the Model Act and most other corporation statutes. Here is the heart of the provision as found in Model Act section 37:

> When the board of directors shall consist of nine or more members, in lieu of electing the whole number of directors annually, the articles of incorporation may provide that the directors be divided into either two or three classes, each class to be as nearly equal in number as possible, the term of office of directors of the first class to expire at the first annual meeting of shareholders after their election, that of the second class to expire at the second annual meeting after their election, and that of the third class, if any, to expire at the third annual meeting after their election.

Those new to corporation law usually are surprised to find that provisions relating to corporation law sometimes are found in state constitutions. That is the situation in Pennsylvania, whose constitution mandates cumulative voting. *Stockholders Committee for Better Management v. Erie Technological Products, Inc.*[3] involved the interesting question of whether a provision in the Pennsylvania corporation statute allowing the classification of directors could be used to circumvent the effect of cumulative voting. Immediately

---

3. Stockholders Comm. for Better Management v. Erie Technological Prods., Inc., 248 F. Supp. 380 (W.D. Pa. 1965).

prior to the time in question, Erie Technological Products, Inc. had a nonclassified board of seven directors. After the plaintiffs gathered enough voting power to elect one of seven directors, the board of directors amended the bylaws to classify the board into three classes, thus making it impossible for the plaintiffs to elect a director. The plaintiffs argued that

> . . . when a Board is classified . . . , and that is done by the directors and a majority group of shareholders with interrelated interests for the purpose and effect of excluding any and all minority representation, then even if such classification is not per se illegal, a court has a right to look to the purpose for which it is done to insure that the Pennsylvania policy of minority representation is not circumvented to the detriment of minority shareholders.[4]

The United States district court hearing the case refused to pick up that challenge, and it allowed the classification of directors to stand on the basis that cumulative voting does not give shareholders the right to elect any particular number of directors, but rather simply gives the shareholders the right to spread an enhanced number of votes among a number of candidates.[5]

Charter Provisions

Modern corporation statutes allow the drafters of corporate charters and charter amendments a virtual free hand in arranging the control of a corporation in any way that suits them. The Model Business Corporation Act contains representative provisions, the most important of which are sections 35, 54, and 59. Section 35

4. *Id.* at 388.
5. That case predated Donahue v. Rodd Electrotype Co., 367 Mass. 578, 328 N.E.2d 505 (1975), which is discussed in chapter 10. See pp. 194–195 *supra*. *Donahue* laid heavy fiduciary duties on shareholders in close corporations, and it is interesting to speculate what effect that case would have had on *Erie Technological Products*.

gives power over the management of a corporation to the board of directors, "except as may be otherwise provided" in the Model Act or charter. Section 54, which is the Model Act's general provision on charters, allows a charter to contain "any provision, not inconsistent with law, . . . for the regulation of the internal affairs of the corporation." And section 59 allows the free amendment of charters at any time.

As a result of those provisions, the power to manage a corporation can be split among its shareholders, directors, and officers in any way desirable. It is even possible to take away all of the board's powers and simply have the shareholders or one of the officers exercise those powers, although that is not practical.[6] It is practical, however, to take power away from the board piecemeal. For example, a corporation's charter might provide that only a shareholders' vote is required for a merger, for the sale of all of a corporation's assets, or for dissolution, each of which usually would require the recommendation of the directors. Or instead of enhancing the power of shareholders, a charter could take authority away from the directors and give it to an officer. A corporation may wish to provide, for example, that all questions relating to a particular line of business will be decided by the president rather than the board.

The most common charter provision that changes the ordinary control relationships is a supermajority voting requirement. Under statutory provisions typified by Model Act sections 40 and 143, the charter (and, in the case of directors, also the bylaws) may require a higher percentage vote of directors or shareholders than the majority vote usually specified in the statute. The supermajority requirement can be used for all actions by shareholders or directors, but usually it is limited to specified actions of particular importance. In one corporation that might be the election of officers, in another the

6. See pp. 148–149 *supra*, for a discussion of the related question of operating without a board and also for a discussion of the Model Act's purported requirement to have a board even if it is given no power.

sale of a specified corporate asset. As a means of impeding hostile tender offers, many publicly held companies have adopted charter provisions that require 80 to 90 percent majorities to approve mergers and other transactions with shareholders having a specified amount of common stock, for example, 10 percent.

When drafting a supermajority provision, it usually is desirable to protect the provision from amendment by a vote of the shareholders or directors that is less than the supermajority called for by the provision. That is done by specifying in the charter that a supermajority vote is required to amend the charter provision that contains the supermajority requirement.

Removal of Directors

The removal of directors is a special issue that sometimes needs handling in a charter provision. In a close corporation, there often are two conflicting desires on the part of shareholders with respect to the removal of directors. First, the shareholders wish to have unlimited power to remove nonshareholder directors at will. Second, each shareholder wants to have substantial protection against being removed personally as a director. Most modern statutes provide that the shareholders may remove directors "with or without cause" at any meeting called for the purpose.[7] That gives the shareholders the power they wish to have over nonshareholder directors, but it provides them little personal protection.

That raises the question of whether, under a statute like the one referred to above, a corporation's charter could provide that directors who also are shareholders could be removed only for cause. The answer seems clearly to be no, since the statutory language seems unequivocally to permit shareholders to remove any or all directors without cause. One way to give shareholders substantial protection against being removed as directors is to provide for a

7. *See, e.g.*, MODEL BUSINESS CORP. ACT § 39.

supermajority vote for the removal without cause of any director who also is a shareholder.

Deadlocks

Deadlocks at either the shareholder or the director level can create some of a corporation's most serious problems. There are many possible unpleasant scenarios involving deadlocks. The one that usually comes to mind is a corporation whose actions are deadlocked; it is unable to act. That can be a serious problem for a corporation and its shareholders, but it is far from the worst deadlock scenario. It must be remembered that the president has the power to act for the corporation on any matter that is within the corporation's usual course of business,[8] so that when the board is deadlocked, the president can operate relatively unfettered. Since the president typically also is a board member, that means that he or she can put into play many of the wishes of one board faction, perhaps to the substantial detriment of some shareholders.

Probably the worst deadlock scenarios occur when the shareholders are deadlocked and cannot replace a board that is dominated by one shareholder faction. *Hall v. Hall*[9] offers a good example. Musselman and Hall Contractors, Inc. was owned equally by Edward and Harry Hall, and prior to Edward's death, Edward and Harry were its only directors. After Edward died, Harry appointed his own wife to the vacant directorship, and then he and his wife appointed themselves as the corporation's only officers. After that happened, Edward's widow, who now owned 50 percent of the corporation's stock, complained that Harry Hall refused to attend a shareholders' meeting, and she sued to enjoin him from continuing in that refusal. The trial court found against the plaintiff,

8. See pp. 158–160 *supra*. As indicated there, a corporation's chief executive officer almost certainly will have that same power, whether he or she holds the office of president.
9. Hall v. Hall, 506 S.W.2d 42 (Mo. Ct. App. 1974).

and the Missouri Court of Appeals upheld the trial court, suggesting among other things that the proper remedy was a suit for dissolution of the corporation under the Missouri corporation statute.

We soon shall turn to a consideration of the dissolution remedy for deadlocks, but before doing so it will be helpful to continue the discussion of the worst deadlock scenario. The situation in *Hall v. Hall* was bad for Edward's widow, since she was left without a voice in corporate affairs. But her situation could have been even worse. In Missouri, where the Halls' corporation was incorporated, preemptive rights[10] are granted by the corporation statute, unless limited or done away with in the charter. Without preemptive rights covering all issuances of shares, and assuming the Halls' corporation had authorized but unissued shares, Harry Hall and his wife could have issued additional shares to themselves, thus forcing Edward's widow into a minority position. Then, using the technique of a freeze-out merger, which will be discussed in the following chapter, Harry and his wife could have forced Edward's widow out of the corporation entirely. That may be, indeed, the very worst deadlock scenario.

Perhaps the best way to solve the problem of additional issuances of shares to favored shareholders, in addition to preemptive rights,[11] is to authorize in a corporation's charter only the shares the corporation initially will issue to its first shareholders, thus requiring a charter amendment, with the attendant vote of the shareholders, for the issuance of any additional shares.

Let us now go back to the typical statutory response to deadlocks, which is dissolution. Model Business Corporation Act section 97 basically provides that if the corporation is harmed because the directors are deadlocked and the shareholders are unable to break the deadlock, or if the shareholders have been deadlocked through

10. A preemptive right is the right to purchase a pro rata portion of new issuances of a corporation's stock.

11. A problem with preemptive rights is that often they are limited to certain issuances of shares, for example those in exchange for cash. *See, e.g.*, MODEL BUSINESS CORP. ACT § 26A

two annual meeting dates so that they have been unable to elect new directors, then the court, upon application of a shareholder, may dissolve the corporation. Since dissolution usually is not an acceptable alternative to most of the shareholders, the usual effect of that provision is to force some compromise before the court acts.

Contractual Arrangements

Contractual arrangements are the most common tool used to arrange control within a corporation. Those arrangements take various forms, but most of them can be categorized as voting trusts, shareholders' agreements, or employment contracts.

Voting Trusts

The classic voting trust is a trust formed in the ordinary way under trust law that has voting stock as its corpus. The shareholders who wish to participate in the trust serve as the grantors by transferring to a trustee legal title to their shares. The trustee then votes the shares and otherwise acts for the benefit of the former shareholders, who now are the beneficiaries of the trust. The voting trust is an old device, going back at least as far as the mid-nineteenth century. At first it operated strictly under common law, but now the voting trust has come under supervision in corporation statutes. Commonly, modern statutes, typified by Model Business Corporation Act section 34, set a ten-year duration on voting trusts, require that the trust agreement be in writing, and require that a copy of the agreement be given to the corporation whose shares are held in trust.

The voting trust is not a popular device for controlling a corporation, partly because of its limited duration under modern statutes, but mostly because establishing a voting trust is such a drastic measure. Few shareholders wish to divest themselves of all control over their shares just for the sake of shareholder unity. For that reason, shareholder agreements, in which the drafters attempt to secure that unity while at the same time allowing shareholders reasonable control of their own shares, are much more popular than are voting trusts.

There is a risk, however, that if the drafter of a shareholders' agreement is not careful, the agreement may be held to be a voting trust and, what is more important, an illegal and void voting trust because the agreement does not meet the statutory requirement for a voting trust. The Delaware Supreme Court has established these tests for determining if what purports to be a voting agreement will be treated as a voting trust: "(1) the voting rights of the stock are separated from the other attributes of ownership; (2) the voting rights granted are intended to be irrevocable for a definite period of time; and (3) the principal purpose of the grant of voting rights is to acquire voting control of the corporation."[12]

The leading case is *Abercrombie v. Davies.*[13] In that case, six shareholders of American Independent Oil Company who together owned a majority of its stock entered into an agreement with eight persons who were to represent the shareholders' interests as "agents" for a period of ten years. Under the agreement, the shareholders delivered their stock certificates to the agents, endorsed for transfer, along with irrevocable proxies. The agreement gave the agents the power to transfer the stock to themselves and create a voting trust if they wished. The agreement also provided that if seven of the eight agents could not agree as to how to vote the stock on a particular matter, they were to choose an arbitrator to resolve any disagreement.

After certain of the agents allegedly violated the agreement, the question of the agreement's enforceability came ultimately before the Delaware Supreme Court. After reciting the Delaware tests for the existence of a voting trust, the court found:

---

12. Lehman v. Cohen, 222 A.2d 800, 805 (Del. 1966).

13. Abercrombie v. Davies, 36 Del. Ch. 371, 130 A.2d 338 (1957).

> (1) that the voting rights of the pooled stock have been divorced from the beneficial ownership, which is retained by the stockholders; (2) that the voting rights have been transferred to fiduciaries denominated Agents; (3) that the transfer of such rights is, through the medium of irrevocable proxies, effective for a period of ten years; (4) that all voting rights in respect of all the stock are pooled in the agents as a group . . . ; and (5) that on its face the agreement has for its principal object the voting control of American.[14]

"These elements," the court said, "are the elements of a voting trust."[15] That conclusion was fatal to the enforceability of the agreement, since the provisions in the Delaware corporation statute governing voting trusts were not complied with. (To comply, a copy of the agreement would have had to have been filed with the corporation and the record title to the shares that were subject to the trust would have had to have been transferred to the agents.)

There are not a large number of cases involving purported voting trusts, so it is difficult to tell just where a court would draw the line between a voting agreement or some other scheme among shareholders and a voting trust. It is fair to say, however, that the various attributes of the arrangement among the shareholders and the agents in *Abercrombie* came close, as a matter of simple fact, to the classic attributes of a voting trust. It should not be too surprising, therefore, that that is what the Delaware Supreme Court considered the arrangements to be. In other cases involving arrangements that arguably were voting trusts but that were far from the facts of *Abercrombie*, that court has not been quick to invalidate the arrangements on the grounds that they constitued voting trusts.[16]

---

14. *Id.* at 381, 130 A.2d at 344–45.
15. *Id.*
16. Two of the most famous such cases are Ringling Bros.-Barnum & Bailey Combined Shows, Inc. v. Ringling, 29 Del. Ch. 610, 53 A.2d 441 (1947); and Lehrman v. Cohen, 222 A.2d 800 (Del. 1966).

Shareholders' Agreements

Agreements among shareholders can contain provisions governing anything the parties wish, so long as the agreement does not constitute an illegal voting trust and so long as it does not violate public policy. Questions of public policy usually arise when a shareholders' agreement intrudes into areas governed by a state's corporation statute. Considering that all corporate issues ultimately are resolvable either by the shareholders or the directors, agreements among shareholders almost always relate to matters within the bailiwick of one or the other of those groups.

Agreements among shareholders relating to actions within the statutory province of shareholders generally do not run into problems on public policy grounds. The general rule is that shareholders may vote their shares in any way they wish. While it is true that shareholders, especially those in close corporations, have fiduciary duties toward their fellow shareholders,[17] those duties generally do not limit a shareholder's ability to look out for his or her own interest. If, therefore, shareholders believe it is in their interest to agree on such matters as whom they will vote for as directors or to whom and under what conditions they may sell their shares, the state typically will take no interest in the matter. And, in fact, agreements among shareholders on such matters are common.

The problem arises when agreements among persons who are both shareholders and directors relate to matters over which the corporation statute gives the directors control. It is the job of directors to represent all of the shareholders equally, and in so doing they exercise fiduciary responsibilities to all of the shareholders. Therefore, courts usually do not favor agreements binding directors to act in the future in agreed-upon ways.

If courts wish, however, they can allow substantial leeway to shareholders and directors in close corporations, and sometimes

17 See pp. 191–195 *supra*.

courts will uphold agreements that seem on their face to violate public policy as reflected in the corporation statute. A leading case is *Galler v. Galler*,[18] decided by the Illinois Supreme Court in 1964. Benjamin and Isadore Galler owned equal shares in the Galler Drug Company. In 1955 they entered into an agreement containing a number of terms relating to the conduct of their corporation's affairs. For our purposes, the most important of those was the agreement that the corporation would pay specified dividends each year according to a formula set forth in the agreement, and that upon the death of either partner, a sum equal to twice his salary as an officer would be paid to his widow over a five-year period. After the death of Benjamin, Isadore refused to follow the agreement, and Benjamin's widow sued.

The lower courts split on the issue of the agreement's enforceability, with the court of appeals holding that the agreement was void, in part because of its "substantial disregard of the provisions of the Corporation Act." The Illinois Supreme Court reversed, finding the agreement to be enforceable in its entirety. As to its dividend and widow's allowance provisions, the court's analysis focused only on their reasonableness in a close corporation. Significantly, the court was not at all bothered that each of those provisions covered matters requiring action by the board of directors under the Illinois corporation statute. The court's rationale was that:

> It would admittedly facilitate judicial supervision of corporate behavior if a strict adherence to the provisions of the Business Corporation Act were required in all cases without regard to the practical exigencies peculiar to the close corporation. However, courts have long ago quite realistically, we feel, relaxed their attitudes concerning statutory compliance when dealing with close corporate behavior, permitting "slight deviations" from corporate "norms" in order to give legal efficacy to common business practice.[19]

---

18. Galler v. Galler, 32 Ill. 2d 16, 203 N.E.2d 577 (1964).
19. *Id.* at 28–29, 203 N.E.2d at 584.

In thinking about *Galler*, two things should be kept in mind. First, in that case each of the corporation's shareholders had signed the agreement, so that the interest of no other shareholder was at stake in the court's decision. When fewer than all the shareholders sign, the chance that a court will treat an agreement the way the Illinois court did in *Galler* is significantly reduced. Second, whether or not a court will treat an agreement that way is impossible to predict, for neither *Galler* nor any other case lays down rules for courts to follow in deciding whether to look the other way when shareholders choose to ignore the corporation statute. As a result, *Galler* is much more useful to lawyers litigating about the enforceability of a shareholders' agreement than it is to careful lawyers drafting one. At the drafting stage, few experienced corporation lawyers would take much comfort from *Galler*.

Employment Contracts

One contractual arrangement that can be used to distribute corporate control is the employment contract. Since in a close corporation shareholders often wish to work full time in their corporation, such contracts can be used along with other devices to distribute control among the shareholders. Employment agreements also can be used, of course, to place limited control in the hands of nonshareholders who will serve as officers. There are, however, significant limitations on the protections available through employment contracts, and a number of things to consider in drafting them.

Corporation statutes universally provide that a corporation's officers are to be chosen by its directors and that the officers may be removed by the directors at will. Partially for that reason, specific performance is not a remedy that will be available to an officer if a corporation breaks his or her employment contract, except perhaps in the most extraordinary circumstances. Model Business Corporation Act section 51 speaks directly to the issue: "Any officer or agent may be removed by the board of directors whenever in its judgment the best interests of the corporation will be served thereby, but such removal shall be without prejudice to the contract rights, if any, of the person so removed."

To offer much protection to an officer, a salary escalator must be built into an employment contract. The simplest way to do that is to provide for minimum annual percentage increases. In financial terms, the next big choice for the drafter of an employment contract is whether to provide for liquidated damages. Although a provision for liquidated damages is not always desirable, it may make a breach of the contract too unpalatable for a board to contemplate.

Especially if breaking an employment contract is likely to cost the corporation a substantial amount of money, an officer faces the possibility that the corporation will change his or her job, or the duties incident to the job, in an attempt to force the officer to resign. That, in fact, often is the first thing corporate managers think of when faced with getting rid of an unwanted officer who has an employment contract. Not surprisingly, since most employment contracts are drafted by the corporation's lawyer, a usual provision in employment contracts calls for the person signing the contract to "hold such offices and perform such services as the board of directors shall provide." That obviously provides an officer with little protection.

Some protection comes from specifying the office to be held, but not so much protection as may at first seem. At the time an employment contract for the president is signed, for example, the president may be the chief executive officer. If the board of directors wants to force the president's resignation, the first thing it likely will do is elect a chairman of the board and make him or her the chief executive officer. That may be followed by other actions, such as the election of a vice chairman who is made chief operating officer and the removal from the president of all duties of significance. While it is true that a court may, if it wishes, interpret such corporate actions as breaches of the president's contract, there can be no assurance that that will be the case.

The best way to avoid such problems is to describe an officer's corporate role in functional terms, such as chief executive officer, chief operating officer, chief financial officer, and so on. A long-term employment contract that does that, and that has a reasonable salary escalator and perhaps a good liquidated damages clause, can give an officer substantial protection.

As a result of the increased takeover activity in recent years, many corporations have entered into so-called golden parachute contracts with their principal executives. Those contracts typically provide that if there is a change of control (as defined) and if the executive is discharged without cause or his or her duties are significantly changed, then the executive is entitled upon leaving the company to the continuation of his or her compensation, bonuses, and other benefits for a stipulated period notwithstanding any other employment the executive may secure. The Internal Revenue Code, however, by imposing confiscatory taxes, does limit the aggregate amounts that may be paid under such contracts.

CHAPTER THIRTEEN

Mergers and Acquisitions

This chapter is titled "Mergers and Acquisitions" because that is the accepted phrase to describe what the chapter is about. The title is, however, a misnomer, because mergers and acquisitions are not two different things. Mergers are simply one form of acquisition. A better but too long title for the chapter might be "Mergers, Consolidations, Acquisitions of Assets, Tender Offers, and Negotiated Purchases of Stock," because those are the topics of the chapter.

Forms of Acquisitions

Mergers

In a merger, the board of directors of each corporation involved in the merger (and that can be more than two) agrees on a plan of merger, the outline for which will be found in the corporation statute.[1] That plan provides which corporation is to survive and which corporation or corporations are to be merged out of existence. It also establishes what the shareholders of the nonsurviving (and, if desired, also of the surviving) corporation or corporations are to receive in exchange for their shares. Typically, they will receive cash or some new security. After approval by the boards, the

1. *See, e.g.*, MODEL BUSINESS CORP. ACT § 71.

merger plan usually is submitted to the shareholders of each corporation,[2] but there are exceptions. For example, under "short-form" merger provisions found in many corporation statutes, no shareholder approval is required if the surviving corporation owns 90 or 95 percent of the stock of a corporation to be merged out of existence.[3] After any required shareholder approval, articles of merger are filed with the state office handling corporate filings. Under some statutes the merger is effective when the articles are filed, and in others it is effective either upon the issuance by the state of a certificate of merger or on a date specified in the certificate of merger.[4] By virtue of provisions in the corporation statute, the surviving corporation will by law take all the assets and be subject to all the liabilities of each nonsurviving corporation.[5] Shareholders who vote against a merger have so-called appraisal rights, under which they can ask a court to appraise their shares and after which they can receive the appraised value of their shares in cash.[6]

Consolidations

A consolidation is very much like a merger. The only real difference is that in a consolidation no corporation survives. Rather, out of the consolidation a new corporation is formed. Consolidations are typically done when for some reason, usually psychological, it is important to one or more groups of people having an interest in a corporation not to have that corporation "taken over" by another. That factor is most often encountered when dealing with nonprofit corporations. Consolidations have been so rarely entered into by business corporations that the drafters of the Revised Model Business Corporation Act chose not to provide for them.

---

2. *See, e.g., id.* § 73.
3. *See, e.g., id.* § 75, which sets its test at 90 percent.
4. *See, e.g., id.* § 76, which follows that latter course.
5. *See, e.g., id.* § 76.
6. *See, e.g., id.* §§ 80, 81.

Assets Acquisitions

A surviving corporation in a merger does not mind assuming the known liabilities of a corporation it is acquiring, because they can be taken into account in determining the purchase price. Contingent liabilities, such as might arise from products liability, are another story. To avoid contingent liabilities, corporations often wish to acquire another corporation's business by purchasing its assets. Here the board of directors of each corporation first agrees to the purchase terms. Often the acquiring corporation will agree to buy all the other corporation's assets and assume all its known liabilities. Under most corporation statutes, the shareholders of the selling corporation will have to approve the plan, but the purchasing corporation's shareholders will not.[7] (If, however, the purchasing corporation has shares traded on a stock exchange, the rules of the exchange may require a shareholders' vote.) As in the case of mergers and consolidations, corporation statutes typically give appraisal rights to shareholders of the selling corporation who vote against an assets acquisition.[8] After the purchase, the selling corporation can stay in existence or it can liquidate and distribute to its shareholders the consideration received from the sale of assets. As discussed below in the section on de facto mergers, contingent liabilities cannot always be avoided even in an assets purchase, because a court will sometimes allow a plaintiff to follow the assets and collect contingent liabilities from an acquiring corporation.

---

7. *See, e.g., id.* § 79. If, however, (1) the selling corporation is to receive shares of the purchasing corporation's stock in exchange for its assets and (2) the purchasing corporation does not have sufficient authorized but unissued shares, then the purchasing corporation's shareholders will have to approve a charter amendment increasing the number of authorized shares.
8. *See, e.g., id.* §§ 80, 81.

Tender Offers

In a tender offer, the management of one corporation offers the shareholders of another corporation the opportunity to tender their shares to the acquiring corporation in exchange for something else, usually cash or shares in the acquiring corporation. A distinguishing characteristic of a tender offer is that it is not a negotiated deal between the acquiring corporation and the shareholders of the target corporation (although management of the target corporation may, in effect, negotiate on their behalf).[9] Rather, the acquiring corporation publicly announces its offer to the target's shareholders on a "take it or leave it" basis. Since negotiation typically is more effective than the delivery of a nonnegotiable offer, tender offers are

---

9. Courts are not agreed on the definition of a tender offer. The fullest statement of what constitutes a tender offer is this eight-factor test, which originated with the Securities and Exchange Commission and has been adopted by some courts:

> "(1) active and widespread solicitation of public shareholders for the shares of an issuer;
>
> (2) solicitation made for a substantial percentage of the issuer's stock;
>
> (3) offer to purchase made at a premium over the prevailing market price;
>
> (4) terms of the offer are firm rather than negotiable;
>
> (5) offer contingent on the tender of a fixed number of shares, often subject to a fixed maximum number to be purchased;
>
> (6) offer open only for a limited period of time;
>
> (7) offeree subjected to pressure to sell his stock;
>
> . . . .
>
> [(8)] public announcements of a purchasing program concerning the target company precede or accompany rapid accumulation of large amounts of the target company's securities." . . .

Hanson Trust PLC v. SCM Corp., 774 F.2d 47, 56–57 (2d Cir. 1985) (reciting and discussing the test and its adoption by other courts, while rejecting the test itself), quoting Wellman v. Dixon, 475 F. Supp. 783, 823–24 (S.D.N.Y. 1979).

used only when face-to-face negotiation with the target's shareholders is not practical. In almost all close corporations negotiation is possible, so tender offers are confined almost exclusively to publicly held corporations. Tender offers may be either friendly or hostile, meaning that the management of the target corporation either supports or does not support the takeover.

Tender offers are subject to extensive regulation under the Securities Exchange Act of 1934, and that regulation is discussed in a companion book, also published by the Practising Law Institute, called *Understanding the Securities Laws* (2d ed. 1990). So far as corporation law is concerned, tender offers are simply the purchase by a corporation of shares in another corporation, accomplished in some cases by the issuance of a corporation's own shares to the target's shareholders. Corporation statutes, typified by Model Business Corporation Act section 4(g), universally give corporations the power to buy shares in other corporations. A simple board of directors' resolution is all that is required to authorize such a purchase, assuming, if shares of the acquiring corporation are to be exchanged with the target's shareholders, that sufficient authorized but unissued shares are available in the acquiring corporation's charter. The issuance of shares, of course, is an everyday corporate activity, covered in chapter 5, that necessarily is engaged in by all corporations. There are, then, no special rules in state corporation law that govern the issuance of shares in a tender offer.

There is, however, some specialized regulation of tender offers under state law. Target corporations and corporations that feared they would be targets have engaged in a wide variety of activities designed to prevent a takeover. In a later section of this chapter, we shall examine the judicial response to takeover defenses. In that same section we also shall look at the special statutes passed by state legislatures in response to tender offers, and at the treatment of those responses by the United States Supreme Court after constitutional challenges.

Negotiated Purchases of Stock

A corporation can acquire another corporation by purchasing its stock in a negotiated transaction. In a close corporation, the acquiring corporation can negotiate directly with the shareholders of the corporation it wishes to acquire and buy their shares for whatever they will take for them. Alternatively, an acquiring corporation can buy stock directly from the target itself, which may be either a close or a publicly held corporation. If the target corporation has sufficient authorized but unissued stock available to sell, the sale will require only the approval of the target's board of directors, not its shareholders (except, again, for applicable stock exchange rules). By that means the acquiring corporation can acquire a percentage of the target's stock sufficient to give it control of the target, but it cannot of course acquire all of it. After making that type of purchase or after a tender offer or negotiated purchase that leaves minority shareholders, an acquiring corporation may have the target enter into a merger with the acquiring corporation itself or with a subsidiary of the acquiring corporation, thus "freezing out" the minority. The acquiring corporation does that by forcing the minority to take in exchange for shares whatever the merger agreement provides. Freeze-out mergers will be discussed later in this chapter.

Acquisitions Through Subsidiaries and Share Exchanges

To accomplish various ends, an acquiring corporation often will do an acquisition through a subsidiary. For corporations that typically operate through subsidiaries rather than divisions (Exxon Corporation being a well-known example of the former and General Motors Corporation of the latter), that is entirely natural. But even corporations that wish ultimately to own directly the assets of another corporation may do the initial acquiring merger through a subsidiary, probably one formed for the purpose, and then merge the subsidiary with the parent. The most common reason for that would be to avoid the corporation law requirement of going to the acquiring corporation's shareholders for approval. That is avoided because in the first merger (between the target and the acquiring corporation's subsidiary) it is the shareholders of those two corporations who have to approve, not those of the subsidiary's parent; and in the second merger (between the subsidiary and the parent) no shareholder approval usually will be necessary because of the short-form merger provisions, discussed above, that are often found in corporation statutes.

One final item remains to be discussed about using subsidiaries in mergers. Take the case of an acquiring corporation that wants to operate the acquired business as a subsidiary. One way to accomplish the acquisition is to form a subsidiary and then have the target corporation merge into the subsidiary (with the shareholders of the target corporation receiving in exchange for their shares whatever the plan of merger provides, typically cash or stock of the parent corporation). Those are called three-cornered mergers, and they are allowed by all corporation statutes. One problem with them is that from a housekeeping standpoint, the newly formed subsidiary has to be set up from scratch. Typically, one of the most expensive and troublesome aspects of that is qualifying the subsidiary to do business in some or all jurisdictions where the target corporation is qualified.

It would be nice, therefore, if the acquired corporation could be the survivor in the merger and the acquiring corporation could be its sole owner after the merger. That is possible under some statutes, including the Model Business Corporation Act.[10] The procedure is called a three-cornered reverse merger, and it works like this. As in

10. The statutory provision that allows this is quite opaque to the uninitiated. The Model Act is typical in that regard. Its authorizing provision is in section 71, which is the section outlining what is to be in the plan of merger. That section provides that the plan of merger shall set forth: "The manner and basis of converting the shares of each corporation into shares, obligations or other securities of the surviving corporation *or of any other corporation* or, in whole

the ordinary three-cornered merger, the acquiring corporation's subsidiary and the target corporation agree on a plan of merger. Here the difference is twofold: (1) the plan says that the target corporation is to survive and (2) the plan provides that upon the effectiveness of the merger, (a) all the outstanding stock of the acquiring corporation's subsidiary (which is owned, of course, by the acquiring corporation) is automatically converted into stock of the target corporation, and (b) all the outstanding stock of the target corporation is automatically converted into whatever the parties agree. Usually the stock is "converted" into a right to receive cash or into stock of the acquiring corporation. Thus, as soon as the merger is effective those "conversions" take place and the acquiring corporation ends up the sole owner of the acquired corporation. The conversions, which often seem at first glance to be bits of legerdemain, happen for a simple series of reasons: The plan of merger says they happen, the plan of merger is in accordance with the corporation statute, and the corporation statute is constitutional.

Notice that in the typical three-cornered reverse merger, the acquiring corporation forms a subsidiary whose only purpose is to agree upon the merger and then be merged out of existence. Out of a desire to provide the same result as in a three-cornered reverse merger, but with streamlined mechanics that do not require a new subsidiary to be formed, the drafters of the Model Business Corporation Act wrote into their statute a procedure called a share exchange. Under Model Act section 72A, the procedures for a share exchange are almost identical to those for a merger. The boards of directors of the acquiring corporation and of the target agree on a plan of share exchange. In that plan, the boards typically provide that all the outstanding common shares of the target will be exchanged for cash or some security issued by the acquiring corporation. The plan is then submitted to the shareholders of the target.

---

or in part, into cash or other property." It is the italicized phrase that provides the necessary authorization.

Upon the approval of the shareholders, articles of share exchange are filed in the appropriate state office, and the share exchange becomes effective. At that point, all that is left is exchanging the stock certificates held by the target's shareholders for cash or for the certificates representing the securities of the acquiring corporation that the target's shareholders received in the exchange. That is a purely mechanical task, however, and it has no effect on the share exchange itself. Whether the shareholders of the target submit their stock certificates for exchange, they cease to be shareholders in the target under the terms of the plan of exchange. As in mergers, consolidations, and assets acquisitions, the recourse of the target's shareholders, besides voting against the transaction, is to seek court appraisal of their shares.[11]

De Facto Merger Doctrine

The de facto merger doctrine is a judicially created vehicle that courts sometimes use to treat an assets acquisition as if it were a merger. The doctrine is invoked to protect either the interests of the shareholders of the selling corporation or those of its creditors. In the first instance the shareholders may bring suit asking a court to treat an assets sale as if it were a merger for the purpose of granting them the appraisal rights they would have had in a merger (the rights to have a court appraise their shares and to be paid the appraisal price in cash).[12] That type of suit can occur only where a corporation statute grants appraisal rights to shareholders in mergers but not in assets sales. Under Model Business Corporation Act sections 80 and 81, shareholders have appraisal rights when a corporation sells all or substantially all of its assets other than in the regular course of business.

11. That is provided for in Model Act sections 80 and 81.
12. For a representative case, *see* Rath v. Rath Packing Co., 257 Iowa 1277, 136 N.W.2d 410 (1965).

In the second instance, creditors, typically tort claimants, of the selling corporation may ask a court to treat an assets sale as if it were a merger for the purpose of allowing them to collect their debt or damages from the acquiring corporation.[13] For two reasons, that is the most worrisome application of the de facto merger doctrine from the point of view of acquiring corporations. First, it is impossible to tell what a corporation's contingent liabilities may be, particularly those that may arise from products liability. Second, the de facto merger doctrine is an equitable doctrine without clear rules governing its application. In large measure, application depends on how a court views both the facts and the equities of an individual situation.[14]

In order to protect the acquiring corporation from contingent liabilities, one or more of the following arrangements often is made in connection with an assets sale:

1. The acquiring corporation will hold back a portion of the purchase price and have a right to set off the held-back funds against any of the seller's contingent liabilities that it is forced to pay.

---

13. A leading case is Knapp v. North Am. Rockwell Corp., 506 F.2d 361 (3d Cir. 1974).
14. Tort law as well as corporation law may be brought into play to allow a plaintiff to "follow the assets" after an assets acquisition. A major example is the product-line theory, and Ray v. Alad Corp., 560 P.2d 3 (Cal. 1977), which involved an assets acquisition of a company that produced ladders, is an important case. There the California Supreme Court said:

    > We . . . conclude that a party which acquires a manufacturing business and continues the output of its line of products under the circumstances here presented assumes strict tort liability for defects in units of the same product line previously manufactured and distributed by the entity from which the business was acquired.

    Id. at 11.

2. A portion of the purchase price will be held in escrow by some third party, with the acquiring corporation having setoff rights.
3. Some financially secure corporation or persons (typically the parent or some corporation affiliated with the seller, or some or all of its shareholders) will agree to indemnify the acquiring corporation against de facto merger doctrine liabilities.
4. The selling corporation will agree to remain in existence and not dividend or distribute to its shareholders proceeds of the assets sale for some period of years.

The first three of those means are designed to avoid the financial consequences of the de facto merger doctrine, while the last is an attempt to prevent even the invocation of the doctrine.

Freeze-out Mergers

A freeze-out merger is a merger done to force minority shareholders out of a corporation. The typical first step in a freeze-out merger is for the majority shareholders of a corporation to form a new corporation and then exchange their shares in the old corporation for all the shares of the new one. The new corporation thus will hold a majority of shares in the old corporation and can control shareholder votes. As a second step, the two corporations enter into a merger under the terms of which the minority shareholders of the old corporation receive cash or some debt security in exchange for their shares. The minority shareholders can, of course, ask a court to appraise their shares if they believe the financial settlement they are to receive is unfair.[15] But so far as the corporation statutes are

15. See p. 234 *supra*.

concerned, the minority shareholders have no right to remain shareholders of the old corporation if the plan of merger provides otherwise.

In a number of cases, shareholders who wished to remain shareholders of a corporation have sued in an attempt to do so. One of the best known such cases is *Singer v. Magnavox,*[16] in which the Delaware Supreme Court ruled that a freeze-out merger on a cash basis, done for the sole purpose of freezing out minority shareholders, is "an abuse of the corporate process" for which the minority shareholders have a cause of action. Under *Singer*, the legality of such a merger had to be tested on two bases: (a) its entire fairness to the minority (which requirement came out of earlier Delaware case law), and (b) whether there was a valid business purpose for the merger.

After *Singer,* Delaware courts issued a number of opinions honing the Singer doctrine. Then the Delaware Supreme Court ruled in *Weinberger v. UOP, Inc.*[17] that the business-purpose requirement of Singer would "no longer be of any force or effect." While doing away with the valid business purpose test, *Weinberger* bolstered the fairness test and at the same time provided a somewhat more liberal appraisal remedy than shareholders had previously had available.

The *Singer* doctrine is not dead outside Delaware, however, because during the years *Singer* was alive in Delaware it influenced the courts of other states. The most helpful case is *Perl v. IU International Corp.,*[18] in which the Supreme Court of Hawaii adopted *Singer* as the law of Hawaii. Most courts have not confronted the questions involved in *Singer, Weinberger,* and *Perl.* While most courts likely will follow Delaware's current thinking on those questions, what a particular court outside Delaware will do is by no means certain.

---

16. Singer v. Magnavox, 380 A.2d 969 (Del. 1977).
17. Weinberger v. UOP, Inc., 457 A.2d 701 (Del. 1983).
18. Perl v. IU Int'l Corp., 61 Hawaii 622, 607 P.2d 1036 (1980).

State Regulation of Tender Offers

As indicated in the first section of this chapter, there is some specialized regulation of tender offers under state law in addition to substantial regulation under the federal securities laws.[19] The state regulation takes two forms: (1) that flowing from the response of courts to defensive measures taken by corporations in an attempt to avoid being taken over; (2) that flowing from state legislatures in the form of statutes designed to regulate takeovers.

Judicial Response to Tender Offer Defenses

Tender offer defenses take a wide variety of forms. They might involve acquiring as a subsidiary a corporation that would cause antitrust problems for an acquiring corporation. They might involve entering into a contract with another company providing that if a majority of the corporation's stock is acquired in a hostile tender offer, the corporation will sell its most desirable assets under terms specified in the contract. They might involve the filing of lawsuits against an acquiring corporation in an attempt either to stop a tender offer on legal grounds or to cause enough delay that the acquiring corporation gives up. All those defensive tactics and the others that corporations use have two things in common: First, the basic corporate actions involved are common everyday actions under contract or corporation law. Second, the actions are taken or at least approved by the board of directors. For those reasons, when courts examine defensive tactics the focus of their attention is not on legal questions relating to the basic actions themselves, but rather on whether the directors properly discharged their fiduciary duties in adopting or approving the actions.

---

19. For a discussion of that federal regulation, see L. SODERQUIST, UNDERSTANDING THE SECURITIES LAWS (2d ed. 1990), which also is published by the Practising Law Institute.

We have already discussed the business judgment rule in chapter 9, and with that background it will come as no surprise that the specific focus of courts in reviewing directors' conduct in the context of tender offer defenses is on that rule. The most helpful case, both for its own handling of the issues before the court and for its discussion of other cases, is *Moran v. Household International, Inc.*,[20] which the Delaware Supreme Court decided in 1985. The facts were these:

> On August 14, 1984, the Board of Directors of Household International, Inc. adopted [a Preferred Share Purchase Rights Plan] by a fourteen to two vote. The intricacies of the Rights Plan are contained in a 48-page document entitled "Rights Agreement". Basically, the Plan provides that Household common shareholders are entitled to the issuance of one Right per common share under certain triggering conditions. There are two triggering events that can activate the Rights. The first is the announcement of a tender offer for 30 percent of Household's shares . . . and the second is the acquisition of 20 percent of Household's shares by any single entity or group . . . .
>
> If an announcement of a tender offer for 30 percent of Household's shares is made, the Rights are issued and are immediately exercisable to purchase 1/100 share of new preferred stock for $100 and are redeemable by the Board for $.50 per Right. If 20 percent of Household's shares are acquired by anyone, the Rights are issued and become non-redeemable and are exercisable to purchase 1/100 of a share of preferred. If a Right is not exercised for preferred, and thereafter, a merger or consolidation occurs, the Rights holder can exercise each Right to purchase $200 of the common stock of the tender offeror for $100. That "flip-over" provision of the Rights Plan is at the heart of the controversy.[21]

Shortly after Household's directors adopted the rights plan, one of its directors and his corporation, which was a major shareholder of Household and which had suggested the possibility of acquiring Household, joined in a suit challenging the adoption of the plan.

20. Moran v. Household Int'l, Inc., 500 A.2d 1346 (Del. 1985).
21. *Id.* at 1349.

The evidence indicated and the chancery court found that the board did not adopt the plan in response to any specific bid for the corporation, "but as a preventive mechanism to ward off future advances."[22] The chancery court ruled in favor of Household, sending the case to the Delaware Supreme Court.

That court's decision turned on whether the directors were entitled to the protection of the business judgment rule in adopting the rights plan. Its discussion of Delaware law on the rule in the context of defensive maneuvers is succinct:

> The business judgment rule is a "presumption that in making a business decision the directors of a corporation acted on an informed basis." *Aronson v. Lewis,* Del. Supr., 473 A.2d 805, 812 (1984). Notwithstanding, in *Unocal* [*Corp. v. Mesa Petroleum Co.*] we held that when the business judgment rule applies to adoption of a defensive mechanism, the initial burden will lie with the directors. The "directors must show that they had reasonable grounds for believing that a danger to corporate policy and effectiveness existed. . . . [T]hey satisfy that burden 'by showing good faith and reasonable investigation. . . .' " *Unocal,* 493 A.2d at 955 . . . . In addition, the directors must show that the defensive mechanism was "reasonable in relation to the threat posed." *Unocal,* 493 A.2d at 955. Moreover, that proof is materially enhanced, as we noted in *Unocal,* where, as here, a majority of the board favoring the proposal consisted of outside independent directors who have acted in accordance with the foregoing standards. Then, the burden shifts back to the plaintiffs who have the ultimate burden of persuasion to show a breach of the directors' fiduciary duties.[23]

Applying those standards to the facts, the Delaware Supreme Court found that the Household directors did have the benefit of the business judgment rule. It found further that the directors had not breached their fiduciary duty, in that they had passed the rights plan "in the good faith belief that it was necessary to protect Household

---

22. *Id.*
23. *Id.* at 1356.

from coercive acquisition techniques,"[24] such as two-tiered tender offers, in which, after the acquiring corporation has amassed enough stock to secure voting control, it forces the other shareholders out of the corporation in a freeze-out merger on terms dictated by it.

Most courts deciding cases involving defenses to tender offers have shown the same unwillingness to fault directors for those maneuvers as did the Delaware Supreme Court in *Moran*. That judicial response has been applauded by those who believe that the large number of corporate takeovers that America has seen in the last two decades is bad for its economic life, largely because those takeovers divert the energy of corporations and their managers away from the efficient provision of goods and services and into merely wasteful power struggles for control. The defense-oriented judicial response has not been appreciated, of course, by those who believe in the purported societal benefits of tender offers, benefits that arguably flow from a Darwinian survival of the fittest in which poorly managed corporations are swallowed up by better managed ones. That judicial response often has not been appreciated by shareholders either, especially when defensive maneuvering has prevented them from selling their shares at a premium in response to a tender offer.

State Legislation Regulating Tender Offers

Federal regulation of tender offers began in 1968 when Congress passed the Williams Act.[25] That same year state legislatures began passing their own statutes, most of which were designed to thwart tender offers either by substantive regulation or procedural roadblocks. By the 1980s, over two-thirds of the states had passed such statutes.

---

24. *Id.* at 1357.

25. The Williams Act added Securities Exchange Act of 1934, §§ 13(d), (e), 14(d), (e), (f). The Williams Act is discussed briefly at pp. 259–260 *infra*.

It was widely thought that most of those state statutes were unconstitutional under either the commerce or supremacy clauses of the United States Constitution, but most court challenges were rendered moot before they could get even as far as a court of appeals. Finally, in 1982, the United States Supreme Court ruled on the constitutionality of the Illinois statute, which was similar to many others, in the case of *Edgar v. MITE Corp.*[26] Here is how the Court summarized the Illinois statute:

> Under the Illinois Act any takeover for the shares of a target company must be registered with the Secretary of State. A target company is defined as a corporation or other issuer of securities of which shareholders located in Illinois own 10% of the class of equity securities subject to the offer, or for which any two of the following three conditions are met: the corporation has its principal executive office in Illinois, is organized under the laws of Illinois, or has at least 10% of its stated capital and paid-in surplus represented in the state. An offer becomes registered 20 days after a registration statement is filed with the Secretary unless the Secretary calls a hearing. The Secretary may call a hearing at any time during the 20-day waiting period to adjudicate the substantive fairness of the offer if he believes it is necessary to protect the shareholders of the target company, and a hearing must be held if requested by a majority of a target company's outside directors or by Illinois shareholders who own 10% of the class of securities subject to the offer. If the Secretary does hold a hearing, he is directed by the statute to deny registration to a tender offer if he finds that it "fails to provide full and fair disclosure to the offerees of all material information concerning the take-over offer, or that the take-over offer is inequitable or would work or tend to work a fraud or deceit upon the offerees . . . ."[27]

After analyzing the effects of that statute, a majority of the Court found that it violated the commerce clause:

> The Commerce Clause . . . permits only incidental regulation of interstate commerce by the states; direct regulation is prohibited. The Illinois Act violates those principles for two reasons. First, it directly

26. Edgar v. MITE Corp., 457 U.S. 624 (1982).
27. *Id.* at 626.

> regulates and prevents, unless its terms are satisfied, interstate tender offers which in turn would generate interstate transactions. Second, the burden the Act imposes on interstate commerce is excessive in light of the local interests the Act purports to further.[28]

Justice White, who wrote the opinion of the Court, also concluded that the Illinois statute violated the supremacy clause in that it attempted to regulate in areas that had been preempted by the Williams Act, but he was not able to gather sufficient votes to make that the Court's opinion. Three justices refused to reach any conclusion on the substantive issues in the case on grounds of mootness.

In the years after *MITE,* a substantial number of states replaced their statutes with new ones that were designed to avoid the problems in the Illinois statute disclosed by the Supreme Court in *MITE.* In 1987, the Supreme Court examined the constitutionality of one of those second-generation statutes in *CTS Corp. v. Dynamics Corp. of America.*[29] The statute involved in CTS was a so-called control share acquisition statute that had been passed by the Indiana legislature:

> The Act focuses on the acquisition of "control shares" in an issuing public corporation.[30] Under the Act, an entity acquires "control shares" whenever it acquires shares that, but for the operation of the Act, would bring its voting power in the corporation to or above any of three thresholds: 20%, 33⅓%, or 50%. An entity that acquires control shares does not necessarily acquire voting rights. Rather, it gains those rights only "to the extent granted by resolution approved by the shareholders of the issuing public corporation." Section 9 requires a majority vote of all disinterested shareholders holding each class of stock for passage of such a resolution. The practical effect of

---

28. *Id.* at 640.
29. CTS Corp. v. Dynamics Corp. of Am., 481 U.S. 69 (1987).
30. Under the statute, an "issuing public corporation" is a corporation having at least 100 shareholders that is incorporated in Indiana, that has its principal office or principal place of business or substantial assets in Indiana, and that has certain other substantial nexuses with Indiana, such as the number (10,000) or percentage (10 percent) of its shareholders who are resident there.

> that requirement is to condition acquisition of control of a corporation on approval of a majority of the pre-existing disinterested shareholders.[31]

The Supreme Court found that the Indiana statute did not violate either the supremacy or the commerce clause, and as could be expected, as soon as that opinion was issued state legislatures began passing statutes that were copies or near copies. Since many corporations that a particular legislature wanted to protect were incorporated in another state, some of those statutes apply to foreign corporations. In that way, those statutes go beyond the Indiana statute, which applied only to Indiana corporations, and their constitutionality is subject to serious question.[32]

Also subject to question on constitutional grounds are various types of post-*MITE* statutes that do not fit the Indiana mold. For example, a number of states, including Delaware and New York, have adopted statutes that preclude mergers and other types of transactions with entities that have acquired specified amounts of voting stock (in Delaware it is 15 percent) for a period of time (three years in Delaware) unless certain conditions are satisfied, such as approval of directors prior to the acquisition of the threshold percentage of stock. Such statutes effectively preclude a would-be hostile offeror from merging with the target and from using the target's assets to finance the acquisition.

Some of those statutes cause substantial problems for lawyers who represent acquiring corporations. If they counsel compliance,

---

31. CTS Corp. v. Dynamics Corp. of Am., 481 U.S. at 73–74.
32. *See, e.g.*, Tyson Foods, Inc. v. McReynolds, 865 F.2d 99(6th Cir. 1989), which declared Tennessee's control share acquisition statute unconstitutional as it relates to other than Tennessee corporations.

even though they believe a statute to be unconstitutional, their client risks losing a takeover bid because of a statute that could have been ignored. On the other hand, if they counsel noncompliance, they and their client may face serious problems if a court disagrees on the issue of constitutionality. Those problems are especially serious in states whose statutes carry criminal penalties.

CHAPTER FOURTEEN

Introduction to Securities Law

Many and various corporate transactions have securities law implications. So pervasive, in fact, is the involvement of securities law in corporate transactions that it is impossible to practice corporate law without also practicing securities law, at least to a limited extent. Any lawyer handling corporate matters needs to have a good basic understanding of the Securities Act of 1933 (the Securities Act), along with at least rudimentary knowledge of some of the provisions in the Securities Exchange Act of 1934 (the Exchange Act). In addition, the corporate lawyer needs to know something of the securities laws of the state or states involved in the lawyer's corporate transactions.

As mentioned in the preceding chapter, another book published by the Practising Law Institute is designed to provide the corporate practitioner with the necessary introduction to the Securities Act and the Exchange Act. That is *Understanding the Securities Laws* (2d ed. 1990), and it is by one of the authors of this book. With that other book in mind, we shall in this chapter merely highlight some of the aspects of the Securities Act and the Exchange Act in an attempt to sensitize the reader to the existence of securities law issues.

Securities Act of 1933

The basic thrust of the Securities Act is the regulation of offers and sales of securities. Anytime a corporation, or anyone else for that matter, offers or sells securities, the application of the Securities Act has to be considered.[1] At the most basic level, the analysis under that Act can be quite simple. Central to the Securities Act are its provisions mandating the registration of securities under specified circumstances. Under those provisions, a registration statement must be filed with the Securities and Exchange Commission before a security may be offered, the registration statement must be effective before a security may be sold, and prospectuses must be prepared and used in prescribed ways, in each case unless an exemption is available (assuming the "jurisdictional means" requirement, relating to use of the mails or some means or instrument of interstate commerce, is met).[2] The usual Securities Act analysis of a particular transaction, then, basically goes like this:

1. Does the transaction involve a security?
2. Is the security being offered or sold?
3. Is a registration exemption available?

The first of those issues is much trickier than it may at first seem. Many commercial schemes that the uninitiated would never dream involve a security—from those relating to warehouse receipts for scotch whiskey to condominium time-sharing plans—may in fact involve one. Basically, if such a transaction involves the investment of money in a common enterprise, with profits to come solely from

1. It is critical to understand that the Securities Act relates to resales of securities by shareholders as well as to the issuance of securities by corporations and other issuers.
2. The main provision covering the requirement of registration and prospectus delivery is Securities Act § 5.

the efforts of others, a security (in the form of an "investment contract") exists.[3]

The resolution of the second issue listed above—"Is a security being offered or sold?"—usually is quite straightforward. But not always. A pledge of stock offers an interesting example. For most purposes, of course, a pledge is not a sale. In *Rubin v. United States*,[4] however, the United States Supreme Court found that for purposes of the Securities Act, a pledge of a security is a sale of that security.

The question of whether a transaction involves a sale is raised in perhaps its most interesting form in connection with corporate mergers and assets acquisitions where the acquiring corporation pays for the acquisition with its own securities. The tricky thing here is that the shareholders of the acquired corporation, who may ultimately receive the acquiring corporation's securities, personally have no dealings with the acquiring corporation. They may vote to approve or disapprove the merger or asset sale, but that can be viewed simply as a part of the decision-making process within their own corporation. What the questions come down to are two:

1. When the shareholders are asked to vote, are the acquiring corporation's securities being offered to them?
2. When the securities come to them, have the securities been sold?[5]

Under the Securities Act, the answer to both those questions is yes.[6]

The third issue above—"Is a registration exemption available?"—is the one that most often requires attention by the average

3. Of course, determining what is a "common enterprise," what are "profits," and what "solely" means present many difficulties (for example, "solely" means, among other things, something like "mainly").
4. Rubin v. United States, 449 U.S. 424 (1981).
5. Under Securities Act § 2(3), which defines the word "sale," a contract of sale is a sale. Therefore, the sale actually occurs when the acquiring corporation has contracted to issue the securities.
6. The Securities and Exchange Commission gives those answers in Securities Act rule 145.

corporation lawyer. Whereas the resolution of the other two issues requires little attention in the garden variety corporate transaction, such is not the case with the issue of whether or not a registration exemption exists. And the correct resolution of that issue is critical for two reasons.

First, if a transaction involves an offer or sale of securities, an exemption usually is essential. Since registration typically takes months of effort and entails hundreds of thousands of dollars in expenses, rarely is registration a practical possibility. Second, the offer or sale of unregistered securities without an exemption can result in crippling criminal and civil liabilities.

The Securities Act and its rules offer corporate practitioners many choices of exemptions for their clients. Those exemptions cover both the original sale of securities by their issuers and resales by shareholders. Regrettably, however, none of the exemptions can easily be understood simply by reading the statute or rules. In all cases, some further learning is required if a lawyer is to help a client secure an exemption.

The Securities Act is a criminal statute, the violation of which can result in imprisonment for five years and a $10,000 fine.[7] Those penalties typically would be imposed in two types of situations: the unlawful sale of unregistered securities[8] and the sale of securities by means of various types of fraudulent conduct.[9] In addition to its criminal penalties, the Securities Act contains provisions granting injured securities purchasers civil remedies for materially false or

7. Securities Act § 24. The Exchange Act is a criminal statute also. Exchange Act § 32 sets out its criminal penalties.
8. Securities Act § 5.
9. *Id.* § 17(a).

misleading statements contained in registration statements[10] or disseminated by other means,[11] and also when securities are sold without compliance with the registration or prospectus delivery requirements.[12]

Securities Exchange Act of 1934

The Exchange Act is much broader in its coverage of securities law than is the Securities Act. As its name indicates, the Exchange Act regulates securities exchanges. It also regulates securities firms and other securities professionals. In those respects, the Exchange Act is the province of a relatively small number of securities lawyers. But in addition, the Exchange Act contains provisions that apply broadly to publicly held companies, and other provisions that apply to anyone who engages in securities transactions. In the rest of this chapter, we shall introduce some of the Exchange Act provisions most often encountered by corporation lawyers.

Registration and Periodic Reporting Under the Exchange Act

The Exchange Act mandates the registration of securities under two distinct circumstances. First, an issuer must register securities under Exchange Act section 12(b) when the securities are to be traded on a stock exchange. Second, an issuer must register securities under that Act when the issuer meets certain tests with respect to number of shareholders and amount of assets. Under Exchange Act section 12(g)(1), read along with Exchange Act rule 12g-1, an issuer must register a class of equity securities when the securities are

10. *Id.* § 11.
11. *Id.* § 12(2).
12. *Id.* § 12(1).

held of record by at least 500 persons and the issuer has assets exceeding $5 million.

By registering securities under the Exchange Act, an issuer becomes a "reporting company." That is, it becomes subject to the periodic reporting requirements of section 13(a). Under that section and its rules, reporting companies must file a wide variety of reports with the Securities and Exchange Commission on a continuing basis. The most common of those reports are the form 10-K annual report, the form 10-Q quarterly report, and the form 8-K current report, which is filed upon the occurrence of specified material events.[13]

Regulation of Proxy Solicitations

Proxy voting by shareholders is a fact of life for most publicly held corporations. State corporation laws require annual meetings, and typically such corporations cannot satisfy quorum requirements unless most shareholders are represented by proxy holders. For that reason, management usually solicits proxies from a corporation's shareholders at least annually and whenever a special shareholders' meeting is called. In addition to that ordinary use of proxies, those attempting to take over the management of a corporation sometimes solicit proxies from shareholders to gather needed votes.

At the heart of the Exchange Act's regulation of proxy solicitations is section 14(a), which makes it illegal to violate the Commission's proxy rules with respect to the solicitation of a proxy to vote any security (other than an exempted security) that is registered under the Exchange Act. Those rules are voluminous and generate

13. There is one other way, besides registration of securities under the Exchange Act, for companies to become subject to the reporting requirements of the Exchange Act. Under Exchange Act section 15(d), read along with regulation 15D, a company that has registered securities under the Securities Act is subject to the same section 13 filing requirements as are companies that have securities registered under the Exchange Act.

much work for a corporation's lawyers and accountants in connection with each meeting of a publicly held corporation's shareholders.

Any security holder may solicit proxies from fellow security holders. In a large corporation, however, printing and postage costs alone may be several hundred dollars for a single mailing, which makes direct solicitation impractical in most cases. In light of that, the Commission adopted rule 14a-8, which requires management to include in its proxy statement proposals made by security holders, along with 500-word supporting statements, when certain conditions are met. Those conditions cover such things as timeliness, amount of securities held by the proposer, and the subject of the proposal.

The most important proxy rule, at least in terms of danger of litigation, is rule 14a-9. That rule is the Commission's antifraud provision in the proxy area, and basically it prohibits soliciting a proxy with respect to a security that is registered under the Exchange Act on the basis of materially false or misleading information.

Regulation of Tender Offers

The Exchange Act subjects tender offers for publicly held companies to substantial regulation under legislation passed in 1968, known as the Williams Act. That Act added to the Exchange Act sections 13(d) and (e) and 14(d), (e), and (f). Section 13(d) is aimed at tender offers only indirectly. It requires a person who owns more that 5 percent of a class of equity security registered under the Exchange Act to provide certain information to the issuer and to the Commission within ten days after the acquisition of securities that triggers the reporting requirement. The other Williams Act provision in section 13 is section 13(e). It gives the Commission the power to regulate repurchases by issuers of their own equity securities.

The centerpiece of the Williams Act is section 14(d). Under that provision, it is unlawful, unless certain filings are made, to make a tender offer for an Exchange Act-registered equity security and certain other securities[14] if success in the offer would result in ownership of more than 5 percent of the class. Section 14(d) also contains a limited amount of substantive regulation of tender offers. For example, it provides that securities deposited in response to a tender offer may be withdrawn within seven days after the date of the original tender offer, and after sixty days have elapsed following that date.

The Williams Act also contains an antifraud provision, section 14(e), that makes it unlawful to make a tender offer on the basis of materially false or misleading information. Unlike other provisions in the Williams Act, that section relates not only to tender offers for specified types of securities (basically those registered under the Exchange Act), but to tender offers for any kind of security.

Section 14(f) is a specialized provision that calls for certain disclosures to the Commission and to security holders when a majority of a corporation's directorships are to be filled, otherwise than at a meeting of security holders, following an acquisition of securities that is subject to the requirements of section 13(d) or 14(d). The usual trigger of that provision is the filling of vacant directorships by sitting directors, which generally is allowed under state corporation law. That provision is intended to deal with the situation in which control of the corporation is sold and, as a part of the transaction, it is agreed that the existing directors will resign seriatim and that the remaining directors will elect new directors who are chosen by the entity acquiring control.

---

14. These are an insurance company's equity securities that would be required to be registered under the Exchange Act save for a registration exemption and equity securities issued by a closed-end investment company registered under the Investment Company Act of 1940.

Fraud in the Purchase or Sale of Securities: Rule 10b-5

Exchange Act rule 10b-5 is the Commission's most important antifraud weapon. It makes it unlawful to make any materially untrue or misleading statement in connection with the purchase or sale of any security; "to employ any device, scheme, or artifice to defraud"; or "to engage in any act, practice, or course of business which operates or would operate as a fraud or deceit upon any person." Although by its terms rule 10b-5 is a criminal provision, courts consistently have implied a private right of action under it.

The most frequent use of rule 10b-5 has been in insider trading cases, typically those in which an officer, director, or other person in a fiduciary relationship with a corporation buys or sells the company's securities when in the possession of material, nonpublic information. But the rule also is used in at least five other situations:

1. When a corporation issues misleading information to the public, or keeps silent when it has a duty to disclose;
2. When an insider selectively discloses material, nonpublic information to another person, who then trades based on the inside information;
3. When a person mismanages a corporation in ways that are connected with the purchase or sale of securities;
4. When a securities firm or another person manipulates the market for a security traded in the over-the-counter market; and
5. When a securities firm or securities professional engages in certain other forms of conduct connected with the purchase or sale of securities.[15]

15. Jacobs, *The Role of Securities Exchange Act Rule 10b-5 in the Regulation of Corporate Management,* 59 CORNELL L. REV. 27, 29 (1973).

Liability for Short-Swing Profits: Section 16(b)

Exchange Act section 16(b) is designed to minimize the unfair use of inside information. Basically, under that provision profits made by insiders from transactions involving publicly traded stock, when a purchase and a sale are made within less than six months of each other, must be disgorged and paid over to the issuer.

Section 16(a) is an important adjunct to section 16(b). That section requires beneficial owners of more than 10 percent of any class of equity security (other than an exempted security) that is registered under the Exchange Act and officers and directors of issuers of such securities to file reports with the Commission and relevant securities exchanges concerning their holdings of all equity securities of such issuers.

Section 16(b) is somewhat complicated. It provides that:

(1) Any profit,
(2) By any person subject to the reporting requirements of section 16(a),
(3) Realized on any purchase and sale, or sale and purchase,
(4) Within any period of less than six months,
(5) Of any non-exempt equity security of an issuer that has an equity security registered under the Exchange Act

"shall inure to and be recoverable by the issuer."[16] An issuer may sue to recover those so-called short-swing profits, or any security holder of the issuer may sue derivatively to recover the profits when after a request the issuer fails to bring suit within sixty days or when it fails diligently to prosecute a claim once filed.

Section 16(b) causes substantial problems for corporate insiders when they are not fully apprised of its provisions. The section creates problems for corporations also, since typically the managers of a corporation do not relish the bad relations that may be created

16. An exception exists when the security was purchased in good faith in connection with a debt previously contracted.

when one of their shareholders demands that short-swing profits be disgorged from an officer, director, or substantial shareholder who has run afoul of section 16(b) because of a lack of knowledge or an inattention to detail. As a result, careful corporation lawyers often make sure that those who are subject to the reporting requirements of section 16(a) and the disgorgement requirements of section 16(b) are fully aware of those requirements.

APPENDIX A

Model Business Corporation Act

(As amended through 1978)

Table of Sections

§ 21. Determination of Amount of Stated Capital.
§ 22. Expenses of Organization, Reorganization and Financing.
§ 23. Shares Represented by Certificates and Uncertificated Shares.
§ 24. Fractional Shares.
§ 25. Liability of Subscribers and Shareholders.
§ 26. Shareholders' Preemptive Rights.
§ 26A. Shareholders' Preemptive Rights [Alternative].
§ 27. By-Laws.
§ 27A. By-Laws and Other Powers in Emergency [Optional].
§ 28. Meetings of Shareholders.
§ 29. Notice of Shareholders' Meetings.
§ 30. Closing of Transfer Books and Fixing Record Date.
§ 31. Voting Record.
§ 32. Quorum of Shareholders.
§ 33. Voting of Shares.
§ 34. Voting Trusts and Agreements Among Shareholders.
§ 35. Board of Directors.
§ 36. Number and Election of Directors.
§ 37. Classification of Directors.
§ 38. Vacancies.
§ 39. Removal of Directors.
§ 40. Quorum of Directors.
§ 41. Director Conflicts of Interest.
§ 42. Executive and Other Committees.
§ 43. Place and Notice of Directors' Meetings; Committee Meetings.
§ 44. Action by Directors Without a Meeting.
§ 45. Dividends.
§ 46. Distributions from Capital Surplus.
§ 47. Loans to Employees and Directors.
§ 48. Liability of Directors in Certain Cases.
§ 49. Provisions Relating to Actions by Shareholders.
§ 50. Officers.
§ 51. Removal of Officers.
§ 52. Books and Records; Financial Reports to Shareholders; Examination of Records.

FORMATION OF CORPORATIONS

§ 53. Incorporators.

§ 54. Articles of Incorporation.
§ 55. Filing of Articles of Incorporation.
§ 56. Effect of Issuance of Certificate of Incorporation.
§ 57. Organization Meeting of Directors.

AMENDMENT

§ 58. Right to Amend Articles of Incorporation.
§ 59. Procedure to Amend Articles of Incorporation.
§ 60. Class Voting on Amendments.
§ 61. Articles of Amendment.
§ 62. Filing of Articles of Amendment.
§ 63. Effect of Certificate of Amendment.
§ 64. Restated Articles of Incorporation.
§ 65. Amendment of Articles of Incorporation in Reorganization Proceedings.
§ 66. Restriction on Redemption or Purchase of Redeemable Shares.
§ 67. Cancellation of Redeemable Shares by Redemption or Purchase.
§ 68. Cancellation of Other Reacquired Shares.
§ 69. Reduction of Stated Capital in Certain Cases.
§ 70. Special Provisions Relating to Surplus and Reserves.

MERGER AND CONSOLIDATION

§ 71. Procedure for Merger.
§ 72. Procedure for Consolidation.
§ 72A. Procedure for Share Exchange.
§ 73. Approval by Shareholders.
§ 74. Articles of Merger, Consolidation or Exchange.
§ 75. Merger of Subsidiary Corporation.
§ 76. Effect of Merger, Consolidation or Exchange.
§ 77. Merger, Consolidation or Exchange of Shares Between Domestic and Foreign Corporations.

SALE OF ASSETS

§ 78. Sale of Assets in Regular Course of Business and Mortgage or Pledge of Assets.
§ 79. Sale of Assets Other Than in Regular Course of Business.

§ 80. Right of Shareholders to Dissent and Obtain Payment for Shares.
§ 81. Procedures for Protection of Dissenters' Rights.

DISSOLUTION

§ 82. Voluntary Dissolution by Incorporators.
§ 83. Voluntary Dissolution by Consent of Shareholders.
§ 84. Voluntary Dissolution by Act of Corporation.
§ 85. Filing of Statement of Intent to Dissolve.
§ 86. Effect of Statement of Intent to Dissolve.
§ 87. Procedure after Filing of Statement of Intent to Dissolve.
§ 88. Revocation of Voluntary Dissolution Proceedings by Consent of Shareholders.
§ 89. Revocation of Voluntary Dissolution Proceedings by Act of Corporation.
§ 90. Filing of Statement of Revocation of Voluntary Dissolution Proceedings.
§ 91. Effect of Statement of Revocation of Voluntary Dissolution Proceedings.
§ 92. Articles of Dissolution.
§ 93. Filing of Articles of Dissolution.
§ 94. Involuntary Dissolution.
§ 95. Notification to Attorney General.
§ 96. Venue and Process.
§ 97. Jurisdiction of Court to Liquidate Assets and Business of Corporation.
§ 98. Procedure in Liquidation of Corporation by Court.
§ 99. Qualifications of Receivers.
§ 100. Filing of Claims in Liquidation Proceedings.
§ 101. Discontinuance of Liquidation Proceedings.
§ 102. Decree of Involuntary Dissolution.
§ 103. Filing of Decree of Dissolution.
§ 104. Deposit with State Treasurer of Amount Due Certain Shareholders.
§ 105. Survival of Remedy after Dissolution.

FOREIGN CORPORATIONS

§ 106. Admission of Foreign Corporation.
§ 107. Powers of Foreign Corporation.

§ 108. Corporate Name of Foreign Corporation.
§ 109. Change of Name by Foreign Corporation.
§ 110. Application for Certificate of Authority.
§ 111. Filing of Application for Certificate of Authority.
§ 112. Effect of Certificate of Authority.
§ 113. Registered Office and Registered Agent of Foreign Corporation.
§ 114. Change of Registered Office or Registered Agent of Foreign Corporation.
§ 115. Service of Process on Foreign Corporation.
§ 116. Amendment to Articles of Incorporation of Foreign Corporation.
§ 117. Merger of Foreign Corporation Authorized to Transact Business in This State.
§ 118. Amended Certificate of Authority.
§ 119. Withdrawal of Foreign Corporation.
§ 120. Filing of Application for Withdrawal.
§ 121. Revocation of Certificate of Authority.
§ 122. Issuance of Certificate of Revocation.
§ 123. Application to Corporations Heretofore Authorized to Transact Business in This State.
§ 124. Transacting Business Without Certificate of Authority.

ANNUAL REPORTS

§ 125. Annual Report of Domestic and Foreign Corporations.
§ 126. Filing of Annual Report of Domestic and Foreign Corporations.

FEES, FRANCHISE TAXES AND CHARGES

§ 127. Fees, Franchise Taxes and Charges to Be Collected by Secretary of State.
§ 128. Fees for Filing Documents and Issuing Certificates.
§ 129. Miscellaneous Charges.
§ 130. License Fees Payable by Domestic Corporations.
§ 131. License Fees Payable by Foreign Corporations.
§ 132. Franchise Taxes Payable by Domestic Corporations.
§ 133. Franchise Taxes Payable by Foreign Corporations.
§ 134. Assessment and Collection of Annual Franchise Taxes.

PENALTIES

MISCELLANEOUS PROVISIONS

.... *BUSINESS CORPORATION ACT

§ 1. Short Title

This Act shall be known and may be cited as the"........* Business Corporation Act."

§ 2. Definitions

As used in this Act, unless the context otherwise requires, the term:

(a) "Corporation" or "domestic corporation" means a corporation for profit subject to the provisions of this Act, except a foreign corporation.

* Supply name of State.

(b) "Foreign corporation" means a corporation for profit organized under laws other than the laws of this State for a purpose or purposes for which a corporation may be organized under this Act.

(c) "Articles of incorporation" means the original or restated articles of incorporation or articles of consolidation and all amendments thereto including articles of merger.

(d) "Shares" means the units into which the proprietary interests in a corporation are divided.

(e) "Subscriber" means one who subscribes for shares in a corporation, whether before or after incorporation.

(f) "Shareholder" means one who is a holder of record of shares in a corporation. If the articles of incorporation or the by-laws so provide, the board of directors may adopt by resolution a procedure whereby a shareholder of the corporation may certify in writing to the corporation that all or a portion of the shares registered in the name of such shareholder are held for the account of a specified person or persons. The resolution shall set forth (1) the classification of shareholder who may certify, (2) the purpose or purposes for which the certification may be made, (3) the form of certification and information to be contained therein, (4) if the certification is with respect to a record date or closing of the stock transfer books within which the certification must be received by the corporation and (5) such other provisions with respect to the procedure as are deemed necessary or desirable. Upon receipt by the corporation of a certification complying with the procedure, the persons specified in the certification shall be deemed, for the purpose or purposes set forth in the certification, to be the holders of record of the number of shares specified in place of the shareholder making the certification.

(g) "Authorized shares" means the shares of all classes which the corporation is authorized to issue.

(h) "Treasury shares" means shares of a corporation which have been issued, have been subsequently acquired by and belong to the corporation, and have not, either by reason of the acquisition or thereafter, been cancelled or restored to the status of authorized but unissued shares. Treasury shares shall be deemed to be "issued" shares, but not "outstanding" shares.

(i) "Net assets" means the amount by which the total assets of a corporation exceed the total debts of the corporation.

(j) "Stated capital" means, at any particular time, the sum of (1) the par value of all shares of the corporation having a par value that have been issued, (2) the amount of the consideration received by the corporation for all shares of the corporation without par value that have been issued, except such part of the consideration therefor as may have been allocated to capital surplus in a manner permitted by law, and (3) such amounts not included in clauses (1) and (2) of this paragraph as have been transferred to stated capital of the corporation, whether upon the issue of shares as a share dividend or otherwise, minus all reductions from such sum as have been effected in a manner permitted by law. Irrespective of the manner of designation thereof by the laws under which a foreign corporation is organized, the stated capital of a foreign corporation shall be determined on the same basis and in the same manner as the stated capital of a domestic corporation, for the purpose of computing fees, franchise taxes and other charges imposed by this Act.

(k) "Surplus" means the excess of the net assets of a corporation over its stated capital.

(l) "Earned surplus" means the portion of the surplus of a corporation equal to the balance of its net profits, income, gains and losses from the date of incorporation, or from the latest date when a deficit was eliminated by an application of its capital surplus or stated capital or otherwise, after deducting subsequent distributions to shareholders and transfers to stated capital and capital surplus to the extent such distributions and transfers are made out of earned surplus. Earned surplus shall include also any portion of surplus allocated to earned surplus in mergers, consolidations or acquisitions of all or substantially all of the outstanding shares or of the property and assets of another corporation, domestic or foreign.

(m) "Capital surplus" means the entire surplus of a corporation other than its earned surplus.

(n) "Insolvent" means inability of a corporation to pay its debts as they become due in the usual course of its business.

(o) "Employee" includes officers but not directors. A director may accept duties which make him also an employee.

§ 3. Purposes

Corporations may be organized under this Act for any lawful purpose or purposes, except for the purpose of banking or insurance.

§ 4. General Powers

Each corporation shall have power:

(a) To have perpetual succession by its corporate name unless a limited period of duration is stated in its articles of incorporation.

(b) To sue and be sued, complain and defend, in its corporate name.

(c) To have a corporate seal which may be altered at pleasure, and to use the same by causing it, or a facsimile thereof, to be impressed or affixed or in any other manner reproduced.

(d) To purchase, take, receive, lease, or otherwise acquire, own, hold, improve, use and otherwise deal in and with, real or personal property, or any interest therein, wherever situated.

(e) To sell, convey, mortgage, pledge, lease, exchange, transfer and otherwise dispose of all or any part of its property and assets.

(f) To lend money and use its credit to assist its employees.

(g) To purchase, take, receive, subscribe for, or otherwise acquire, own, hold, vote, use, employ, sell, mortgage, lend, pledge, or otherwise dispose of, and otherwise use and deal in and with, shares or other interests in, or obligations of, other domestic or foreign corporations, associations, partnerships or individuals, or direct or indirect obligations of the United States or of any other government, state, territory, governmental district or municipality or of any instrumentality thereof.

(h) To make contracts and guarantees and incur liabilities, borrow money at such rates of interest as the corporation may determine, issue its notes, bonds, and other obligations, and secure any of its obligations by mortgage or pledge of all or any of its property, franchises and income.

(i) To lend money for its corporate purposes, invest and reinvest its funds, and take and hold real and personal property as security for the payment of funds so loaned or invested.

(j) To conduct its business, carry on its operations and have offices and exercise the powers granted by this Act, within or without this State.

(k) To elect or appoint officers and agents of the corporation, and define their duties and fix their compensation.

(l) To make and alter by-laws, not inconsistent with its articles of incorporation or with the laws of this State, for the administration and regulation of the affairs of the corporation.

(m) To make donations for the public welfare or for charitable, scientific or educational purposes.

(n) To transact any lawful business which the board of directors shall find will be in aid of governmental policy.

(o) To pay pensions and establish pension plans, pension trusts, profit sharing plans, stock bonus plans, stock option plans and other incentive plans for any or all of its directors, officers and employees.

(p) To be a promoter, partner, member, associate, or manager of any partnership, joint venture, trust or other enterprise.

(q) To have and exercise all powers necessary or convenient to effect its purposes.

§ 5. Indemnification of Officers, Directors, Employees and Agents

(a) A corporation shall have power to indemnify any person who was or is a party or is threatened to be made a party to any threatened, pending or completed action, suit or proceeding, whether civil, criminal, administrative or investigative (other than an action by or in the right of the corporation) by reason of the fact that he is or was a director, officer, employee or agent of the corporation, or is or was serving at the request of the corporation as a director, officer, employee or agent of another corporation, partnership, joint venture, trust or other enterprise, against expenses (including attorneys' fees), judgments, fines and amounts paid in settlement actually and reasonably incurred by him in connection with such action, suit or proceeding if he acted in good faith and in a manner he reasonably believed to be in or not opposed to the best interests of the corporation, and, with respect to any criminal action or proceeding, had no reasonable cause to believe his conduct was unlawful. The termination of any action, suit or proceeding by judgment, order, settlement, conviction, or upon a plea of nolo contendere or its equivalent, shall not, of itself, create a presumption that the person did not act in good faith and in a manner which he reasonably believed to be in or not opposed to the best interests of the corporation, and, with respect to any criminal action or proceeding, had reasonable cause to believe that his conduct was unlawful.

(b) A corporation shall have power to indemnify any person who was or is a party or is threatened to be made a party to any threatened, pending or completed action or suit by or in the right of the corporation to procure a judgment in its favor by reason of the fact that he is or was a director, officer, employee or agent of the corporation, or is or was serving at the request of the corporation as a director, officer, employee or agent of another corporation, partnership, joint venture, trust or other enterprise against expenses (including attorneys' fees) actually and reasonably incurred by him in connection with the defense or settlement of such action or suit if he acted in good faith and in a manner he reasonably believed to be in or not opposed to the best interests of the corporation and except that no indemnification shall be made in respect of any claim, issue or matter as to which such person shall have been adjudged to be liable for negligence or misconduct in the performance of his duty to the corporation unless and only to the extent that the court in which such action or suit was brought shall determine upon application that, despite the adjudication of liability but in view of all circumstances of the case, such person is fairly and reasonably entitled to indemnity for such expenses which such court shall deem proper.

(c) To the extent that a director, officer, employee or agent of a corporation has been successful on the merits or otherwise in defense of any action, suit or proceeding referred to in subsections (a) or (b), or in defense of any claim, issue or matter therein, he shall be indemnified against expenses (including attorneys' fees) actually and reasonably incurred by him in connection therewith.

(d) Any indemnification under subsections (a) or (b) (unless ordered by a court) shall be made by the corporation only as authorized in the specific case upon a determination that indemnification of the director, officer, employee or agent is proper in the circumstances because he has met the applicable standard of conduct set forth in subsections (a) or (b). Such determination shall be made (1) by the board of directors by a majority vote of a quorum consisting of directors who were not parties to such action, suit or proceeding, or (2) if such a quorum is not obtainable, or, even if obtainable a quorum of disinterested directors so directs, by independent legal counsel in a written opinion, or (3) by the shareholders.

(e) Expenses (including attorneys' fees) incurred in defending a civil or criminal action, suit or proceeding may be paid by the corporation in advance of the final disposition of such action, suit or proceeding as authorized in the manner provided in subsection (d) upon receipt of an undertaking by or on behalf of the director, officer, employee or agent to repay such amount unless it shall ultimately be determined that he is entitled to be indemnified by the corporation as authorized in this section.

(f) The indemnification provided by this section shall not be deemed exclusive of any other rights to which those indemnified may be entitled under any by-law, agreement, vote of shareholders or disinterested directors or otherwise, both as to action in his official capacity and as to action in another capacity while holding such office, and shall continue as to a person who has ceased to be a director, officer, employee or agent and shall inure to the benefit of the heirs, executors and administrators of such a person.

(g) A corporation shall have power to purchase and maintain insurance on behalf of any person who is or was a director, officer, employee or agent of the corporation, or is or was serving at the request of the corporation as a director, officer, employee or agent of another corporation, partnership, joint venture, trust or other enterprise against any liability asserted against him and incurred by him in any such capacity or arising out of his status as such, whether or not the corporation would have the power to indemnify him against such liability under the provisions of this section.

§ 6. Right of Corporation to Acquire and Dispose of Its Own Shares

A corporation shall have the right to purchase, take, receive or otherwise acquire, hold, own, pledge, transfer or otherwise dispose of its own shares, but purchases of its own shares, whether direct or indirect, shall be made only to the extent of unreserved and unrestricted earned surplus available therefor, and, if the articles of incorporation so permit or with the affirmative vote of the holders of a majority of all shares entitled to vote thereon, to the extent of unreserved and unrestricted capital surplus available therefor.

To the extent that earned surplus or capital surplus is used as the measure of the corporation's right to purchase its own shares, such surplus shall be restricted so long as such shares are held as treasury shares, and upon the disposition or cancellation of any such shares the restriction shall be removed pro tanto.

Notwithstanding the foregoing limitation, a corporation may purchase or otherwise acquire its own shares for the purpose of:

(a) Eliminating fractional shares.

(b) Collecting or compromising indebtedness to the corporation.

(c) Paying dissenting shareholders entitled to payment for their shares under the provisions of this Act.

(d) Effecting, subject to the other provisions of this Act, the retirement of its redeemable shares by redemption or by purchase at not to exceed the redemption price.

No purchase of or payment for its own shares shall be made at a time when the corporation is insolvent or when such purchase or payment would make it insolvent.

§ 7. Defense of Ultra Vires

No act of a corporation and no conveyance or transfer of real or personal property to or by a corporation shall be invalid by reason of the fact that the corporation was without capacity or power to do such act or to make or receive such conveyance or transfer, but such lack of capacity or power may be asserted:

(a) In a proceeding by a shareholder against the corporation to enjoin the doing of any act or the transfer of real or personal property by or to the corporation. If the unauthorized act or transfer sought to be enjoined is being, or is to be, performed or made pursuant to a contract to which the corporation is a party, the court may, if all of the parties to the contract are parties to the proceeding and if it deems the same to be equitable, set aside and enjoin the performance of such contract, and in so doing may allow to the corporation or to the other parties to the contract, as the case may be, compensation for the loss or damage sustained by either of them which may result from the action of the court in setting aside and enjoining the performance of such contract, but anticipated profits to be derived from the performance of the contract shall not be awarded by the court as a loss or damage sustained.

(b) In a proceeding by the corporation, whether acting directly or through a receiver, trustee, or other legal representative, or through shareholders in a representative suit, against the incumbent or former officers or directors of the corporation.

(c) In a proceeding by the Attorney General, as provided in this Act, to dissolve the corporation, or in a proceeding by the Attorney General to enjoin the corporation from the transaction of unauthorized business.

§ 8. Corporate Name

The corporate name:

(a) Shall contain the word "corporation," "company," "incorporated" or "limited," or shall contain an abbreviation of one of such words.

(b) Shall not contain any word or phrase which indicates or implies that it is organized for any purpose other than one or more of the purposes contained in its articles of incorporation.

(c) Shall not be the same as, or deceptively similar to, the name of any domestic corporation existing under the laws of this State or any foreign corporation authorized to transact business in this State, or a name the exclusive right to which is, at the time, reserved in the manner provided in this Act, or the name of a corporation which has in effect a registration of its corporate name as provided in this Act, except that this provision shall not apply if the applicant files with the Secretary of State either of the following: (1) the written consent of such other corporation or holder of a reserved or registered name to use the same or deceptively similar name and one or more words are added to make such name distinguishable from such other name, or (2) a certified copy of a final decree of a court of competent jurisdiction establishing the prior right of the applicant to the use of such name in this State.

A corporation with which another corporation, domestic or foreign, is merged, or which is formed by the reorganization or consolidation of one or more domestic or foreign corporations or upon a sale, lease or other disposition to or exchange with, a domestic corporation of all or substantially all the assets of another corporation, domestic or foreign, including its name, may have the same name as that used in this State by any of such corporations if such other corporation was organized under the laws of, or is authorized to transact business in, this State.

§ 9. Reserved Name

The exclusive right to the use of a corporate name may be reserved by:

(a) Any person intending to organize a corporation under this Act.

(b) Any domestic corporation intending to change its name.

(c) Any foreign corporation intending to make application for a certificate of authority to transact business in this State.

(d) Any foreign corporation authorized to transact business in this State and intending to change its name.

(e) Any person intending to organize a foreign corporation and intending to have such corporation make application for a certificate of authority to transact business in this State.

The reservation shall be made by filing with the Secretary of State an application to reserve a specified corporate name, executed by the applicant. If the Secretary of State finds that the name is available for corporate use, he shall reserve the same for the exclusive use of the applicant for a period of one hundred and twenty days.

The right to the exclusive use of a specified corporate name so reserved may be transferred to any other person or corporation by filing in the office of the Secretary of State a notice of such transfer, executed by the applicant for whom the name was reserved, and specifying the name and address of the transferee.

§ 10. Registered Name

Any corporation organized and existing under the laws of any state or territory of the United States may register its corporate name under this Act, provided its corporate name is not the same as, or deceptively similar to, the name of any domestic corporation existing under the laws of this State, or the name of any foreign corporation authorized to transact business in this State, or any corporate name reserved or registered under this Act.

Such registration shall be made by:

(a) Filing with the Secretary of State (1) an application for registration executed by the corporation by an officer thereof, setting forth the name of the corporation, the state or territory under the laws of which it is incorporated, the date of its incorporation, a statement that it is carrying on or doing business, and a brief statement of the business in which it is engaged, and (2) a certificate setting forth that such corporation is in good standing under the laws of the state or territory wherein it is organized, executed by the Secretary of State of such state or territory or by such other official as may have custody of the records pertaining to corporations, and

(b) Paying to the Secretary of State a registration fee in the amount of . . . . for each month, or fraction thereof, between the date of filing such application and December 31st of the calendar year in which such application is filed.

Such registration shall be effective until the close of the calendar year in which the application for registration is filed.

§ 11. Renewal of Registered Name

A corporation which has in effect a registration of its corporate name, may renew such registration from year to year by annually filing an application for renewal setting forth the facts required to be set forth in an original application for registration and a certificate of good standing as required for the original registration and by paying a fee of . . . . A renewal application may be filed between the first day of October and the thirty-first day of December in each year, and shall extend the registration for the following calendar year.

§ 12. Registered Office and Registered Agent

Each corporation shall have and continuously maintain in this State:

(a) A registered office which may be, but need not be, the same as its place of business.

(b) A registered agent, which agent may be either an individual resident in this State whose business office is identical with such registered office, or a domestic corporation, or a foreign corporation authorized to transact business in this State, having a business office identical with such registered office.

§ 13. Change of Registered Office or Registered Agent

A corporation may change its registered office or change its registered agent, or both, upon filing in the office of the Secretary of State a statement setting forth:

(a) The name of the corporation.

(b) The address of its then registered office.

(c) If the address of its registered office is to be changed, the address to which the registered office is to be changed.

(d) The name of its then registered agent.

(e) If its registered agent is to be changed, the name of its successor registered agent.

(f) That the address of its registered office and the address of the business office of its registered agent, as changed, will be identical.

(g) That such change was authorized by resolution duly adopted by its board of directors.

Such statement shall be executed by the corporation by its president, or a vice president, and verified by him, and delivered to the Secretary of State. If the Secretary of State finds that such statement conforms to the provisions of this Act, he shall file such statement in his office, and upon such filing the change of address of the registered office, or the appointment of a new registered agent, or both, as the case may be, shall become effective.

Any registered agent of a corporation may resign as such agent upon filing a written notice thereof, executed in duplicate, with the Secretary of State, who shall forthwith mail a copy thereof to the corporation at its registered office. The appointment of such agent shall terminate upon the expiration of thirty days after receipt of such notice by the Secretary of State.

If a registered agent changes his or its business address to another place within the same . . . .* , he or it may change such address and the address of the registered office of any corporation of which he or it is registered agent by filing a statement as required above except that it need be signed only by the registered agent and need not be responsive to (e) or (g) and must recite that a copy of the statement has been mailed to the corporation.

§ 14. Service of Process on Corporation

The registered agent so appointed by a corporation shall be an agent of such corporation upon whom any process, notice or demand required or permitted by law to be served upon the corporation may be served.

Whenever a corporation shall fail to appoint or maintain a registered agent in this State, or whenever its registered agent cannot with reasonable diligence be found at the registered office, then the Secretary of State shall be an agent of such corporation upon whom any such process, notice, or demand may be served. Service on the Secretary of State of any such process, notice, or demand shall be made by delivering to and leaving with him, or with any clerk having charge of the corporation department of his office, duplicate copies of such process, notice or demand. In the event any such process, notice or demand is served on the Secretary of State, he shall immediately cause one of the copies thereof to be forwarded by registered mail, addressed to the corporation at its registered office. Any service so had on the Secretary of State shall be returnable in not less than thirty days.

The Secretary of State shall keep a record of all processes, notices and demands served upon him under this section, and shall record therein the time of such service and his action with reference thereto.

---

* Supply designation of jurisdiction, such as county, etc., in accordance with local practice.

Nothing herein contained shall limit or affect the right to serve any process, notice or demand required or permitted by law to be served upon a corporation in any other manner now or hereafter permitted by law.

§ 15. Authorized Shares

Each corporation shall have power to create and issue the number of shares stated in its articles of incorporation. Such shares may be divided into one or more classes, any or all of which classes may consist of shares with par value or shares without par value, with such designations, preferences, limitations, and relative rights as shall be stated in the articles of incorporation. The articles of incorporation may limit or deny the voting rights of or provide special voting rights for the shares of any class to the extent not inconsistent with the provisions of this Act.

Without limiting the authority herein contained, a corporation, when so provided in its articles of incorporation, may issue shares of preferred or special classes:

(a) Subject to the right of the corporation to redeem any of such shares at the price fixed by the articles of incorporation for the redemption thereof.

(b) Entitling the holders thereof to cumulative, noncumulative or partially cumulative dividends.

(c) Having preference over any other class or classes of shares as to the payment of dividends.

(d) Having preference in the assets of the corporation over any other class or classes of shares upon the voluntary or involuntary liquidation of the corporation.

(e) Convertible into shares of any other class or into shares of any series of the same or any other class, except a class having prior or superior rights and preferences as to dividends or distribution of assets upon liquidation, but shares without par value shall not be converted into shares with par value unless that part of the stated capital of the corporation represented by such shares without par value is, at the time of conversion, at least equal to the aggregate par value of the shares into which the shares without par value are to be converted or the amount of any such deficiency is transferred from surplus to stated capital.

§ 16. Issuance of Shares of Preferred or Special Classes in Series

If the articles of incorporation so provide, the shares of any preferred or special class may be divided into and issued in series. If the shares of any such class are to be issued in series, then each series shall be so designated as to distinguish the shares thereof from the shares of all other series and classes. Any or all of the series of any such class and the variations in the relative rights and preferences as between different series may be fixed and determined by the articles of incorporation, but all shares of the same class shall be identical except as to the following relative rights and preferences, as to which there may be variations between different series:

(A) The rate of dividend.

(B) Whether shares may be redeemed and, if so, the redemption price and the terms and conditions of redemption.

(C) The amount payable upon shares in event of voluntary and involuntary liquidation.

(D) Sinking fund provisions, if any, for the redemption or purchase of shares.

(E) The terms and conditions, if any, on which shares may be converted.

(F) Voting rights, if any.

If the articles of incorporation shall expressly vest authority in the board of directors, then, to the extent that the articles of incorporation shall not have established series and fixed and determined the variations in the relative rights and preferences as between series, the board of directors shall have authority to divide any or all of such classes into series and, within the limitations set forth in this section and in the articles of incorporation, fix and determine the relative rights and preferences of the shares of any series so established.

In order for the board of directors to establish a series, where authority so to do is contained in the articles of incorporation, the board of directors shall adopt a resolution setting forth the designation of the series and fixing and determining the relative rights and preferences thereof, or so much thereof as shall not be fixed and determined by the articles of incorporation.

Prior to the issue of any shares of a series established by resolution adopted by the board of directors, the corporation shall file in the office of the Secretary of State a statement setting forth:

(a) The name of the corporation.

(b) A copy of the resolution establishing and designating the series, and fixing and determining the relative rights and preferences thereof.

(c) The date of adoption of such resolution.

(d) That such resolution was duly adopted by the board of directors.

Such statement shall be executed in duplicate by the corporation by its president or a vice president and by its secretary or an assistant secretary, and verified by one of the officers signing such statement, and shall be delivered to the Secretary of State. If the Secretary of State finds that such statement conforms to law, he shall, when all franchise taxes and fees have been paid as in this Act prescribed:

(1) Endorse on each of such duplicate originals the word "Filed," and the month, day, and year of the filing thereof.

(2) File one of such duplicate originals in his office.

(3) Return the other duplicate original to the corporation or its representative.

Upon the filing of such statement by the Secretary of State, the resolution establishing and designating the series and fixing and determining the relative rights and preferences thereof shall become effective and shall constitute an amendment of the articles of incorporation.

§ 17. Subscriptions for Shares

A subscription for shares of a corporation to be organized shall be irrevocable for a period of six months, unless otherwise provided by the terms of the subscription agreement or unless all of the subscribers consent to the revocation of such subscription.

Unless otherwise provided in the subscription agreement, subscriptions for shares, whether made before or after the organization of a corporation, shall be paid in full at such time, or in such installments and at such times, as shall be determined by the board of directors. Any call made by the board of directors for payment on subscriptions shall be uniform as to all shares of the same class or as to all shares of the same series, as the case may be. In case of default in the payment of any installment or call when such payment is due, the corporation may proceed to collect the amount due in the same manner as any debt due the corporation. The by-laws may prescribe other penalties for failure to pay installments or calls that may become due, but no penalty working a forfeiture of a subscription, or of the amounts paid thereon, shall be declared as against any subscriber unless the amount due thereon shall remain unpaid for a period of twenty days after written demand has been made therefor. If mailed, such written demand shall be deemed to be made when deposited in the United States mail in a sealed envelope addressed to the subscriber at his last post-office address known to the corporation, with postage thereon prepaid. In the event of the sale of any shares by reason of any forfeiture, the excess of proceeds realized over the amount due and unpaid on such shares shall be paid to the delinquent subscriber or to his legal representative.

§ 18. Consideration for Shares

Shares having a par value may be issued for such consideration expressed in dollars, not less than the par value thereof, as shall be fixed from time to time by the board of directors.

Shares without par value may be issued for such consideration expressed in dollars as may be fixed from time to time by the board of directors unless the articles of incorporation reserve to the shareholders the right to fix the consideration. In the event that such right be reserved as to any shares, the shareholders shall, prior to the issuance of such shares, fix the consideration to be received for such shares, by a vote of the holders of a majority of all shares entitled to vote thereon.

Treasury shares may be disposed of by the corporation for such consideration expressed in dollars as may be fixed from time to time by the board of directors.

That part of the surplus of a corporation which is transferred to stated capital upon the issuance of shares as a share dividend shall be deemed to be the consideration for the issuance of such shares.

In the event of the issuance of shares upon the conversion or exchange of indebtedness or shares, the consideration for the shares so issued shall be (1) the principal sum of, and accrued interest on, the indebtedness so exchanged or converted, or the stated capital then represented by the shares so exchanged or converted, and (2) that part of surplus, if any, transferred to stated capital upon the issuance of shares for the shares so exchanged or converted, and (3) any additional consideration paid to the corporation upon the issuance of shares for the indebtedness or shares so exchanged or converted.

§ 19. Payment for Shares

The consideration for the issuance of shares may be paid, in whole or in part, in money, in other property, tangible or intangible, or in labor or services actually performed for the corporation. When payment of the consideration for which shares are to be issued shall have been received by the corporation, such shares shall be deemed to be fully paid and nonassessable.

Neither promissory notes nor future services shall constitute payment or part payment for the issuance of shares of a corporation.

In the absence of fraud in the transaction, the judgment of the board of directors or the shareholders, as the case may be, as to the value of the consideration received for shares shall be conclusive.

§ 20. Stock Rights and Options

Subject to any provisions in respect thereof set forth in its articles of incorporation, a corporation may create and issue, whether or not in connection with the issuance and sale of any of its shares or other securities, rights or options entitling the holders thereof to purchase from the corporation shares of any class or classes. Such rights or options shall be evidenced in such manner as the board of directors shall approve and, subject to the provisions of the articles of incorporation, shall set forth the terms upon which, the time or times within which and the price or prices at which such shares may be purchased from the corporation upon the exercise of any such right or option. If such rights or options are to be issued to directors, officers or employees as such of the corporation or of any subsidiary thereof, and not to the shareholders generally, their issuance shall be approved by the affirmative vote of the holders of a majority of the shares entitled to vote thereon or shall be authorized by and consistent with a plan approved or ratified by such a vote of shareholders. In the absence of fraud in the transaction, the judgment of the board of directors as to the adequacy of the consideration received for such rights or options shall be conclusive. The price or prices to be received for any shares having a par value, other than treasury shares to be issued upon the exercise of such rights or options, shall not be less than the par value thereof.

§ 21. Determination of Amount of Stated Capital

In case of the issuance by a corporation of shares having a par value, the consideration received therefor shall constitute stated capital to the extent of the par value of such shares, and the excess, if any, of such consideration shall constitute capital surplus.

In case of the issuance by a corporation of shares without par value, the entire consideration received therefor shall constitute stated capital unless the corporation shall determine as provided in this section that only a part thereof shall be stated capital. Within a period of sixty days after the issuance of any shares without par value, the board of directors may allocate to capital surplus any portion of the consideration received for the issuance of such shares. No such allocation shall be made of any portion of the consideration received for shares without par value having a preference in the assets of the corporation in the event of involuntary liquidation except the amount, if any, of such consideration in excess of such preference.

If shares have been or shall be issued by a corporation in merger or consolidation or in acquisition of all or substantially all of the outstanding shares or of the property and assets of another corporation, whether domestic or foreign, any amount that would otherwise constitute capital surplus under the foregoing provisions of this section may instead be allocated to earned surplus by the board of directors of the issuing corporation except that its aggregate earned surplus shall not exceed the sum of the earned surpluses as defined in this Act of the issuing corporation and of all other corporations, domestic or foreign, that were merged or consolidated or of which the shares or assets were acquired.

The stated capital of a corporation may be increased from time to time by resolution of the board of directors directing that all or a part of the surplus of the corporation be transferred to stated capital. The board of directors may direct that the amount of the surplus so transferred shall be deemed to be stated capital in respect of any designated class of shares.

§ 22. Expenses of Organization, Reorganization and Financing

The reasonable charges and expenses of organization or reorganization of a corporation, and the reasonable expenses of and compensation for the sale or underwriting of its shares, may be paid or allowed by such corporation out of the consideration received by it in payment for its shares without thereby rendering such shares not fully paid or assessable.

§ 23. Shares Represented by Certificates and Uncertificated Shares

The shares of a corporation shall be represented by certificates or shall be uncertificated shares. Certificates shall be signed by the chairman or vice-chairman of the board of directors or the president or a vice president and by the treasurer or an assistant treasurer or the secretary or an assistant secretary of the corporation, and may be sealed with the seal of the corporation or a facsimile thereof. Any and all signatures upon a certificate may be a facsimile. In case any officer, transfer agent or registrar who has signed or whose facsimile signature has been placed upon such certificate shall have ceased to be such officer, transfer agent or registrar before such certificate is issued, it may be issued by the corporation with the same effect as if he were such officer, transfer agent or registrar at the date of its issue.

Every certificate representing shares issued by a corporation which is authorized to issue shares of more than one class shall set forth upon the face or back of the certificate, or shall state that the corporation will furnish to any shareholder upon request and without charge, a full statement of the designations, preferences, limitations, and relative rights of the shares of each class authorized to be issued, and if the corporation is authorized to issue any preferred or special class in series, the variations in the relative rights and preferences between the shares of each such series so far as the same have been fixed and determined and the authority of the board of directors to fix and determine the relative rights and preferences of subsequent series.

Each certificate representing shares shall state upon the face thereof:

(a) That the corporation is organized under the laws of this State.

(b) The name of the person to whom issued.

(c) The number and class of shares, and the designation of the series, if any, which such certificate represents.

(d) The par value of each share represented by such certificate, or a statement that the shares are without par value.

No certificate shall be issued for any share until such share is fully paid.

Unless otherwise provided by the articles of incorporation or by-laws, the board of directors of a corporation may provide by resolution that some or all of any or all classes and series of its shares shall be uncertificated shares, provided that such resolution shall not apply to shares represented by a certificate until such certificate is surrendered to the corporation. Within a reasonable time after the issuance or transfer of uncertificated shares, the corporation shall send to the registered owner thereof a written notice containing the information required to be set forth or stated on certificates pursuant to the second and third paragraphs of this section. Except as otherwise expressly provided by law, the rights and obligations of the holders of uncertificated shares and the rights and obligations of the holders of certificates representing shares of the same class and series shall be identical.

§ 24. Fractional Shares

A corporation may (1) issue fractions of a share, either represented by a certificate or uncertificated, (2) arrange for the disposition of fractional interests by those entitled thereto, (3) pay in cash the fair value of fractions of a share as of the time when those entitled to receive such fractions are determined, or (4) issue scrip in registered or bearer form which shall entitle the holder to receive a certificate for a full share or an uncertificated full share upon the surrender of such scrip aggregating a full share. A certificate for a fractional share or an uncertificated fractional share shall, but scrip shall not unless otherwise provided therein, entitle the holder to exercise voting rights, to receive dividends thereon, and to participate in any of the assets of the corporation in the event of liquidation. The board of directors may cause scrip to be issued subject to the condition that it shall become void if not exchanged for certificates representing full shares or uncertificated full shares before a specified date, or subject to the condition that the shares for which scrip is exchangeable may be sold by the corporation and the proceeds thereof distributed to the holders of scrip, or subject to any other conditions which the board of directors may deem advisable.

§ 25. Liability of Subscribers and Shareholders

A holder of or subscriber to shares of a corporation shall be under no obligation to the corporation or its creditors with respect to such shares other than the obligation to pay to the corporation the full consideration for which such shares were issued or to be issued.

Any person becoming an assignee or transferee of shares or of a subscription for shares in good faith and without knowledge or notice that the full consideration therefor has not been paid shall not be personally liable to the corporation or its creditors for any unpaid portion of such consideration.

An executor, administrator, conservator, guardian, trustee, assignee for the benefit of creditors, or receiver shall not be personally liable to the corporation as a holder of or subscriber to shares of a corporation but the estate and funds in his hands shall be so liable.

No pledgee or other holder of shares as collateral security shall be personally liable as a shareholder.

§ 26. Shareholders' Preemptive Rights

The shareholders of a corporation shall have no preemptive right to acquire unissued or treasury shares of the corporation, or securities of the corporation convertible into or carrying a right to subscribe to or acquire shares, except to the extent, if any, that such right is provided in the articles of incorporation.

§ 26A. Shareholders' Preemptive Rights [Alternative]

Except to the extent limited or denied by this section or by the articles of incorporation, shareholders shall have a preemptive right to acquire unissued or treasury shares or securities convertible into such shares or carrying a right to subscribe to or acquire shares.

Unless otherwise provided in the articles of incorporation,

(a) No preemptive right shall exist

(1) to acquire any shares issued to directors, officers or employees pursuant to approval by the affirmative vote of the holders of a majority of the shares entitled to vote thereon or when authorized by and consistent with a plan theretofore approved by such a vote of shareholders; or

(2) to acquire any shares sold otherwise than for cash.

(b) Holders of shares of any class that is preferred or limited as to dividends or assets shall not be entitled to any preemptive right.

(c) Holders of shares of common stock shall not be entitled to any preemptive right to shares of any class that is preferred or limited as to dividends or assets or to any obligations, unless convertible into shares of common stock or carrying a right to subscribe to or acquire shares of common stock.

(d) Holders of common stock without voting power shall have no preemptive right to shares of common stock with voting power.

(e) The preemptive right shall be only an opportunity to acquire shares or other securities under such terms and conditions as the board of directors may fix for the purpose of providing a fair and reasonable opportunity for the exercise of such right.

§ 27. By-Laws

The initial by-laws of a corporation shall be adopted by its board of directors. The power to alter, amend or repeal the by-laws or adopt new by-laws, subject to repeal or change by action of the shareholders, shall be vested in the board of directors unless reserved to the shareholders by the articles of incorporation. The by-laws may contain any provisions for the regulation and management of the affairs of the corporation not inconsistent with law or the articles of incorporation.

§ 27A. By-Laws and Other Powers in Emergency [Optional]

The board of directors of any corporation may adopt emergency by-laws, subject to repeal or change by action of the shareholders, which shall, notwithstanding any different provision elsewhere in this Act or in the articles of incorporation or by-laws, be operative during any emergency in the conduct of the business of the corporation resulting from an attack on the United States or any nuclear or atomic disaster. The emergency by-laws may make any provision that may be practical and necessary for the circumstances of the emergency, including provisions that:

(a) A meeting of the board of directors may be called by any officer or director in such manner and under such conditions as shall be prescribed in the emergency by-laws;

(b) The director or directors in attendance at the meeting, or any greater number fixed by the emergency by-laws, shall constitute a quorum; and

(c) The officers or other persons designated on a list approved by the board of directors before the emergency, all in such order of priority and subject to such conditions, and for such period of time (not longer than reasonably necessary after the termination of the emergency) as may be provided in the emergency by-laws or in the resolution approving the list shall, to the extent required to provide a quorum at any meeting of the board of directors, be deemed directors for such meeting.

The board of directors, either before or during any such emergency, may provide, and from time to time modify, lines of succession in the event that during such an emergency any or all officers or agents of the corporation shall for any reason be rendered incapable of discharging their duties.

The board of directors, either before or during any such emergency, may, effective in the emergency, change the head office or designate several alternative head offices or regional offices, or authorize the officers so to do.

To the extent not inconsistent with any emergency by-laws so adopted, the by-laws of the corporation shall remain in effect during any such emergency and upon its termination the emergency by-laws shall cease to be operative.

Unless otherwise provided in emergency by-laws, notice of any meeting of the board of directors during any such emergency may be given only to such of the directors as it may be feasible to reach at the time and by such means as may be feasible at the time, including publication or radio.

To the extent required to constitute a quorum at any meeting of the board of directors during any such emergency, the officers of the corporation who are present shall, unless otherwise provided in emergency by-laws, be deemed, in order of rank and within the same rank in order of seniority, directors for such meeting.

No officer, director or employee acting in accordance with any emergency by-laws shall be liable except for willful misconduct. No officer, director or employee shall be liable for any action taken by him in good faith in such an emergency in furtherance of the ordinary business affairs of the corporation even though not authorized by the by-laws then in effect.

§ 28. Meetings of Shareholders

Meetings of shareholders may be held at such place within or without this State as may be stated in or fixed in accordance with the by-laws. If no other place is stated or so fixed, meetings shall be held at the registered office of the corporation.

An annual meeting of the shareholders shall be held at such time as may be stated in or fixed in accordance with the by-laws. If the annual meeting is not held within any thirteen-month period the

Court of . . . . may, on the application of any shareholder, summarily order a meeting to be held.

Special meetings of the shareholders may be called by the board of directors, the holders of not less than one-tenth of all the shares entitled to vote at the meeting, or such other persons as may be authorized in the articles of incorporation or the by-laws.

§ 29. Notice of Shareholders' Meetings

Written notice stating the place, day and hour of the meeting and, in case of a special meeting, the purpose or purposes for which the meeting is called, shall be delivered not less than ten nor more than fifty days before the date of the meeting, either personally or by mail, by or at the direction of the president, the secretary, or the officer or persons calling the meeting, to each shareholder of record entitled to vote at such meeting. If mailed, such notice shall be deemed to be delivered when deposited in the United States mail addressed to the shareholder at his address as it appears on the stock transfer books of the corporation, with postage thereon prepaid.

§ 30. Closing of Transfer Books and Fixing Record Date

For the purpose of determining shareholders entitled to notice of or to vote at any meeting of shareholders or any adjournment thereof, or entitled to receive payment of any dividend, or in order to make a determination of shareholders for any other proper purpose, the board of directors of a corporation may provide that the stock transfer books shall be closed for a stated period but not to exceed, in any case, fifty days. If the stock transfer books shall be closed for the purpose of determining shareholders entitled to notice of or to vote at a meeting of shareholders, such books shall be closed for at least ten days immediately preceding such meeting. In lieu of closing the stock transfer books, the by-laws, or in the absence of an applicable by-law the board of directors, may fix in advance a date as the record date for any such determination of shareholders, such date in any case to be not more than fifty days and, in case of a meeting of shareholders, not less than ten days prior to the date on which the particular action, requiring such determination of shareholders, is to be taken. If the stock transfer books are not closed and no record date is fixed for the determination of shareholders entitled to notice of or to vote at a meeting of shareholders, or shareholders entitled to receive payment of a dividend, the date on which notice of the meeting is mailed or the date on which the resolution of the board of directors declaring such dividend is adopted, as the case may be, shall be the record date for such determination of shareholders. When a determination of shareholders entitled to vote at any meeting of shareholders has been made as provided in this section, such determination shall apply to any adjournment thereof.

§ 31. Voting Record

The officer or agent having charge of the stock transfer books for shares of a corporation shall make a complete record of the shareholders entitled to vote at such meeting or any adjournment thereof, arranged in alphabetical order, with the address of and the number of shares held by each. Such record shall be produced and kept open at the time and place of the meeting and shall be subject to the inspection of any shareholder during the whole time of the meeting for the purposes thereof.

Failure to comply with the requirements of this section shall not affect the validity of any action taken at such meeting.

An officer or agent having charge of the stock transfer books who shall fail to prepare the record of shareholders, or produce and keep it open for inspection at the meeting, as provided in this section, shall be liable to any shareholder suffering damage on account of such failure, to the extent of such damage.

§ 32. Quorum of Shareholders

Unless otherwise provided in the articles of incorporation, a majority of the shares entitled to vote, represented in person or by proxy, shall constitute a quorum at a meeting of shareholders, but in no event shall a quorum consist of less than one-third of the shares entitled to vote at the meeting. If a quorum is present, the affirmative vote of the majority of the shares represented at the meeting and entitled to vote on the subject matter shall be the act of the shareholders, unless the vote of a greater number or voting by classes is required by this Act or the articles of incorporation or by-laws.

§ 33. Voting of Shares

Each outstanding share, regardless of class, shall be entitled to one vote on each matter submitted to a vote at a meeting of shareholders, except as may be otherwise provided in the articles of incorporation. If the articles of incorporation provide for more or less than one vote for any share, on any matter, every reference in this Act to a majority or other proportion of shares shall refer to such a majority or other proportion of votes entitled to be cast.

Neither treasury shares, nor shares held by another corporation if a majority of the shares entitled to vote for the election of directors of such other corporation is held by the corporation, shall be voted at any meeting or counted in determining the total number of outstanding shares at any given time.

A shareholder may vote either in person or by proxy executed in writing by the shareholder or by his duly authorized attorney-in-fact. No proxy shall be valid after eleven months from the date of its execution, unless otherwise provided in the proxy.

[Either of the following prefatory phrases may be inserted here: "The articles of incorporation may provide that" or "Unless the articles of incorporation otherwise provide"] . . . at each election for directors every shareholder entitled to vote at such election shall have the right to vote, in person or by proxy, the number of shares owned by him for as many persons as there are directors to be elected and for whose election he has a right to vote, or to cumulate his votes by giving one candidate as many votes as the number of such directors multiplied by the number of his shares shall equal, or by distributing such votes on the same principle among any number of such candidates.

Shares standing in the name of another corporation, domestic or foreign, may be voted by such officer, agent or proxy as the by-laws of such other corporation may prescribe, or, in the absence of such provision, as the board of directors of such other corporation may determine.

Shares held by an administrator, executor, guardian or conservator may be voted by him, either in person or by proxy, without a transfer of such shares into his name. Shares standing in the name of a trustee may be voted by him, either in person or by proxy, but no trustee shall be entitled to vote shares held by him without a transfer of such shares into his name.

Shares standing in the name of a receiver may be voted by such receiver, and shares held by or under the control of a receiver may be voted by such receiver without the transfer thereof into his name if authority so to do be contained in an appropriate order of the court by which such receiver was appointed.

A shareholder whose shares are pledged shall be entitled to vote such shares until the shares have been transferred into the name of the pledgee, and thereafter the pledgee shall be entitled to vote the shares so transferred.

On and after the date on which written notice of redemption of redeemable shares has been mailed to the holders thereof and a sum sufficient to redeem such shares has been deposited with a bank or trust company with irrevocable instruction and authority to pay the redemption price to the holders thereof upon surrender of certificates therefor, such shares shall not be entitled to vote on any matter and shall not be deemed to be outstanding shares.

§ 34. Voting Trusts and Agreements Among Shareholders

Any number of shareholders of a corporation may create a voting trust for the purpose of conferring upon a trustee or trustees the right to vote or otherwise represent their shares, for a period of not to exceed ten years, by entering into a written voting trust agreement specifying the terms and conditions of the voting trust, by depositing a counterpart of the agreement with the corporation at its registered office, and by transferring their shares to such trustee or trustees for the purposes of the agreement. Such trustee or trustees shall keep a record of the holders of voting trust certificates evidencing a beneficial interest in the voting trust, giving the names and addresses of all such holders and the number and class of the shares in respect of which the voting trust certificates held by each are issued, and shall deposit a copy of such record with the corporation at its registered office. The counterpart of the voting trust agreement and the copy of such record so deposited with the corporation shall be subject to the same right of examination by a shareholder of the corporation, in person or by agent or attorney, as are the books and records of the corporation, and such counterpart and such copy of such record shall be subject to examination by any holder of record of voting trust certificates, either in person or by agent or attorney, at any reasonable time for any proper purpose.

Agreements among shareholders regarding the voting of their shares shall be valid and enforceable in accordance with their terms. Such agreements shall not be subject to the provisions of this section regarding voting trusts.

§ 35. Board of Directors

All corporate powers shall be exercised by or under authority of, and the business and affairs of a corporation shall be managed under the direction of, a board of directors except as may be otherwise provided in this Act or the articles of incorporation. If any such provision is made in the articles of incorporation, the powers and duties conferred or imposed upon the board of directors by this Act shall be exercised or performed to such extent and by such person or persons as shall be provided in the articles of incorporation. Directors need not be residents of this State or shareholders of the corporation unless the articles of incorporation or by-laws so require. The articles of incorporation or by-laws may prescribe other qualifications for directors. The board of directors shall have authority to fix the compensation of directors unless otherwise provided in the articles of incorporation.

A director shall perform his duties as a director, including his duties as a member of any committee of the board upon which he may serve, in good faith, in a manner he reasonably believes to be in the best interests of the corporation, and with such care as an ordinarily prudent person in a like position would use under similar circumstances. In performing his duties, a director shall be entitled to rely on information, opinions, reports or statements, including financial statements and other financial data, in each case prepared or presented by:

(a) one or more officers or employees of the corporation whom the director reasonably believes to be reliable and competent in the matters presented,

(b) counsel, public accountants or other persons as to matters which the director reasonably believes to be within such person's professional or expert competence, or

(c) a committee of the board upon which he does not serve, duly designated in accordance with a provision of the articles of incorporation or the by-laws, as to matters within its designated authority, which committee the director reasonably believes to merit confidence, but he shall not be considered to be acting in good faith if he has knowledge concerning the matter in question that would cause such reliance to be unwarranted. A person who so performs his duties shall have no liability by reason of being or having been a director of the corporation.

A director of a corporation who is present at a meeting of its board of directors at which action on any corporate matter is taken shall be presumed to have assented to the action taken unless his dissent shall be entered in the minutes of the meeting or unless he shall file his written dissent to such action with the secretary of the meeting before the adjournment thereof or shall forward such dissent by registered mail to the secretary of the corporation immediately after the adjournment of the meeting. Such right to dissent shall not apply to a director who voted in favor of such action.

§ 36. Number and Election of Directors

The board of directors of a corporation shall consist of one or more members. The number of directors shall be fixed by, or in the manner provided in, the articles of incorporation or the by-laws, except as to the number constituting the initial board of directors, which number shall be fixed by the articles of incorporation. The number of directors may be increased or decreased from time to time by amendment to, or in the manner provided in, the articles of incorporation or the by-laws, but no decrease shall have the effect of shortening the term of any incumbent director. In the absence of a by-law providing for the number of directors, the number shall be the same as that provided for in the articles of incorporation. The names and addresses of the members of the first board of directors shall be stated in the articles of incorporation. Such persons shall hold office until the first annual meeting of shareholders, and until their successors shall have been elected and qualified. At the first annual meeting of shareholders and at each annual meeting thereafter the shareholders shall elect directors to hold office until the next succeeding annual meeting, except in case of the classification of directors as permitted by this Act. Each director shall hold office for the term for which he is elected and until his successor shall have been elected and qualified.

§ 37. Classification of Directors

When the board of directors shall consist of nine or more members, in lieu of electing the whole number of directors annually, the articles of incorporation may provide that the directors be divided into either two or three classes, each class to be as nearly equal in number as possible, the term of office of directors of the first class to expire at the first annual meeting of shareholders after their election, that of the second class to expire at the second annual meeting after their election, and that of the third class, if any, to expire at the third annual meeting after their election. At each annual meeting after such classification the number of directors equal to the number of the class whose term expires at the time of such meeting shall be elected to hold office until the second succeeding annual meeting, if there be two classes, or until the third succeeding annual meeting, if there be three classes. No classification of directors shall be effective prior to the first annual meeting of shareholders.

§ 38. Vacancies

Any vacancy occurring in the board of directors may be filled by the affirmative vote of a majority of the remaining directors though less than a quorum of the board of directors. A director elected to fill a vacancy shall be elected for the unexpired term of his predecessor in office. Any directorship to be filled by reason of an increase in the number of directors may be filled by the board of directors for a term of office continuing only until the next election of directors by the shareholders.

§ 39. Removal of Directors

At a meeting of shareholders called expressly for that purpose, directors may be removed in the manner provided in this section. Any director or the entire board of directors may be removed, with or without cause, by a vote of the holders of a majority of the shares then entitled to vote at an election of directors.

In the case of a corporation having cumulative voting, if less than the entire board is to be removed, no one of the directors may be removed if the votes cast against his removal would be sufficient to elect him if then cumulatively voted at an election of the entire board of directors, or, if there be classes of directors, at an election of the class of directors of which he is a part.

Whenever the holders of the shares of any class are entitled to elect one or more directors by the provisions of the articles of incorporation, the provisions of this section shall apply, in respect to the removal of a director or directors so elected, to the vote of the holders of the outstanding shares of that class and not to the vote of the outstanding shares as a whole.

§ 40. Quorum of Directors

A majority of the number of directors fixed by or in the manner provided in the by-laws or in the absence of a by-law fixing or providing for the number of directors, then of the number stated in the articles of incorporation, shall constitute a quorum for the transaction of business unless a greater number is required by the articles of incorporation or the by-laws. The act of the majority of the directors present at a meeting at which a quorum is present shall be the act of the board of directors, unless the act of a greater number is required by the articles of incorporation or the by-laws.

§ 41. Director Conflicts of Interest

No contract or other transaction between a corporation and one or more of its directors or any other corporation, firm, association or entity in which one or more of its directors are directors or officers or are financially interested, shall be either void or voidable because of such relationship or interest or because such director or directors are present at the meeting of the board of directors or a committee thereof which authorizes, approves or ratifies such contract or transaction or because his or their votes are counted for such purpose, if:

(a) the fact of such relationship or interest is disclosed or known to the board of directors or committee which authorizes, approves or ratifies the contract or transaction by a vote or consent sufficient for the purpose without counting the votes or consents of such interested directors; or

(b) the fact of such relationship or interest is disclosed or known to the shareholders entitled to vote and they authorize, approve or ratify such contract or transaction by vote or written consent; or

(c) the contract or transaction is fair and reasonable to the corporation.

Common or interested directors may be counted in determining the presence of a quorum at a meeting of the board of directors or a committee thereof which authorizes, approves or ratifies such contract or transaction.

§ 42. Executive and Other Committees

If the articles of incorporation or the by-laws so provide, the board of directors, by resolution adopted by a majority of the full board of directors, may designate from among its members an executive committee and one or more other committees each of which, to the extent provided in such resolution or in the articles of incorporation or the by-laws of the corporation, shall have and may exercise all the authority of the board of directors, except that no such committee shall have authority to (i) declare dividends or distributions, (ii) approve or recommend to shareholders actions or proposals required by this Act to be approved by shareholders, (iii) designate candidates for the office of director, for purposes of proxy solicitation or otherwise, or fill vacancies on the board of directors or any committee thereof, (iv) amend the by-laws, (v) approve a plan of merger not requiring shareholder approval, (vi) reduce earned or capital surplus, (vii) authorize or approve the reacquisition of shares unless pursuant to a general formula or method specified by the board of directors, or (viii) authorize or approve the issuance or sale of, or any contract to issue or sell, shares or designate the terms of a series of a class of shares, provided that the board of directors, having acted regarding general authorization for the issuance or sale of shares, or any contract therefor, and, in the case of a series, the designation thereof, may, pursuant to a general formula or method specified by the board by resolution or by adoption of a stock option or other plan, authorize a committee to fix the terms of any contract for the sale of the shares and to fix the terms upon which such shares may be issued or sold, including, without limitation, the price, the dividend rate, provisions for redemption, sinking fund, conversion, voting or preferential rights, and provisions for other features of a class of shares, or a series of a class of shares, with full power in such committee to adopt any final resolution setting forth all the terms thereof and to authorize the statement of the terms of a series for filing with the Secretary of State under this Act.

Neither the designation of any such committee, the delegation thereto of authority, nor action by such committee pursuant to such authority shall alone constitute compliance by any member of the board of directors, not a member of the committee in question, with his responsibility to act in good faith, in a manner he reasonably believes to be in the best interests of the corporation, and with such care as an ordinarily prudent person in a like position would use under similar circumstances.

§ 43. Place and Notice of Directors' Meetings; Committee Meetings

Meetings of the board of directors, regular or special, may be held either within or without this State.

Regular meetings of the board of directors or any committee designated thereby may be held with or without notice as prescribed in the by-laws. Special meetings of the board of directors or any committee designated thereby shall be held upon such notice as is prescribed in the by-laws. Attendance of a director at a meeting shall constitute a waiver of notice of such meeting, except where a director attends a meeting for the express purpose of objecting to the transaction of any business because the meeting is not lawfully called or convened. Neither the business to be transacted at, nor the purpose of, any regular or special meeting of the board of directors or any committee designated thereby need be specified in the notice or waiver of notice of such meeting unless required by the by-laws.

Except as may be otherwise restricted by the articles of incorporation or by-laws, members of the board of directors or any committee designated thereby may participate in a meeting of such board or committee by means of a conference telephone or similar communications equipment by means of which all persons participating in the meeting can hear each other at the same time and participation by such means shall constitute presence in person at a meeting.

§ 44. Action by Directors Without a Meeting

Unless otherwise provided by the articles of incorporation or by-laws, any action required by this Act to be taken at a meeting of the directors of a corporation, or any action which may be taken at a meeting of the directors or of a committee, may be taken without a meeting if a consent in writing, setting forth the action so taken, shall be signed by all of the directors, or all of the members of the committee, as the case may be. Such consent shall have the same effect as a unanimous vote.

§ 45. Dividends

The board of directors of a corporation may, from time to time, declare and the corporation may pay dividends in cash, property, or its own shares, except when the corporation is insolvent or when the payment thereof would render the corporation insolvent or when the declaration or payment thereof would be contrary to any restriction contained in the articles of incorporation, subject to the following provisions:

(a) Dividends may be declared and paid in cash or property only out of the unreserved and unrestricted earned surplus of the corporation, except as otherwise provided in this section.

[Alternative] (a) Dividends may be declared and paid in cash or property only out of the unreserved and unrestricted earned surplus of the corporation, or out of the unreserved and unrestricted net earnings of the current fiscal year and the next preceding fiscal year taken as a single period, except as otherwise provided in this section.

(b) If the articles of incorporation of a corporation engaged in the business of exploiting natural resources so provide, dividends may be declared and paid in cash out of the depletion reserves, but each such dividend shall be identified as a distribution of such reserves and the amount per share paid from such reserves shall be disclosed to the shareholders receiving the same concurrently with the distribution thereof.

(c) Dividends may be declared and paid in its own treasury shares.

(d) Dividends may be declared and paid in its own authorized but unissued shares out of any unreserved and unrestricted surplus of the corporation upon the following conditions:

(1) If a dividend is payable in its own shares having a par value, such shares shall be issued at not less than the par value thereof and there shall be transferred to stated capital at the time such dividend is paid an amount of surplus equal to the aggregate par value of the shares to be issued as a dividend.

(2) If a dividend is payable in its own shares without par value, such shares shall be issued at such stated value as shall be fixed by the board of directors by resolution adopted at the time such dividend is declared, and there shall be transferred to stated capital at the time such dividend is paid an amount of surplus equal to the aggregate stated value so fixed in respect of such shares; and the amount per share so transferred to stated capital shall be disclosed to the shareholders receiving such dividend concurrently with the payment thereof.

(e) No dividend payable in shares of any class shall be paid to the holders of shares of any other class unless the articles of incorporation so provide or such payment is authorized by the affirmative vote or the written consent of the holders of at least a majority of the outstanding shares of the class in which the payment is to be made.

A split-up or division of the issued shares of any class into a greater number of shares of the same class without increasing the stated capital of the corporation shall not be construed to be a share dividend within the meaning of this section.

§ 46. Distributions from Capital Surplus

The board of directors of a corporation may, from time to time, distribute to its shareholders out of capital surplus of the corporation a portion of its assets, in cash or property, subject to the following provisions:

(a) No such distribution shall be made at a time when the corporation is insolvent or when such distribution would render the corporation insolvent.

(b) No such distribution shall be made unless the articles of incorporation so provide or such distribution is authorized by the affirmative vote of the holders of a majority of the outstanding shares of each class whether or not entitled to vote thereon by the provisions of the articles of incorporation of the corporation.

(c) No such distribution shall be made to the holders of any class of shares unless all cumulative dividends accrued on all preferred or special classes of shares entitled to preferential dividends shall have been fully paid.

(d) No such distribution shall be made to the holders of any class of shares which would reduce the remaining net assets of the corporation below the aggregate preferential amount payable in event of involuntary liquidation to the holders of shares having preferential rights to the assets of the corporation in the event of liquidation.

(e) Each such distribution, when made, shall be identified as a distribution from capital surplus and the amount per share disclosed to the shareholders receiving the same concurrently with the distribution thereof.

The board of directors of a corporation may also, from time to time, distribute to the holders of its outstanding shares having a cumulative preferential right to receive dividends, in discharge of their cumulative dividend rights, dividends payable in cash out of the capital surplus of the corporation, if at the time the corporation has no earned surplus and is not insolvent and would not thereby be rendered insolvent. Each such distribution when made, shall be identified as a payment of cumulative dividends out of capital surplus.

§ 47. Loans to Employees and Directors

A corporation shall not lend money to or use its credit to assist its directors without authorization in the particular case by its shareholders, but may lend money to and use its credit to assist any employee of the corporation or of a subsidiary, including any such employee who is a director of the corporation, if the board of directors decides that such loan or assistance may benefit the corporation.

§ 48. Liability of Directors in Certain Cases

In addition to any other liabilities, a director shall be liable in the following circumstances unless he complies with the standard provided in this Act for the performance of the duties of directors:

(a) A director who votes for or assents to the declaration of any dividend or other distribution of the assets of a corporation to its shareholders contrary to the provisions of this Act or contrary to any restrictions contained in the articles of incorporation, shall be liable to the corporation, jointly and severally with all other directors so voting or assenting, for the amount of such dividend which is paid or the value of such assets which are distributed in excess of the amount of such dividend or distribution which could have been paid or distributed without a violation of the provisions of this Act or the restrictions in the articles of incorporation.

(b) A director who votes for or assents to the purchase of the corporation's own shares contrary to the provisions of this Act shall be liable to the corporation, jointly and severally with all other directors so voting or assenting, for the amount of consideration paid for such shares which is in excess of the maximum amount which could have been paid therefor without a violation of the provisions of this Act.

(c) A director who votes for or assents to any distribution of assets of a corporation to its shareholders during the liquidation of the corporation without the payment and discharge of, or making adequate provision for, all known debts, obligations, and liabilities of the corporation shall be liable to the corporation, jointly and severally with all other directors so voting or assenting, for the value of such assets which are distributed, to the extent that such debts, obligations and liabilities of the corporation are not thereafter paid and discharged.

Any director against whom a claim shall be asserted under or pursuant to this section for the payment of a dividend or other distribution of assets of a corporation and who shall be held liable thereon, shall be entitled to contribution from the shareholders who accepted or received any such dividend or assets, knowing such dividend or distribution to have been made in violation of this Act, in proportion to the amounts received by them.

Any director against whom a claim shall be asserted under or pursuant to this section shall be entitled to contribution from the other directors who voted for or assented to the action upon which the claim is asserted.

§ 49. Provisions Relating to Actions by Shareholders

No action shall be brought in this State by a shareholder in the right of a domestic or foreign corporation unless the plaintiff was a holder of record of shares or of voting trust certificates therefor at the time of the transaction of which he complains, or his shares or voting trust certificates thereafter devolved upon him by operation of law from a person who was a holder of record at such time.

In any action hereafter instituted in the right of any domestic or foreign corporation by the holder or holders of record of shares of such corporation or of voting trust certificates therefor, the court having jurisdiction, upon final judgment and a finding that the action was brought without reasonable cause, may require the plaintiff or plaintiffs to pay to the parties named as defendant the reasonable expenses, including fees of attorneys, incurred by them in the defense of such action.

In any action now pending or hereafter instituted or maintained in the right of any domestic or foreign corporation by the holder or holders of record of less than five per cent of the outstanding shares of any class of such corporation or of voting trust certificates therefor, unless the shares or voting trust certificates so held have a market value in excess of twenty-five thousand dollars, the corporation in whose right such action is brought shall be entitled at any time before final judgment to require the plaintiff or plaintiffs to give security for the reasonable expenses, including fees of attorneys, that may be incurred by it in connection with such action or may be incurred by other parties named as defendant for which it may become legally liable. Market value shall be determined as of the date that the plaintiff institutes the action or, in the case of an intervenor, as of the date that he becomes a party to the action. The amount of such security may from time to time be increased or decreased, in the discretion of the court, upon showing that the security provided has or may become inadequate or is excessive. The corporation shall have recourse to such security in such amount as the court having jurisdiction shall determine upon the termination of such action, whether or not the court finds the action was brought without reasonable cause.

§ 50. Officers

The officers of a corporation shall consist of a president, one or more vice presidents as may be prescribed by the by-laws, a secretary, and a treasurer, each of whom shall be elected by the board of directors at such time and in such manner as may be prescribed by the by-laws. Such other officers and assistant officers and agents as may be deemed necessary may be elected or appointed by the board of directors or chosen in such other manner as may be prescribed by the by-laws. Any two or more offices may be held by the same person, except the offices of president and secretary.

All officers and agents of the corporation, as between themselves and the corporation, shall have such authority and perform such duties in the management of the corporation as may be provided in the by-laws, or as may be determined by resolution of the board of directors not inconsistent with the by-laws.

§ 51. Removal of Officers

Any officer or agent may be removed by the board of directors whenever in its judgment the best interests of the corporation will be served thereby, but such removal shall be without prejudice to the contract rights, if any, of the person so removed. Election or appointment of an officer or agent shall not of itself create contract rights.

§ 52. Books and Records; Financial Reports to Shareholders; Examination of Records

Each corporation shall keep correct and complete books and records of account and shall keep minutes of the proceedings of its shareholders and board of directors and shall keep at its registered office or principal place of business, or at the office of its transfer agent or registrar, a record of its shareholders, giving the names and addresses of all shareholders and the number and class of the shares held by each. Any books, records and minutes may be in written form or in any other form capable of being converted into written form within a reasonable time.

Any person who shall have been a holder of record of shares or of voting trust certificates therefor at least six months immediately preceding his demand or shall be the holder of record of, or the holder of record of voting trust certificates for, at least five per cent of all the outstanding shares of the corporation, upon written demand stating the purpose thereof, shall have the right to examine, in person, or by agent or attorney, at any reasonable time or times, for any proper purpose its relevant books and records of account, minutes, and record of shareholders and to make extracts therefrom.

Any officer or agent who, or a corporation which, shall refuse to allow any such shareholder or holder of voting trust certificates, or his agent or attorney, so to examine and make extracts from its books and records of account, minutes, and record of shareholders, for any proper purpose, shall be liable to such shareholder or holder of voting trust certificates in a penalty of ten per cent of the value of the shares owned by such shareholder, or in respect of which such voting trust certificates are issued, in addition to any other damages or remedy afforded him by law. It shall be a defense to any action for penalties under this section that the person suing therefor has within two years sold or offered for sale any list of shareholders or of holders of voting trust certificates for shares of such corporation or any other corporation or has aided or abetted any person in procuring any list of shareholders or of holders of voting trust certificates for any such purpose, or has improperly used any information secured through any prior examination of the books and records of account, or minutes, or record of shareholders or of holders of voting trust certificates for shares of such corporation or any other corporation, or was not acting in good faith or for a proper purpose in making his demand.

Nothing herein contained shall impair the power of any court of competent jurisdiction, upon proof by a shareholder or holder of voting trust certificates of proper purpose, irrespective of the period of time during which such shareholder or holder of voting trust certificates shall have been a shareholder of record or a holder of record of voting trust certificates, and irrespective of the number of shares held by him or represented by voting trust certificates held by him, to compel the production for examination by such shareholder or holder of voting trust certificates of the books and records of account, minutes and record of shareholders of a corporation.

Each corporation shall furnish to its shareholders annual financial statements, including at least a balance sheet as of the end of each fiscal year and a statement of income for such fiscal year, which shall be prepared on the basis of generally accepted accounting principles, if the corporation prepares financial statements for such fiscal year on that basis for any purpose, and may be consolidated statements of the corporation and one or more of its subsidiaries. The financial statements shall be mailed by the corporation to each of its shareholders within 120 days after the close of each fiscal year and, after such mailing and upon written request, shall be mailed by the corporation to any shareholder (or holder of a voting trust certificate for its shares) to whom a copy of the most recent annual financial statements has not previously been mailed. In the case of statements audited by a public accountant, each copy shall be accompanied by a report setting forth his opinion thereon; in other cases, each copy shall be accompanied by a statement of the president or the person in charge of the corporation's financial accounting records (1) stating his reasonable belief as to whether or not the financial statements were prepared in accordance with generally accepted accounting principles and, if not, describing the basis of presentation, and (2) describing any respects in which the financial statements were not prepared on a basis consistent with those prepared for the previous year.

§ 53. Incorporators

One or more persons, or a domestic or foreign corporation, may act as incorporator or incorporators of a corporation by signing and delivering in duplicate to the Secretary of State articles of incorporation for such corporation.

§ 54. Articles of Incorporation

The articles of incorporation shall set forth:

(a) The name of the corporation.

(b) The period of duration, which may be perpetual.

(c) The purpose or purposes for which the corporation is organized which may be stated to be, or to include, the transaction of any or all lawful business for which corporations may be incorporated under this Act.

(d) The aggregate number of shares which the corporation shall have authority to issue; if such shares are to consist of one class only, the par value of each of such shares, or a statement that all of such shares are without par value; or, if such shares are to be divided into classes, the number of shares of each class, and a statement of the par value of the shares of each such class or that such shares are to be without par value.

(e) If the shares are to be divided into classes, the designation of each class and a statement of the preferences, limitations and relative rights in respect of the shares of each class.

(f) If the corporation is to issue the shares of any preferred or special class in series, then the designation of each series and a statement of the variations in the relative rights and preferences as between series insofar as the same are to be fixed in the articles of incorporation, and a statement of any authority to be vested in the board of directors to establish series and fix and determine the variations in the relative rights and preferences as between series.

(g) If any preemptive right is to be granted to shareholders, the provisions therefor.

(h) Any provision, not inconsistent with law, which the incorporators elect to set forth in the articles of incorporation for the regulation of the internal affairs of the corporation, including any provision restricting the transfer of shares and any provision which under this Act is required or permitted to be set forth in the by-laws.

(i) The address of its initial registered office, and the name of its initial registered agent at such address.

(j) The number of directors constituting the initial board of directors and the names and addresses of the persons who are to serve as directors until the first annual meeting of shareholders or until their successors be elected and qualify.

(k) The name and address of each incorporator.

It shall not be necessary to set forth in the articles of incorporation any of the corporate powers enumerated in this Act.

§ 55. Filing of Articles of Incorporation

Duplicate originals of the articles of incorporation shall be delivered to the Secretary of State. If the Secretary of State finds that the articles of incorporation conform to law, he shall, when all fees have been paid as in this Act prescribed:

(a) Endorse on each of such duplicate originals the word "Filed," and the month, day and year of the filing thereof.

(b) File one of such duplicate originals in his office.

(c) Issue a certificate of incorporation to which he shall affix the other duplicate original.

The certificate of incorporation, together with the duplicate original of the articles of incorporation affixed thereto by the Secretary of State, shall be returned to the incorporators or their representative.

§ 56. Effect of Issuance of Certificate of Incorporation

Upon the issuance of the certificate of incorporation, the corporate existence shall begin, and such certificate of incorporation shall be conclusive evidence that all conditions precedent required to be performed by the incorporators have been complied with and that the corporation has been incorporated under this Act, except as against this State in a proceeding to cancel or revoke the certificate of incorporation or for involuntary dissolution of the corporation.

§ 57. Organization Meeting of Directors

After the issuance of the certificate of incorporation an organization meeting of the board of directors named in the articles of incorporation shall be held, either within or without this State, at the call of a majority of the directors named in the articles of incorporation, for the purpose of adopting by-laws, electing officers and transacting such other business as may come before the meeting. The directors calling the meeting shall give at least three days' notice thereof by mail to each director so named, stating the time and place of the meeting.

§ 58. Right to Amend Articles of Incorporation

A corporation may amend its articles of incorporation, from time to time, in any and as many respects as may be desired, so long as its articles of incorporation as amended contain only such provisions as might be lawfully contained in original articles of incorporation at the time of making such amendment, and, if a change in shares or the rights of shareholders, or an exchange, reclassification or cancellation of shares or rights of shareholders is to be made, such provisions as may be necessary to effect such change, exchange, reclassification or cancellation.

In particular, and without limitation upon such general power of amendment, a corporation may amend its articles of incorporation, from time to time, so as:

(a) To change its corporate name.

(b) To change its period of duration.

(c) To change, enlarge or diminish its corporate purposes.

(d) To increase or decrease the aggregate number of shares, or shares of any class, which the corporation has authority to issue.

(e) To increase or decrease the par value of the authorized shares of any class having a par value, whether issued or unissued.

(f) To exchange, classify, reclassify or cancel all or any part of its shares, whether issued or unissued.

(g) To change the designation of all or any part of its shares, whether issued or unissued, and to change the preferences, limitations, and the relative rights in respect of all or any part of its shares, whether issued or unissued.

(h) To change shares having the par value, whether issued or unissued, into the same or a different number of shares without par value, and to change shares without par value, whether issued or unissued, into the same or a different number of shares having a par value.

(i) To change the shares of any class, whether issued or unissued and whether with or without par value, into a different number of shares of the same class or into the same or a different number of shares, either with or without par value, of other classes.

(j) To create new classes of shares having rights and preferences either prior and superior or subordinate and inferior to the shares of any class then authorized, whether issued or unissued.

(k) To cancel or otherwise affect the right of the holders of the shares of any class to receive dividends which have accrued but have not been declared.

(l) To divide any preferred or special class of shares, whether issued or unissued, into series and fix and determine the designations of such series and the variations in the relative rights and preferences as between the shares of such series.

(m) To authorize the board of directors to establish, out of authorized but unissued shares, series of any preferred or special class of shares and fix and determine the relative rights and preferences of the shares of any series so established.

(n) To authorize the board of directors to fix and determine the relative rights and preferences of the authorized but unissued shares of series theretofore established in respect of which either the relative rights and preferences have not been fixed and determined or the relative rights and preferences theretofore fixed and determined are to be changed.

(o) To revoke, diminish, or enlarge the authority of the board of directors to establish series out of authorized but unissued shares of any preferred or special class and fix and determine the relative rights and preferences of the shares of any series so established.

(p) To limit, deny or grant to shareholders of any class the preemptive right to acquire additional or treasury shares of the corporation, whether then or thereafter authorized.

§ 59. Procedure to Amend Articles of Incorporation

Amendments to the articles of incorporation shall be made in the following manner:

(a) The board of directors shall adopt a resolution setting forth the proposed amendment and, if shares have been issued, directing that it be submitted to a vote at a meeting of shareholders, which may be either the annual or a special meeting. If no shares have been issued, the amendment shall be adopted by resolution of the board of directors and the provisions for adoption by shareholders shall not apply. The resolution may incorporate the proposed amendment in restated articles of incorporation which contain a statement that except for the designated amendment the restated articles of incorporation correctly set forth without change the corresponding provisions of the articles of incorporation as theretofore amended, and that the restated articles of incorporation together with the designated amendment supersede the original articles of incorporation and all amendments thereto.

(b) Written notice setting forth the proposed amendment or a summary of the changes to be effected thereby shall be given to each shareholder of record entitled to vote thereon within the time and in the manner provided in this Act for the giving of notice of meetings of shareholders. If the meeting be an annual meeting, the proposed amendment of such summary may be included in the notice of such annual meeting.

(c) At such meeting a vote of the shareholders entitled to vote thereon shall be taken on the proposed amendment. The proposed amendment shall be adopted upon receiving the affirmative vote of the holders of a majority of the shares entitled to vote thereon, unless any class of shares is entitled to vote thereon as a class, in which event the proposed amendment shall be adopted upon receiving the affirmative vote of the holders of a majority of the shares of each class of shares entitled to vote thereon as a class and of the total shares entitled to vote thereon.

Any number of amendments may be submitted to the shareholders, and voted upon by them, at one meeting.

§ 60. Class Voting on Amendments

The holders of the outstanding shares of a class shall be entitled to vote as a class upon a proposed amendment, whether or not entitled to vote thereon by the provisions of the articles of incorporation, if the amendment would:

(a) Increase or decrease the aggregate number of authorized shares of such class.

(b) Increase or decrease the par value of the shares of such class.

(c) Effect an exchange, reclassification or cancellation of all or part of the shares of such class.

(d) Effect an exchange, or create a right of exchange, of all or any part of the shares of another class into the shares of such class.

(e) Change the designations, preferences, limitations or relative rights of the shares of such class.

(f) Change the shares of such class, whether with or without par value, into the same or a different number of shares, either with or without par value, of the same class or another class or classes.

(g) Create a new class of shares having rights and preferences prior and superior to the shares of such class, or increase the rights and preferences or the number of authorized shares, of any class having rights and preferences prior or superior to the shares of such class.

(h) In the case of a preferred or special class of shares, divide the shares of such class into series and fix and determine the designation of such series and the variations in the relative rights and preferences between the shares of such series, or authorize the board of directors to do so.

(i) Limit or deny any existing preemptive rights of the shares of such class.

(j) Cancel or otherwise affect dividends on the shares of such class which have accrued but have not been declared.

§ 61. Articles of Amendment

The articles of amendment shall be executed in duplicate by the corporation by its president or a vice president and by its secretary or an assistant secretary, and verified by one of the officers signing such articles, and shall set forth:

(a) The name of the corporation.

(b) The amendments so adopted.

(c) The date of the adoption of the amendment by the shareholders, or by the board of directors where no shares have been issued.

(d) The number of shares outstanding, and the number of shares entitled to vote thereon, and if the shares of any class are entitled to vote thereon as a class, the designation and number of outstanding shares entitled to vote thereon of each such class.

(e) The number of shares voted for and against such amendment, respectively, and, if the shares of any class are entitled to vote thereon as a class, the number of shares of each such class voted for and against such amendment, respectively, or if no shares have been issued, a statement to that effect.

(f) If such amendment provides for an exchange, reclassification or cancellation of issued shares, and if the manner in which the same shall be effected is not set forth in the amendment, then a statement of the manner in which the same shall be effected.

(g) If such amendment effects a change in the amount of stated capital, then a statement of the manner in which the same is effected and a statement, expressed in dollars, of the amount of stated capital as changed by such amendment.

§ 62. Filing of Articles of Amendment

Duplicate originals of the articles of amendment shall be delivered to the Secretary of State. If the Secretary of State finds that the articles of amendment conform to law, he shall, when all fees and franchise taxes have been paid as in this Act prescribed:

(a) Endorse on each of such duplicate originals the word "Filed," and the month, day and year of the filing thereof.

(b) File one of such duplicate originals in his office.

(c) Issue a certificate of amendment to which he shall affix the other duplicate original.

The certificate of amendment, together with the duplicate original of the articles of amendment affixed thereto by the Secretary of State, shall be returned to the corporation or its representative.

§ 63. Effect of Certificate of Amendment

The amendment shall become effective upon the issuance of the certificate of amendment by the Secretary of State, or on such later date, not more than thirty days subsequent to the filing thereof with the Secretary of State, as shall be provided for in the articles of amendment.

No amendment shall affect any existing cause of action in favor of or against such corporation, or any pending suit to which such corporation shall be a party, or the existing rights of persons other than shareholders; and, in the event the corporate name shall be changed by amendment, no suit brought by or against such corporation under its former name shall abate for that reason.

§ 64. Restated Articles of Incorporation

A domestic corporation may at any time restate its articles of incorporation as theretofore amended, by a resolution adopted by the board of directors.

Upon the adoption of such resolution, restated articles of incorporation shall be executed in duplicate by the corporation by its president or a vice president and by its secretary or assistant secretary and verified by one of the officers signing such articles and shall set forth all of the operative provisions of the articles of incorporation as theretofore amended together with a statement that the restated articles of incorporation correctly set forth without change the corresponding provisions of the articles of incorporation as theretofore amended and that the restated articles of incorporation supersede the original articles of incorporation and all amendments thereto.

Duplicate originals of the restated articles of incorporation shall be delivered to the Secretary of State. If the Secretary of State finds that such restated articles of incorporation conform to law, he shall, when all fees and franchise taxes have been paid as in this Act prescribed:

(1) Endorse on each of such duplicate originals the word "Filed," and the month, day and year of the filing thereof.

(2) File one of such duplicate originals in his office.

(3) Issue a restated certificate of incorporation, to which he shall affix the other duplicate original.

The restated certificate of incorporation, together with the duplicate original of the restated articles of incorporation affixed thereto by the Secretary of State, shall be returned to the corporation or its representative.

Upon the issuance of the restated certificate of incorporation by the Secretary of State, the restated articles of incorporation shall become effective and shall supersede the original articles of incorporation and all amendments thereto.

§ 65. Amendment of Articles of Incorporation in Reorganization Proceedings

Whenever a plan of reorganization of a corporation has been confirmed by decree or order of a court of competent jurisdiction in proceedings for the reorganization of such corporation, pursuant to the provisions of any applicable statute of the United States relating to reorganizations of corporations, the articles of incorporation of the corporation may be amended, in the manner provided in this section, in as many respects as may be necessary to carry out the plan and put it into effect, so long as the articles of incorporation as amended contain only such provisions as might be lawfully contained in original articles of incorporation at the time of making such amendment.

In particular and without limitation upon such general power of amendment, the articles of incorporation may be amended for such purpose so as to:

(A) Change the corporate name, period of duration or corporate purposes of the corporation;

(B) Repeal, alter or amend the by-laws of the corporation;

(C) Change the aggregate number of shares or shares of any class, which the corporation has authority to issue;

(D) Change the preferences, limitations and relative rights in respect of all or any part of the shares of the corporation, and classify, reclassify or cancel all or any part thereof, whether issued or unissued;

(E) Authorize the issuance of bonds, debentures or other obligations of the corporation, whether or not convertible into shares of any class or bearing warrants or other evidences of optional rights to purchase or subscribe for shares of any class, and fix the terms and conditions thereof; and

(F) Constitute or reconstitute and classify or reclassify the board of directors of the corporation, and appoint directors and officers in place of or in addition to all or any of the directors or officers then in office.

Amendments to the articles of incorporation pursuant to this section shall be made in the following manner:

(a) Articles of amendment approved by decree or order of such court shall be executed and verified in duplicate by such person or persons as the court shall designate or appoint for the purpose, and shall set forth the name of the corporation, the amendments of the articles of incorporation approved by the court, the date of the decree or order approving the articles of amendment, the title of the proceedings in which the decree or order was entered, and a statement that such decree or order was entered by a court having jurisdiction of the proceedings for the reorganization of the corporation pursuant to the provisions of an applicable statute of the United States.

(b) Duplicate originals of the articles of amendment shall be delivered to the Secretary of State. If the Secretary of State finds that the articles of amendment conform to law, he shall, when all fees and franchise taxes have been paid as in this Act prescribed:

(1) Endorse on each of such duplicate originals the word "Filed," and the month, day and year of the filing thereof.

(2) File one of such duplicate originals in his office.

(3) Issue a certificate of amendment to which he shall affix the other duplicate original.

The certificate of amendment, together with the duplicate original of the articles of amendment affixed thereto by the Secretary of State, shall be returned to the corporation or its representative.

The amendment shall become effective upon the issuance of the certificate of amendment by the Secretary of State, or on such later date, not more than thirty days subsequent to the filing thereof with the Secretary of State, as shall be provided for in the articles of amendment without any action thereon by the directors or shareholders of the corporation and with the same effect as if the amendments had been adopted by unanimous action of the directors and shareholders of the corporation.

§ 66. Restriction on Redemption or Purchase of Redeemable Shares

No redemption or purchase of redeemable shares shall be made by a corporation when it is insolvent or when such redemption or purchase would render it insolvent, or which would reduce the net assets below the aggregate amount payable to the holders of shares having prior or equal rights to the assets of the corporation upon involuntary dissolution.

§ 67. Cancellation of Redeemable Shares by Redemption or Purchase

When redeemable shares of a corporation are redeemed or purchased by the corporation, the redemption or purchase shall effect a cancellation of such shares, and a statement of cancellation shall be filed as provided in this section. Thereupon such shares shall be restored to the status of authorized but unissued shares, unless the articles of incorporation provide that such shares when redeemed or purchased shall not be reissued, in which case the filing of the statement of cancellation shall constitute an amendment to the articles of incorporation and shall reduce the number of shares of the class so cancelled which the corporation is authorized to issue by the number of shares so cancelled.

The statement of cancellation shall be executed in duplicate by the corporation by its president or a vice president and by its secretary or an assistant secretary, and verified by one of the officers signing such statement, and shall set forth:

(a) The name of the corporation.

(b) The number of redeemable shares cancelled through redemption or purchase, itemized by classes and series.

(c) The aggregate number of issued shares, itemized by classes and series, after giving effect to such cancellation.

(d) The amount, expressed in dollars, of the stated capital of the corporation after giving effect to such cancellation.

(e) If the articles of incorporation provide that the cancelled shares shall not be reissued, the number of shares which the corporation will have authority to issue itemized by classes and series, after giving effect to such cancellation.

Duplicate originals of such statement shall be delivered to the Secretary of State. If the Secretary of State finds that such statement conforms to law, he shall, when all fees and franchise taxes have been paid as in this Act prescribed:

(1) Endorse on each of such duplicate originals the word "Filed," and the month, day and year of the filing thereof.

(2) File one of such duplicate originals in his office.

(3) Return the other duplicate original to the corporation or its representative.

Upon the filing of such statement of cancellation, the stated capital of the corporation shall be deemed to be reduced by that part of the stated capital which was, at the time of such cancellation, represented by the shares so cancelled.

Nothing contained in this section shall be construed to forbid a cancellation of shares or a reduction of stated capital in any other manner permitted by this Act.

§ 68. Cancellation of Other Reacquired Shares

A corporation may at any time, by resolution of its board of directors, cancel all or any part of the shares of the corporation of any class reacquired by it, other than redeemable shares redeemed or purchased, and in such event a statement of cancellation shall be filed as provided in this section.

The statement of cancellation shall be executed in duplicate by the corporation by its president or a vice president and by its secretary or an assistant secretary, and verified by one of the officers signing such statement, and shall set forth:

(a) The name of the corporation.

(b) The number of reacquired shares cancelled by resolution duly adopted by the board of directors, itemized by classes and series, and the date of its adoption.

(c) The aggregate number of issued shares, itemized by classes and series, after giving effect to such cancellation.

(d) The amount, expressed in dollars, of the stated capital of the corporation after giving effect to such cancellation.

Duplicate originals of such statement shall be delivered to the Secretary of State. If the Secretary of State finds that such statement conforms to law, he shall, when all fees and franchise taxes have been paid as in this Act prescribed:

(1) Endorse on each of such duplicate originals the word "Filed," and the month, day and year of the filing thereof.

(2) File one of such duplicate originals in his office.

(3) Return the other duplicate original to the corporation or its representative.

Upon the filing of such statement of cancellation, the stated capital of the corporation shall be deemed to be reduced by that part of the stated capital which was, at the time of such cancellation, represented by the shares so cancelled, and the shares so cancelled shall be restored to the status of authorized but unissued shares.

Nothing contained in this section shall be construed to forbid a cancellation of shares or a reduction of stated capital in any other manner permitted by this Act.

§ 69. Reduction of Stated Capital in Certain Cases

A reduction of the stated capital of a corporation, where such reduction is not accompanied by any action requiring an amendment of the articles of incorporation and not accompanied by a cancellation of shares, may be made in the following manner:

(A) The board of directors shall adopt a resolution setting forth the amount of the proposed reduction and the manner in which the reduction shall be effected, and directing that the question of such reduction be submitted to a vote at a meeting of shareholders, which may be either an annual or a special meeting.

(B) Written notice, stating that the purpose or one of the purposes of such meeting is to consider the question of reducing the stated capital of the corporation in the amount and manner proposed by the board of directors, shall be given to each shareholder of record entitled to vote thereon within the time and in the manner provided in this Act for the giving of notice of meetings of shareholders.

(C) At such meeting a vote of the shareholders entitled to vote thereon shall be taken on the question of approving the proposed reduction of stated capital, which shall require for its adoption the affirmative vote of the holders of a majority of the shares entitled to vote thereon.

When a reduction of the stated capital of a corporation has been approved as provided in this section, a statement shall be executed in duplicate by the corporation by its president or a vice president and by its secretary or an assistant secretary, and verified by one of the officers signing such statement, and shall set forth:

(a) The name of the corporation.

(b) A copy of the resolution of the shareholders approving such reduction, and the date of its adoption.

(c) The number of shares outstanding, and the number of shares entitled to vote thereon.

(d) The number of shares voted for and against such reduction, respectively.

(e) A statement of the manner in which such reduction is effected, and a statement, expressed in dollars, of the amount of stated capital of the corporation after giving effect to such reduction.

Duplicate originals of such statement shall be delivered to the Secretary of State. If the Secretary of State finds that such statement conforms to law, he shall, when all fees and franchise taxes have been paid as in this Act prescribed:

(1) Endorse on each of such duplicate originals the word "Filed," and the month, day and year of the filing thereof.

(2) File one of such duplicate originals in his office.

(3) Return the other duplicate original to the corporation or its representative.

Upon the filing of such statement, the stated capital of the corporation shall be reduced as therein set forth.

No reduction of stated capital shall be made under the provisions of this section which would reduce the amount of the aggregate stated capital of the corporation to an amount equal to or less than the aggregate preferential amounts payable upon all issued shares having a preferential right in the assets of the corporation in the event of involuntary liquidation, plus the aggregate par value of all issued shares having a par value but no preferential right in the assets of the corporation in the event of involuntary liquidation.

§ 70. Special Provisions Relating to Surplus and Reserves

The surplus, if any, created by or arising out of a reduction of the stated capital of a corporation shall be capital surplus.

The capital surplus of a corporation may be increased from time to time by resolution of the board of directors directing that all or a part of the earned surplus of the corporation be transferred to capital surplus.

A corporation may, by resolution of its board of directors, apply any part or all of its capital surplus to the reduction or elimination of any deficit arising from losses, however incurred, but only after first eliminating the earned surplus, if any, of the corporation by applying such losses against earned surplus and only to the extent that such losses exceed the earned surplus, if any. Each such application of capital surplus shall, to the extent thereof, effect a reduction of capital surplus.

A corporation may, by resolution of its board of directors, create a reserve or reserves out of its earned surplus for any proper purpose or purposes, and may abolish any such reserve in the same manner. Earned surplus of the corporation to the extent so reserved shall not be available for the payment of dividends or other distributions by the corporation except as expressly permitted by this Act.

§ 71. Procedure for Merger

Any two or more domestic corporations may merge into one of such corporations pursuant to a plan of merger approved in the manner provided in this Act.

The board of directors of each corporation shall, by resolution adopted by each such board, approve a plan of merger setting forth:

(a) The names of the corporations proposing to merge, and the name of the corporation into which they propose to merge, which is hereinafter designated as the surviving corporation.

(b) The terms and conditions of the proposed merger.

(c) The manner and basis of converting the shares of each corporation into shares, obligations or other securities of the surviving corporation or of any other corporation or, in whole or in part, into cash or other property.

(d) A statement of any changes in the articles of incorporation of the surviving corporation to be effected by such merger.

(e) Such other provisions with respect to the proposed merger as are deemed necessary or desirable.

§ 72. Procedure for Consolidation

Any two or more domestic corporations may consolidate into a new corporation pursuant to a plan of consolidation approved in the manner provided in this Act.

The board of directors of each corporation shall, by a resolution adopted by each such board, approve a plan of consolidation setting forth:

(a) The names of the corporations proposing to consolidate, and the name of the new corporation into which they propose to consolidate, which is hereinafter designated as the new corporation.

(b) The terms and conditions of the proposed consolidation.

(c) The manner and basis of converting the shares of each corporation into shares, obligations or other securities of the new corporation or of any other corporation or, in whole or in part, into cash or other property.

(d) With respect to the new corporation, all of the statements required to be set forth in articles of incorporation for corporations organized under this Act.

(e) Such other provisions with respect to the proposed consolidation as are deemed necessary or desirable.

§ 72-A. Procedure for Share Exchange

All the issued or all the outstanding shares of one or more classes of any domestic corporation may be acquired through the exchange of all such shares of such class or classes by another domestic or foreign corporation pursuant to a plan of exchange approved in the manner provided in this Act.

The board of directors of each corporation shall, by resolution adopted by each such board, approve a plan of exchange setting forth:

(a) The name of the corporation the shares of which are proposed to be acquired by exchange and the name of the corporation to acquire the shares of such corporation in the exchange, which is hereinafter designated as the acquiring corporation.

(b) The terms and conditions of the proposed exchange.

(c) The manner and basis of exchanging the shares to be acquired for shares, obligations or other securities of the acquiring corporation or any other corporation, or, in whole or in part, for cash or other property.

(d) Such other provisions with respect to the proposed exchange as are deemed necessary or desirable.

The procedure authorized by this Section shall not be deemed to limit the power of a corporation to acquire all or part of the shares of any class or classes of a corporation through a voluntary exchange or otherwise by agreement with the shareholders.

§ 73. Approval by Shareholders

(a) The board of directors of each corporation in the case of a merger or consolidation, and the board of directors of the corporation the shares of which are to be acquired in the case of an exchange, upon approving such plan of merger, consolidation or exchange, shall, by resolution, direct that the plan be submitted to a vote at a meeting of its shareholders, which may be either an annual or a special meeting. Written notice shall be given to each shareholder of record, whether or not entitled to vote at such meeting, not less than twenty days before such meeting, in the manner provided in this Act for the giving of notice of meetings of shareholders, and, whether the meeting be an annual or a special meeting, shall state that the purpose or one of the purposes is to consider the proposed plan of merger, consolidation or exchange. A copy or a summary of the plan of merger, consolidation or exchange, as the case may be, shall be included in or enclosed with such notice.

(b) At each such meeting, a vote of the shareholders shall be taken on the proposed plan. The plan shall be approved upon receiving the affirmative vote of the holders of a majority of the shares entitled to vote thereon of each such corporation, unless any class of shares of any such corporation is entitled to vote thereon as a class, in which event as to such corporation, the plan shall be approved upon receiving the affirmative vote of the holders of a majority of the shares of each class of shares entitled to vote thereon as a class and of the total shares entitled to vote thereon. Any class of shares of any such corporation shall be entitled to vote as a class if any such plan contains any provision which, if contained in a proposed amendment to articles of incorporation, would entitle such class of shares to vote as a class and, in the case of an exchange, if the class is included in the exchange.

(c) After such approval by a vote of the shareholders of each such corporation, and at any time prior to the filing of the articles of merger, consolidation or exchange, the merger, consolidation or exchange may be abandoned pursuant to provisions therefor, if any, set forth in the plan.

(d) (1) Notwithstanding the provisions of subsections (a) and (b), submission of a plan of merger to a vote at a meeting of shareholders of a surviving corporation shall not be required if:

(i) the articles of incorporation of the surviving corporation do not differ except in name from those of the corporation before the merger,

(ii) each holder of shares of the surviving corporation which were outstanding immediately before the effective date of the merger is to hold the same number of shares with identical rights immediately after,

(iii) the number of voting shares outstanding immediately after the merger, plus the number of voting shares issuable on conversion of other securities issued by virtue of the terms of the merger and on exercise of rights and warrants so issued, will not exceed by more than 20 percent the number of voting shares outstanding immediately before the merger, and

(iv) the number of participating shares outstanding immediately after the merger, plus the number of participating shares issuable on conversion of other securities issued by virtue of the terms of the merger and on exercise of rights and warrants so issued, will not exceed by more than 20 percent the number of participating shares outstanding immediately before the merger.

(2) As used in this subsection:

(i) "voting shares" means shares which entitle their holders to vote unconditionally in elections of directors;

(ii) "participating shares" means shares which entitle their holders to participate without limitation in distribution of earnings or surplus.

§ 74. Articles of Merger, Consolidation or Exchange*

* Section 74 appears here as it does in the report that announced the most recent amendments to this section. See Conard, Amendments of Model Business Corporation Act Affecting Dissenters' Rights, 33 Bus. Law. 2587 (1978). Section 74 also appears in this form in the latest edition of the Model Business Corporation Act published by the American Law Institute — American Bar Association Committee on Continuing Professional Education. See ABA Committee on Corporate Laws, Model Business Corporation Act (with revisions through January 1, 1979) and Professional Corporation Supplement.

It seems, however, that in amending and restating Section 74 in 1978, the ABA Committee on Corporate Laws partially overlooked amendments to the section adopted in 1976. See ABA Committee on Corporate Laws, Changes in the Model Business Corporation Act Affecting Dissenters' Rights, 32 Bus. Law 1855, 1859 (1977); ABA Committee on Corporate Laws, Final Changes in the Model Business Corporation Act Revising Sections 63, 73, 74, 76, 77, 80 and Adding a New Section — 72-A, 31 Bus. Law. 1747, 1749-50 (1976); Conard, *supra*, at 2589-90. These amendments, which affected subsections (a), (b) and (c), took account of the procedure for share exchanges, added in 1976 by Section 72-A. As Section 74 now appears to stand, subsections (b) and (c) refer to share exchanges, but subsection (a) does not.

(a) Upon receiving the approvals required by sections 71, 72 and 73, articles of merger or articles of consolidation shall be executed in duplicate by each corporation by its president or a vice president and by its secretary or an assistant secretary, and verified by one of the officers of each corporation signing such articles, and shall set forth:

(1) The plan of merger or the plan of consolidation;

(2) As to each corporation, either (i) the number of shares outstanding, and, if the shares of any class are entitled to vote as a class, the designation and number of outstanding shares of each such class, or (ii) a statement that the vote of shareholders is not required by virtue of subsection 73(d);

(3) As to each corporation the approval of whose shareholders is required, the number of shares voted for and against such plan, respectively, and, if the shares of any class are entitled to vote as a class, the number of shares of each such class voted for and against such plan, respectively.

Subsection (a) should probably read as follows:

(a) Upon receiving the approvals required by sections 71, 72, 72-A and 73, articles of merger, articles of consolidation or articles of exchange shall be executed in duplicate by each corporation by its president or a vice president and by its secretary or an assistant secretary, and verified by one of the officers of each corporation signing such articles, and shall set forth:

(1) The plan of merger, consolidation or exchange;

(2) As to each corporation, either (i) the number of shares outstanding, and, if the shares of any class are entitled to vote as a class, the designation and number of outstanding shares of each such class, or (ii) a statement that the vote of shareholders is not required by virtue of subsection 73(d);

(3) As to each corporation the approval of whose shareholders is required, the number of shares voted for and against such plan, respectively, and, if the shares of any class are entitled to vote as a class, the number of shares of each such class voted for and against such plan, respectively;

(4) As to the acquiring corporation in a plan of exchange, a statement that the adoption of the plan and performance of its terms were duly approved by its board of directors and such other requisite corporate action, if any, as may be required of it.

[Eds.]

(b) Duplicate originals of the articles of merger, consolidation or exchange shall be delivered to the Secretary of State. If the Secretary of State finds that such articles conform to law, he shall, when all fees and franchise taxes have been paid as in this Act prescribed:

(1) Endorse on each of such duplicate originals the word "Filed," and the month, day and year of the filing thereof.

(2) File one of such duplicate originals in his office.

(3) Issue a certificate of merger, consolidation or exchange to which he shall affix the other duplicate original.

(c) The certificate of merger, consolidation or exchange together with the duplicate original of the articles affixed thereto by the Secretary of State, shall be returned to the surviving, new or acquiring corporation, as the case may be, or its representative.

§ 75. Merger of Subsidiary Corporation

Any corporation owning at least ninety per cent of the outstanding shares of each class of another corporation may merge such other corporation into itself without approval by a vote of the shareholders of either corporation. Its board of directors shall, by resolution, approve a plan of merger setting forth:

(A) The name of the subsidiary corporation and the name of the corporation owning at least ninety per cent of its shares, which is hereinafter designated as the surviving corporation.

(B) The manner and basis of converting the shares of the subsidiary corporation into shares, obligations or other securities of the surviving corporation or of any other corporation or, in whole or in part, into cash or other property.

A copy of such plan of merger shall be mailed to each shareholder of record of the subsidiary corporation.

Articles of merger shall be executed in duplicate by the surviving corporation by its president or a vice president and by its secretary or an assistant secretary, and verified by one of its officers signing such articles, and shall set forth:

(a) The plan of merger;

(b) The number of outstanding shares of each class of the subsidiary corporation and the number of such shares of each class owned by the surviving corporation; and

(c) The date of the mailing to shareholders of the subsidiary corporation of a copy of the plan of merger.

On and after the thirtieth day after the mailing of a copy of the plan of merger to shareholders of the subsidiary corporation or upon the waiver thereof by the holders of all outstanding shares duplicate originals of the articles of merger shall be delivered to the Secretary of State. If the Secretary of State finds that such articles conform to law, he shall, when all fees and franchise taxes have been paid as in this Act prescribed:

(1) Endorse on each of such duplicate originals the word "Filed," and the month, day and year of the filing thereof,

(2) File one of such duplicate originals in his office, and

(3) Issue a certificate of merger to which he shall affix the other duplicate original.

The certificate of merger, together with the duplicate original of the articles of merger affixed thereto by the Secretary of State, shall be returned to the surviving corporation or its representative.

§ 76. Effect of Merger, Consolidation or Exchange

A merger, consolidation or exchange shall become effective upon the issuance of a certificate of merger, consolidation or exchange by the Secretary of State, or on such later date, not more than thirty days subsequent to the filing thereof with the Secretary of State, as shall be provided for in the plan.

When a merger or consolidation has become effective:

(a) The several corporations parties to the plan of merger or consolidation shall be a single corporation, which, in the case of a merger, shall be that corporation designated in the plan of merger as the surviving corporation, and, in the case of a consolidation, shall be the new corporation provided for in the plan of consolidation.

(b) The separate existence of all corporations parties to the plan of merger or consolidation, except the surviving or new corporation, shall cease.

(c) Such surviving or new corporation shall have all the rights, privileges, immunities and powers and shall be subject to all the duties and liabilities of a corporation organized under this Act.

(d) Such surviving or new corporation shall thereupon and thereafter possess all the rights, privileges, immunities, and franchises, of a public as well as of a private nature, of each of the merging or consolidating corporations; and all property, real, personal and mixed, and all debts due on whatever account, including subscriptions to shares, and all other choses in action, and all and every other interest of or belonging to or due to each of the corporations so merged or consolidated, shall be taken and deemed to be transferred to and vested in such single corporation without further act or deed; and the title to any real estate, or any interest therein, vested in any of such corporations shall not revert or be in any way impaired by reason of such merger or consolidation.

(e) Such surviving or new corporation shall thenceforth be responsible and liable for all the liabilities and obligations of each of the corporations so merged or consolidated; and any claim existing or action or proceeding pending by or against any of such corporations may be prosecuted as if such merger or consolidation had not taken place, or such surviving or new corporation may be substituted in its place. Neither the rights of creditors nor any liens upon the property of any such corporation shall be impaired by such merger or consolidation.

(f) In the case of a merger, the articles of incorporation of the surviving corporation shall be deemed to be amended to the extent, if any, that changes in its articles of incorporation are stated in the plan of merger; and, in the case of a consolidation, the statements set forth in the articles of consolidation and which are required or permitted to be set forth in the articles of incorporation of corporations organized under this Act shall be deemed to be the original articles of incorporation of the new corporation.

When a merger, consolidation or exchange has become effective, the shares of the corporation or corporations party to the plan that are, under the terms of the plan, to be converted or exchanged, shall cease to exist, in the case of a merger or consolidation, or be deemed to be exchanged in the case of an exchange; and the holders of such shares shall thereafter be entitled only to the shares, obligations, other securities, cash or other property into which they shall have been converted or for which they shall have been exchanged, in accordance with the plan, subject to any rights under Section 80 of this Act.

§ 77. Merger, Consolidation or Exchange of Shares Between Domestic and Foreign Corporations

One or more foreign corporations and one or more domestic corporations may be merged or consolidated, or participate in an exchange, in the following manner, if such merger, consolidation or exchange is permitted by the laws of the state under which each such foreign corporation is organized:

(a) Each domestic corporation shall comply with the provisions of this Act with respect to the merger, consolidation or exchange, as the case may be, of domestic corporations and each foreign corporation shall comply with the applicable provisions of the laws of the state under which it is organized.

(b) If the surviving or new corporation in a merger or consolidation is to be governed by the laws of any state other than this State, it shall comply with the provisions of this Act with respect to foreign corporations if it is to transact business in this State, and in every case it shall file with the Secretary of State of this State:

(1) An agreement that it may be served with process in this State in any proceeding for the enforcement of any obligation of any domestic corporation which is a party to such merger or consolidation and

in any proceeding for the enforcement of the rights of a dissenting shareholder of any such domestic corporation against the surviving or new corporation;

(2) An irrevocable appointment of the Secretary of State of this State as its agent to accept service of process in any such proceeding; and

(3) An agreement that it will promptly pay to the dissenting shareholders of any such domestic corporation, the amount, if any, to which they shall be entitled under provisions of this Act with respect to the rights of dissenting shareholders.

§ 78. Sale of Assets in Regular Course of Business and Mortgage or Pledge of Assets

The sale, lease, exchange, or other disposition of all, or substantially all, the property and assets of a corporation in the usual and regular course of its business and the mortgage or pledge of any or all property and assets of a corporation whether or not in the usual and regular course of business may be made upon such terms and conditions and for such consideration, which may consist in whole or in part of cash or other property, including shares, obligations or other securities of any other corporation, domestic or foreign, as shall be authorized by its board of directors; and in any such case no authorization or consent of the shareholders shall be required.

§ 79. Sale of Assets Other Than in Regular Course of Business

A sale, lease, exchange, or other disposition of all, or substantially all, the property and assets, with or without the goodwill, of a corporation, if not in the usual and regular course of its business, may be made upon such terms and conditions and for such consideration, which may consist in whole or in part of cash or other property, including shares, obligations or other securities of any other corporation, domestic or foreign, as may be authorized in the following manner:

(a) The board of directors shall adopt a resolution recommending such sale, lease, exchange, or other disposition and directing the submission thereof to a vote at a meeting of shareholders, which may be either an annual or a special meeting.

(b) Written notice shall be given to each shareholder of record, whether or not entitled to vote at such meeting, not less than twenty days before such meeting, in the manner provided in this Act for the giving of notice of meetings of shareholders, and, whether the meeting be an annual or a special meeting, shall state that the purpose, or one of the purposes is to consider the proposed sale, lease, exchange, or other disposition.

(c) At such meeting the shareholders may authorize such sale, lease, exchange, or other disposition and may fix, or may authorize the board of directors to fix, any or all of the terms and conditions thereof and the consideration to be received by the corporation therefor. Such authorization shall require the affirmative vote of the holders of a majority of the shares of the corporation entitled to vote thereon, unless any class of shares is entitled to vote thereon as a class, in which event such authorization shall require the affirmative vote of the holders of a majority of the shares of each class of shares entitled to vote as a class thereon and of the total shares entitled to vote thereon.

(d) After such authorization by a vote of shareholders, the board of directors nevertheless, in its discretion, may abandon such sale, lease, exchange, or other disposition of assets, subject to the rights of third parties under any contracts relating thereto, without further action or approval by shareholders.

§ 80. Right of Shareholders to Dissent and Obtain Payment for Shares

(a) Any shareholder of a corporation shall have the right to dissent from, and to obtain payment for his shares in the event of, any of the following corporate actions:

(1) Any plan of merger or consolidation to which the corporation is a party, except as provided in subsection (c);

(2) Any sale or exchange of all or substantially all of the property and assets of the corporation not made in the usual or regular course of its business, including a sale in dissolution, but not including a sale pursuant to an order of a court having jurisdiction in the premises or a sale for cash on terms requiring that all or substantially all of the net proceeds of sale be distributed to the shareholders in accordance with their respective interests within one year after the date of sale;

(3) Any plan of exchange to which the corporation is a party as the corporation the shares of which are to be acquired;

(4) Any amendment of the articles of incorporation which materially and adversely affects the rights appurtenant to the shares of the dissenting shareholders in that it:

(i) alters or abolishes a preferential right of such shares;

(ii) creates, alters or abolishes a right in respect of the redemption of such shares, including a provision respecting a sinking fund for the redemption or repurchase of such shares;

(iii) alters or abolishes a preemptive right of the holder of such shares to acquire shares or other securities;

(iv) excludes or limits the right of the holder of such shares to vote on any matter, or to cumulate his votes, except as such right may be limited by dilution through the issuance of shares or other securities with similar voting rights; or

(5) Any other corporate action taken pursuant to a shareholder vote with respect to which the articles of incorporation, the bylaws, or a resolution of the board of directors directs that dissenting shareholders shall have a right to obtain payment for their shares.

(b) (1) A record holder of shares may assert dissenters' rights as to less than all of the shares registered in his name only if he dissents with respect to all the shares beneficially owned by any one person, and discloses the name and address of the person or persons on whose behalf he dissents. In that event, his rights shall be determined as if the shares as to which he has dissented and his other shares were registered in the names of different shareholders.

(2) A beneficial owner of shares who is not the record holder may assert dissenters' rights with respect to shares held on his behalf, and shall be treated as a dissenting shareholder under the terms of this section and section 31 if he submits to the corporation at the time of or before the assertion of these rights a written consent of the record holder.

(c) The right to obtain payment under this section shall not apply to the shareholders of the surviving corporation in a merger if a vote of the shareholders of such corporation is not necessary to authorize such merger.

(d) A shareholder of a corporation who has a right under this section to obtain payment for his shares shall have no right at law or in equity to attack the validity of the corporate action that gives rise to his right to obtain payment, nor to have the action set aside or rescinded, except when the corporate action is unlawful or fraudulent with regard to the complaining shareholder or to the corporation.

§ 81. Procedures for Protection of Dissenters' Rights

(a) As used in this section:

(1) "Dissenter" means a shareholder or beneficial owner who is entitled to and does assert dissenters' rights under section 80, and who has performed every act required up to the time involved for the assertion of such rights.

(2) "Corporation" means the issuer of the shares held by the dissenter before the corporate action, or the successor by merger or consolidation of that issuer.

(3) "Fair value" of shares means their value immediately before the effectuation of the corporate action to which the dissenter objects, excluding any appreciation or depreciation in anticipation

of such corporate action unless such exclusion would be inequitable.

(4) "Interest" means interest from the effective date of the corporate action until the date of payment, at the average rate currently paid by the corporation on its principal bank loans, or, if none, at such rate as is fair and equitable under all the circumstances.

(b) If a proposed corporate action which would give rise to dissenters' rights under section 80(a) is submitted to a vote at a meeting of shareholders, the notice of meeting shall notify all shareholders that they have or may have a right to dissent and obtain payment for their shares by complying with the terms of this section, and shall be accompanied by a copy of sections 80 and 81 of this Act.

(c) If the proposed corporate action is submitted to a vote at a meeting of shareholders, any shareholder who wishes to dissent and obtain payment for his shares must file with the corporation, prior to the vote, a written notice of intention to demand that he be paid fair compensation for his shares if the proposed action is effectuated, and shall refrain from voting his shares in approval of such action. A shareholder who fails in either respect shall acquire no right to payment for his shares under this section or section 80.

(d) If the proposed corporate action is approved by the required vote at a meeting of shareholders, the corporation shall mail a further notice to all shareholders who gave due notice of intention to demand payment and who refrained from voting in favor of the proposed action. If the proposed corporate action is to be taken without a vote of shareholders, the corporation shall send to all shareholders who are entitled to dissent and demand payment for their shares a notice of the adoption of the plan of corporate action. The notice shall (1) state where and when a demand for payment must be sent and certificates of certificated shares must be deposited in order to obtain payment, (2) inform holders of uncertificated shares to what extent transfer of shares will be restricted from the time that demand for payment is received, (3) supply a form for demanding payment which includes a request for certification of the date on which the shareholder, or the person on whose behalf the shareholder dissents, acquired beneficial ownership of the shares, and (4) be accompanied by a copy of sections 80 and 81 of this Act. The time set for the demand and deposit shall be not less than 30 days from the mailing of the notice.

(e) A shareholder who fails to demand payment, or fails (in the case of certificated shares) to deposit certificates, as required by a notice pursuant to subsection (d) shall have no right under this section or section 80 to receive payment for his shares. If the shares are not represented by certificates, the corporation may restrict their transfer from the time of receipt of demand for payment until effectuation of the proposed corporate action, or the release of restrictions under the terms of subsection (f). The dissenter shall retain all other rights of a shareholder until these rights are modified by effectuation of the proposed corporate action.

(f) (1) Within 60 days after the date set for demanding payment and depositing certificates, if the corporation has not effectuated the proposed corporate action and remitted payment for shares pursuant to paragraph (3), it shall return any certificates that have been deposited, and release uncertificated shares from any transfer restrictions imposed by reason of the demand for payment.

(2) When uncertificated shares have been released from transfer restrictions, and deposited certificates have been returned, the corporation may at any later time send a new notice conforming to the requirements of subsection (d), with like effect.

(3) Immediately upon effectuation of the proposed corporate action, or upon receipt of demand for payment if the corporate action has already been effectuated, the corporation shall remit to dissenters who have made demand and (if their shares are certificated) have deposited their certificates the amount which the corporation estimates to be the fair value of the shares, with interest if any has accrued. The remittance shall be accompanied by:

(i) the corporation's closing balance sheet and statement of income for a fiscal year ending not more than 16 months before the date of remittance, together with the latest available interim financial statements;

(ii) a statement of the corporation's estimate of fair value of the shares; and

(iii) a notice of the dissenter's right to demand supplemental payment, accompanied by a copy of sections 80 and 81 of this Act.

(g) (1) If the corporation fails to remit as required by subsection (f), or if the dissenter believes that the amount remitted is less than the fair value of his shares, or that the interest is not correctly determined, he may send the corporation his own estimate of the value of the shares or of the interest, and demand payment of the deficiency.

(2) If the dissenter does not file such an estimate within 30 days after the corporation's mailing of its remittance, he shall be entitled to no more than the amount remitted.

(h) (1) Within 60 days after receiving a demand for payment pursuant to subsection (g), if any such demands for payment remain unsettled, the corporation shall file in an appropriate court a petition requesting that the fair value of the shares and interest thereon be determined by the court.

(2) An appropriate court shall be a court of competent jurisdiction in the county of this state where the registered office of the corporation is located. If, in the case of a merger or consolidation or exchange of shares, the corporation is a foreign corporation without a registered office in this state, the petition shall be filed in the county where the registered office of the domestic corporation was last located.

(3) All dissenters, wherever residing, whose demands have not been settled shall be made parties to the proceeding as in an action against their shares. A copy of the petition shall be served on each such dissenter; if a dissenter is a nonresident, the copy may be served on him by registered or certified mail or by publication as provided by law.

(4) The jurisdiction of the court shall be plenary and exclusive. The court may appoint one or more persons as appraisers to receive evidence and recommend a decision on the question of fair value. The appraisers shall have such power and authority as shall be specified in the order of their appointment or in any amendment thereof. The dissenters shall be entitled to discovery in the same manner as parties in other civil suits.

(5) All dissenters who are made parties shall be entitled to judgment for the amount by which the fair value of their shares is found to exceed the amount previously remitted, with interest.

(6) If the corporation fails to file a petition as provided in paragraph (1) of this subsection, each dissenter who made a demand and who has not already settled his claim against the corporation shall be paid by the corporation the amount demanded by him, with interest, and may sue therefor in an appropriate court.

(i) (1) The costs and expenses of any proceeding under subsection (h), including the reasonable compensation and expenses of appraisers appointed by the court, shall be determined by the court and assessed against the corporation, except that any part of the costs and expenses may be apportioned and assessed as the court may deem equitable against all or some of the dissenters who are parties and whose action in demanding supplemental payment the court finds to be arbitrary, vexatious, or not in good faith.

(2) Fees and expenses of counsel and of experts for the respective parties may be assessed as the court may deem equitable against the corporation and in favor of any or all dissenters if the corporation failed to comply substantially with the requirements of this section, and may be assessed against either the corporation or a dissenter, in favor of any other party, if the court finds that the party against whom the fees and expenses are assessed acted arbitrarily, vexatiously, or not in good faith in respect to the rights provided by this section and section 80.

(3) If the court finds that the services of counsel for any dissenter were of substantial benefit to other dissenters similarly situated, and

should not be assessed against the corporation, it may award to these counsel reasonable fees to be paid out of the amounts awarded to the dissenters who were benefitted.

(j) (1) Notwithstanding the foregoing provisions of this section, the corporation may elect to withhold the remittance required by subsection (f) from any dissenter with respect to shares of which the dissenter (or the person on whose behalf the dissenter acts) was not the beneficial owner on the date of the first announcement to news media or to shareholders of the terms of the proposed corporate action. With respect to such shares, the corporation shall, upon effectuating the corporate action, state to each dissenter its estimate of the fair value of the shares, state the rate of interest to be used (explaining the basis thereof), and offer to pay the resulting amounts on receiving the dissenter's agreement to accept them in full satisfaction.

(2) If the dissenter believes that the amount offered is less than the fair value of the shares and interest determined according to this section, he may within 30 days after the date of mailing of the corporation's offer, mail the corporation his own estimate of fair value and interest, and demand their payment. If the dissenter fails to do so, he shall be entitled to no more than the corporation's offer.

(3) If the dissenter makes a demand as provided in paragraph (2), the provisions of subsections (h) and (i) shall apply to further proceedings on the dissenter's demand.

§ 82. Voluntary Dissolution by Incorporators

A corporation which has not commenced business and which has not issued any shares, may be voluntarily dissolved by its incorporators at any time in the following manner:

(a) Articles of dissolution shall be executed in duplicate by a majority of the incorporators, and verified by them, and shall set forth:

(1) The name of the corporation.

(2) The date of issuance of its certificate of incorporation.

(3) That none of its shares has been issued.

(4) That the corporation has not commenced business.

(5) That the amount, if any, actually paid in on subscriptions for its shares, less any part thereof disbursed for necessary expenses, has been returned to those entitled thereto.

(6) That no debts of the corporation remain unpaid.

(7) That a majority of the incorporators elect that the corporation be dissolved.

(b) Duplicate originals of the articles of dissolution shall be delivered to the Secretary of State. If the Secretary of State finds that the articles of dissolution conform to law, he shall, when all fees and franchise taxes have been paid as in this Act prescribed:

(1) Endorse on each of such duplicate originals the word "Filed," and the month, day and year of the filing thereof.

(2) File one of such duplicate originals in his office.

(3) Issue a certificate of dissolution to which he shall affix the other duplicate original.

The certificate of dissolution, together with the duplicate original of the articles of dissolution affixed thereto by the Secretary of State, shall be returned to the incorporators or their representative. Upon the issuance of such certificate of dissolution by the Secretary of State, the existence of the corporation shall cease.

§ 83. Voluntary Dissolution by Consent of Shareholders

A corporation may be voluntarily dissolved by the written consent of all of its shareholders.

Upon the execution of such written consent, a statement of intent to dissolve shall be executed in duplicate by the corporation by its president or a vice president and by its secretary or an assistant secretary, and verified by one of the officers signing such statement, which statement shall set forth:

(a) The name of the corporation.

(b) The names and respective addresses of its officers.

(c) The names and respective addresses of its directors.

(d) A copy of the written consent signed by all shareholders of the corporation.

(e) A statement that such written consent has been signed by all shareholders of the corporation or signed in their names by their attorneys thereunto duly authorized.

§ 84. Voluntary Dissolution by Act of Corporation

A corporation may be dissolved by the act of the corporation, when authorized in the following manner:

(a) The board of directors shall adopt a resolution recommending that the corporation be dissolved, and directing that the question of such dissolution be submitted to a vote at a meeting of shareholders, which may be either an annual or a special meeting.

(b) Written notice shall be given to each shareholder of record entitled to vote at such meeting within the time and in the manner provided in this Act for the giving of notice of meetings of shareholders, and, whether the meeting be an annual or special meeting, shall state that the purpose, or one of the purposes, of such meeting is to consider the advisability of dissolving the corporation.

(c) At such meeting a vote of shareholders entitled to vote thereat shall be taken on a resolution to dissolve the corporation. Such resolution shall be adopted upon receiving the affirmative vote of the holders of a majority of the shares of the corporation entitled to vote thereon, unless any class of shares is entitled to vote thereon as a class, in which event the resolution shall be adopted upon receiving the affirmative vote of the holders of a majority of the shares of each class of shares entitled to vote thereon as a class and of the total shares entitled to vote thereon.

(d) Upon the adoption of such resolution, a statement of intent to dissolve shall be executed in duplicate by the corporation by its president or a vice president and by its secretary or an assistant secretary, and verified by one of the officers signing such statement, which statement shall set forth:

(1) The name of the corporation.

(2) The names and respective addresses of its officers.

(3) The names and respective addresses of its directors.

(4) A copy of the resolution adopted by the shareholders authorizing the dissolution of the corporation.

(5) The number of shares outstanding, and, if the shares of any class are entitled to vote as a class, the designation and number of outstanding shares of each such class.

(6) The number of shares voted for and against the resolution, respectively, and, if the shares of any class are entitled to vote as a class, the number of shares of each such class voted for and against the resolution, respectively.

§ 85. Filing of Statement of Intent to Dissolve

Duplicate originals of the statement of intent to dissolve, whether by consent of shareholders or by act of the corporation, shall be delivered to the Secretary of State. If the Secretary of State finds that such statement conforms to law, he shall, when all fees and franchise taxes have been paid as in this Act prescribed:

(a) Endorse on each of such duplicate originals the word "Filed," and the month, day and year of the filing thereof.

(b) File one of such duplicate originals in his office.

(c) Return the other duplicate original to the corporation or its representative.

§ 86. Effect of Statement of Intent to Dissolve

Upon the filing by the Secretary of State of a statement of intent to dissolve, whether by consent of shareholders or by act of the corporation, the corporation shall cease to carry on its business, except insofar as may be necessary for the winding up thereof, but its corporate existence shall continue until a certificate of dissolution has been issued by the Secretary of State or until a decree dissolving the corporation has been entered by a court of competent jurisdiction as in this Act provided.

§ 87. Procedure after Filing of Statement of Intent to Dissolve

After the filing by the Secretary of State of a statement of intent to dissolve:

(a) The corporation shall immediately cause notice thereof to be mailed to each known creditor of the corporation.

(b) The corporation shall proceed to collect its assets, convey and dispose of such of its properties as are not to be distributed in kind to its shareholders, pay, satisfy and discharge its liabilities and obligations and do all other acts required to liquidate its business and affairs, and, after paying or adequately providing for the payment of all its obligations, distribute the remainder of its assets, either in cash or in kind, among its shareholders according to their respective rights and interests.

(c) The corporation, at any time during the liquidation of its business and affairs, may make application to a court of competent jurisdiction within the state and judicial subdivision in which the registered office or principal place of business of the corporation is situated, to have the liquidation continued under the supervision of the court as provided in this Act.

§ 88. Revocation of Voluntary Dissolution Proceedings by Consent of Shareholders

By the written consent of all of its shareholders, a corporation may, at any time prior to the issuance of a certificate of dissolution by the Secretary of State, revoke voluntary dissolution proceedings theretofore taken, in the following manner:

Upon the execution of such written consent, a statement of revocation of voluntary dissolution proceedings shall be executed in duplicate by the corporation by its president or a vice president and by its secretary or an assistant secretary, and verified by one of the officers signing such statement, which statement shall set forth:

(a) The name of the corporation.

(b) The names and respective addresses of its officers.

(c) The names and respective addresses of its directors.

(d) A copy of the written consent signed by all shareholders of the corporation revoking such voluntary dissolution proceedings.

(e) That such written consent has been signed by all shareholders of the corporation or signed in their names by their attorneys thereunto duly authorized.

§ 89. Revocation of Voluntary Dissolution Proceedings by Act of Corporation

By the act of the corporation, a corporation may, at any time prior to the issuance of a certificate of dissolution by the Secretary of State, revoke voluntary dissolution proceedings theretofore taken, in the following manner:

(a) The board of directors shall adopt a resolution recommending that the voluntary dissolution proceedings be revoked, and directing that the question of such revocation be submitted to a vote at a special meeting of shareholders.

(b) Written notice, stating that the purpose or one of the purposes of such meeting is to consider the advisability of revoking the voluntary dissolution proceedings, shall be given to each shareholder of record entitled to vote at such meeting within the time and in the manner provided in this Act for the giving of notice of special meetings of shareholders.

(c) At such meeting a vote of the shareholders entitled to vote thereat shall be taken on a resolution to revoke the voluntary dissolution proceedings, which shall require for its adoption the affirmative vote of the holders of a majority of the shares entitled to vote thereon.

(d) Upon the adoption of such resolution, a statement of revocation of voluntary dissolution proceedings shall be executed in duplicate by the corporation by its president or a vice president and by its secretary or an assistant secretary, and verified by one of the officers signing such statement, which statement shall set forth:

(1) The name of the corporation.

(2) The names and respective addresses of its officers.

(3) The names and respective addresses of its directors.

(4) A copy of the resolution adopted by the shareholders revoking the voluntary dissolution proceedings.

(5) The number of shares outstanding.

(6) The number of shares voted for and against the resolution, respectively.

§ 90. Filing of Statement of Revocation of Voluntary Dissolution Proceedings

Duplicate originals of the statement of revocation of voluntary dissolution proceedings, whether by consent of shareholders or by act of the corporation, shall be delivered to the Secretary of State. If the Secretary of State finds that such statement conforms to law, he shall, when all fees and franchise taxes have been paid as in this Act prescribed:

(a) Endorse on each of such duplicate originals the word "Filed," and the month, day and year of the filing thereof.

(b) File one of such duplicate originals in his office.

(c) Return the other duplicate original to the corporation or its representative.

§ 91. Effect of Statement of Revocation of Voluntary Dissolution Proceedings

Upon the filing by the Secretary of State of a statement of revocation of voluntary dissolution proceedings, whether by consent of shareholders or by act of the corporation, the revocation of the voluntary dissolution proceedings shall become effective and the corporation may again carry on its business.

§ 92. Articles of Dissolution

If voluntary dissolution proceedings have not been revoked, then when all debts, liabilities and obligations of the corporation have been paid and discharged, or adequate provision has been made therefor, and all of the remaining property and assets of the corporation have been distributed to its shareholders, articles of dissolution shall be executed in duplicate by the corporation by its president or a vice president and by its secretary or an assistant secretary, and verified by one of the officers signing such statement, which statement shall set forth:

(a) The name of the corporation.

(b) That the Secretary of State has theretofore filed a statement of intent to dissolve the corporation, and the date on which such statement was filed.

(c) That all debts, obligations and liabilities of the corporation have been paid and discharged or that adequate provision has been made therefor.

(d) That all the remaining property and assets of the corporation have been distributed among its shareholders in accordance with their respective rights and interests.

(e) That there are no suits pending against the corporation in any court, or that adequate provision has been made for the satisfaction of any judgment, order or decree which may be entered against it in any pending suit.

§ 93. Filing of Articles of Dissolution

Duplicate originals of such articles of dissolution shall be delivered to the Secretary of State. If the Secretary of State finds that such articles of dissolution conform to law, he shall, when all fees and franchise taxes have been paid as in this Act prescribed:

(a) Endorse on each of such duplicate originals the word "Filed," and the month, day and year of the filing thereof.

(b) File one of such duplicate originals in his office.

(c) Issue a certificate of dissolution to which he shall affix the other duplicate original.

The certificate of dissolution, together with the duplicate original of the articles of dissolution affixed thereto by the Secretary of State, shall be returned to the representative of the dissolved corporation.

Upon the issuance of such certificate of dissolution the existence of the corporation shall cease, except for the purpose of suits, other proceedings and appropriate corporate action by shareholders, directors and officers as provided in this Act.

§ 94. Involuntary Dissolution

A corporation may be dissolved involuntarily by a decree of the .... court in an action filed by the Attorney General when it is established that:

(a) The corporation has failed to file its annual report within the time required by this Act, or has failed to pay its franchise tax on or before the first day of August of the year in which such franchise tax becomes due and payable; or

(b) The corporation procured its articles of incorporation through fraud; or

(c) The corporation has continued to exceed or abuse the authority conferred upon it by law; or

(d) The corporation has failed for thirty days to appoint and maintain a registered agent in this State; or

(e) The corporation has failed for thirty days after change of its registered office or registered agent to file in the office of the Secretary of State a statement of such change.

§ 95. Notification to Attorney General

The Secretary of State, on or before the last day of December of each year, shall certify to the Attorney General the names of all corporations which have failed to file their annual reports or to pay franchise taxes in accordance with the provisions of this Act, together with the facts pertinent thereto. He shall also certify, from time to time, the names of all corporations which have given other cause for dissolution as provided in this Act, together with the facts pertinent thereto. Whenever the Secretary of State shall certify the name of a corporation to the Attorney General as having given any cause for dissolution, the Secretary of State shall concurrently mail to the corporation at its registered office a notice that such certification has been made. Upon the receipt of such certification, the Attorney General shall file an action in the name of the State against such corporation for its dissolution. Every such certificate from the Secretary of State to the Attorney General pertaining to the failure of a corporation to file an annual report or pay a franchise tax shall be taken and received in all courts as prima facie evidence of the facts therein stated. If, before action is filed, the corporation shall file its annual report or pay its franchise tax, together with all penalties thereon, or shall appoint or maintain a registered agent as provided in this Act, or shall file with the Secretary of State the required statement of change of registered office or registered agent, such fact shall be forthwith certified by the Secretary of State to the Attorney General and he shall not file an action against such corporation for such cause. If, after action is filed, the corporation shall file its annual report or pay its franchise tax, together with all penalties thereon, or shall appoint or maintain a registered agent as provided in this Act, or shall file with the Secretary of State the required statement of change of registered office or registered agent, and shall pay the costs of such action, the action for such cause shall abate.

§ 96. Venue and Process

Every action for the involuntary dissolution of a corporation shall be commenced by the Attorney General either in the .... court of the county in which the registered office of the corporation is situated, or in the .... court of .... county. Summons shall issue and be served as in other civil actions. If process is returned not found, the Attorney General shall cause publication to be made as in other civil cases in some newspaper published in the county where the registered office of the corporation is situated, containing a notice of the pendency of such action, the title of the court, the title of the action, and the date on or after which default may be entered. The Attorney General may include in one notice the names of any number of corporations against which actions are then pending in the same court. The Attorney General shall cause a copy of such notice to be mailed to the corporation at its registered office within ten days after the first publication thereof. The certificate of the Attorney General of the mailing of such notice shall be prima facie evidence thereof. Such notice shall be published at least once each week for two successive weeks, and the first publication thereof may begin at any time after the summons has been returned. Unless a corporation shall have been served with summons, no default shall be taken against it earlier than thirty days after the first publication of such notice.

§ 97. Jurisdiction of Court to Liquidate Assets and Business of Corporation

The . . . . courts shall have full power to liquidate the assets and business of a corporation:

(a) In an action by a shareholder when it is established:

(1) That the directors are deadlocked in the management of the corporate affairs and the shareholders are unable to break the deadlock, and that irreparable injury to the corporation is being suffered or is threatened by reason thereof; or

(2) That the acts of the directors or those in control of the corporation are illegal, oppressive or fraudulent; or

(3) That the shareholders are deadlocked in voting power, and have failed, for a period which includes at least two consecutive annual meeting dates, to elect successors to directors whose terms have expired or would have expired upon the election of their successors; or

(4) That the corporate assets are being misapplied or wasted.

(b) In an action by a creditor:

(1) When the claim of the creditor has been reduced to judgment and an execution thereon returned unsatisfied and it is established that the corporation is insolvent; or

(2) When the corporation has admitted in writing that the claim of the creditor is due and owing and it is established that the corporation is insolvent.

(c) Upon application by a corporation which has filed a statement of intent to dissolve, as provided in this Act, to have its liquidation continued under the supervision of the court.

(d) When an action has been filed by the Attorney General to dissolve a corporation and it is established that liquidation of its business and affairs should precede the entry of a decree of dissolution.

Proceedings under clause (a), (b) or (c) of this section shall be brought in the county in which the registered office or the principal office of the corporation is situated.

It shall not be necessary to make shareholders parties to any such action or proceeding unless relief is sought against them personally.

§ 98. Procedure in Liquidation of Corporation by Court

In proceedings to liquidate the assets and business of a corporation the court shall have power to issue injunctions, to appoint a receiver or receivers pendente lite, with such powers and duties as the court, from time to time, may direct, and to take such other proceedings as may be requisite to preserve the corporate assets wherever situated, and carry on the business of the corporation until a full hearing can be had.

After a hearing had upon such notice as the court may direct to be given to all parties to the proceedings and to any other parties in interest designated by the court, the court may appoint a liquidating receiver or receivers with authority to collect the assets of the corporation, including all amounts owing to the corporation by subscribers on account of any unpaid portion of the consideration for the issuance of shares. Such liquidating receiver or receivers shall have authority, subject to the order of the court, to sell, convey and dispose of all or any part of the assets of the corporation wherever situated, either at public or private sale. The assets of the corporation or the proceeds resulting from a sale, conveyance or other disposition thereof shall be applied to the expenses of such liquidation and to the payment of the liabilities and obligations of the corporation, and any remaining assets or proceeds shall be distributed among its shareholders according to their respective rights and interests. The order appointing such liquidating receiver or receivers shall state their powers and duties. Such powers and duties may be increased or diminished at any time during the proceedings.

The court shall have power to allow from time to time as expenses of the liquidation compensation to the receiver or receivers and to attorneys in the proceeding, and to direct the payment thereof out of the assets of the corporation or the proceeds of any sale or disposition of such assets.

A receiver of a corporation appointed under the provisions of this section shall have authority to sue and defend in all courts in his own name as receiver of such corporation. The court appointing such receiver shall have exclusive jurisdiction of the corporation and its property, wherever situated.

§ 99. Qualifications of Receivers

A receiver shall in all cases be a natural person or a corporation authorized to act as receiver, which corporation may be a domestic corporation or a foreign corporation authorized to transact business in this State, and shall in all cases give such bond as the court may direct with such sureties as the court may require.

§ 100. Filing of Claims in Liquidation Proceedings

In proceedings to liquidate the assets and business of a corporation the court may require all creditors of the corporation to file with the clerk of the court or with the receiver, in such form as the court may prescribe, proofs under oath of their respective claims. If the court requires the filing of claims it shall fix a date, which shall be not less than four months from the date of the order, as the last day for the filing of claims, and shall prescribe the notice that shall be given to creditors and claimants of the date so fixed. Prior to the date so fixed, the court may extend the time for the filing of claims. Creditors and claimants failing to file proofs of claim on or before the date so fixed may be barred, by order of court, from participating in the distribution of the assets of the corporation.

§ 101. Discontinuance of Liquidation Proceedings

The liquidation of the assets and business of a corporation may be discontinued at any time during the liquidation proceedings when it is established that cause for liquidation no longer exists. In such event the court shall dismiss the proceedings and direct the receiver to redeliver to the corporation all its remaining property and assets.

§ 102. Decree of Involuntary Dissolution

In proceedings to liquidate the assets and business of a corporation, when the costs and expenses of such proceedings and all debts, obligations and liabilities of the corporation shall have been paid and discharged and all of its remaining property and assets distributed to its shareholders, or in case its property and assets are not sufficient to satisfy and discharge such costs, expenses, debts and obligations, all the property and assets have been applied so far as they will go to their payment, the court shall enter a decree dissolving the corporation, whereupon the existence of the corporation shall cease.

§ 103. Filing of Decree of Dissolution

In case the court shall enter a decree dissolving a corporation, it shall be the duty of the clerk of such court to cause a certified copy of the decree to be filed with the Secretary of State. No fee shall be charged by the Secretary of State for the filing thereof.

§ 104. Deposit with State Treasurer of Amount Due Certain Shareholders

Upon the voluntary or involuntary dissolution of a corporation, the portion of the assets distributable to a creditor or shareholder who is unknown or cannot be found, or who is under disability and there is no person legally competent to receive such distributive portion, shall be reduced to cash and deposited with the State Treasurer and shall be paid over to such creditor or shareholder or to his legal representative upon proof satisfactory to the State Treasurer of his right thereto.

§ 105. Survival of Remedy After Dissolution

The dissolution of a corporation either (1) by the issuance of a certificate of dissolution by the Secretary of State, or (2) by a decree of court when the court has not liquidated the assets and business of the corporation as provided in this Act, or (3) by expiration of its period of duration, shall not take away or impair any remedy available to or against such corporation, its directors, officers, or shareholders, for any right or claim existing, or any liability incurred, prior to such dissolution if action or other proceeding thereon is commenced within two years after the date of such dissolution. Any such action or proceeding by or against the corporation may be prosecuted or defended by the corporation in its corporate name. The shareholders, directors and officers shall have power to take such corporate or other action as shall be appropriate to protect such remedy, right or claim. If such corporation was dissolved by the expiration of its period of duration, such corporation may amend its articles of incorporation at any time during such period of two years so as to extend its period of duration.

§ 106. Admission of Foreign Corporation

No foreign corporation shall have the right to transact business in this State until it shall have procured a certificate of authority so to do from the Secretary of State. No foreign corporation shall be entitled to procure a certificate of authority under this Act to transact in this State any business which a corporation organized under this Act is not permitted to transact. A foreign corporation shall not be denied a certificate of authority by reason of the fact that the laws of the state or country under which such corporation is organized governing its organization and internal affairs differ from the laws of this State, and nothing in this Act contained shall be construed to authorize this State to regulate the organization or the internal affairs of such corporation.

Without excluding other activities which may not constitute transacting business in this State, a foreign corporation shall not be considered to be transacting business in this State, for the purposes of this Act, by reason of carrying on in this State any one or more of the following activities:

(a) Maintaining or defending any action or suit or any administrative or arbitration proceeding, or effecting the settlement thereof or the settlement of claims or disputes.

(b) Holding meetings of its directors or shareholders or carrying on other activities concerning its internal affairs.

(c) Maintaining bank accounts.

(d) Maintaining offices or agencies for the transfer, exchange and registration of its securities, or appointing and maintaining trustees or depositaries with relation to its securities.

(e) Effecting sales through independent contractors.

(f) Soliciting or procuring orders, whether by mail or through employees or agents or otherwise, where such orders require acceptance without this State before becoming binding contracts.

(g) Creating as borrower or lender, or acquiring, indebtedness or mortgages or other security interests in real or personal property.

(h) Securing or collecting debts or enforcing any rights in property securing the same.

(i) Transacting any business in interstate commerce.

(j) Conducting an isolated transaction completed within a period of thirty days and not in the course of a number of repeated transactions of like nature.

§ 107. Powers of Foreign Corporation

A foreign corporation which shall have received a certificate of authority under this Act shall, until a certificate of revocation or of withdrawal shall have been issued as provided in this Act, enjoy the same, but no greater, rights and privileges as a domestic corporation organized for the purposes set forth in the application pursuant to which such certificate of authority is issued; and, except as in this Act otherwise provided, shall be subject to the same duties, restrictions, penalties and liabilities now or hereafter imposed upon a domestic corporation of like character.

§ 108. Corporate Name of Foreign Corporation

No certificate of authority shall be issued to a foreign corporation unless the corporate name of such corporation:

(a) Shall contain the word "corporation," "company," "incorporated," or "limited," or shall contain an abbreviation of one of such words, or such corporation shall, for use in this State, add at the end of its name one of such words or an abbreviation thereof.

(b) Shall not contain any word or phrase which indicates or implies that it is organized for any purpose other than one or more of the purposes contained in its articles of incorporation or that it is authorized or empowered to conduct the business of banking or insurance.

(c) Shall not be the same as, or deceptively similar to, the name of any domestic corporation existing under the laws of this State or any foreign corporation authorized to transact business in this State, or a name the exclusive right to which is, at the time, reserved in the manner provided in this Act, or the name of a corporation which has in effect a registration of its name as provided in this Act, except that this provision shall not apply if the foreign corporation applying for a certificate of authority files with the Secretary of State any one of the following:

(1) a resolution of its board of directors adopting a fictitious name for use in transacting business in this State which fictitious name is not deceptively similar to the name of any domestic corporation or of any foreign corporation authorized to transact business in this State or to any name reserved or registered as provided in this Act, or

(2) the written consent of such other corporation or holder of a reserved or registered name to use the same or deceptively similar name and one or more words are added to make such name distinguishable from such other name, or

(3) a certified copy of a final decree of a court of competent jurisdiction establishing the prior right of such foreign corporation to the use of such name in this State.

§ 109. Change of Name by Foreign Corporation

Whenever a foreign corporation which is authorized to transact business in this State shall change its name to one under which a certificate of authority would not be granted to it on application therefor, the certificate of authority of such corporation shall be suspended and it shall not thereafter transact any business in this State until it has changed its name to a name which is available to it under the laws of this State or has otherwise complied with the provisions of this Act.

§ 110. Application for Certificate of Authority

A foreign corporation, in order to procure a certificate of authority to transact business in this State, shall make application therefor to the Secretary of State, which application shall set forth:

(a) The name of the corporation and the state or country under the laws of which it is incorporated.

(b) If the name of the corporation does not contain the word "corporation," "company," "incorporated," or "limited," or does not contain an abbreviation of one of such words, then the name of the corporation with the word or abbreviation which it elects to add thereto for use in this State.

(c) The date of incorporation and the period of duration of the corporation.

(d) The address of the principal office of the corporation in the state or country under the laws of which it is incorporated.

(e) The address of the proposed registered office of the corporation in this State, and the name of its proposed registered agent in this State at such address.

(f) The purpose or purposes of the corporation which it proposes to pursue in the transaction of business in this State.

(g) The names and respective addresses of the directors and officers of the corporation.

(h) A statement of the aggregate number of shares which the corporation has authority to issue, itemized by classes, par value of shares, shares without par value, and series, if any, within a class.

(i) A statement of the aggregate number of issued shares itemized by classes, par value of shares, shares without par value, and series, if any, within a class.

(j) A statement, expressed in dollars, of the amount of stated capital of the corporation, as defined in this Act.

(k) An estimate, expressed in dollars, of the value of all property to be owned by the corporation for the following year, wherever located, and an estimate of the value of the property of the corporation to be located within this State during such year, and an estimate, expressed in dollars, of the gross amount of business which will be transacted by the corporation during such year, and an estimate of the gross amount thereof which will be transacted by the corporation at or from places of business in this State during such year.

(l) Such additional information as may be necessary or appropriate in order to enable the Secretary of State to determine whether such corporation is entitled to a certificate of authority to transact business in this State and to determine and assess the fees and franchise taxes payable as in this Act prescribed.

Such application shall be made on forms prescribed and furnished by the Secretary of State and shall be executed in duplicate by the corporation by its president or a vice president and by its secretary or an assistant secretary, and verified by one of the officers signing such application.

§ 111. Filing of Application for Certificate of Authority

Duplicate originals of the application of the corporation for a certificate of authority shall be delivered to the Secretary of State, together with a copy of its articles of incorporation and all amendments thereto, duly authenticated by the proper officer of the state or country under the laws of which it is incorporated.

If the Secretary of State finds that such application conforms to law, he shall, when all fees and franchise taxes have been paid as in this Act prescribed:

(a) Endorse on each of such documents the word "Filed," and the month, day and year of the filing thereof.

(b) File in his office one of such duplicate originals of the application and the copy of the articles of incorporation and amendments thereto.

(c) Issue a certificate of authority to transact business in this State to which he shall affix the other duplicate original application.

The certificate of authority, together with the duplicate original of the application affixed thereto by the Secretary of State, shall be returned to the corporation or its representative.

§ 112. Effect of Certificate of Authority.

Upon the issuance of a certificate of authority by the Secretary of State, the corporation shall be authorized to transact business in this State for those purposes set forth in its application, subject, however, to the right of this State to suspend or to revoke such authority as provided in this Act.

§ 113. Registered Office and Registered Agent of Foreign Corporation

Each foreign corporation authorized to transact business in this State shall have and continuously maintain in this State:

(a) A registered office which may be, but need not be, the same as its place of business in this State.

(b) A registered agent, which agent may be either an individual resident in this State whose business office is identical with such registered office, or a domestic corporation, or a foreign corporation authorized to transact business in this State, having a business office identical with such registered office.

§ 114. Change of Registered Office or Registered Agent of Foreign Corporation

A foreign corporation authorized to transact business in this State may change its registered office or change its registered agent, or both, upon filing in the office of the Secretary of State a statement setting forth:

(a) The name of the corporation.

(b) The address of its then registered office.

(c) If the address of its registered office be changed, the address to which the registered office is to be changed.

(d) The name of its then registered agent.

(e) If its registered agent be changed, the name of its successor registered agent.

(f) That the address of its registered office and the address of the business office of its registered agent, as changed, will be identical.

(g) That such change was authorized by resolution duly adopted by its board of directors.

Such statement shall be executed by the corporation by its president or a vice president, and verified by him, and delivered to the Secretary of State. If the Secretary of State finds that such statement conforms to the provisions of this Act, he shall file such statement in his office, and upon such filing the change of address of the registered office, or the appointment of a new registered agent, or both, as the case may be, shall become effective.

Any registered agent of a foreign corporation may resign as such agent upon filing a written notice thereof, executed in duplicate, with the Secretary of State, who shall forthwith mail a copy thereof to the corporation at its principal office in the state or country under the laws of which it is incorporated. The appointment of such agent shall terminate upon the expiration of thirty days after receipt of such notice by the Secretary of State.

If a registered agent changes his or its business address to another place within the same ....*, he or it may change such address and the address of the registered office of any corporation of which he or it is registered agent by filing a statement as required above except that it need be signed only by the registered agent and need not be responsive to (e) or (g) and must recite that a copy of the statement has been mailed to the corporation.

§ 115. Service of Process on Foreign Corporation

The registered agent so appointed by a foreign corporation authorized to transact business in this State shall be an agent of such corporation upon whom any process, notice or demand required or permitted by law to be served upon the corporation may be served.

Whenever a foreign corporation authorized to transact business in this State shall fail to appoint or maintain a registered agent in this State, or whenever any such registered agent cannot with reasonable diligence be found at the registered office, or whenever the certificate of authority of a foreign corporation shall be suspended or revoked, then the Secretary of State shall be an agent of such corporation upon whom any such process, notice, or demand may be served. Service on the Secretary of State of any such process, notice

* Supply designation of jurisdiction, such as county, etc., in accordance with local practice.

or demand shall be made by delivering to and leaving with him, or with any clerk having charge of the corporation department of his office, duplicate copies of such process, notice or demand. In the event any such process, notice or demand is served on the Secretary of State, he shall immediately cause one of such copies thereof to be forwarded by registered mail, addressed to the corporation at its principal office in the state or country under the laws of which it is incorporated. Any service so had on the Secretary of State shall be returnable in not less than thirty days.

The Secretary of State shall keep a record of all processes, notices and demands served upon him under this section, and shall record therein the time of such service and his action with reference thereto.

Nothing herein contained shall limit or affect the right to serve any process, notice or demand, required or permitted by law to be served upon a foreign corporation in any other manner now or hereafter permitted by law.

§ 116. Amendment to Articles of Incorporation of Foreign Corporation

Whenever the articles of incorporation of a foreign corporation authorized to transact business in this State are amended, such foreign corporation shall, within thirty days after such amendment becomes effective, file in the office of the Secretary of State a copy of such amendment duly authenticated by the proper officer of the state or country under the laws of which it is incorporated; but the filing thereof shall not of itself enlarge or alter the purpose or purposes which such corporation is authorized to pursue in the transaction of business in this State, nor authorize such corporation to transact business in this State under any other name than the name set forth in its certificate of authority.

§ 117. Merger of Foreign Corporation Authorized to Transact Business in This State

Whenever a foreign corporation authorized to transact business in this State shall be a party to a statutory merger permitted by the laws of the state or country under the laws of which it is incorporated, and such corporation shall be the surviving corporation, it shall, within thirty days after such merger becomes effective, file with the Secretary of State a copy of the articles of merger duly authenticated by the proper officer of the state or country under the laws of which such statutory merger was effected; and it shall not be necessary for such corporation to procure either a new or amended certificate of authority to transact business in this State unless the name of such corporation be changed thereby or unless the corporation desires to pursue in this State other or additional purposes than those which it is then authorized to transact in this State.

§ 118. Amended Certificate of Authority

A foreign corporation authorized to transact business in this State shall procure an amended certificate of authority in the event it changes its corporate name, or desires to pursue in this State other or additional purposes than those set forth in its prior application for a certificate of authority, by making application therefor to the Secretary of State.

The requirements in respect to the form and contents of such application, the manner of its execution, the filing of duplicate originals thereof with the Secretary of State, the issuance of an amended certificate of authority and the effect thereof, shall be the same as in the case of an original application for a certificate of authority.

§ 119. Withdrawal of Foreign Corporation

A foreign corporation authorized to transact business in this State may withdraw from this State upon procuring from the Secretary of State a certificate of withdrawal. In order to procure such certificate of withdrawal, such foreign corporation shall deliver to the Secretary of State an application for withdrawal, which shall set forth:

(a) The name of the corporation and the state or country under the laws of which it is incorporated.

(b) That the corporation is not transacting business in this State.

(c) That the corporation surrenders its authority to transact business in this State.

(d) That the corporation revokes the authority of its registered agent in this State to accept service of process and consents that service of process in any action, suit or proceeding based upon any cause of action arising in this State during the time the corporation was authorized to transact business in this State may thereafter be made on such corporation by service thereof on the Secretary of State.

(e) A post-office address to which the Secretary of State may mail a copy of any process against the corporation that may be served on him.

(f) A statement of the aggregate number of shares which the corporation has authority to issue, itemized by classes, par value of shares, shares without par value, and series, if any, within a class, as of the date of such application.

(g) A statement of the aggregate number of issued shares, itemized by classes, par value of shares, shares without par value, and series, if any, within a class, as of the date of such application.

(h) A statement, expressed in dollars, of the amount of stated capital of the corporation, as of the date of such application.

(i) Such additional information as may be necessary or appropriate in order to enable the Secretary of State to determine and assess any unpaid fees or franchise taxes payable by such foreign corporation as in this Act prescribed.

The application for withdrawal shall be made on forms prescribed and furnished by the Secretary of State and shall be executed by the corporation by its president or a vice president and by its secretary or an assistant secretary, and verified by one of the officers signing the application, or, if the corporation is in the hands of a receiver or trustee, shall be executed on behalf of the corporation by such receiver or trustee and verified by him.

§ 120. Filing of Application for Withdrawal

Duplicate originals of such application for withdrawal shall be delivered to the Secretary of State. If the Secretary of State finds that such application conforms to the provisions of this Act, he shall, when all fees and franchise taxes have been paid as in this Act prescribed:

(a) Endorse on each of such duplicate originals the word "Filed," and the month, day and year of the filing thereof.

(b) File one of such duplicate originals in his office.

(c) Issue a certificate of withdrawal to which he shall affix the other duplicate original.

The certificate of withdrawal, together with the duplicate original of the application for withdrawal affixed thereto by the Secretary of State, shall be returned to the corporation or its representative. Upon the issuance of such certificate of withdrawal, the authority of the corporation to transact business in this State shall cease.

§ 121. Revocation of Certificate of Authority

The certificate of authority of a foreign corporation to transact business in this State may be revoked by the Secretary of State upon the conditions prescribed in this section when:

(a) The corporation has failed to file its annual report within the time required by this Act, or has failed to pay any fees, franchise taxes or penalties prescribed by this Act when they have become due and payable; or

(b) The corporation has failed to appoint and maintain a registered agent in this State as required by this Act; or

(c) The corporation has failed, after change of its registered office or registered agent, to file in the office of the Secretary of State a statement of such change as required by this Act; or

(d) The corporation has failed to file in the office of the Secretary of State any amendment to its articles of incorporation or any articles of merger within the time prescribed by this Act; or

(e) A misrepresentation has been made of any material matter in any application, report, affidavit, or other document submitted by such corporation pursuant to this Act.

No certificate of authority of a foreign corporation shall be revoked by the Secretary of State unless (1) he shall have given the corporation not less than sixty days' notice thereof by mail addressed to its registered office in this State, and (2) the corporation shall fail prior to revocation to file such annual report, or pay such fees, franchise taxes or penalties, or file the required statement of change of registered agent or registered office, or file such articles of amendment or articles of merger, or correct such misrepresentation.

§ 122. Issuance of Certificate of Revocation

Upon revoking any such certificate of authority, the Secretary of State shall:

(a) Issue a certificate of revocation in duplicate.

(b) File one of such certificates in his office.

(c) Mail to such corporation at its registered office in this State a notice of such revocation accompanied by one of such certificates.

Upon the issuance of such certificate of revocation, the authority of the corporation to transact business in this State shall cease.

§ 123. Application to Corporations Heretofore Authorized to Transact Business in This State

Foreign corporations which are duly authorized to transact business in this State at the time this Act takes effect, for a purpose or purposes for which a corporation might secure such authority under this Act, shall, subject to the limitations set forth in their respective certificates of authority, be entitled to all the rights and privileges applicable to foreign corporations procuring certificates of authority to transact business in this State under this Act, and from the time this Act takes effect such corporations shall be subject to all the limitations, restrictions, liabilities, and duties prescribed herein for foreign corporations procuring certificates of authority to transact business in this State under this Act.

§ 124. Transacting Business Without Certificate of Authority

No foreign corporation transacting business in this State without a certificate of authority shall be permitted to maintain any action, suit or proceeding in any court of this State, until such corporation shall have obtained a certificate of authority. Nor shall any action, suit or proceeding be maintained in any court of this State by any successor or assignee of such corporation on any right, claim or demand arising out of the transaction of business by such corporation in this State, until a certificate of authority shall have been obtained by such corporation or by a corporation which has acquired all or substantially all of its assets.

The failure of a foreign corporation to obtain a certificate of authority to transact business in this State shall not impair the validity of any contract or act of such corporation, and shall not prevent such corporation from defending any action, suit or proceeding in any court of this State.

A foreign corporation which transacts business in this State without a certificate of authority shall be liable to this State, for the years or parts thereof during which it transacted business in this State without a certificate of authority, in an amount equal to all fees and franchise taxes which would have been imposed by this Act upon such corporation had it duly applied for and received a certificate of authority to transact business in this State as required by this Act and thereafter filed all reports required by this Act, plus all penalties imposed by this Act for failure to pay such fees and franchise taxes. The Attorney General shall bring proceedings to recover all amounts due this State under the provisions of this Section.

§ 125. Annual Report of Domestic and Foreign Corporations

Each domestic corporation, and each foreign corporation authorized to transact business in this State, shall file, within the time prescribed by this Act, an annual report setting forth:

(a) The name of the corporation and the state or country under the laws of which it is incorporated.

(b) The address of the registered office of the corporation in this State, and the name of its registered agent in this State at such address, and, in case of a foreign corporation, the address of its principal office in the state or country under the laws of which it is incorporated.

(c) A brief statement of the character of the business in which the corporation is actually engaged in this State.

(d) The names and respective addresses of the directors and officers of the corporation.

(e) A statement of the aggregate number of shares which the corporation has authority to issue, itemized by classes, par value of shares, shares without par value, and series, if any, within a class.

(f) A statement of the aggregate number of issued shares, itemized by classes, par value of shares, shares without par value, and series, if any, within a class.

(g) A statement, expressed in dollars, of the amount of stated capital of the corporation, as defined in this Act.

(h) A statement, expressed in dollars, of the value of all the property owned by the corporation, wherever located, and the value of the property of the corporation located within this State, and a statement, expressed in dollars, of the gross amount of business transacted by the corporation for the twelve months ended on the thirty-first day of December preceding the date herein provided for the filing of such report and the gross amount thereof transacted by the corporation at or from places of business in this State. If, on the thirty-first day of December preceding the time herein provided for the filing of such report, the corporation had not been in existence for a period of twelve months, or in the case of a foreign corporation had not been authorized to transact business in this State for a period of twelve months, the statement with respect to business transacted shall be furnished for the period between the date of incorporation or the date of its authorization to transact business in this State, as the case may be, and such thirty-first day of December. If all the property of the corporation is located in this State and all of its business is transacted at or from places of business in this State, or if the corporation elects to pay the annual franchise tax on the basis of its entire stated capital, then the information required by this subparagraph need not be set forth in such report.

(i) Such additional information as may be necessary or appropriate in order to enable the Secretary of State to determine and assess the proper amount of franchise taxes payable by such corporation.

Such annual report shall be made on forms prescribed and furnished by the Secretary of State, and the information therein contained shall be given as of the date of the execution of the report, except as to the information required by subparagraphs (g), (h) and (i) which shall be given as of the close of business on the thirty-first day of December next preceding the date herein provided for the filing of such report. It shall be executed by the corporation by its president, a vice president, secretary, and assistant secretary, or treasurer, and verified by the officer executing the report, or, if the corporation is in the hands of a receiver or trustee, it shall be executed on behalf of the corporation and verified by such receiver or trustee.

§ 126. Filing of Annual Report of Domestic and Foreign Corporations

Such annual report of a domestic or foreign corporation shall be delivered to the Secretary of State between the first day of January and the first day of March of each year, except that the first annual report of a domestic or foreign corporation shall be filed between the first day of January and the first day of March of the year next succeeding the calendar year in which its certificate of incorporation or its certificate of authority, as the case may be, was issued by the Secretary of State. Proof to the satisfaction of the Secretary of State that prior to the first day of March such report was deposited in the United States mail in a sealed envelope, properly addressed, with postage prepaid, shall be deemed a compliance with this requirement. If the Secretary of State finds that such report conforms to the requirements of this Act, he shall file the same. If he finds that it does not so conform, he shall promptly return the same to the corporation for any necessary corrections, in which event the penalties hereinafter prescribed for failure to file such report within the time hereinabove provided shall not apply, if such report is corrected to conform to the requirements of this Act and returned to the Secretary of State within thirty days from the date on which it was mailed to the corporation by the Secretary of State.

§ 127. Fees, Franchise Taxes and Charges to Be Collected by Secretary of State

The Secretary of State shall charge and collect in accordance with the provisions of this Act:

(a) Fees for filing documents and issuing certificates.

(b) Miscellaneous charges.

(c) License fees.

(d) Franchise taxes.

§ 128. Fees for Filing Documents and Issuing Certificates

The Secretary of State shall charge and collect for:

(a) Filing articles of incorporation and issuing a certificate of incorporation, ... dollars.

(b) Filing articles of amendment and issuing a certificate of amendment, ... dollars.

(c) Filing restated articles of incorporation, ... dollars.

(d) Filing articles of merger or consolidation and issuing a certificate of merger or consolidation, ... dollars.

(e) Filing an application to reserve a corporate name, ... dollars.

(f) Filing a notice of transfer of a reserved corporate name, ... dollars.

(g) Filing a statement of change of address of registered office or change of registered agent, or both, ... dollars.

(h) Filing a statement of the establishment of a series of shares, ... dollars.

(i) Filing a statement of cancellation of shares, ... dollars.

(j) Filing a statement of reduction of stated capital, ... dollars.

(k) Filing a statement of intent to dissolve, ... dollars.

(l) Filing a statement of revocation of voluntary dissolution proceedings, ... dollars.

(m) Filing articles of dissolution, ... dollars.

(n) Filing an application of a foreign corporation for a certificate of authority to transact business in this State and issuing a certificate of authority, ... dollars.

(o) Filing an application of a foreign corporation for an amended certificate of authority to transact business in this State and issuing an amended certificate of authority, ... dollars.

(p) Filing a copy of an amendment to the articles of incorporation of a foreign corporation holding a certificate of authority to transact business in this State, ... dollars.

(q) Filing a copy of articles of merger of a foreign corporation holding a certificate of authority to transact business in this State, ... dollars.

(r) Filing an application for withdrawal of a foreign corporation and issuing a certificate of withdrawal, ... dollars.

(s) Filing any other statement or report, except an annual report, of a domestic or foreign corporation, ... dollars.

§ 129. Miscellaneous Charges

The Secretary of State shall charge and collect:

(a) For furnishing a certified copy of any document, instrument, or paper relating to a corporation, ... cents per page and . . . . dollars for the certificate and affixing the seal thereto.

(b) At the time of any service of process on him as resident agent of a corporation, ... dollars, which amount may be recovered as taxable costs by the party to the suit or action causing such service to be made if such party prevails in the suit or action.

§ 130. License Fees Payable by Domestic Corporations

The Secretary of State shall charge and collect from each domestic corporation license fees, based upon the number of shares which it will have authority to issue or the increase in the number of shares which it will have authority to issue, at the time of:

(a) Filing articles of incorporation;

(b) Filing articles of amendment increasing the number of authorized shares; and

(c) Filing articles of merger or consolidation increasing the number of authorized shares which the surviving or new corporation, if a domestic corporation, will have the authority to issue above the aggregate number of shares which the constituent domestic corporations and constituent foreign corporations authorized to transact business in this State had authority to issue.

The license fees shall be at the rate of . . . . cents per share up to and including the first 10,000 authorized shares, ... cents per share for each authorized share in excess of 10,000 shares up to and including 100,000 shares, and . . . . cents per share for each authorized share in excess of 100,000 shares, whether the shares are of par value or without par value.

The license fees payable on an increase in the number of authorized shares shall be imposed only on the increased number of shares, and the number of previously authorized shares shall be taken into account in determining the rate applicable to the increased number of authorized shares.

§ 131. License Fees Payable by Foreign Corporations

The Secretary of State shall charge and collect from each foreign corporation license fees, based upon the proportion represented in this State of the number of shares which it has authority to issue or the increase in the number of shares which it has authority to issue, at the time of:

(a) Filing an application for a certificate of authority to transact business in this State;

(b) Filing articles of amendment which increased the number of authorized shares; and

(c) Filing articles of merger or consolidation which increased the number of authorized shares which the surviving or new corporation, if a foreign corporation, has authority to issue above the aggregate number of shares which the constituent domestic corporations and constituent foreign corporations authorized to transact business in this State had authority to issue.

The license fees shall be at the rate of .... cents per share up to and including the first 10,000 authorized shares represented in this State, ... cents per share for each authorized share in excess of 10,000 shares up to and including 100,000 shares represented in this State, and .... cents per share for each authorized share in excess of 100,000 shares represented in this State, whether the shares are of par value or without par value.

The license fees payable on an increase in the number of authorized shares shall be imposed only on the increased number of such shares represented in this State, and the number of previously authorized shares represented in this State shall be taken into account in determining the rate applicable to the increased number of authorized shares.

The number of authorized shares represented in this State shall be that proportion of its total authorized shares which the sum of the value of its property located in this State and the gross amount of business transacted by it at or from places of business in this State bears to the sum of the value of all of its property, wherever located, and the gross amount of its business, wherever transacted. Such proportion shall be determined from information contained in the application for a certificate of authority to transact business in this State until the filing of an annual report and thereafter from information contained in the latest annual report filed by the corporation.

§ 132. Franchise Taxes Payable by Domestic Corporations

The Secretary of State shall charge and collect from each domestic corporation an initial franchise tax at the time of filing its articles of incorporation at the rate of one-twelfth of one-half of the license fee payable by such corporation under the provisions of this Act at the time of filing its articles of incorporation, for each calendar month, or fraction thereof, between the date of the issuance of the certificate of incorporation by the Secretary of State and the first day of July of the next succeeding calendar year.

The Secretary of State shall charge and collect from each domestic corporation an annual franchise tax, payable in advance for the period from July 1 in each year to July 1 in the succeeding year, beginning July 1 in the calendar year in which such corporation is required to file its first annual report under this Act, at the rate of .... of .... per cent of the amount represented in this State of the stated capital of the corporation, as disclosed by the latest report filed by the corporation with the Secretary of State.

The amount represented in this State of the stated capital of the corporation shall be that proportion of its stated capital which the sum of the value of its property located in this State and the gross amount of business transacted by it at or from places of business in this State bears to the sum of the value of all of its property, wherever located, and the gross amount of its business, wherever transacted, except as follows:

(a) If the corporation elects in its annual report in any year to pay its annual franchise tax on its entire stated capital, all franchise taxes accruing against the corporation after the filing of such annual report shall be assessed accordingly until the corporation elects otherwise in an annual report for a subsequent year.

(b) If the corporation fails to file its annual report in any year within the time prescribed by this Act, the proportion of its stated capital represented in this State shall be deemed to be its entire stated capital, unless its annual report is thereafter filed and its franchise tax thereafter adjusted by the Secretary of State in accordance with the provisions of this Act, in which case the proportion shall likewise be adjusted to the same proportion that would have prevailed if the corporation had filed its annual report within the time prescribed by this Act.

§ 133. Franchise Taxes Payable by Foreign Corporations

The Secretary of State shall charge and collect from each foreign corporation authorized to transact business in this State an initial franchise tax at the time of filing its application for a certificate of authority at the rate of one-twelfth of one-half of the license fee payable by such corporation under the provisions of this Act at the time of filing such application, for each month, or fraction thereof, between the date of the issuance of the certificate of authority by the Secretary of State and the first day of July of the next succeeding calendar year.

The Secretary of State shall charge and collect from each foreign corporation authorized to transact business in this State an annual franchise tax, payable in advance for the period from July 1 in each year to July 1 in the succeeding year, beginning July 1 in the calendar year in which such corporation is required to file its first annual report under this Act, at the rate of . . . . per cent of the amount represented in this State of the stated capital of the corporation, as disclosed by the latest annual report filed by the corporation with the Secretary of State.

The amount represented in this State of the stated capital of the corporation shall be that proportion of its stated capital which the sum of the value of its property located in this State and the gross amount of business transacted by it at or from places of business in this State bears to the sum of the value of all of its property, wherever located, and the gross amount of its business, wherever transacted, except as follows:

(a) If the corporation elects in its annual report in any year to pay its annual franchise tax on its entire stated capital, all franchise taxes accruing against the corporation after the filing of such annual report shall be assessed accordingly until the corporation elects otherwise in an annual report for a subsequent year.

(b) If the corporation fails to file its annual report in any year within the time prescribed by this Act, the proportion of its stated capital represented in this State shall be deemed to be its entire stated capital, unless its annual report is thereafter filed and its franchise tax thereafter adjusted by the Secretary of State in accordance with the provisions of this Act, in which case the proportion shall likewise be adjusted to the same proportion that would have prevailed if the corporation had filed its annual report within the time prescribed by this Act.

§ 134. Assessment and Collection of Annual Franchise Taxes

It shall be the duty of the Secretary of State to collect all annual franchise taxes and penalties imposed by, or assessed in accordance with, this Act.

Between the first day of March and the first day of June of each year, the Secretary of State shall assess against each corporation, domestic and foreign, required to file an annual report in such year, the franchise tax payable by it for the period from July 1 of such year to July 1 of the succeeding year in accordance with the provisions of this Act, and, if it has failed to file its annual report within the time prescribed by this Act, the penalty imposed by this Act upon such corporation for its failure so to do; and shall mail a written notice to each corporation against which such tax is assessed, addressed to such corporation at its registered office in this State, notifying the corporation (1) of the amount of franchise tax assessed against it for the ensuing year and the amount of penalty, if any, assessed against it for failure to file its annual report; (2) that objections, if any, to such assessment will be heard by the officer making the assessment on or before the fifteenth day of June of such year, upon receipt of a request from the corporation; and (3) that such tax and penalty shall be payable to the Secretary of State on the first day of July next succeeding the date of the notice. Failure to receive such notice shall not relieve the corporation of its obligation to pay the tax and any penalty assessed, or invalidate the assessment thereof.

The Secretary of State shall have power to hear and determine objections to any assessment of franchise tax at any time after such assessment and, after hearing, to change or modify any such assessment. In the event of any adjustment of franchise tax with respect to which a penalty has been assessed for failure to file an annual report, the penalty shall be adjusted in accordance with the provisions of this Act imposing such penalty.

All annual franchise taxes and all penalties for failure to file annual reports shall be due and payable on the first day of July of each year. If the annual franchise tax assessed against any corporation subject to the provisions of this Act, together with all penalties assessed thereon, shall not be paid to the Secretary of State on or before the thirty-first day of July of the year in which such tax is due and payable, the Secretary of State shall certify such fact to the Attorney General on or before the fifteenth day of November of such year, whereupon the Attorney General may institute an action against such corporation in the name of this State, in any court of competent jurisdiction, for the recovery of the amount of such franchise tax and penalties, together with the cost of suit, and prosecute the same to final judgment.

For the purpose of enforcing collection, all annual franchise taxes assessed in accordance with this Act, and all penalties assessed thereon and all interest and costs that shall accrue in connection with the collection thereof, shall be a prior and first lien on the real and personal property of the corporation from and including the first day of July of the year when such franchise taxes become due and payable until such taxes, penalties, interest, and costs shall have been paid.

§ 135. Penalties Imposed upon Corporations

Each corporation, domestic or foreign, that fails or refuses to file its annual report for any year within the time prescribed by this Act shall be subject to a penalty of ten per cent of the amount of the franchise tax assessed against it for the period beginning July 1 of the year in which such report should have been filed. Such penalty shall be assessed by the Secretary of State at the time of the assessment of the franchise tax. If the amount of the franchise tax as originally assessed against such corporation be thereafter adjusted in accordance with the provisions of this Act, the amount of the penalty shall be likewise adjusted to ten per cent of the amount of the adjusted franchise tax. The amount of the franchise tax and the amount of the penalty shall be separately stated in any notice to the corporation with respect thereto.

If the franchise tax assessed in accordance with the provisions of this Act shall not be paid on or before the thirty-first day of July, it shall be deemed to be delinquent, and there shall be added a penalty of one per cent for each month or part of month that the same is delinquent, commencing with the month of August.

Each corporation, domestic or foreign, that fails or refuses to answer truthfully and fully within the time prescribed by this Act interrogatories propounded by the Secretary of State in accordance with the provisions of this Act, shall be deemed to be guilty of a misdemeanor and upon conviction thereof may be fined in any amount not exceeding five hundred dollars.

§ 136. Penalties Imposed upon Officers and Directors

Each officer and director of a corporation, domestic or foreign, who fails or refuses within the time prescribed by this Act to answer truthfully and fully interrogatories propounded to him by the Secretary of State in accordance with the provisions of this Act, or who signs any articles, statement, report, application or other document filed with the Secretary of State which is known to such officer or director to be false in any material respect, shall be deemed to be guilty of a misdemeanor, and upon conviction thereof may be fined in any amount not exceeding . . . . dollars.

§ 137. Interrogatories by Secretary of State

The Secretary of State may propound to any corporation, domestic or foreign, subject to the provisions of this Act, and to any officer or director thereof, such interrogatories as may be reasonably necessary and proper to enable him to ascertain whether such corporation has complied with all the provisions of this Act applicable to such corporation. Such interrogatories shall be answered within thirty days after the mailing thereof, or within such additional time as shall be fixed by the Secretary of State, and the answers thereto shall be full and complete and shall be made in writing and under oath. If such interrogatories be directed to an individual they shall be answered by him, and if directed to a corporation they shall be answered by the president, vice president, secretary or assistant secretary thereof. The Secretary of State need not file any document to which such interrogatories relate until such interrogatories be answered as herein provided, and not then if the answers thereto disclose that such document is not in conformity with the provisions of this Act. The Secretary of State shall certify to the Attorney General, for such action as the Attorney General may deem appropriate, all interrogatories and answers thereto which disclose a violation of any of the provisions of this Act.

§ 138. Information Disclosed by Interrogatories

Interrogatories propounded by the Secretary of State and the answers thereto shall not be open to public inspection nor shall the

Secretary of State disclose any facts or information obtained therefrom except insofar as his official duty may require the same to be made public or in the event such interrogatories or the answers thereto are required for evidence in any criminal proceedings or in any other action by this State.

§ 139. Powers of Secretary of State

The Secretary of State shall have the power and authority reasonably necessary to enable him to administer this Act efficiently and to perform the duties therein imposed upon him.

§ 140. Appeal from Secretary of State

If the Secretary of State shall fail to approve any articles of incorporation, amendment, merger, consolidation or dissolution, or any other document required by this Act to be approved by the Secretary of State before the same shall be filed in his office, he shall, within ten days after the delivery thereof to him, give written notice of his disapproval to the person or corporation, domestic or foreign, delivering the same, specifying the reasons therefor. From such disapproval such person or corporation may appeal to the .... court of the county in which the registered office of such corporation is, or is proposed to be, situated by filing with the clerk of such court a petition setting forth a copy of the articles or other document sought to be filed and a copy of the written disapproval thereof by the Secretary of State; whereupon the matter shall be tried de novo by the court, and the court shall either sustain the action of the Secretary of State or direct him to take such action as the court may deem proper.

If the Secretary of State shall revoke the certificate of authority to transact business in this State of any foreign corporation, pursuant to the provisions of this Act, such foreign corporation may likewise appeal to the .... court of the county where the registered office of such corporation in this State is situated, by filing with the clerk of such court a petition setting forth a copy of its certificate of authority to transact business in this State and a copy of the notice of revocation given by the Secretary of State; whereupon the matter shall be tried de novo by the court, and the court shall either sustain the action of the Secretary of State or direct him to take such action as the court may deem proper.

Appeals from all final orders and judgments entered by the . . . . court under this section in review of any ruling or decision of the Secretary of State may be taken as in other civil actions.

§ 141. Certificates and Certified Copies to Be Received in Evidence

All certificates issued by the Secretary of State in accordance with the provisions of this Act, and all copies of documents filed in his office in accordance with the provisions of this Act when certified by him, shall be taken and received in all courts, public offices, and official bodies as prima facie evidence of the facts therein stated. A certificate by the Secretary of State under the great seal of this State, as to the existence or nonexistence of the facts relating to corporations shall be taken and received in all courts, public offices, and official bodies as prima facie evidence of the existence or nonexistence of the facts therein stated.

§ 142. Forms to Be Furnished by Secretary of State

All reports required by this Act to be filed in the office of the Secretary of State shall be made on forms which shall be prescribed and furnished by the Secretary of State. Forms for all other documents to be filed in the office of the Secretary of State shall be furnished by the Secretary of State on request therefor, but the use thereof, unless otherwise specifically prescribed in this Act, shall not be mandatory.

§ 143. Greater Voting Requirements

Whenever, with respect to any action to be taken by the shareholders of a corporation, the articles of incorporation require the vote or concurrence of the holders of a greater proportion of the shares, or of any class or series thereof, then required by this Act with respect to such action, the provisions of the articles of incorporation shall control.

§ 144. Waiver of Notice

Whenever any notice is required to be given to any shareholder or director of a corporation under the provisions of this Act or under the provisions of the articles of incorporation or by-laws of the corporation, a waiver thereof in writing signed by the person or persons entitled to such notice, whether before or after the time stated therein, shall be equivalent to the giving of such notice.

§ 145. Action by Shareholders Without a Meeting

Any action required by this Act to be taken at a meeting of the shareholders of a corporation, or any action which may be taken at a meeting of the shareholders, may be taken without a meeting if a consent in writing, setting forth the action so taken, shall be signed by all of the shareholders entitled to vote with respect to the subject matter thereof.

Such consent shall have the same effect as a unanimous vote of shareholders, and may be stated as such in any articles or document filed with the Secretary of State under this Act.

§ 146. Unauthorized Assumption of Corporate Powers

All persons who assume to act as a corporation without authority so to do shall be jointly and severally liable for all debts and liabilities incurred or arising as a result thereof.

§ 147. Application to Existing Corporations

The provisions of this Act shall apply to all existing corporations organized under any general act of this State providing for the organization of corporations for a purpose or purposes for which a corporation might be organized under this Act, where the power has been reserved to amend, repeal or modify the act under which such corporation was organized and where such act is repealed by this Act.

§ 148. Application to Foreign and Interstate Commerce

The provisions of this Act shall apply to commerce with foreign nations and among the several states only insofar as the same may be permitted under the provisions of the Constitution of the United States.

§ 149. Reservation of Power

The . . . .* shall at all times have power to prescribe such regulations, provisions and limitations as it may deem advisable, which regulations, provisions and limitations shall be binding upon any and all corporations subject to the provisions of this Act, and the . . . .* shall have power to amend, repeal or modify this Act at pleasure.

§ 150. Effect of Repeal of Prior Acts

The repeal of a prior act by this Act shall not affect any right accrued or established, or any liability or penalty incurred, under the provisions of such act, prior to the repeal thereof.

§ 151. Effect of Invalidity of Part of This Act

If a court of competent jurisdiction shall adjudge to be invalid or unconstitutional any clause, sentence, paragraph, section or part of this Act, such judgment or decree shall not affect, impair, invalidate or nullify the remainder of this Act, but the effect thereof shall be confined to the clause, sentence, paragraph, section or part of this Act so adjudged to be invalid or unconstitutional.

---

* Insert name of legislative body.

§ 152. Repeal of Prior Acts

(Insert appropriate provisions) . . . .

APPENDIX B

Reading Financial Statements

The most basic and most often encountered financial statements are the balance sheet and the income statement. They are discussed below somewhat fully. Two subsidiary statements, the retained earnings statement and the statement of changes in financial position, are mentioned briefly.

Balance Sheet

The balance sheet shows a company's assets and liabilities plus the equity in the business held by its owners at a particular point in time, such as at the close of business on December 31. The simplest corporate balance sheet possible, showing only totals and leaving out all detail, might look like:

ACADEMAIR, INC.
Balance Sheet
December 31, 1992

ASSETS	$385,000	LIABILITIES	$285,000
		SHAREHOLDERS' EQUITY	$100,000
		Total Liabilities and Shareholders' Equity	$385,000

In that example, the assets are equal to the liabilities plus the shareholders' equity (which might be called "proprietor's equity" in a proprietorship or "partners' capital" in a partnership). That is always true for a balance sheet, because what a balance sheet shows is simply how much the company owns (its assets), how much it owes (its liabilities), and how much is left over for the company's owners. The following two equations may be helpful:

$$\text{assets} = \text{liabilities} + \text{equity}; \quad \text{assets} - \text{liabilities} = \text{equity}$$

With that background, we now can turn to a balance sheet showing details. A more detailed version of the balance sheet shown above might look like this:

ACADEMAIR, INC.
Balance Sheet
December 31, 1992

ASSETS		LIABILITIES	
Current Assets		Current Liabilities	
Cash	$ 50,000	Accounts payable	$ 60,000
Accounts receivable (net of allowance for bad debts of $5,000)	75,000	Notes payable (including current portion of long-term debt)	40,000
Inventory (FIFO)	125,000	Income taxes payable	25,000
Total current assets	$250,000	Total current liabilities	$125,000
Fixed Assets		Long-term liabilities	
Land	$ 50,000	5-year notes payable	$160,000
Building	75,000		
Equipment	50,000	Total Liabilities	$285,000
Less: Accumulated depreciation	$ 50,000		
Net fixed assets	$125,000	SHAREHOLDERS' EQUITY	
Intangibles: Patents	$ 10,000		
		Common stock ($1.00 par value; 1,000 shares authorized, issued, and outstanding)	$ 1,000
		Paid-in capital in excess of par value	49,000
		Retained earnings	50,000
		Total Shareholders' Equity	$100,000
Total Assets	$385,000	Total Liabilities and Shareholders' Equity	$385,000

Even without further discussion, it is now possible to "read" a good deal of that balance sheet, since much of the detail that has been added is self-explanatory. In order better to understand that detail, however, some explanation is in order.

Assets

The assets of the corporation are shown under three headings: current assets, fixed assets, and intangibles. Current assets consist of cash and those items such as accounts receivable that are normally expected to be converted into cash within one year. Fixed assets are the company's more or less permanent physical assets, such as its land, buildings, machinery, and equipment. Intangible assets include, among other things, such items as patents and trademarks. Current assets and fixed assets are discussed below.

Current Assets

Cash. Cash includes not only currency, which a company might keep in "petty cash," but also bank deposits and other "cash equivalents."

Accounts receivable. If a company sells goods or services on credit, the amounts owing from purchasers are "accounts receivable." The company must anticipate, however, that some of the accounts receivable will not be received. An account, which might be called "allowance for bad debts," is therefore established in the company's books and set off against or subtracted from the accounts receivable shown in the balance sheet. That is necessary in order to present a fair picture of how much the company likely will receive from its credit sales.

Inventory. In a manufacturing company, inventory includes raw materials, work in process, and finished goods. Other types of companies have other types of inventory. For example, a retail store has in inventory only the purchased goods it sells. Service companies, of course, have no inventory. In preparing a balance sheet, a company must first determine what its inventory is (preferably by physically counting it) and then place a value on that inventory. The generally accepted method of valuation is to record the inventory at its cost or market value, whichever is lower (here "market value" is not retail value, but what it would cost the company to replace the inventory). For simplicity, we shall ignore the methods a manufacturing company would use in measuring the cost of goods that are in various stages of the manufacturing process and deal only with the valuation of purchased goods that a company has in inventory. The following are two common ways to measure the "cost" of inventory that has been purchased at different times and at varying prices.

(a) *First-in, first-out* (FIFO). Under the FIFO method of valuation, the items of inventory that are purchased first are deemed to be sold first. Therefore, under that method the most recent purchase prices are deemed to represent the cost of the items remaining in inventory. For example, suppose that the purchases and sales of a particular item are as follows:

	Quantity	Cost per Item	Total Cost
January Purchase	100	$0.60	$ 60
March Purchase	500	0.70	350
June Purchase	300	0.80	240
September Purchase	100	0.90	90
Total Purchases	1,000		$740
Less sales	700		
Ending inventory	300		

Under the FIFO method of valuation, the cost of the ending inventory of 300 items would be deemed to be $250 ($.90 each for 100 and $.80 each for 200). Obviously, in times of rising prices, use of the FIFO method will result in inventory's being shown on the balance sheet at the highest possible amount.

(b) *Last-in, first-out* (LIFO). Under the LIFO method of valuation, the items of inventory that are purchased last are deemed to be sold first, and so the cost of the ending inventory is deemed to be the cost of the items that were purchased first. In the situation described above, the cost of the ending inventory of 300 items would be deemed to be $200 ($ .60 each for 100 items and $.70 each for 200 items).

Fixed Assets

As indicated above, fixed assets include such items as land, buildings, machinery, and equipment. Fixed assets typically are shown on the balance sheet at their cost less accumulated depreciation. "Depreciation" is the term used to describe the allocation of the cost of certain fixed assets, such as buildings, machinery, and equipment, over their estimated useful lives. The term "depletion" rather than "depreciation" is used in the case of "wasting assets," such as oil and gas fields. "Amortization" is the term used when intangible assets, such as patents or trademarks, are involved. Land is not depreciated, since it does not have (at least for accounting purposes) a limited useful life.

When a fixed asset is depreciated, the cost of the asset is allocated over its expected useful life, and each annual installment of depreciation is added to an account in the company's books called "accumulated depreciation." On the balance sheet, accumulated depreciation is set off against the total fixed assets (shown at their total cost at time of purchase). Notice that appreciation in the value of assets, which is likely for certain assets in times of rising prices, is not reflected on the balance sheet.

Several methods are used to calculate depreciation. Here are the two most frequently encountered:

Straight-line method. The straight-line depreciation method is the most common for other than tax purposes. Under that method, depreciation is calculated by dividing the cost of the asset, less its salvage value, by the estimated useful life of the asset. For example, a computer costing $50,000, with a salvage value of $10,000 and an estimated useful life of five years, would have annual depreciation of $8,000 ($50,000 – $10,000 = $40,000; $40,000 / 5 = $8,000), or 20 percent per year.

Double declining balance method. Under the double declining balance method, depreciation is calculated by taking twice the straight-line depreciation percentage rate and multiplying that percentage rate by either the initial cost of the asset, which is what is done the first year depreciation is calculated, or in succeeding years by each declining balance figure that results from subtracting previously calculated depreciation from the initial cost. Salvage value does not enter into the computation, but under this method an asset is not depreciated below a reasonable salvage value. Using the example above, the depreciation percentage rate would be 40 percent (20 percent doubled). That rate multiplied by $50,000 (the initial cost of the computer) gives a result of $20,000, which would be the amount of depreciation for the first year. For the following year, depreciation would be calculated by multiplying the "declining balance" of $30,000 ($50,000 – $20,000) by 40 percent to give a result of $12,000. That method of calculating annual depreciation would continue until a reasonable salvage figure is reached.

The double declining balance method, and certain other methods not discussed here, are called accelerated depreciation methods because they produce a greater amount of depreciation in the initial years of an asset's life than does the straight-line method.

Liabilities

The second portion of the balance sheet consists of the liabilities of the company. Liabilities are usually separated into two categories: current liabilities and long-term liabilities. Current liabilities consist of those debts that are to be paid within a year. Accounts payable, short-term notes payable, and income taxes payable are typical current liabilities. Long-term liabilities are often in the form of long term notes or bonds, but include any debt that is not due within one year. In the case of a debt that is partially due within one year and partially due in future years, the portion of the debt payable within one year is shown as a current liability and the rest as a long-term liability.

Equity

The third and final portion of a balance sheet represents the owners' equity. In the case of a corporation, that portion is subdivided into three categories. Those categories are given various names in state corporation statutes. In the Model Business Corporation Act and many other statutes they are called stated capital, capital surplus, and earned surplus. Regardless of the names used in corporation statutes, however, accountants use their own terms on balance sheets. Thus, what a corporation statute calls stated capital is shown on the above balance sheet as "common stock," capital surplus is shown as "paid-in capital in excess of par value," and earned surplus as "retained earnings." In the discussion below, we shall use the "lawyers' terms" commonly found in statutes.

To explain the terms fully would take more space than is warranted here, particularly since they are discussed in chapter 5. Briefly, stated capital is calculated by multiplying the number of shares of stock outstanding by the par value of each share. (In this discussion of stated capital and both categories of surplus, we shall ignore stock without par value and also ignore the possibility of transfers between the categories of shareholders' equity, which is allowed by corporation statutes in some circumstances.) In the case of the balance sheet shown above, the par value of the corporation's common stock is one dollar per share and 1,000 shares have been issued, yielding a stated capital of $1,000. For current purposes, par value is perhaps best explained as being simply an arbitrary dollar figure assigned to the stock, the major purpose of which is to determine the amount of stated capital. The importance of that is that corporation statutes place restrictions on what a corporation can do with its stated capital.

Capital surplus is basically the difference between what shareholders paid the corporation for their stock and the par value of the stock. In the case of the balance sheet shown above, it appears that the 1,000 shares of common stock were sold by the corporation for $50 each, or $50,000 in total ($49,000 shown in "paid-in capital in excess of par value" plus $1,000 shown in "common stock"). As in the case of stated capital, corporation statutes restrict what a corporation can do with its capital surplus, although the restrictions differ from those for stated capital.

Again ignoring transfers between categories of shareholders' equity, earned surplus shows the total amount of profits and losses of the corporation since its formation, decreased by any dividends paid the shareholders (since dividends are usually payable only out of earned surplus). One might ask what happens if the corporation has had losses rather than profits. In that case, earned surplus is shown as a negative number (indicated by placing the number in parentheses).

Income Statement

Unlike the balance sheet, which shows a company's financial status at a particular point in time (such as on December 31), the income statement shows the results of a company's operations over a period of time (such as for the year ending December 31). Stated simply, it shows the company's revenues and expenses, and how much the company made in profits. An income statement for Academair, Inc. might look like this:

ACADEMAIR, INC.
Income Statement
Year Ended December 31, 1992

Net sales		$500,000
Cost of goods sold and operating expenses		
Cost of goods sold		$304,000
Depreciation		15,000
Selling and administrative expenses		100,000
		$419,000
	Operating Income	$ 81,000
Interest on long-term notes		13,000
Income before income taxes		$ 68,000
Income taxes		18,000
	Net income	$ 50,000
Net income per share (1,000 shares outstanding)		$50

Some explanation of specific income statement items may be helpful.

Net sales. Net sales are calculated by totaling all sales during the period, and then subtracting the sales price of all returned goods and all allowances made because of damaged or defective goods.

Cost of goods sold. Calculating the cost of goods sold begins where calculating the cost of ending inventory for balance sheet purposes ends. In the case of goods that are sold in the form in which they were purchased, the cost of goods sold during a period (assuming there is no inventory at the beginning of the period) is calculated by subtracting the cost of ending inventory from the total cost of the purchased goods. In our example above relating to inventory valuation, the total cost of the purchases of the item in question were $740. Under the FIFO method of valuation, the cost of ending inventory was $250 and under the LIFO method, $200. Under those methods, the cost of goods sold for that item would be $490 ($740 minus $250) and $540 ($740 minus $200).

Obviously, the cost of goods sold has a direct effect on the amount of income shown on a company's income statement. As can easily be seen, the amount of income shown may vary, sometimes to a great extent, depending on the method of inventory valuation used.

Depreciation. We have already discussed depreciation as it is shown on the balance sheet. There, the total amount of depreciation over the past life of fixed assets is shown as a setoff from the total cost of those assets. On the income statement, only depreciation for the period covered by the statement is shown. In the case of the above income statement, that is one year's depreciation.

By using an accelerated depreciation method, such as the double declining balance method, the depreciation over the first few years of an asset's life will be much greater than it would be if the straightline method were used. That, of course, will result in lower income—and lower taxes—during those years. A company's decisions with respect to the estimated useful life of assets also affects the amount of depreciation, and therefore income, shown on its income statement. For example, within the limits of what are called "generally accepted accounting principles," a company might estimate the useful life of a particular piece of machinery as five years, or ten years, or any number of years in between, thus causing a possible variation in depreciation of as much as 100 percent.

Selling and administrative expenses. Selling and administrative expenses are exactly what one would expect. That item generally encompasses all the expenses of a company not included under another heading (called "line items" on financial statements) on the income statement.

Interest on long-term notes. The interest accrued on long-term debt during the period covered by an income statement is generally shown as a line item separate from other expenses. In the case of Academair, Inc., the long-term debt is in the form of notes. In the case of other corporations, it could be represented by other debt instruments, such as bonds.

Income taxes. Income taxes are also shown as a separate line item, allowing the reader of the income statement to see at a glance what the company's income was both before and after taxes.

Net income per share. This item is simply net income divided by the number of shares outstanding.

Retained Earnings Statement

The retained earnings statement shows increases and decreases in the corporation's earned surplus (called retained earnings by most accountants) during the period covered by the income statement it accompanies. In the case of a statement showing changes during a calendar year, it would show (1) the amount of earned surplus on January 1, (2) any additions to earned surplus arising from profits during the year, (3) any decreases arising from dividends paid to shareholders, or from transfers to capital surplus or stated capital, and (4) the amount of earned surplus on December 31.

Statement of Cash Flows

The statement of cash flows covers the same period as the income statement it accompanies and shows (1) from what sources the company received its funds (net income, for example) and (2) how its funds were used (such as for dividends and purchases of equipment).

The financial statements shown above do not include all of the items one will find on other financial statements; and the discussion of these statements and the accounting concepts they embody was simplified. One will find, however, that even the most complicated balance sheets and income statements for the largest corporations are, in the main, simply more detailed versions of the statements included here. If one understands these simple statements, one will understand more complex ones to a fair degree.

Model Business Corporation Act Offical Forms: By-Laws—Long Form

Form No. 51

BY-LAWS OF

. . . .

Article I. Offices

The principal office of the corporation in the State of .... shall be located in the City of ...., County of .... The corporation may have such other offices, either within or without the State of ...., as the board of directors may designate or as the business of the corporation may require from time to time.

The registered office of the corporation, required by the .... Business Corporation Act to be maintained in the State of .... may be, but need not be, identical with the principal office in the State of ...., and the address of the registered office may be changed from time to time by the board of directors. [§ 12] [§ 13, Clause (g)]*

* Numbers in [brackets] are references to Sections of the Model Business Corporation Act.

Article II. Shareholders

Section 1. Annual Meeting. The annual meeting of the shareholders shall be held on the . . . . in the month of . . . . in each year, beginning with the year 19 . . . ., at the hour of . . . . . . o'clock . . . . M., or at such other time on such other day within such month as shall be fixed by the board of directors, for the purpose of electing directors and for the transaction of such other business as may come before the meeting. If the day fixed for the annual meeting shall be a legal holiday in the State of . . . ., such meeting shall be held on the next succeeding business day. If the election of directors shall not be held on the day designated herein for any annual meeting of the shareholders, or at any adjournment thereof, the board of directors shall cause the election to be held at a special meeting of the shareholders as soon thereafter as conveniently may be. [§ 28] [§ 36]

Section 2. Special Meetings. Special meetings of the shareholders, for any purpose or purposes, unless otherwise prescribed by statute, may be called by the president or by the board of directors, and shall be called by the president at the request of the holders of not less than one-tenth of all outstanding shares of the corporation entitled to vote at the meeting. [§ 28]

Section 3. Place of Meeting. The board of directors may designate any place, either within or without the State of . . . . , as the place of meeting for any annual meeting or for any special meeting called by the board of directors. A waiver of notice signed by all shareholders entitled to vote at a meeting may designate any place, either within or without the State of . . . . , as the place for the holding of such meeting. If no designation is made, or if a special meeting be otherwise called, the place of meeting shall be the principal office of the corporation in the State of . . . . [§ 28]

Section 4. Notice of Meeting. Written notice stating the place, day and hour of the meeting and, in case of a special meeting, the purpose or purposes for which the meeting is called, shall, unless otherwise prescribed by statute, be delivered not less than ten nor more than fifty days before the date of the meeting, either personally or by mail, by or at the direction of the president, or the secretary, or the officer or other persons calling the meeting, to each shareholder of record entitled to vote at such meeting. If mailed, such notice shall be deemed to be delivered when deposited in the United States mail, addressed to the shareholder at his address as it appears on the stock transfer books of the corporation, with postage thereon prepaid. [§ 29]

Section 5. Closing of Transfer Books or Fixing of Record Date. For the purpose of determining shareholders entitled to notice of or to vote at any meeting of shareholders or any adjournment thereof, or shareholders entitled to receive payment of any dividend, or in order to make a determination of shareholders for any other proper purpose, the board of directors of the corporation may provide that the stock transfer books shall be closed for a stated period but not to exceed, in any case, fifty days. If the stock transfer books shall be closed for the purpose of determining shareholders entitled to notice of or to vote at a meeting of shareholders, such books shall be closed for at least ten days immediately preceding such meeting. In lieu of closing the stock transfer books, the board of directors may fix in advance a date as the record date for any such determination of shareholders, such date in any case to be not more than fifty days and, in case of a meeting of shareholders, not less than ten days prior to the date on which the particular action, requiring such determination of shareholders, is to be taken. If the stock transfer books are not closed and no record date is fixed for the determination of shareholders entitled to notice of or to vote at a meeting of shareholders, or shareholders entitled to receive payment of a dividend, the date on which notice of the meeting is mailed or the date on which the resolution of the board of directors declaring such dividend is adopted, as the case may be, shall be the record date for such determination of shareholders. When a determination of shareholders entitled to vote at any meeting of shareholders has been made as provided in this section, such determination shall apply to any adjournment thereof. [§ 30]

Section 6. Voting Record. The officer or agent having charge of the stock transfer books for shares of the corporation shall make a complete record of the shareholders entitled to vote at each meeting of shareholders or any adjournment thereof, arranged in alphabetical order, with the address of and the number of shares held by each. Such record shall be produced and kept open at the time and place of the meeting and shall be subject to the inspection of any shareholder during the whole time of the meeting for the purposes thereof. [§ 31]

Section 7. Quorum. A majority of the outstanding shares of the corporation entitled to vote, represented in person or by proxy, shall constitute a quorum at a meeting of shareholders. If less than a majority of the outstanding shares are represented at a meeting, a majority of the shares so represented may adjourn the meeting from time to time without further notice. At such adjourned meeting at which a quorum shall be present or represented, any business may be transacted which might have been transacted at the meeting as originally noticed. The shareholders present at a duly organized meeting may continue to transact business until adjournment, notwithstanding the withdrawal of enough shareholders to leave less than a quorum. [§ 32]

Section 8. Proxies. At all meetings of shareholders, a shareholder may vote in person or by proxy executed in writing by the shareholder or by his duly authorized attorney-in-fact. Such proxy shall be filed with the secretary of the corporation before or at the time of the meeting. No proxy shall be valid after eleven months from the date of its execution, unless otherwise provided in the proxy. [§ 33]

Section 9. Voting of Shares. Subject to the provisions of Section 12 of this Article II, each outstanding share entitled to vote shall be entitled to one vote upon each matter submitted to a vote at a meeting of shareholders. [§ 33]

Section 10. Voting of Shares by Certain Holders. Shares standing in the name of another corporation may be voted by such officer, agent or proxy as the by-laws of such corporation may prescribe, or, in the absence of such provision, as the board of directors of such other corporation may determine. [§ 33]

Shares held by an administrator, executor, guardian or conservator may be voted by him, either in person or by proxy, without a transfer of such shares into his name. Shares standing in the name of a trustee may be voted by him, either in person or by proxy, but no trustee shall be entitled to vote shares held by him without a transfer of such shares into his name. [§ 33]

Shares standing in the name of a receiver may be voted by such receiver, and shares held by or under the control of a receiver may be voted by such receiver without the transfer thereof into his name if authority so to do be contained in an appropriate order of the court by which such receiver was appointed. [§ 33]

A shareholder whose shares are pledged shall be entitled to vote such shares until the shares have been transferred into the name of the pledgee, and thereafter the pledgee shall be entitled to vote the shares so transferred. [§ 33]

Neither treasury shares of its own stock held by the corporation, nor shares held by another corporation if a majority of the shares entitled to vote for the election of directors of such other corporation are held by the corporation, shall be voted at any meeting or counted in determining the total number of outstanding shares at any given time for purposes of any meeting. [§ 33]

Section 11. Informal Action by Shareholders. Any action required or permitted to be taken at a meeting of the shareholders may be taken without a meeting if a consent in writing, setting forth the action so taken, shall be signed by all of the shareholders entitled to vote with respect to the subject matter thereof. [§ 145]

[Optional Section.] *Section 12. Cumulative Voting.* At each election for directors every shareholder entitled to vote at such election shall have the right to vote, in person or by proxy, the number of shares owned by him for as many persons as there are directors to be elected and for whose election he has a right to vote, or to cumulate his votes by giving one candidate as many votes as the number of such directors multiplied by the number of his shares shall equal, or by distributing such votes on the same principle among any number of such candidates. [§ 33]

Article III. Board of Directors

Section 1. General Powers. The business and affairs of the corporation shall be managed by its board of directors. [§ 35]

Section 2. Number, Tenure and Qualifications. The number of directors of the corporation shall be . . . . Each director shall hold office until the next annual meeting of shareholders and until his successor shall have been elected and qualified. Directors need not be residents of the State of . . . . or shareholders of the corporation. [§ 35] [§ 36]

Section 3. Regular Meetings. A regular meeting of the board of directors shall be held without other notice than this by-law immediately after, and at the same place as, the annual meeting of shareholders. The board of directors may provide, by resolution, the time and place, either within or without the State of . . . ., for the holding of additional regular meetings without other notice than such resolution. [§ 43]

Section 4. Special Meetings. Special meetings of the board of directors may be called by or at the request of the president or any two directors. The person or persons authorized to call special meetings of the board of directors may fix any place, either within or without the State of . . . . , as the place for holding any special meeting of the board of directors called by them. [§ 43]

Section 5. Notice. Notice of any special meeting shall be given at least two days previously thereto by written notice delivered personally or mailed to each director at his business address, or by telegram. If mailed, such notice shall be deemed to be delivered when deposited in the United States mail, so addressed, with postage thereon prepaid. If notice be given by telegram, such notice shall be deemed to be delivered when the telegram is delivered to the telegraph company. Any director may waive notice of any meeting. The attendance of a director at a meeting shall constitute a waiver of notice of such meeting, except where a director attends a meeting for the express purpose of objecting to the transaction of any business because the meeting is not lawfully called or convened. Neither the business to be transacted at, nor the purpose of, any regular or special meeting of the board of directors need be specified in the notice or waiver of notice of such meeting. [§ 43]

Section 6. Quorum. A majority of the number of directors fixed by Section 2 of this Article III shall constitute a quorum for the transaction of business at any meeting of the board of directors, but if less than such majority is present at a meeting, a majority of the directors present may adjourn the meeting from time to time without further notice. [§ 40]

Section 7. Manner of Acting. The act of the majority of the directors present at a meeting at which a quorum is present shall be the act of the board of directors. [§ 40]

Section 8. Action Without a Meeting. Any action required or permitted to be taken by the board of directors at a meeting may be taken without a meeting if a consent in writing, setting forth the action so taken, shall be signed by all of the directors. [§ 44]

Section 9. Vacancies. Any vacancy occurring in the board of directors may be filled by the affirmative vote of a majority of the remaining directors though less than a quorum of the board of directors. A director elected to fill a vacancy shall be elected for the unexpired term of his predecessor in office. Any directorship to be filled by reason of an increase in the number of directors may be filled by election by the board of directors for a term of office continuing only until the next election of directors by the shareholders. [§ 38]

Section 10. Compensation. By resolution of the board of directors, each director may be paid his expenses, if any, of attendance at each meeting of the board of directors, and may be paid a stated salary as director or a fixed sum for attendance at each meeting of the board of directors or both. No such payment shall preclude any director from serving the corporation in any other capacity and receiving compensation therefor. [§ 35]

Section 11. Presumption of Assent. A director of the corporation who is present at a meeting of the board of directors at which action on any corporate matter is taken shall be presumed to have assented to the action taken unless his dissent shall be entered in the minutes of the meeting or unless he shall file his written dissent to such action with the person acting as the secretary of the meeting before the adjournment thereof or shall forward such dissent by registered mail to the secretary of the corporation immediately after the adjournment of the meeting. Such right to dissent shall not apply to a director who voted in favor of such action. [§ 48]

Article IV. Officers

Section 1. Number. The officers of the corporation shall be a president, one or more vice-presidents (the number thereof to be determined by the board of directors), a secretary, and a treasurer, each of whom shall be elected by the board of directors. Such other officers and assistant officers as may be deemed necessary may be elected or appointed by the board of directors. Any two or more offices may be held by the same person, except the offices of president and secretary. [§ 50]

Section 2. Election and Term of Office. The officers of the corporation to be elected by the board of directors shall be elected annually by the board of directors at the first meeting of the board of directors held after each annual meeting of the shareholders. If the election of officers shall not be held at such meeting, such election shall be held as soon thereafter as conveniently may be. Each officer shall hold office until his successor shall have been duly elected and shall have qualified or until his death or until he shall resign or shall have been removed in the manner hereinafter provided. [§ 50]

Section 3. Removal. Any officer or agent may be removed by the board of directors whenever in its judgment the best interests of the corporation will be served thereby, but such removal shall be without prejudice to the contract rights, if any, of the person so removed. Election or appointment of an officer or agent shall not of itself create contract rights. [§ 51]

Section 4. Vacancies. A vacancy in any office because of death, resignation, removal, disqualification or otherwise, may be filled by the board of directors for the unexpired portion of the term.

Section 5. President. The president shall be the principal executive officer of the corporation and, subject to the control of the board of directors, shall in general supervise and control all of the business and affairs of the corporation. He shall, when present, preside at all meetings of the shareholders and of the board of directors. He may sign, with the secretary or any other proper officer of the corporation thereunto authorized by the board of directors, certificates for shares of the corporation and deeds, mortgages, bonds, contracts, or other instruments which the board of directors has authorized to be executed, except in cases where the signing and execution thereof shall be expressly delegated by the board of directors or by these By-Laws to some other officer or agent of the corporation, or shall be required by law to be otherwise signed or executed; and in general shall perform all duties incident to the officer of president and such other duties as may be prescribed by the board of directors from time to time. [§ 23]

Section 6. The Vice-Presidents. In the absence of the president or in the event of his death, inability or refusal to act, the vice-president (or in the event there be more than one vice-president, the vice-presidents in the order designated at the time of their election, or in the absence of any designation, then in the order of their election) shall perform the duties of the president, and when so acting, shall have all the powers of and be subject to all the restrictions upon the president. Any vice-president may sign, with the secretary or an assistant secretary, certificates for shares of the corporation; and shall perform such other duties as from time to time may be assigned to him by the president or by the board of directors. [§ 23]

Section 7. The Secretary. The secretary shall: (a) keep the minutes of the proceedings of the shareholders and of the board of directors in one or more books provided for that purpose; (b) see that all notices are duly given in accordance with the provisions of these By-Laws or as required by law; (c) be custodian of the corporate records and of the seal of the corporation and see that the seal of the corporation is affixed to all documents the execution of which on behalf of the corporation under its seal is duly authorized; (d) keep a register of the post office address of each shareholder which shall be furnished to the secretary by such shareholder; (e) sign with the president, or a vice-president, certificates for shares of the corporation, the issuance of which shall have been authorized by resolution of the board of directors; (f) have general charge of the stock transfer books of the corporation; and (g) in general perform all duties incident to the office of secretary and such other duties as from time to time may be assigned to him by the president or by the board of directors. [§ 23]

Section 8. The Treasurer. The treasurer shall: (a) have charge and custody of and be responsible for all funds and securities of the corporation; (b) receive and give receipts for moneys due and payable to the corporation from any source whatsoever, and deposit all such moneys in the name of the corporation in such banks, trust companies or other depositaries as shall be selected in accordance with the provisions of Article V of these By-Laws; and (c) in general perform all of the duties incident to the office of treasurer and such other duties as from time to time may be assigned to him by the president or by the board of directors. If required by the board of directors, the treasurer shall give a bond for the faithful discharge of his duties in such sum and with such surety or sureties as the board of directors shall determine.

Section 9. Assistant Secretaries and Assistant Treasurers. The assistant secretaries, when authorized by the board of directors, may sign with the president or a vice-president certificates for shares of the corporation the issuance of which shall have been authorized by a resolution of the board of directors. The assistant treasurers shall respectively, if required by the board of directors, give bonds for the faithful discharge of their duties in such sums and with such sureties as the board of directors shall determine. The assistant secretaries and assistant treasurers, in general, shall perform such duties as shall be assigned to them by the secretary or the treasurer, respectively, or by the president or the board of directors. [§ 23]

Section 10. Salaries. The salaries of the officers shall be fixed from time to time by the board of directors and no officer shall be prevented from receiving such salary by reason of the fact that he is also a director of the corporation.

Article V. Contracts, Loans, Checks and Deposits

Section 1. Contracts. The board of directors may authorize any officer or officers, agent or agents, to enter into any contract or execute and deliver any instrument in the name of and on behalf of the corporation, and such authority may be general or confined to specific instances.

Section 2. Loans. No loans shall be contracted on behalf of the corporation and no evidences of indebtedness shall be issued in its name unless authorized by a resolution of the board of directors. Such authority may be general or confined to specific instances.

Section 3. Checks, Drafts, etc. All checks, drafts or other orders for the payment of money, notes or other evidences of indebtedness issued in the name of the corporation shall be signed by such officer or officers, agent or agents of the corporation and in such manner as shall from time to time be determined by resolution of the board of directors.

Section 4. Deposits. All funds of the corporation not otherwise employed shall be deposited from time to time to the credit of the corporation in such banks, trust companies or other depositaries as the board of directors may select.

Article VI. Certificates for Shares and Their Transfer

Section 1. Certificates for Shares. Certificates representing shares of the corporation shall be in such form as shall be determined by the board of directors. Such certificates shall be signed by the president or a vice-president and by the secretary or an assistant secretary and sealed with the corporate seal or a facsimile thereof. The signatures of such officers upon a certificate may be facsimiles if the certificate is manually signed on behalf of a transfer agent or a registrar other than the corporation itself or one of its employees.

Each certificate for shares shall be consecutively numbered or otherwise identified. The name and address of the person to whom the shares represented thereby are issued, with the number of shares and date of issue, shall be entered on the stock transfer books of the corporation. All certificates surrendered to the corporation for transfer shall be cancelled and no new certificate shall be issued until the former certificate for a like number of shares shall have been surrendered and cancelled, except that in case of a lost, destroyed or mutilated certificate a new one may be issued therefor upon such terms and indemnity to the corporation as the board of directors may prescribe. [§ 23] [§ 52]

Section 2. Transfer of Shares. Transfer of shares of the corporation shall be made only on the stock transfer books of the corporation by the holder of record thereof or by his legal representative, who shall furnish proper evidence of authority to transfer, or by his attorney thereunto authorized by power of attorney duly executed and filed with the secretary of the corporation, and on surrender for cancellation of the certificate for such shares. The person in whose name shares stand on the books of the corporation shall be deemed by the corporation to be the owner thereof for all purposes.

Article VII. Fiscal Year

The fiscal year of the corporation shall begin on the first day of January and end on the thirty-first day of December in each year.

Article VIII. Dividends

The board of directors may, from time to time, declare and the corporation may pay dividends on its outstanding shares in the manner and upon the terms and conditions provided by law and its Articles of Incorporation. [§ 45]

Article IX. Corporate Seal

The board of directors shall provide a corporate seal which shall be circular in form and shall have inscribed thereon the name of the corporation and the state of incorporation and the words "Corporate Seal." [§ 4, Clause (c)]

Article X. Waiver of Notice

Whenever any notice is required to be given to any shareholder or director of the corporation under the provisions of these By-Laws or under the provisions of the Articles of Incorporation or under the provisions of the .... Business Corporation Act, a waiver thereof in writing signed by the person or persons entitled to such notice, whether before or after the time stated therein, shall be deemed equivalent to the giving of such notice. [§ 144]

Article XI. Amendments

These By-Laws may be altered, amended or repealed and new By-Laws may be adopted by the board of directors or by the shareholders at any regular or special meeting. [§ 27]

[Optional] Article XII. Executive Committee

Section 1. Appointment. The board of directors by resolution adopted by a majority of the full board, may designate two or more of its members to constitute an executive committee. The designation of such committee and the delegation thereto of authority shall not operate to relieve the board of directors, or any member thereof, of any responsibility imposed by law. [§ 42]

Section 2. Authority. The executive committee, when the board of directors is not in session shall have and may exercise all of the authority of the board of directors except to the extent, if any, that such authority shall be limited by the resolution appointing the executive committee and except also that the executive committee shall not have the authority of the board of directors in reference to amending the articles of incorporation, adopting a plan of merger or consolidation, recommending to the shareholders the sale, lease or other disposition of all or substantially all of the property and assets of the corporation otherwise than in the usual and regular course of its business, recommending to the shareholders a voluntary dissolution of the corporation or a revocation thereof, or amending the By-Laws of the corporation. [§ 42]

Section 3. Tenure and Qualifications. Each member of the executive committee shall hold office until the next regular annual meeting of the board of directors following his designation and until his successor is designated as a member of the executive committee and is elected and qualified.

Section 4. Meetings. Regular meetings of the executive committee may be held without notice at such times and places as the executive committee may fix from time to time by resolution. Special meetings of the executive committee may be called by any member thereof upon not less than one day's notice stating the place, date and hour of the meeting, which notice may be written or oral, and if mailed, shall be deemed to be delivered when deposited in the United States mail addressed to the member of the executive committee at his business address. Any member of the executive committee may waive notice of any meeting and no notice of any meeting need be given to any member thereof who attends in person. The notice of a meeting of the executive committee need not state the business proposed to be transacted at the meeting.

Section 5. Quorum. A majority of the members of the executive committee shall constitute a quorum for the transaction of business at any meeting thereof, and action of the executive committee must be authorized by the affirmative vote of a majority of the members present at a meeting at which a quorum is present.

Section 6. Action Without a Meeting. Any action required or permitted to be taken by the executive committee at a meeting may be taken without a meeting if a consent in writing, setting forth the action so taken, shall be signed by all of the members of the executive committee. [§ 44]

Section 7. Vacancies. Any vacancy in the executive committee may be filled by a resolution adopted by a majority of the full board of directors.

Section 8. Resignations and Removal. Any member of the executive committee may be removed at any time with or without cause by resolution adopted by a majority of the full board of directors. Any member of the executive committee may resign from the executive committee at any time by giving written notice to the president or secretary of the corporation, and unless otherwise specified therein, the acceptance of such resignation shall not be necessary to make it effective.

Section 9. Procedure. The executive committee shall elect a presiding officer from its members and may fix its own rules of procedure which shall not be inconsistent with these By-Laws. It shall keep regular minutes of its proceedings and report the same to the board of directors for its information at the meeting thereof held next after the proceedings shall have been taken.

Article XIII. Emergency By-Laws [§ 27-A]

The Emergency By-Laws provided in this Article XIII shall be operative during any emergency in the conduct of the business of the corporation resulting from an attack on the United States or any nuclear or atomic disaster, notwithstanding any different provision in the preceding Articles of the By-Laws or in the Articles of Incorporation of the corporation or in the . . . . Business Corporation Act. To the extent not inconsistent with the provisions of this Article, the By-Laws provided in the preceding Articles shall remain in effect during such emergency and upon its termination the Emergency By-Laws shall cease to be operative.

During any such emergency:

(a) A meeting of the board of directors may be called by any officer or director of the corporation. Notice of the time and place of the meeting shall be given by the person calling the meeting to such of the directors as it may be feasible to reach by any available means of communication. Such notice shall be given at such time in advance of the meeting as circumstances permit in the judgment of the person calling the meeting.

(b) At any such meeting of the board of directors, a quorum shall consist of . . . . [here insert the particular provisions desired].

(c) The board of directors, either before or during any such emergency, may provide, and from time to time modify, lines of succession in the event that during such an emergency any or all officers or agents of the corporation shall for any reason be rendered incapable of discharging their duties.

(d) The board of directors, either before or during any such emergency, may, effective in the emergency, change the head office or designate several alternative head offices or regional offices, or authorize the officers so to do.

No officer, director or employee acting in accordance with these Emergency By-Laws shall be liable except for willful misconduct.

These Emergency By-Laws shall be subject to repeal or change by further action of the board of directors or by action of the shareholders, but no such repeal or change shall modify the provisions of the next preceding paragraph with regard to action taken prior to the time of such repeal or change. Any amendment of these Emergency By-Laws may make any further or different provision that may be practical and necessary for the circumstances of the emergency.

Tables of Authorities

(References are to pages.)

Cases

A

B

C

O

P

Q

R

S

Federal Law

Internal Revenue Code of 1986, as amended

Securities Act of 1933

Securities Exchange Act of 1934

United States Code Sections

Model and Uniform Laws

Model Business Corporation Act

Revised Model Business Corporation Act

Revised Uniform Limited Partnership Act (1976)

Uniform Limited Partnership Act (1916)

Uniform Partnership Act

State Law

California

Index

Index

Index

E

F

G

Index